IMPERFECT EQUALITY

RECONSTRUCTING AMERICA SERIES
Paul Cimbala, series editor

IMPERFECT EQUALITY

*African Americans and the Confines
of White Racial Attitudes
in Post-Emancipation Maryland*

RICHARD PAUL FUKE

Fordham University Press
New York
1999

ISBN 0-8232-1962-3 (hardcover)
ISBN 0-8232-1963-1 (paperback)
ISSN 1523-4606
Reconstructing America, no. 2

Library of Congress Cataloging-in-Publication Data

Fuke, Richard Paul, 1940–
    Imperfect equality : African Americans and the confines of white
racial attitudes in post-emancipation Maryland / Richard Paul Fuke.
        p.   cm.—(Reconstructing America ; no. 2)
    Includes bibliographical references and index.
    ISBN 0-8232-1962-3 (hc).—ISBN 0-8232-1963-1 (pbk)
    1. Afro-Americans—Civil rights—Maryland—History—19th century.
2. Freedmen—Maryland—History.   3. Whites—Maryland—Attitudes—
History—19th century.   4. Reconstruction—Maryland.   5. Maryland—
Race relations.   I. Title.   II. Series: Reconstructing America
(Series) ; no. 2.
E185.93.M2F85   1999
305.896′0730752—dc21   99-24308
                                                                                                 CIP

Printed in the United States of America
99   00   01   02   03   5   4   3   2   1
First Edition

To Phebe Jacobsen

CONTENTS

TABLES

ILLUSTRATIONS

Illustrations follow page 68.

Baltimore Street between St. Paul and Calvert Streets, ca. 1870

Baltimore Street, ca. 1870

Judge Hugh Lennox Bond

Indenture papers, 1864

Labor contract, 1865

Labor contract, 1866

Baltimore Association broadside

Baltimore Association letter

Baltimore Gazette, March 22, 1866

Sharp Street Methodist Episcopal Church (Colored)

A washerwoman and child

Maryland, 1865

Governor Augustus W. Bradford

Oden Bowie

Archibald Stirling, Jr.

John L. Thomas, Jr.

Baltimore Street, ca. 1870

The Chesapeake Marine and Railway Drydock Company

The Douglass Institute

ACKNOWLEDGMENTS

I started writing this book in 1964. Since then I have received a research grant from the Social Sciences and Humanities Research Council of Canada and several grants from Wilfrid Laurier University. I very much appreciate this support and wish to extend my thanks to both institutions.

Over the thirty-five years, many colleagues have generously read portions of the manuscript and offered their comments. I would especially like to thank John Hope Franklin at Duke University, Loren Schweninger at the University of North Carolina at Greensboro, Douglas Lorimer at Wilfrid Laurier University, Craig Simpson at the University of Western Ontario, and Ira Berlin and Herman Belz at the University of Maryland. Their suggestions have helped me greatly, especially as I have struggled to define the parameters of Radical Republican ideology. I would also like to thank Paul Cimbala, for his cooperation and support.

In addition, many people in many libraries have helped me in the process of preparing this book. The staffs at the National Archives in Washington, D.C., the Maryland State Archives in Annapolis, Maryland, the Maryland Historical Society and the Enoch Pratt Free Library in Baltimore, the Baltimore City Archives, and the Baltimore City Hall have extended their energetic assistance not only in retrieving the documents upon which this book is based but in sharing with me their interest in and insights into African American history in Maryland.

Above all, I wish to extend my heartfelt gratitude to Phebe Jacobsen, senior archivist, retired, at the Maryland State Archives in Annapolis. From the time when the initial phase of this research led to my master's degree at the University of Maryland, Phebe has provided unstinting assistance and support. Her quiet, determined professionalism has at key junctures of this project encouraged me to continue and reminded me to keep my standards high. I deeply appreciate her guidance and for that reason dedicate this book to her.

INTRODUCTION

I

ON NOVEMBER 1, 1864, Governor Augustus W. Bradford proclaimed Maryland's new constitution which freed more than eighty-seven thousand slaves. This momentous event heralded months of confrontation and adjustment between blacks and whites and redefined race relations in the state for decades to come. As elsewhere in the South, this process presented both opportunities and obstacles. On the one hand, freed slaves and already free blacks exercised newfound freedom, while on the other, the whites with whom they lived and worked did much to obstruct them. Some wished to see blacks win greater economic, civil, and political rights; most others did not. Even the avowed friends of black progress debated how far they should challenge the assumptions behind Maryland's pre-emancipation race relations.[1]

For their part, black Marylanders sought to make the most of their freedom. Although those affected directly by the proclamation constituted only half of Maryland's black population, slavery had defined the lives of every black person in the state. After November 1, 1864, freed and already free people everywhere moved quickly to escape its restrictions, asserting whatever autonomy they could over their working and personal lives. Thousands left their homes to reunite with families or to contract with employers of their choice. Others challenged apprenticeship laws that bound the labor of their children to white employers. Some rented land and a few acquired acres of their own. Many moved to Baltimore or Washington.

White opposition to black aspirations was equally forthright. The refusal of conservative Unionists and pro-Southern Democrats to contenance anything for freed slaves beyond a strict reading of the Thirteenth Amendment was immediate, vociferous, and hardly surprising.[2] Less predictable but equally important were "radical" Unionists and Republicans whose pro-Northern Reconstruction policies contained inner limitations that ultimately undermined the very people they were intended to help. As exponents of what Eric Foner has called the ideology of "free soil, free labor, and free men," Maryland radicals supported civil and political rights for black citizens and strove to provide them with the basic essentials—including education—of free and self-reliant labor. But few escaped the economic and racial assumptions of the time that limited the assistance of even the most ardent supporters of expanded civil rights.[3]

Essentially, in an era wedded to the efficacy of self-help and laissez-faire, white radicals collaborated with conservatives—often unintentionally—to fashion a postwar society that left blacks very much to their own devices. For example, although determined to win them fair working conditions for remunerative wages, radicals nonetheless stopped well short of the "forty acres and a mule" so ardently sought by a virtually landless black population. As much as they might applaud land ownership in principle, most radicals agreed that ex-slaves should begin their tutelage as free laborers under contract to fair employers. Only with such training and the accumulation of modest capital could they expect to acquire land and the responsibilities that went with it.[4]

Whether they liked it or not, black Marylanders depended for their success on this combination of white attitudes. When blacks could compel conservatives to recognize their priorities or when radicals lent their support, they found room to maneuver. When the former rejected their efforts and the latter refused to support them wholeheartedly, they did not find room. In the end, the newfound mobility of the work force notwithstanding, rural employers dictated wages and the terms of sharecropping agreements. The United States Army and Freedmen's Bureau helped freed people to find work at steady wages and to build schools. Radical politicians challenged Maryland's apprenticeship laws, fought for the repeal of discriminatory legislation, and supported universal manhood suffrage. But at the same time, both promoted contract labor, accepted wage levels defined by planters, rejected any notion of racial equality, and adhered generally to a mid-nineteenth-century laissez-faire philosophy.

Combined, their own assertiveness, white conservatism, and racial constraint constituted the environment in which rural blacks sought to build a better world. At times a reform dynamic emerged, as their vision, in cooperation with that of white radicals, accomplished significant changes in state law and custom; at others, frustration and failure undermined their best efforts as conservative opposition and radicals' caution undercut the prospect of greater change. In either case, with or without help, black Marylanders found it necessary to rely increasingly on their own efforts to resist outright opposition and to make the most of whatever support they could find.

The same combination of factors shaped race relations in Baltimore. At the time of emancipation, only two thousand of the city's more than twenty thousand black residents were slaves. The remainder constituted the United States' largest urban free black population at the time.[5] For decades, this tight-knit community had occupied a special status free from many of the restraints confronting free blacks in the tidewater counties. Black men provided Baltimore with most of its waiters and much of its unskilled day labor; women, its domestic service. In some trades—ship caulking and brick making especially—black labor predominated. In areas of the city occupied entirely by black residents, a small professional class provided barbers, ministers, doctors, undertakers, teachers, and musicians.[6]

Emancipation opened prospects for urban change. Several thousand rural black men, women, and children migrated immediately to Baltimore in search of employment. Others, forced off farms and plantations by masters no longer willing to care for them, joined the trek cityward hoping to find relief from municipal, state, or federal authorities. Baltimore's postwar economy proved sufficiently resilient to absorb most of these people into the work force, and in the process facilitated a significant shift in the demographics of black labor in the state.

As in the tidewater counties, black Baltimoreans—both new and old—confronted the prejudices of the white community. Like their rural counterparts, urban conservative Unionists and Democrats opposed black progress of any sort, and radical Unionists and Republicans—although far more numerous in Baltimore than elsewhere in the state—remained steadfastly attached to a philosophy of black self-help with minimal assistance from whites. Furthermore, even the staunchest supporters of urban black residents' economic, civil, and educational rights refused to countenance integration in churches, meeting halls, and public transportation facilities. Nor did they advocate anything approaching what was called—in the parlance of the day—"social equality."

Certainly, the work of the army, the Freedmen's Bureau, and radical politicians assisted rural and urban freed and already free blacks in making real and lasting accomplishments. In the end, however, these proved insufficient in number and strength to challenge the power of deep-seated racial attitudes. The ultimate effect of conservative strength and radical restraint was to undermine both black aspirations and the efforts of radicals to cultivate even modest reform. Equally clearly, they compelled black Marylanders to pursue their own course. By 1870, they had, for better or worse, constructed their own society in alliance with their white supporters whenever possible. To make matters worse, by the time the Fifteenth Amendment to the United States Constitution was approved, radical influence in Maryland had all but disappeared and the effects of its handiwork remained confined to that which it had accomplished between 1864 and 1867. These changes proved insufficient for black people and their remaining white friends to mount a frontal assault on the bastion of white supremacy. As conservative Governor Thomas Swann was fond of putting it, "This is a white man's country."[7]

II

The several chapters in this book examine the interaction among black Marylanders' effort to expand their freedom, conservative whites' determination to resist it, and radicals' carefully crafted reform agenda. This work complements many recent books and articles—primarily economic or econometric—that examine the choices available to freed slaves in the post-emancipation South and the forces that ultimately defined them. Some works point to new opportunities in wage labor, sharecropping, the purchase of land, and migration to different neighborhoods, counties, or cities. Others argue that despite such newfound mobility and autonomy, blacks failed to change their historically subservient relationship to whites; that even the acquisition of land did little more than supplement their basic, subsistence-oriented economy.[8]

Did freed and already free laborers enter an open market where they could pursue improved working conditions and higher wages, or did sharecropping and other mechanisms of labor-management relations— even those advocated by laborers' supporters—force them into a subordinate economic relationship with their ex-masters and employers? If we judge from the Maryland evidence, it is clear that both forces were at work; that black farm laborers sought whatever autonomy they could amidst the opposing forces of a free market and coerced labor. This conclusion supports the findings of others. Roger Ransom and Richard Sutch interpret freedmen's partial withdrawal from plantations as a response to limited post-emancipation "incentives," and Eric Foner defines a black autonomy that was neither totally free nor totally regulated. According to Gavin Wright, ex-slaves adopted a family-oriented strategy that constituted a part of the "balance" between the competing claims of labor and management, and Barbara Fields sees their focus on family autonomy as that of "a subsistence-oriented peasantry."[9]

But in other ways, Maryland differed from most Southern states. For one thing, it had never left the Union. Despite attack by Confederate forces on several occasions, its pro-Northern government remained in place. For another, between 1861 and 1867, white radicals enjoyed access to political power. Finally, by November 1, 1864, half of Maryland's black population had already been free for some time. Unlike most slaveholding states, Maryland had for years possessed a large free black population in both its rural and urban midst.

Such experience offered a unique perspective on post-emancipation race relations, one that revealed the crucial importance of pre-emancipation white attitudes toward free blacks. For among the many difficulties black Marylanders confronted was whites' long-accustomed familiarity with and professed contempt for a large and subservient free black population which, in effect, emancipation simply doubled in size. Indeed, for decades, the more than eighty-three thousand free blacks in Maryland before November 1, 1864, had toiled as wage laborers, sharecroppers, and small landowners under agreements similar to those that came to shape post-emancipation labor-management relations.[10] Truly, whites had, in the words of Ira Berlin:

> created the institutions, standards of personal relations, and patterns of thought which helped them control free Negroes, extort their labor, and maintain social distance between the races. Faced with a greatly enlarged free black population after the Civil War, whites almost instinctively applied the lessons of the past. . . . [W]ith almost a century of experience to draw on, whites had little need to grope.[11]

Such attitudes were important throughout the Reconstruction South in helping shape white treatment of freed blacks, but they had a devastating impact in Maryland where the pre-emancipation black population had reached such large proportions. Significantly, none of the historical forces that had led to the manumission of so many black Marylanders prior to 1864—the influence of the American Revolution, proximity to the antislavery North, and the shift away from labor-intensive staple crop production—resulted in a corresponding emancipation of white Marylanders' minds.

For in the final analysis, the aspirations of black Marylanders failed to find a sufficiently sympathetic audience among whites to assure their realization. The intransigent opposition of conservatives and the ideological constraints of radicals combined to present black people with only limited opportunities to live on an equal basis with their white neighbors and compelled them to develop their own separate, semi-autonomous, and perforce, second-class society. It was, to repeat, essentially a question of white racial attitudes. Black Marylanders could assert much, but their prospect of translating such assertion into meaningful change remained defined by the extent of whites' support for that change.

White Marylanders in the 1860s were simply not prepared to contemplate—to say nothing of approve—legislation or social programs designed to force the issue of racial equality. Conservatives opposed anything more than a rudimentary acceptance of emancipation. Radicals obviously sought more but they too stopped well short of what black people fervently hoped for. That rural planters should prove recalcitrant is hardly surprising. Their opinions were well known and consistently articulated. As for radicals, they did not regard black people as equal to whites, at least not yet, and believed firmly that any effort to legislate such equality was mistaken. "We do not encourage any benevolence toward them," wrote Baltimore Criminal Court judge and prominent radical Hugh Lennox Bond in April 1865, "which does not tend to make the colored man feel his duty and capacity to support himself. Whatever can educate his mind and equip his body for self-care is in the right direction. Everything else tends to lager houses, idleness, vice."[12] A year later, he added, "If he can get a living let him get it; if he cannot, let him go without, only throw no obstacles in his way."[13] And in 1867, he told a black audience, "Upon *you* is the . . . responsibility of demonstrating . . . your fitness. . . ."[14]

NOTES

1. Among the available literature on Maryland during Reconstruction, the most important to date is Barbara Jeanne Fields, *Slavery and Freedom on the*

Middle Ground: Maryland during the Nineteenth Century (New Haven and London, 1985). Impressive in both its historical and analytical sweep, Fields's book provides a broad account of the suppression of black labor in Maryland in the nineteenth century. As such it offers both more and less than this study. It provides a discussion of the periods both before and after emancipation that are not addressed here, but limits to one chapter its coverage of the period immediately following emancipation. The importance of Fields's emphasis on the class origins of black coercion should also be noted. In *Slavery and Freedom* and elsewhere (especially her chapter in J. Morgan Kousser and James M. McPherson [eds.], *Region, Race, and Reconstruction: Essays in Honor of C. Vann Woodward* [New York, 1982]), Fields argues that class distinctions outweighed racial prejudice in accounting for blacks' relegation to a separate and inferior status in Maryland. This study does not seek to challenge that assertion. Clearly, issues pertaining to class permeated relations between white planters and their ex-slaves and may well indeed have dictated the content of white racism in the state. The point here is rather that racial antagonism, whatever its origins, fueled the opposition of white conservatives to any advancement sought by blacks and undermined the reform philosophy of sympathetic white radicals. The manner in which such prejudice shaped the eventual outcome of post-emancipation race relations in Maryland is the topic of this book, not the nature of its origins.

Charles L. Wagandt's *The Mighty Revolution: Negro Emancipation in Maryland, 1862–1864* (Baltimore, 1964), provides excellent coverage and analysis of the issues leading to emancipation, and Margaret L. Callcott's *The Negro in Maryland Politics, 1870–1912* (Baltimore, 1969) offers similar treatment of the generation after the passage of the Fifteenth Amendment to the United States Constitution. Leroy Graham's *Baltimore: Nineteenth-Century Black Capital* (Washington, 1982) offers a detailed account of prominent black Baltimoreans and their political activities before and after emancipation. See also Richard O. Curry (ed.), *Radicalism, Racism, and Party Realignment: The Border States during Reconstruction* (Baltimore, 1969). William G. Paul's and Joseph Garonzik's doctoral dissertations, "The Shadow of Equality: The Negro in Baltimore, 1864–1911" (University of Wisconsin, 1972), and "Urbanization and the Black Population of Baltimore, 1850–1870" (State University of New York at Stony Brook, 1974) contain much that is helpful, but like Fields, Paul deals with a broad sweep of time and devotes relatively little attention to immediate post-emancipation issues. His study is also confined to the city of Baltimore. Garonzik offers a detailed, quantified study of urban neighborhoods, similarly confined to Baltimore, which supports some of the demographic material found in this study. Jean H. Baker's *The Politics of Continuity: Maryland Political Parties from 1858 to 1870* (Baltimore, 1973), provides important political background to the development of post-emancipation race relations but touches upon the latter themselves only briefly. To find a study (other than that of Fields) that confronts directly questions relating to freed slaves and their progress, one must return to Jeffrey R. Brackett's *Progress of the Colored People of Maryland since the War* (Baltimore, 1890), an informative but dated rendition of events in the Reconstruction period and after. For other secondary literature related to this study, see the bibliography.

Two recent published collections of primary documents enhance greatly our access to the events surrounding emancipation in the state. Both are volumes in the series *Freedom: A Documentary History of Emancipation, 1861– 1867, Selected from the Holdings of the National Archives of the United States.* The first is edited by Ira Berlin, Barbara J. Fields, Thaviola Glymph, Joseph P. Reidy, and Leslie S. Rowland, and is entitled Series 1: Volume 1: *The Destruction of Slavery* (New York, 1985). The second, edited by Ira Berlin, Joseph P. Reidy, and Leslie Rowland, is entitled Series 2: *The Black Military Experience* (New York, 1982). Both volumes contain documents related directly to Maryland, many of which are taken from the records of the United States Army and the Freedmen's Bureau, collections used extensively in this book.

2. Since the 1950s, hundreds of books and articles have addressed Southern white opposition to the aspirations of freed slaves. Some of the best of these appeared in the late 1950s and early to mid 1960s as part of what since has been called the "neo-abolitionist" response to an earlier, conservative historiography. Important studies in this response are: John Hope Franklin, *Reconstruction after the Civil War* (Chicago, 1961); Kenneth Stampp, *The Era of Reconstruction, 1865–1867* (New York, 1965); and Eric McKitrick, *Andrew Johnson and Reconstruction* (Chicago, 1960).

3. Eric Foner, *Free Soil, Free Labor, Free Men: The Ideology of the Republican Party* (New York, 1970). For a discussion of Northern racial attitudes during Reconstruction see: C. Vann Woodward, "Seeds of Failure in Radical Race Policy," in *New Frontiers in American Reconstruction,* ed. Harold M. Hyman (Chicago, 1966), 125–47; William S. McFeely, *Yankee Stepfather: General O. O. Howard and the Freedmen* (New Haven, 1968), 84–106; George M. Fredrickson, *The Black Image in the White Mind: The Debate on Afro-American Character and Destiny, 1817–1914* (New York, 1971); Louis Gerteis, *From Contraband to Freedmen: Federal Policy toward Southern Blacks, 1861– 1865* (Westport, Conn., 1973); Herman Belz, "The New Orthodoxy in Reconstruction Historiography," *Reviews in American History* 1 (March 1973): 106–13; Richard Paul Fuke, "A Reform Mentality: Federal Attitudes toward Black Marylanders, 1864–1868," *Civil War History* (September 1976): 214–35; Eric Foner, *Politics and Ideology in the Age of Civil War* (New York, 1980), 97–127.

4. See Foner, *Politics and Ideology,* 97–127; Paul Gates, "Federal Land

Policy in the South, 1866–1888," *Journal of Southern History* 6 (1940): 303–30; Martin Abbott, "Free Land, Free Labor, and the Freedmen's Bureau," *Agricultural History* (1956); LaWanda Cox, "The Promise of Land for the Freedmen," *Mississippi Valley Historical Review* 45 (December 1958): 413–40; Willie Lee Rose, *Rehearsal for Reconstruction: The Port Royal Experiment* (New York, 1964); Robert F. Horowitz, "Land to the Freedmen: A Vision of Reconstruction," *Ohio History* 86 (summer 1977): 187–99; Edward Magdol, *A Right to the Land: Essays on the Freedmen's Community* (Westport, Conn., 1977); Claude F. Oubre, *Forty Acres and a Mule: The Freedmen's Bureau and Black Landownership* (Baton Rouge, 1978); Richard Paul Fuke, "A School for Freed Labor: The Maryland 'Government Farms,' 1864–1866," *Maryland Historian* (spring/summer, 1985): 11–34.

5. U. S. Bureau of the Census, *Population of the United States in 1870, Compiled from the Original Returns of the Ninth Census* (Washington, D.C. 1872), 163.

6. James M. Wright, *The Free Negro in Maryland, 1634–1860* (New York, 1921), 149–74; Ira Berlin, *Slaves without Masters: The Free Negro in the Antebellum South* (New York, 1974), 217–50; Richard Paul Fuke, "Black Marylanders, 1864–1868" (Ph.D. diss., University of Chicago, 1973), chapter 6.

7. *Baltimore Sun*, June 21, 1866. See also *Baltimore American*, April 6, 1864; "Message of Governor Swann to the General Assembly of Maryland" (Annapolis, 1866), which appears as Document A in *Journal of the Proceedings of the House of Delegates, Extra Session, 1866* (Annapolis, 1866); "Message of Governor Swann to the General Assembly of Maryland," (Annapolis, 1867), which appears as Document A in *Journal of the Proceedings of the House of Delegates, January Session 1867* (Annapolis, 1867). Thomas Swann was born in Alexandria, D.C., in 1806. He attended Columbia College in Washington, D.C., and the University of Virginia. He moved to Baltimore in 1834, where he became the president of the Baltimore and Ohio Railroad Company in 1848. In 1856 he was elected mayor of Baltimore on the American, or "Know-Nothing" Party ticket. In 1864 he was elected governor of Maryland as a Unionist but did not take office until January 1, 1866, upon the completion of Thomas Hicks's term. Although personally opposed to slavery, his politics were conservative and he quickly asserted his opposition to Unionists with radical views toward race relations (*Dictionary of American Biography* [24 vols. and index, New York, 1928–1974], 18:237–38; *Who Was Who in America, Historical Volume, 1607–1896* [Chicago, 1963], 516).

8. The literature on blacks' economic response to emancipation is voluminous and cannot possibly be discussed adequately in a single footnote. Useful review articles include: Harold D. Woodman, "Sequel to Slavery: The New History Views the Postbellum South," *Journal of Southern History* 44 (November 1977): 523–54; and Gavin Wright, "The Strange Career of the New

Southern Economic History," *Reviews in American History* 10 (December 1982): 164–80. Prominent studies stressing the response of blacks to relatively open market conditions include: Robert Higgs, *Competition and Coercion: Blacks in the American Economy, 1865–1914* (Cambridge, Eng., 1977); Stephen DeCanio, *Agriculture in the Postbellum South: The Economics of Production and Supply* (Cambridge, Mass., 1974); Joseph D. Reid, "Sharecropping as an Understandable Market Response—the Postbellum South," *Journal of Economic History* 33 (March 1973): 106–30; and Ralph Shlomowitz, " 'Bound' or 'Free'? Black Labor in Cotton and Sugarcane Farming, 1865–1880," *Journal of Southern History* 50 (November 1984): 570–96. For emphasis on the restricted or coercive nature of the Southern labor system see: Roger L. Ransom and Richard Sutch, *One Kind of Freedom: The Economic Consequences of Emancipation* (Cambridge, Eng., 1977); Jonathan Wiener, *Social Origins of the New South: Alabama, 1860–1885* (Baton Rouge, 1978); Jay R. Mandle, *The Roots of Black Poverty: The Southern Plantation Economy after the Civil War* (Durham, N.C., 1978); William Cohen, "Negro Involuntary Servitude in the South, 1865–1940: A Preliminary Analysis," *Journal of Southern History* 42 (February 1976): 33–60; and Pete Daniel, "The Metamorphosis of Slavery, 1865–1900," *Journal of American History* 66 (June 1979): 88–99.

For a more general discussion of black aspirations see, Edward Magdol, *A Right to the Land: Essays on the Freedmen's Community* (Westport, Conn., 1977), 35–90; William E. Messner, *Freedmen and the Ideology of Free Labor: Louisiana, 1862–1865* (Lafayette, La., 1978), 184–88; Leon F. Litwack, *Been in the Storm So Long: The Aftermath of Slavery* (New York, 1979), 221ff; Elizabeth R. Bethel, *Promiseland: A Century of Life in a Negro Community* (Philadelphia, 1981), 5–9; Eric Foner, *Nothing But Freedom: Emancipation and Its Legacy* (Baton Rouge, 1983), 74–110.

9. Ransom and Sutch maintain that freedmen "possessed the power, not only to shape their own destinies within the society in which they found themselves, but also to change that society, at least in a limited way" (Ransom and Sutch, *One Kind of Freedom*, 6, 1). According to Foner, "Autonomy was the lens through which . . . workers viewed labor conditions during Reconstruction. Those who could rent or purchase land did so; those who could not sought modes of labor that secured the highest degree of personal independence" (Foner, *Nothing But Freedom*, 86). Wright stresses the importance of the family as an organizing unit of black labor and sees blacks' desire to escape the regulation of plantation life as a family-oriented market response (Gavin Wright, *Old South, New South: Revolutions in the Southern Economy since the Civil War* [New York, 1986], 85–86, 90). Fields analyzes the behavior of freedmen who sought to dispose of their labor as they saw fit by "cultivating their own gardens, working for wages just long enough to earn a family subsistence, and refusing to establish themselves on a permanent basis with a single employer" (Fields, *Slavery and Freedom*, 165).

10. Wright, *The Free Negro in Maryland*, 149–74.
11. Berlin, *Slaves without Masters*, 381–82.
12. *American Missionary*, 2nd Ser., 9 (April 1, 1865): 80.
13. *Baltimore American*, November 24, 1866.
14. Ibid., July 1, 1867. Emphasis added. Hugh Lennox Bond was born in 1828 in Baltimore. He graduated from the University of the City of New York in 1848. He returned to Baltimore and was admitted to the bar in 1851. In 1860 he was appointed judge of the Baltimore Criminal Court. A member of the American or "Know-Nothing" Party in the 1850s, he became a strong Unionist after the April 19, 1861, Baltimore attack upon the 6th Massachusetts Regiment (*Dictionary of American Biography* 2:431–32; *Who Was Who in America: Historical Volume, 1607–1896*, 63). See also, Richard Paul Fuke, "Hugh Lennox Bond and Radical Republican Ideology," *Journal of Southern History* 45 (November 1979): 569–86.

IMPERFECT EQUALITY

1

"Twill Be Very Different to Be Free"

I

THROUGHOUT THE TIDEWATER COUNTIES Maryland slaves gathered in the late hours of October 31, 1864, to greet the dawn of freedom. According to one witness, "All Africa was abroad; some on horseback, some in wagons, but nearly all on foot, moving along, singing and joyful."[1] In Baltimore, five hundred cannon greeted the occasion amidst church bells, flags, illuminations, and congratulatory speeches.[2] It was, said the *Baltimore American*, "a source of real joy."[3] Back from Rochester, New York, Frederick Douglass celebrated his return to the land of his bondage. "What a wonderful change a few short years have wrought! I left Maryland a slave; I return to find her . . . a free state . . . clothed in her garments of Liberty and Justice."[4] In humbler but equally eloquent words, a tidewater freedman recalled, "That was the happiest day of my life. . . . [T]will be very different to be free."[5]

Black Marylanders' initial response to emancipation had been anticipated for some time. In a dramatic preview of events to come, many slaves quit their plantations as early as 1863. Reacting to emancipation in the District of Columbia, President Lincoln's emancipation proclamation, and the recruitment of black men into the Union Army, hundreds fled to federal lines. There were many soldiers about—regular regiments assigned to the defense of Washington and special recruiting units intent on enlisting runaways—few of whom paid any heed to the objections of local planters.[6] Once started, whites could do little to halt the exodus of a substantial number of slaves especially from the southern Maryland counties close to Washington. With them these men and women took their strong arms and backs, the pillars of tidewater prosperity. "In our part of the state," observed an eyewitness, "a great deal of our grain and harvests . . . will fall ungathered for want of the necessary labor to save it."[7]

After November 1, 1864, Maryland's entire slave population seized the options hitherto available to a relative few. This they did by either leaving their farms and plantations to live and work elsewhere or engaging with their ex-masters under free contractual arrangements. Among the former, some traveled short distances, others long. Some returned, others did not. But whether they departed or stayed, the import of their behavior was clear. The law that had enslaved them had been repealed and they could now legally move from one place to another and sell their labor under terms that they helped determine.

Among those freed slaves who left, many headed for the city. Washington attracted those abandoning the farms and plantations of Montgomery, Prince George's, Charles, and St. Mary's Counties. Easily accessible, it offered migrants the most convenient alternative to labor in southern Maryland as well as a source of food and shelter in the form of the United States government. As a consequence, explained the *Alexandria Gazette,* "They all go to Washington—at least in the first place."[8] For others, Baltimore offered similar attraction. Here too assistance was available from the federal Bureau of Refugees, Freedmen, and Abandoned Lands, with additional support from the Baltimore Quakers' Friends Association in Aid of Freedmen.[9]

But for each person who migrated to Washington or Baltimore, a dozen more stayed behind. Of these, many remained with their ex-masters and negotiated wage or crop-sharing contracts. "Large numbers of these freedmen," explained the *Baltimore American,* "will remain at their former homes and make the scenes of their compulsory toil their continued dwelling place."[10] Many freedmen in southern Maryland "arranged for the season's work at once," added John Eaton of the Freedmen's Bureau, "when still at their former homes."[11]

Those freedmen on the Edward Lloyd plantation in Talbot County were a case in point. Dozens of farm hands stayed on his several properties after November 1, 1864. They received cash wages, but lived in their old slave quarters, ate their employer's food, and cultivated the same fields that they had as slaves. Bill Sampson, for example, a freedman in his sixties, stayed on at Lloyd's "Home House" farm, earning between ten and fifteen dollars a month in 1865 and 1866. Another slave, Ned Roberts, in his fifties, did the same thing, remaining at "Home House" in 1865 and 1866, for ten dollars a month. On another of Lloyd's properties, "400 Acres Farm," freedman John Lundy decided to remain at seven dollars a month, his friend Henry Blake at five. At

"Hopewell Farm," Charles Skinner, already free and several others free and freed, stayed on at monthly wages of $12.50.[12]

In February 1865, a correspondent to the *Baltimore American* added that most freed blacks "hired out at moderate wages to their old masters or some neighbor, retaining, if practicable, the humble homes to which they were accustomed."[13] A year later, in May 1866, the *National Intelligencer* informed its readers that in Prince George's County "most of the negroes . . . are quietly and cheerfully at work with former masters, upon wages, with the usual allowances of lands, garden spot etc."[14] In November 1867, a tidewater planter explained why his slaves stayed. "They could not be persuaded to leave me during the war nor since and they is said to be the best hands in my neighborhood. If I was a bad master I think they would have found it out and entered the service of some other man."[15]

But as many freed people left their ex-masters to work for new employers as stayed, if not more. An ex-slave intent on leaving his or her employer did not have to move to Washington or Baltimore to do it. This was especially true on the Eastern Shore, where a population decline in some counties was matched by increases in others.[16] Black workers responded to emancipation by leaving the place of their bondage even if it was only to go a short distance. As Resin "Parson" Williams, a free laborer working on the Oden Bowie plantation in Prince George's County, recalled, "When the slaves were made free . . . they were told they need no longer work for their masters unless they so desired. Most of the darkeys quit 'den and dar' and made a quick departure for other parts."[17]

Similar accounts abounded. "I hear of some families," wrote diarist Samuel Harrison of Talbot County, "from which the whole household staff . . . has left. At this moment seven of Genl. Tilghman's former slaves are upon my farm in the house of the free negro Ephraim who cultivates it."[18] "I . . . hired five persons for the year," complained an Eastern Shore planter, "they worked for me a short time but when they found they could get higher wages elsewhere . . . they left me and I was compelled to hire other hands. [T]his was no uncommon occurence."[19] As Freedmen's Bureau agent James M. Johnston saw it, there was "a restless disposition on [the] part of the Freedmen."[20]

In several diary entries of Susanna Warfield of Kent County between January 1865 and November 1867, the problems of the new labor system were evident:

TABLE 1.1

BLACK POPULATION IN TIDEWATER MARYLAND AND BALTIMORE 1860–1870

Southern Maryland County	1860	1870
Anne Arundel	12,196	11,732
Calvert	6,450	5,533
Charles	10,721	9,318
Montgomery	6,973	7,434
Prince George's	13,677	9,780
St. Mary's	8,415	7,726

Eastern Shore County	1860	1870
Caroline	3,525	3,758
Cecil	3,868	4,014
Dorchester	8,807	7,556
Kent	5,920	7,732
Queen Anne	7,546	6,592
Somerset	9,660	9,477
Talbot	6,689	6,666
Worcester	7,219	8,072
Wicomico		4,050

Baltimore City	1860	1870
Baltimore	27,808	39,556

Source: U.S. Bureau of the Census, *A Compendium of the Ninth Census, June 1, 1870* (Washington, 1872), 10–11; U.S. Bureau of the Census, *Population of the United States in 1870, Compiled from the Original Returns of the Ninth Census* . . . (Washington, 1872), 163–65.

—Louisa left me on the 8th of March. I hired her by the day until the 16th. . . . Ellen came, she remained until June—three months—then came Kitty—then Betty—all good for nothing—Ellen impudent, Kitty a thief, Betty lazy and sickly.

—I have Matilda Johnson with me now as cook. She came 1st of this year. This is her 4th month. William Henry, Charlotte's son has been living here—dismissed—George Smith now—John Grahame commenced going to school on Wednesday last. . . . We have Owen Gilroy and Mahaly's son at work here in the Mount Marino field. . . . Murphy McDaniel is here at work also. Matilda left me in August for camp meeting and never came back. I was without a cook seven weeks.

—I went to Baltimore on the 13th and stayed seven days. While I was gone George Holmes turned John Grahame off. He had behaved badly by running out [at] nights. I sent his clothes to him. He was just seventeen when he left. July 2—Juby Smith here in John Grahame's place. . . . Sam Johnson went off in March with Sarah, Mary's sister.

—Hetty my cook left me soon after . . . Mary came to live with me 16th of September. . . . Owen Gilroy and Barnes at work here—Jim also. Jim was married to Eliza in September.[21]

"The Government set the slaves free," said the *Baltimore Gazette* in July 1865, "[and] thousands of negroes left their former masters."[22] Such mobility represented a sharp break from the rigid controls of slavery and constituted an important assertion of what W. R. Cole, Maryland Commissioner of Immigration, called "freedom of change in location."[23] But whether freed slaves moved from their place of bondage or stayed with their ex-masters under new contractual arrangements, both options reflected blacks' new faith in the twin attributes of self-help and self-reliance. "The colored people ought to learn to make the best of the present opportunities," advised prominent black Marylander Henry Highland Garnet, "and use the hands made free by endeavoring to get homes for themselves, wives, and children, and show that they can and will do for themselves."[24]

The emphasis on self-reliance struck a responsive chord in even the poorest farm laborer. When planters hired hands "at fair wages . . . paying them regularly," reported the *Washington Star* in September 1865, "the freedmen work willingly, highly pleased with the improvement in their condition."[25] Black farmhands "have applied to their labor a degree of vigor," added the *Baltimore American* "which shows with what newness of life they have been infused."[26] Such sentiment was echoed by William D. Wallach, editor of the *Washington Star* and owner of a large Dorchester County plantation. Freedmen in his district, he claimed, "are disposed to work faithfully for wages and have had infused into them, by the magic of emancipation, an amount of manliness and energy . . . which the race was here previously thought incapable of manifesting."[27]

The freed negroes on the Eastern Shore of Maryland are laboring much more industriously than was anticipated by those surrounding them who opposed their emancipation. I may justly add that they are also laboring far more intelligently than before—the incentive of wages not only having increased their industry amazingly, but also their perceptive powers: or rather their disposition to use the latter to the advantage of their employers.[28]

For anyone who cared to investigate the situation carefully it was hard to avoid the simple conclusion of one woman that "those who were well paid worked well."[29] Freedmen's Bureau agents reported regularly that black men and women worked hard and dependably when treated fairly by their employers. "Where they have been justly dealt with, and received fair equivalent for their labor," explained one such officer, "their employers report them to be industrious and faithful to their agreements."[30] As Joseph Hall, radical merchant from Calvert County, reported in November 1865, "the colored people of this county . . . [are] a quiet and orderly people disposed to be just in their dealings and willing to work and do the best they can for all that will treat them as they ought to be treated and pay them for their labor. . . . [A]ll they want is to be secure in their just rights."[31]

Where conditions were unsatisfactory; where they were not "justly dealt with," black workers did not hesitate to seek better arrangements. "They complain of not receiving their wages," reported Freedmen's Bureau agent Seldon N. Clark from St. Mary's County in August 1865. "If all the planters in lower Maryland were honest and the freedmen knew it, they would go there willingly and work."[32] A colleague made the same point. "[R]ather than hire themselves out," explained Edward F. O'Brien, they went to the city. The freedmen in St. Mary's County "would rather work for three dollars a month in Washington than work for the traitors here for twelve. . . . [They] will take care of themselves and hire out to whom they please."[33]

The same was true elsewhere. In July 1866 agent James Johnston reported from Kent County that "There is on the part of a great many Freedmen a feeling of distrust towards their former masters and white citizens generally, and the farmers experience great inconvenience in retaining laborers any length of time in their service."[34] From R. G. Rutherford in Montgomery County came the additional explanation: "[I]n some cases . . . Freedmen take a dislike to their employers (generally with cause) and leave before the expiration of their contracts.—Self interest generally induces the farmers to deal fairly with the Freedmen, if they do not it soon becomes known and they can get no laborers."[35] Nor was it necessary to be an agent of the Freedmen's Bureau to see that blacks had certain priorities and were willing to act accordingly. "Are you prepared to part with the most valuable part of this people?" asked a correspondent to the *Chestertown Transcript*, "for it will be this class who will leave if driven to extremities."[36]

In fact, the threat of their departure gave freed people the power to affect such key conditions of their life and work as wages, hours, rations, and various other factors relating to education and family unity. The realization of ambitions in any or all of these categories depended on a number of variables, most of which white employers controlled, but black mobility served as a check on total white authority. Indeed, areas of the state that failed to recognize the priorities of their workers suffered the consequences. "The complaint of a scarcity of labor is well-founded," reported Seldon Clark from southern Maryland in August 1865, "not more than half the usual amount of land is cultivated this year for that reason."[37]

Seizing their advantage, black laborers bargained with white planters for a variety of working agreements. Starting with the standard Freedmen's Bureau–approved contract that offered specified wages and "quarters, full, substantial, and healthy rations, [and] all necessary medical attendance and supplies," they managed to add a number of provisions designed to meet their own needs.[38] On November 26, 1864, Jordan Diggs of Prince George's County signed a contract with John Eamshaw that provided for his family in a number of ways:

> [T]he said Jordan Diggs . . . hereby agrees in consideration of the sum of three hundred dollars . . . to furnish . . . eight working hands himself included, for the term of one year commencing the first day of January 1865. Jordan Diggs, Carlotte Diggs, Narissa Diggs, Hannible Diggs, John Diggs, Thomas Diggs, Wares Diggs, and Anthony Brogden being the names of the hands so furnished. And the same John Eamshaw . . . hereby agrees to furnish . . . said Jordan Diggs and his entire family consisting of the above mentioned eight hands and four young and helpless children with food. . . . And it is hereby further agreed to allow Jordan Diggs . . . to raise poultry on the premises of the farm and also two hogs to be fed by John Eamshaw. . . . And it is further agreed to grant Jordan Diggs the privilege of keeping one milch cow on the premises to be fed by John Eamshaw and also to furnish Jordan Diggs with a sufficiency of firewood to keep him and his family comfortable during

the winter months to cook etc. And it is hereby agreed further to allow Jordan Diggs a sufficient time during the spring and summer months to work his garden which [he is allowed] the liberty of making on the premises, and also a sufficiency of time during the fall to gather vegetables. And it is hereby agreed by John Eamshaw . . . that the wife of Jordan Diggs . . . shall do the cooking for the eight working hands and the four children . . . and it is hereby agreed that the house in which the said Jordan Diggs shall live in shall be free of rent.[39]

Family garden plots were common, as was the right to raise livestock. "I owe Robert Wilson (colored,) eighty-five dollars," explained Thomas Ringgold of Kent County, "and have bargained to give him one hundred dollars and a house and garden for the ensuing year for his family to live in."[40] Other agreements provided specifically for items both large and small. Employers in Sandy Spring, Montgomery County, stipulated an annual ration for one hand as three bushels of corn, three hundred pounds of pork, and an occasional bushel of wheat flour.[41] In July 1866 Bureau agent George E. Henry reported from Prince George's County that "The price generally paid by the farmers for field hands is $10 per month, and board, with a garden, and the privilege of keeping pigs, chickens, etc. In some cases the quarters are furnished and in others they are . . . [not]."[42]

Although wage labor prevailed, sharecropping and renting were also common. Here, too, black workers sought to meet their basic needs in a number of ways. On December 14, 1865, Peter Dorsey, his family, and several other freedmen signed with James Thomas of St. Mary's County to farm thirty-eight acres in tobacco and the "fallow field" in corn, in exchange for a third of the proceeds. Thomas was to provide the seed, implements, and a team of horses.[43] Others reached similar agreements. "[I] Steven Hall Went to Work for Elisha Hance," explained a freedman in Calvert County, "to Work a portion of his land. [H]e agred to find the teame and I was to find the hands and Work the land for half of its products tobacco and Corn and Wheat."[44] "I made an agreement," explained Joseph Molden, also of Calvert County, "to work the farm of Joseph Griffin near Leonard's Creek . . . for one half the crop. He was to [supply] food and deduct the cost from our share."[45]

Some freed people rented land outright. In November 1865, an Eastern Shore observer described a planter who had "divided all [his] outlying lands into tracts of a few acres each, put up a house on each tract and rented the whole to his freedmen."[46] In July 1867, R. G. Rutherford reported from Montgomery County that "some are renting land which they cultivate on their own account. There being every prospect of an abundant harvest, there is no doubt . . . that they will do well."[47] Later that same month, William L. VanDerlip, Bureau agent for Calvert and Anne Arundel Counties, explained. "So many freedmen were cheated in 1865," he said, "that when they were asked to hire for 1866 they refused and the planters were obliged to engage them on shares. [But in 1866] still some of the planters found a way to cheat them. [As a result] the planters are now compelled to rent them sections of their farms at stipulated prices."[48]

Renting in some cases led to an even higher plateau: the actual purchase and thus possession of the land itself. In at least one county, the progression from farmhand to landowner was sufficiently common to attract notice. From Calvert County in June 1866, Seldon Clark reported that many black workers were renting land to "cultivate it for a share of the crop. Those working in this way give one third of the produce as rent." After that, Clark explained, "many blacks lease land with the expectation of buying it at the expiration of their [contracts]. . . . The most encouraging feature of [this process] is that some have already become land-owners."[49] As John Mercer Langston, a prominent Northern black lawyer advised freed Marylanders in 1867, "The secret of success is self-reliance. Get money, get land, sow your own acres."[50]

Indeed, self-reliance seemed to be what most black Marylanders were after whether they reached the pinnacle of landownership or not. As Langston maintained in the same 1867 speech, "Slavery means shirk and liberty means work, and to work for yourself; liberty to feed, [and] clothe . . . yourself and those dependent upon you."[51] This did not necessarily require the ownership of land. Wages, sharecropping, and renting demonstrated, in Henry Highland Garnet's words, "that they can and will do for themselves."[52] Clearly, emancipation brought about a change in emphasis from meeting the needs of the employer to meeting those of the worker and his or her family.

This new focus, although often misconstrued, did not escape the notice of white observers. "The emancipated black," explained the *Chestertown Transcript* in July 1865:

> seems possessed with the idea that he must secure sufficient money from three days work to live the balance of seven in idleness. . . . [N]egroes as

TABLE 1.2

REPRESENTATIVE WAGES PAID TO BLACK FARM LABORERS, 1865–1867

Date	County or region	Adult male per month	Adult female per month	Child 14–18
Nov 64	Prince George's	$12	$5	$5
Nov 64	Charles	10	5	5
Dec 64	Eastern Shore	10–12		
Dec 64	Talbot	12	4	7
Apr 65	Worcester	10		
Aug 65	Southern Maryland	10		
Sep 65	Queen Anne's	10–12		
Oct 65	St. Mary's	12		
Jan 66	Somerset	10	3	
Apr 66	Prince George's	10		
Apr 66	Anne Arundel	10	5	
May 66	Talbot	8–15		
May 66	Montgomery	10		
May 66	Queen Anne's	13	5	
May 66	Calvert	8–12	4–5	
May 66	Kent	10–12	3–4	
Jun 66	Calvert	8		
Jun 66	Montgomery	8		
Jul 66	Prince George's	10–12		
Jul 66	Talbot	10–18		
Jul 66	Kent and Queen Anne's	15–20		
Oct 66	Anne Arundel	8	4	
Oct 66	Montgomery	10–12	5–6	
Feb 67	Montgomery	10–12	5–6	
Feb 67	Montgomery	7–15	6–8	3–8
Feb 67	Montgomery	10–12	5–6	
Feb 67	Montgomery	8–10		
Feb 67	Montgomery	10	2–4	
Feb 67	Montgomery	10	4	
Feb 67	Montgomery	10–12	4–6	4–6
Feb 67	Prince George's	10	3	
Mar 67	Prince George's	10		
Jun 67	Prince George's	10–15		
Jun 67	Prince George's	12		
Oct 67	Anne Arundel	10		2–5

Source: The figures in this table are drawn from a number of sources and consist essentially of wage ranges reported by Freedman's Bureau agents in various parts of the state. These can be found in letters from these officers to their headquarters and appear in the box and book (volume) records of The Records of the Bureau of Refugees, Freedmen, and Abandoned Lands, Record Group 105, District of Maryland and District of Columbia, National Archives, Washington, D.C.

a race will not labor constantly unless constrained. . . . The negro laborer, from the farm hand to the kitchen scullion, seems to have no idea of his obligation to fulfill his contract of hire.[53]

The Democratic *Baltimore Gazette* expressed the point even more vigorously in November 1865 when it claimed that "Very few, if any, of the negroes will consent to settle down to steady and persistent work; many will not work at all; whilst the large majority prefer to alternate a little labor with a large amount of idleness and vagabondism."[54]

Such opinion was typical. Most conservative whites ridiculed blacks' efforts to escape plantation labor and equated such behavior with laziness or "degradation." In December 1865, an Anne Arundel County correspondent to the *Maryland Farmer and Mechanic* claimed that "The negro (half-crazed by the change . . . in his status) will not—with rare exceptions—settle down to a regular and systematic course of industry." An editorial in the same magazine in January 1866, spoke of the "unsettled condition of our negro population, . . . [and] their natural indolence and improvidence." Another correspondent in July 1866 claimed that "liberty has so demoralized the race that they have become a nuisance, and a 'stench in the nostrils of our people,' and ought to be got rid of as quickly as possible." In May 1867, the magazine once again editorialized that black farm workers "seem to have become impressed as of late that every species of field labor is degrading, and that one of the chief blessings of their newly conceded liberty is to do nothing at all, or where necessity obliges them to forego that luxury, to do as little as possible."[55]

Conservative politicians responded in much the same fashion. In January 1867, Oden Bowie, an ex-slaveowner and Democratic chairman of the state senate committee on labor and immigration, wrote that emancipation was "greatly unsettling and demoralizing . . . that hitherto useful and contented class of labor. . . . The black man . . . is admirably fitted for the servile condition which for two centuries he has so advantageously occupied in this country." Once free, "we must conclude that a retrograde instead of an advanced condition, is his unhappy fate." A year later, Governor Thomas Swann addressed the General Assembly on the topic of the "demoralization of negro labor in many parts of the State." And a few days later, Oden Bowie, now governor-elect, showed that a year had done little to change his mind. Addressing the same legislature, he condemned the "vicious idleness into which the freedmen have been inclined."[56]

As the *Baltimore Gazette* explained, what Maryland planters wanted was a work force still attuned to the needs of commercial agriculture. Obviously they were not getting it as freed people refused to reassume the habits of slavery. "You can no more expect the negro to work steadily than you can expect the horse to plow, or the ox to draw, unless he is made to do it," said the *Gazette*. "When rude labor ceases to be controlled by intelligence, it must be replaced."[57] But the *Gazette* and other conservative critics missed the point. There *was* an intelligence at work in tidewater Maryland, that of people trying to determine their own affairs. Clearly, black Marylanders had priorities of their own. They moved about the state and changed employers. They signed contracts and worked their own garden plots. They rented or even purchased land and farmed it with the help of their families. They were a more autonomous people than they had been as slaves.[58]

II

There was, however, a larger context in which black Marylanders' response to emancipation took place. Although their immediate gains brought with them geographic mobility and improved self-reliance, they did so within a system still very much under whites' control. Freed and already free blacks effected important changes in the availability of their labor and its relationship to management, but their work remained exclusively that of unskilled agricultural workers almost totally dependent on white employers.

To start with, the latter held the upper hand in defining contracts. On November 9, a scant eight days after emancipation, planters in Prince George's County held a public meeting in Upper Marlboro to promote the one-year contract and a uniform wage scale. Men were to receive no more than $120 a year plus board, women $60, and boys under eighteen the same.[59] At a similar meeting a few days later, planters in Charles County agreed upon much the same rates, and in Talbot County they settled on a $150 maximum for men, $90 for older boys, and $50 for women.[60] In Charles County, employers adopted the Prince George's scale and added the stipulation that freed slaves be prohibited from renting or leasing "any house or land . . . unless . . . under the control or supervision of the proprietor or owner."[61] These rates proved difficult to enforce precisely, but they served as the norm for tidewater Maryland for the entire period 1864–70.

Such wages contributed to family subsistence but little more. The specifics were amply demonstrated by the farmhands who remained on the Edward Lloyd plantation in Talbot County. In 1866, for example, Ned Roberts earned $120 in wages. At the end of the year, he received only $43.51. The rest went to his employer for clothing, medical expenses, and incidentals. Roberts's case was not unusual. All of Lloyd's workers at one time or another had large amounts deducted from their wages, and in every case their remaining money disappeared quickly. Employers regularly deducted from wages to cover such items as "pik nik to Hickory Hill," "the shoemaker," "camp meeting," and "agricultural fair."[62] Moreover, a typical black farmhand earned from two to five dollars a month less than his white counterpart and no more at all than a slave hired out for wages before emancipation. The 1864–65 wage scale was in fact a carryover from slavery when masters hired out their excess labor.[63]

Sharecropping and renting offered black families greater influence in determining crops and the allocation of their labor, but seldom paid any more money. Generally, sharecroppers and tenants could anticipate the expenditure of their full share for such necessities as housing, food, clothing, and medical care.[64] Moreover, many of those working under such arrangements fell into debt with their employers. "In many cases they rent land," explained Joseph Hall in May 1867, "and at the end of the year . . . [have] nothing, and the landlord has all, and many times [the Negroes are] left in debt besides."[65] William VanDerlip described such a case in Anne Arundel County. "Jones and his wife agreed," he explained, to work the farm of their employer, "on shares of ⅓ the crop. After the crops [sic] was gathered, [he] presented a bill of about $100 for medical services and one for provisions so large that the two aggregated more than ⅓ the crop."[66] In another such instance, sharecropper Joseph Molden of Calvert County complained in December 1867 that his employer Joseph Griffin "gave me the enclosed account book claiming that I was in his debt, and to pay himself the balance . . . he deducted forty-three dollars from my son's wages for this year."[67]

If emancipation and the events that followed did little to shake employers' ultimate control over freed blacks' labor, they did even less to open avenues to better occupations. By 1870, virtually all tidewater black men and women remained unskilled farm laborers or domestic servants. Only a handful had more sophisticated jobs. Villages on the Chesapeake Bay and Potomac River had their black sailors and oyster-men, some of whom did quite well. Black fence makers and black-smiths lived in several rural communities and there were a few independent farmers. But such people were in a small minority. There was nothing in emancipation that suddenly opened new rural occupa-tional vistas. The occupational structure of the tidewater counties re-mained the same as it had for decades. Few freed blacks had jobs that raised them from the lowest level of economic life.[68] Black Marylanders had been poor unskilled workers as slaves and remained so as freedmen with only limited means of improving their situation. Their determina-tion to win for themselves and their families a self-reliant place in the post-emancipation economy ensured enhanced autonomy but not up-ward mobility.

In one sense freed slaves had accomplished much. "Not a single prophecy has been fulfilled," claimed the *Maryland Union* (Caroline County) in January 1865; "Our jail is today and has been for weeks past without a tenant. . . . Neither is our almshouse filled with 'worth-less free negroes,' the number of that class seeking its charitable alms being less than at any former period." In fact, one could, "go further . . . [and] take the entire State. Our statement will hold true throughout its length and breadth."[69] But the going was tough. Not all black people could stay out of almshouses and even those who could found the line between success and failure to be thin. Many who went to Washington or Baltimore in hopes of finding work ended up seeking relief from the federal government or local agencies.[70] Those who moved shorter distances or not at all encountered other problems. For example, the confusion attending emancipation led some planters to curtail opera-tions at least temporarily, resulting in particular hardships in the winter of 1864–65. "Emancipated late last autumn," explained a Prince George's County eyewitness, "they were turned adrift with neither food nor clothes. Many could not find employment."[71] "Many . . . were suddenly turned neck and heels out of doors," added William Wallach, "and for the time being hardly knew where to procure a mouthful of food."[72] According to William F. Taylor, a black Baltimorean who traveled extensively in the tidewater counties, employers "drove them right out into the cold without anything at all to aid or shelter them." If it had not been for other blacks who took these people in, they would have suffered "a great deal of destitution and probable straightout starvation."[73]

In addition to temporary dislocation, many blacks had suddenly to provide for their elderly, infirm, and very young dependents. After emancipation, many planters, especially in southern Maryland, turned such people off their land. Many found shelter with family or friends, but those without found themselves adrift with no place to go except the cities. On November 18, 1864, the Washington correspondent to the *Baltimore American*, reported that "some farmers . . . are devising means of getting rid of such of the slaves . . . [who] are unfit for service."[74] As late as October 1865, homeless freed people drifted into Washington. "Thousands are aged and crippled," explained the *American*, "and driven away from the homes of their former masters to whom they are no longer useful. The influx of freedmen of this class is still very considerable."[75]

Even with work, rural freedmen found it difficult to get by. "The colored men are none of them men of means," wrote a sympathetic Caroline County white in July 1867. "Living as they do by such work as they can find to do from day to day in a farming community it is hard for them to 'make both ends meet.' "[76] "These people," added a Howard County resident, "are poor and have no means, only what is necessary to feed and clothe their families."[77] Some could not even manage that. In August 1866, the *Dorchester News* described conditions found by "an officer of the law" in black homes in the Bucktown district.

> His observation of their condition presents a very discouraging picture. . . . In one house, which was the home of seven persons, the only provision was a peck of green apples and a quart of sour milk. In the next house he found eight persons. Of these, four children were entirely naked, and the only provision found was about one lb. of bacon. . . . In a third house he found a family of four with absolutely nothing to eat: not a single mouthful of any kind of provision.[78]

And among the "contraband" blacks from Washington who found employment cutting wood in Montgomery County, conditions were equally unfortunate. "These men altogether reside in mud hovels," explained Dr. Charles Richardson in December 1866. "Many of them were suffering from nakedness and disease."[79]

TABLE 1.3

BLACK OCCUPATIONS IN KENT COUNTY, 1870

Occupation	Number
Laborers	2,281
Domestic Servants	823
Farmers	51
Ostlers	19
Sailors	13
Carters	10
Merchants	8
Fishermen	7
Teachers	7
Gardeners	6
Ministers	6
Barbers	5
Fencemakers	4
Teamsters	4
Overseers	3
Butcher's Helpers	2
Printer's Helpers	2
Whitewashers	2
Blacksmiths	1
Engineers	1
Errand Boys	1
Foundrymen	1
Grave Diggers	1
Hedge Layers	1
Janitors	1
Laundresses	1
Oystermen	1
Sawyers	1
Shoemakers	1
Steamboat Hands	1

Source: *Ninth Census of the United States, 1870,* Schedule 1—Inhabitants.

III

There were many reasons why emancipation failed to bring about a more thorough economic revolution in the tidewater counties of Maryland. Essentially, they were all part of a larger problem: the absence of an adequate base upon which freedmen could build. Although black people won an important and gratifying degree of self-confidence and autonomy from their freedom, they lacked the wherewithal to translate such progress into substantial economic gain. Clearly contributing to such failure were low wages and the lack of land, but there was much more to it than that. Other forces that might have promoted upward economic mobility did not exist in Reconstruction Maryland. It was a question of spirit and attitude as well as of dollars and acres. Those with the power to effect immediate and real change in the economy did not wish to do so. Almost to a man, Maryland planters believed that blacks were inferior to whites and that their dependent status must be maintained for everyone's sake. White radicals and Freedmen's Bureau agents, for all they sought to do to improve conditions under which black men and women lived and worked, still saw the latter as a subservient labor force that ought to come to terms with its employers as quickly as possible.[80]

That whites regarded freed people in such a fashion was not surprising, given their historical opinion of free blacks. There was nothing in emancipation to compel this opinion to change, and as a consequence the old model became the new. As the Democratic *Port Tobacco Times* put it in November 1864, "This class of labor has heretofore afforded but a poor dependence."[81] "It is an opinion based on conviction," added the *Baltimore Gazette*, "that the freed Negro is not a profitable worker."[82] Radicals knew better. They recognized black Marylanders' eagerness to work hard and their desire to acquire greater autonomy from whites, but they seemed satisfied when such diligence occurred within a modest and gradually progressive context. Radicals approved blacks' new routine of wage labor, sharecropping, and limited landownership. As R. G. Rutherford reported in October 1866, "The result of the freed labor system is satisfactory. . . . [T]he freedmen in this county [Montgomery] are an industrious and well-disposed class of people. They are generally at work and receive fair remuneration for their labor. Some few are working farms on shares and still a smaller number cultivate their own land. . . . The freedmen are generally doing well. Contracts are well-observed."[83]

NOTES

1. From a speech by United States Senator John A. J. Creswell, *Congressional Globe*, 38 Cong., 2 Sess., 120–24 (January 5, 1865).

2. *New York Tribune*, November 2, 1864.

3. *Baltimore American and Commercial Advertiser*, November 2, 1864. Hereafter referred to as *Baltimore American*.

4. *Baltimore American*, November 19, 1864.

5. *American Missionary*, 2d. Ser., 9 (May 1, 1865), 99. This quotation is reproduced here as recalled by "Misses" Haskell and Campbell, American Missionary Association teachers employed in Maryland.

6. For a discussion of wartime military activities in Maryland see, Wagandt, *The Mighty Revolution*, 155–84; and Charles B. Clark, "Suppression and Control of Maryland," *Maryland Historical Magazine* 54 (1959): 241–72. On occasion the army sent brass bands into likely neighborhoods to advertise its presence and as early as September 1863, Governor Bradford complained that "a steamer in government employ is sent into some of the rivers. . . . [The] officer and guard immediately make known their presence, and find means of communicating with slaves on neighboring farms." "[T]hese slaves," Bradford claimed, "usually under the cover of night, are induced to quit their houses, and repair on board the boat." (J. Thomas Scharf, *History of Maryland* [Hartboro, Pa., 1967. Reprint of 1879 edition], 572).

7. *Debates of the Constitutional Convention of the State of Maryland*, 3 vols. (Annapolis, 1864), 1: 124. See also Agnes Kane Callum, comp., *Slave Statistics of St. Mary's County Maryland, 1864, Commissioner George B. Dent* (Baltimore, 1993).

8. Quoted in the *Baltimore Sun*, August 9, 1865.

9. "Communication from Major General Lew Wallace in Relation to the Freedman's Bureau to the General Assembly of Maryland" (Annapolis, 1865), which appears as Document J in Maryland, General Assembly, House of Delegates, *Journal of Proceedings, January Session, 1865* (Annapolis, 1865); Papers of the Friends Association in Aid of Freedmen, Maryland State Archives, Annapolis, Md.

10. *Baltimore American*, January 6, 1865.

11. ". . . A Communication from the Secretary of War, together with the Reports of the Assistant Commissioners of the Freedmen's Bureau . . . ," Document no. 27 contained in U.S. Senate, *Senate Executive Documents for*

the First Session of the Thirty-Ninth Congress of the United States of America, 1865–1866 (Washington, 1866), 2: 151.

12. Lloyd Papers (MS 2001), Maryland Historical Society, Baltimore, Md.

13. *Baltimore American,* February 23, 1865.

14. Quoted in *Baltimore Sun,* May 29, 1866.

15. J. Shepherd to W. L. VanDerlip, November 25, 1866, Volume 47 (Letters Received, Annapolis, July 20, 1866–September 11, 1868), Records of the Bureau of Refugees, Freedmen, and Abandoned Lands, District of Maryland, Record Group 105, National Archives, Washington D.C. Hereafter, Bureau records will be referred to as BRFAL, RG 105, preceded by the pertinent volume or box, and district (Md. or D.C.). The phrase "Letters Received, Assistant Commissioner," will be abbreviated as LRAC.

16. U.S. Census Office, *A Compendium of the Ninth Census* (Washington, 1872), 10–11; U.S. Census Office, *Population of the United States in 1870, Compiled from the Original Returns of the Ninth Census. . . .* (Washington, 1872), 163; Brackett, *Progress of the Colored People in Maryland since the War,* 25.

17. George P. Rawick, ed., *The American Slave: A Composite Autobiography,* 19 vols. (Westport, Conn., 1972), 16:75–76.

18. Harrison Journal (MS 432.1), Maryland Historical Society. "Tell Charlotte not to leave you," Henrietta Barroll of Carroll County advised a friend, "give . . . [her] as much as *others* offer her." (Henrietta Barroll to "Nora," December 17, 1864, Barroll Family Letters (MS 108), Maryland Historical Society).

19. J. L. Belt to T. J. Jackson, April 24, 1867, Box 2 (LRAC, April 1, 1866–August 17, 1868), BRFAL, Md., RG 105.

20. J. M. Johnston to J. F. Chur, July 19, 1866, Ibid.

21. January 6, 1865, May 1, 1866, June ?, and November 8, 1867, Warfield, Susanna Diaries (MS 760), Maryland Historical Society.

22. *Baltimore Gazette,* July 25, 1865.

23. "Report of the Commissioner of Immigration of the State of Maryland to the General Assembly" (Annapolis, 1867), 39–40, which appears as Document N in Maryland, General Assembly, House of Delegates, *Journal of Proceedings, January Session, 1867* (Annapolis, 1867).

24. *Liberator,* 34 (November 25, 1864), 190. Born in 1815, in New Market, Maryland, Garnet escaped slavery with his family in 1826. He went to school in New York State and became a Presbyterian minister in 1842. An outspoken abolitionist, he attracted national attention, especially after an 1843 speech calling upon slaves to kill their masters. In 1864, he became pastor of the Fifteenth Street Presbyterian Church in Washington, D.C. (*Dictionary of American Biography,* 7:154–55; James Grant Wilson and John Fiske, eds., *Appleton's Cyclopedia of American Biography* [New York, 1898], 3:398).

25. *Washington Star*, September 11, 1865.

26. *Baltimore American*, September 28, 1865.

27. Ibid., January 30, 1865.

28. Ibid., February 15, 1865.

29. From unidentified newspaper clipping in the Nathaniel Holmes Morison Scrapbook of Newspaper Articles, 1839–1890, Enoch Pratt Free Library, Baltimore, Md.

30. *Baltimore Sun*, September 1, 1866.

31. J. Hall to S. N. Clark, November 4, 1865, Box 1 (LRAC, September 1865–October 27, 1866), BRFAL, D.C., RG 105.

32. S. N. Clark to J. Eaton Jr., August 21, 1865, State Papers [1865], Maryland State Archives, *Baltimore American*, August 29, 1865; *Liberator*, 35 (September 1, 1865), 139.

33. E. F. O'Brien to S. N. Clark, October 13, 1865, Box 1 (LRAC, September 1865–October 27, 1866), BRFAL, D.C., RG 105.

34. J. M. Johnston to J. F. Chur, July 25, 1866, Box 1 (LRAC, April 1, 1866–August 17, 1868) BRFAL, Md., RG 105.

35. R. G. Rutherford to C. H. Howard, October 27, 1866, Volume 53 (Register of Letters Sent, Rockville, June 5, 1866–October 20, 1867), BRFAL, Md., RG 105.

36. *Chestertown Transcript*, December 17, 1864.

37. S. N. Clark to J. Eaton Jr., August 21, 1865, State Papers [1865], Maryland State Archives.

38. Miscellaneous Contracts, Office of the Assistant Commissioner, BRFAL, D.C., RG 105.

39. Contract contained in Box 12 (Letters Received, Bladensburg, May 1866–December 1867), BRFAL, Md., RG 105.

40. "Communication from Major General Lew Wallace," 48.

41. W. H. Stabler to R. G. Rutherford, February 25, 1867, Volume 52 (Letters Received, Rockville, May 19, 1866–September 24, 1867), BRFAL, Md., RG 105.

42. G. E. Henry to W. W. Rogers, July 14, 1866, Volume 50 (Register of Letters Sent, Bladensburg, June 4, 1866–September 18, 1867), BRFAL, Md., RG 105.

43. E. F. O'Brien to S. N. Clark, January 4, 1866, Box 1 (LRAC, September 1865–October 27, 1866) BRFAL, D.C., RG 105.

44. H. Stockbridge to W. L. VanDerlip, January 25, 1868, Box 11 (Letters Received, Annapolis, July 20, 1866–September 11, 1868), BRFAL, Md., RG 105.

45. J. Molden to S. Ethridge, December 18, 1867, Ibid.

46. From unidentified newspaper clipping in the Nathaniel Holmes Morison Scrapbook of Newspaper Articles, 1839–1890, Enoch Pratt Free Library.

47. R. G. Rutherford to W. W. Rogers, July 19, 1867, Volume 53 (Register of Letters Sent, Rockville, June 5, 1866–October 2, 1867), BRFAL, Md., RG 105.

48. W. L. VanDerlip to W. W. Rogers, July 19, 1867, Volume 48 (Letters Sent, Annapolis, June 28, 1866–March 13, 1868) BRFAL, Md., RG 105.

49. S. N. Clark to C. H. Howard, June 16, 1866, Box 11 (Letters Received, Annapolis, July 20, 1866–September 11, 1868), BRFAL, Md., RG 105; *Baltimore Sun*, June 27, 1866.

50. *Baltimore American*, August 27, 1867. Langston was born a slave in Louisa County, Virginia, in 1829. He was manumitted in 1834 in his master's will—his master was his father—and moved to Ohio where he was raised and educated by a friend of his father. He attended Oberlin, read law in Elyria, Ohio, and was admitted to the bar in 1854. He served as a township clerk, and during the war as a recruiting agent for black troops. Between 1865 and 1868 he served on the Council of Oberlin, and in 1868 was appointed inspector-general of the Freedmen's Bureau. In 1869 he became dean of the law department of Howard University. (*Dictionary of American Biography*, 10: 597–98; W. Augustus Low and Virgil A. Clift, eds., *Encyclopedia of Black America* [New York, 1981], 497).

51. Ibid.

52. *Liberator*, 34, November 25, 1864, 190.

53. *Chestertown Transcript*, July 8, 1865.

54. *Baltimore Gazette*, November 3, 1865.

55. *Maryland Farmer and Mechanic*, 3:1 (January 1866), 8, 1; 3:7 (July 1866), 200–201; 4:5 (May 1867), 131.

56. "Report of the Committee on Labor and Immigration" (Annapolis, 1867), 1, which appears as Document Y in Maryland, General Assembly, Senate, *Journal of Proceedings of the Senate, January Session, 1867* (Annapolis, 1867); "Message of Governor Swann to the General Assembly of Maryland" (Annapolis, 1868), 15, and "Inaugural Address of Governor Oden Bowie to the General Assembly of Maryland, January 8, 1868," 7, which appear as Documents A and D in *Journal of the Proceedings of the House of Delegates of Maryland, January Session, 1868* (Annapolis, 1868). See also A. W. Bradford to O. O. Howard, October 4, 1865, State Papers [1865], Maryland State Archives.

57. *Baltimore Gazette*, November 25, 1865.

58. As Roger L. Ransom and Richard Sutch have explained, one of the ways blacks could effect such determination was to withdraw some of their labor from whites and devote it to concerns of their own. Such withdrawal, they say, was "a voluntary response to the new patterns of incentives in the post-emancipation economy," and cannot be taken as " 'evidence' to support racist characterizations of blacks as lazy, incompetent, and unwilling to work without

compulsion." (Ransom and Sutch, *One Kind of Freedom*, 6). In fact, according to the authors, blacks were generally "emboldened and enheartened by emancipation," and "This optimism was further reinforced when black workers found they possessed the power, not only to shape their own destinies within the society in which they found themselves, but also to change that society, at least in a limited way." (Ransom and Sutch, *One Kind of Freedom*, 1).

59. *Baltimore Sun*, November 14, 1864.

60. Ibid., December 15, 1864.

61. *Baltimore American*, November 21, 1864.

62. Lloyd Papers (MS 2001), Maryland Historical Society; Wilson Account Book (MS 1067), Maryland Historical Society.

63. *Maryland Farmer and Mechanic*, 3 (May 1866): 149–50; *Chestertown Transcript*, July 8, 1865; *Baltimore Sun*, November 14 and 21, 1864.

64. E. F. O'Brien to S. N. Clark, January 4, 1866, Box 1 (LRAC, September 1865–October 27, 1866), BRFAL, D.C., RG 105; W. H. Stabler to R. G. Rutherford, February 25, 1867, Volume 52 (Letters Received, Rockville, May 19, 1866–September 24, 1867), BRFAL, Md., RG 105.

65. J. Hall to W. L. VanDerlip, May 20, 1867, Box 11 (Letters Received, Annapolis, July 20, 1866–September 20, 1868), BRFAL, Md., RG 105.

66. W. L. VanDerlip to W. W. Rogers, October 8, 1867, Ibid.

67. J. Molden to S. Ethridge, December 1867, Ibid.

68. Ninth Census of the United States, 1870, Schedule 1.

69. Quoted in *Baltimore American*, January 16, 1865.

70. See below, chap. 6.

71. S. N. Clark to J. Eaton Jr., August 21, 1865, State Papers [1865], Maryland State Archives.

72. *Baltimore American*, February 15, 1865.

73. Records of the House of Representatives, Committee on the Judiciary, Testimony in Investigation of the Government of Maryland [1867], Record Group 233, National Archives, Washington, D. C.

74. *Baltimore American*, November 19, 1864.

75. Ibid., October 28, 1865.

76. C. B. Boynton to E. M. Gregory, May 23, 1867, Box 1 (LRAC, April 1, 1866–August 17, 1868), BRFAL, Md., RG 105.

77. P. Pollard to E. M. Gregory, June 25, 1867, Ibid.

78. Quoted in *Baltimore Gazette*, August 13, 1866.

79. C. Richardson to C. H. Howard, December 23, 1866, Box 12 (Letters Received, Rockville, May 1866–September 1867), BRFAL, Md., RG 105.

80. For a discussion of white attitudes toward blacks see below, chap. 10.

81. Quoted in *Baltimore Sun*, November 14, 1864.

82. *Baltimore Gazette*, November 25, 1865.

83. R. G. Rutherford to C. H. Howard, October 27, 1866, Volume 53 (Register of Letters Sent, Rockville, June 5, 1866–October 20, 1867), BRFAL, Md., RG 105.

2

The Freedmen's Bureau

I

ALTHOUGH RADICAL POLITICIANS toured the tidewater counties occasionally, the day-to-day link between blacks and those who hoped to insure their economic improvement was maintained principally by federal agents. In some aspects of their work these men sought close cooperation with white and black leaders. In their attack against the forced apprenticeship of black minors, for example, they worked directly with prominent radicals in bringing test cases before state and federal courts.[1] Similar cooperation marked their effort to expand civil and political rights.[2] In education, Northern teachers worked closely with local blacks, the Freedmen's Bureau, and the Baltimore Association for the Moral and Educational Improvement of the Colored People.[3] But in basic economic matters, especially those having to do with contractual relationships between black farm laborers and white employers, federal agents assumed sole responsibility. These were the men actually on the spot who talked directly with local black workers and white employers about the needs and aspirations of both. With considerable means of persuasion at their disposal, it was they who helped shape most effectively the rural transition from slavery to freedom.

Early in the Civil War, the United States Army stationed troops in Baltimore and strategic parts of southern Maryland and the Eastern Shore. Between 1863 and the end of hostilities in 1865, federal soldiers became involved with black Marylanders in a number of ways, including the enlistment of slaves and free blacks, the establishment of the Government Farms in St. Mary's County, and the effort to halt the apprenticeship of black children.[4] Although the army did not attempt to interfere with the contractual relations between freed people and their ex-masters, its action in these other areas marked the beginning of active federal involvement in the state and helped define its nature. Moreover, the army was not entirely unconcerned about blacks' economic problems. In his accumulation of information on apprenticeship, General Lewis ("Lew") Wallace, commander of the 8th Army Corps, headquartered in Baltimore, heard numerous complaints from freed people about intolerable working conditions and from white planters about the "laziness" and "unreliability" of emancipated labor. Such information provided the basis for the insistence by the United States government that Maryland be fully included in the operations of the Bureau of Refugees, Freedmen, and Abandoned Lands.[5]

The Freedmen's Bureau was born only weeks before the end of the war. In a bill passed by Congress in March 1865, the federal government promised protection for blacks "in the Rebel States, or . . . any territory embraced in the operations of the army."[6] Since the area surrounding the nation's capital fell into the second category, the six southern Maryland counties closest to the District of Columbia were included. Until October 1865, blacks in Baltimore, northern and western Maryland, and on the Eastern Shore were without the benefit of Bureau protection. However, in response to reports and complaints of troublesome conditions, the Bureau decided to extend its operations northward. On September 27, 1865, it established an office in Baltimore to cover the rest of Maryland. In March 1866, this area received official Bureau status as the District of Maryland with its own assistant commissioner, George J. Stannard.[7]

Originally scheduled to cease operations one year after the war, the Bureau won a new lease on life in July 1866 when Congress passed its second Freedmen's Bureau bill over the veto of President Andrew Johnson. This act extended the work of the Bureau to 1868 and widened its scope to include all parts of the country with freed slaves. This new provision confirmed the Bureau's authority to expand operations into those parts of Maryland not originally within military lines.[8]

II

The Bureau was fully committed to improving conditions for rural black Marylanders. Its agents were determined to obtain contractual settlements between labor and management satisfactory to black aspirations. "The great object in view," explained Edward O'Brien, "is to afford these freedmen a means of subsistence by procuring for them good homes at fair wages, and by securing to them the legitimate fruits of their labor."[9] Toward the accomplishment of this end Bureau agents worked diligently. Especially prominent were assistant commissioners John Eaton, Charles H. Howard (brother of Oliver Otis), and Edgar M. Gregory, and a corps of field agents and inspectors including Seldon Clark, James Johnston, William McDougall, R. G. Rutherford, George Henry, and Edward O'Brien. Together with blacks, these men did much to assist the latter in gaining an independent foothold as free and self-sufficient farm laborers.

Because Maryland had remained a loyal state throughout the war, emancipated its own slaves, and maintained the uninterrupted jurisdiction of its laws and courts, the Freedmen's Bureau lacked the legal power to impose or enforce contractual agreements among its people. "Heeding all the privileges of Maryland," explained Eaton, "as a State which has respected its constitutional obligations, my endeavor has been to act not so much by direct authority as to secure the best possible administration of bad laws, and to aid as far as I might in . . . exacting good faith between employer and employe[e]."[10] Moreover, since the Bureau did not extend its influence over much of Maryland until 1866, black workers and white employers there had already established working relationships. Only in the counties close to Washington could the Bureau involve itself directly in the making of contracts. Here its agents were responsible for the hiring out of refugees from the District of Columbia and from the Government Farms in St. Mary's County. Whenever possible in these cases, the Bureau insisted on written agreements between the parties involved that included terms set by the government.[11]

But whether privately initiated or federally sponsored, contracts between freed slaves and their ex-masters were of major concern to the Bureau. It was through such agreements that its agents sought to provide black farm laborers with the prerequisites for self-support by ensuring them jobs for themselves and families at fair and regular wages under good working conditions. As Edward O'Brien explained, the Bureau sought to "render the freedmen all they require in obtaining good homes with those who would do them justice."[12] Bureau agents in Maryland were instructed "to do all in their power" to make certain that blacks were treated fairly and that their wages were sufficient for "the support of their families."[13] It was plain to John Eaton that they "would work well anywhere for kind treatment and Fair wages," and that the absence of such in many parts of Maryland was "constantly disturbing the relations of employer and employe[e]."[14]

Understandably, such an assignment proved easiest where the Bureau was intimately involved in the contractual process. In hiring black laborers to planters in southern Maryland, Bureau agents in Washington controlled the initial conditions of employment and could dictate terms satisfactory to their needs and those of workers and their families. In such cases, the Bureau insisted upon written contracts that guaranteed black laborers housing, food, and medical care. Employers were "firmly bound" to honor such terms; the failure to comply resulting in a fine equal to the yearly wages of the employee.[15] In the rest of Maryland where the Bureau did not participate as actively in the making of contracts, its agents lacked such tight control. Nevertheless, they were charged with the investigation of contractual agreements and empowered to "advise" workers and planters in the handling of wage disputes. The order to "adjudicate difficulties between employers and employees so far as is expedient," was a common one for all Maryland agents.[16] And the word "expedient" carried with it real authority. Even in those parts of the state where the Bureau did not control negotiations between labor and management, it could pressure planters into behaving fairly toward their workers by taking recalcitrant employers to court.[17]

Bureau agents clearly had what they perceived to be blacks' best interests at heart. In seeking "fair" contracts, they saw themselves as defenders of freed peoples' newly won emancipation and as shields against a return to the conditions of slavery. Such was especially the case in southern Maryland. In finding suitable locations for the families who had worked on the Government Farms, Edward O'Brien was particularly concerned that their new contracts be good ones. In examining an agreement reached by workers without his advice, O'Brien was irate. "On looking over the instrument," he told his superiors, "you will find that the said Thomas [employer] claims all and the men who work for him get what he chooses to give, a better embodiment of slavery under the guise of freedom I never saw." O'Brien insisted on a better deal for his workers despite stiff white opposition. "With but few exceptions," he complained, the [white] people of the county ask me to approve such contracts and I have steadily refused. I cannot consent to any [such] injustice being committed upon the colored people."[18]

Few Bureau agents were as determinedly outspoken as O'Brien in their defense of the interests of black workers, but almost all shared his insistence that planters give their employees a fair chance to support themselves and families. Moreover, to a man, the agents recognized the threat posed by whites to this goal and did their best to counter it. "My idea of the actions of these people," said O'Brien, "is that they wish to hold out as long as possible with the hope that the freedmen will be compelled to come into their wishes and thus be reduced to that state of dependence from which they have just emerged."[19] Others agreed. "The bad faith of employers has prevented success," explained John Eaton. Freed people, he said, "would work well anywhere for kind treatment and fair wages; but . . . [the worker] can by no means compel the good faith of his white employer."[20]

Bureau agents in rural Maryland devoted much of their time to the investigation of contractual disputes. In southern Maryland especially, they received numerous complaints from unhappy or dissatisfied black workers and tracked down as many as they could. "A great portion of the business of this county [Prince George's]," explained George Henry, "has been to assist the Freedmen in obtaining pay for labor."[21] Individual pleas for assistance varied, but all dealt with planters' failure to honor contractual agreements. "Ezekiel Ridley (colored) makes complaint that Joseph W. Kirby of Piscataway, Prince George Co Md., is indebted to him . . . for services rendered," read a typical 1867 request for Bureau help.[22] "Jefferson Bolts (colored) makes statement that he contracted to work for Horace Keat who resides near Mechanicsville, Montgomery Co. Md., [for] three months"; read another, "that he worked the required . . . Feb., Mar., and Apr. 1867 within nine days when said Keat drove him from his premises, that all he ever received from said Keat in payment for said work is $1.25 in tobacco."[23] "William and Robert Nelson," related a third,

> have entered complaint . . . against Mrs. Sarah Richards of Inglewood, Montgomery County . . . to the effect that she withholds from them wages due for services rendered as farm laborers. . . . These men seem to be honest and hard-working people and having endeavored to obtain a settlement in vain have applied to this office for assistance to enable them to obtain the benefit of their labor.[24]

Of the twenty-two major complaints handled by R. G. Rutherford in Montgomery County between July and December 1866, nine had to do with wages.[25] Of the fifty-two investigated by Henry in Prince George's County between June 8, 1866, and September 12, 1867, thirty-three dealt with "debt for labor."[26] In addition, both agents handled dozens of minor complaints which "by their nature" were never recorded.[27] In Baltimore the Bureau investigated complaints from black migrants, some concerning their new jobs and some, positions left behind in the rural counties.[28] Agents in the city were also responsible for the investigation of contract disputes on the Eastern Shore. Since the Bureau did not establish field offices in this part of the state, its scrutiny of labor conditions there was less thorough than in the counties close to Washington. Nevertheless, inspecting agents inquired of contract conditions, discussed them with both workers and employers, and helped freed people obtain just treatment and fair wages.[29]

As an initial response to black complaints, the Bureau normally sent letters to the employers in question asking why they refused to honor their agreements. "Complaint has been made to me by James Price," wrote Henry to George W. Gardener of Prince George's County, "charging you with violation of contract and non-payment of wages due him when he went away. . . . Will you please inform me by letter as soon as convenient why the contract was broken."[30] In many cases, such a communication, or one like it, led to negotiations between the Bureau and planters that resulted in amicable agreements between the latter and their laborers. "Such cases are generally settled by bringing the parties together," explained R. G. Rutherford. Should moral suasion not work, "the law must be resorted to."[31] In July 1867, Henry reported that he tried his best to settle contract disputes "without recourse to the law," but when such action became necessary, "I have prosecuted . . . and in most of these cases have been successful."[32]

After the passage of the federal Civil Rights Act of 1866, workers could take their own disputes to court, but without the presence of a Bureau agent, stood little chance of winning just treatment. Before the act passed, county judges and magistrates were barred by state law from hearing black testimony in cases involving whites. After the act had passed, many officials either continued to exclude such testimony or refused to treat it seriously. As late as July 1867, Henry explained that "a colored man's oath is not always regarded as of much account . . . and therefore has but little weight against a white man."[33] Therefore, in the absence in Maryland of Bureau courts empowered to handle contract disputes, federal assistance for black plaintiffs before civil tribunals provided the next best thing. Without the support of a Bureau agent, "the freedmen are generally powerless to obtain redress for wrongs," said C. H. Howard in October 1866.[34] With it, the results were often quite different. "[T]he moral effect of the presence of a Bureau officer is good"; explained Henry, "it exercises a powerful influence in preventing abuses."[35]

Indeed, much of the thrust behind the Bureau's major campaign to win universal acceptance of the Civil Rights Act grew from its concern over contracts. Although some of their rhetoric focused on equal rights as a principle, Bureau agents related most effectively to the practical considerations involved. Nor was their point lost among supporters who normally concentrated on ideological arguments. According to the *Baltimore American,* the Civil Rights Act protected black Marylanders' "right to labor" which closely defined meant their "right to choose their occupation and employer, to contract for wages, and to appropriate to their own use the results of their labor." The liberty to work meant "liberty to be paid for work done—liberty to sue for it if not paid—liberty to testify in suits in conformity with the laws of evidence which govern all others." The purpose of the Civil Rights Act, the *American* concluded, was to provide such privileges for black workers by doing "justice where State laws or courts fail to do it."[36]

Thus, in attempting to acquire for freed people fair contracts at good pay and protection for the same under widely accepted laws, the Bureau sought for them their legal equality with whites. As Seldon Clark explained, "Maryland having by a vote of her people, abolished slavery, the freedmen are now a part of her legitimate population and entitled to the protection and benefit of her laws."[37] To accept anything less was to invite a return to the past, and now that he was free, "The Negro would be less than a man not to resort to the *lex talionis* [law of the talon] under such oppression with no other remedy provided."[38] Bureau agents believed that their presence and their work constituted that "other remedy." Their frequent visits, maintained A. W. Bolenius, "[are] beneficial to the interests of the colored population as it [sic] proves to rebel sympathizers that the government is determined to protect the Refugees in their rights."[39]

According to the Bureau, the results of such determination justified the effort. Conditions in Harford County were much improved, reported Henry Von Shirach in June 1866, after he "warned all parties evilly disposed toward their colored fellow-beings," that the government intended "to protect white and black alike in their rights."[40] "The moral effect of the Bureau . . . and the occasional visits of its officers," added James Johnston a month later from Kent County, "have done much towards preserving harmony and preventing abuses." As a result, the condition of the freedmen in his district was "quite as encouraging as [in] any section of the country I have visited."[41] Similar reports came from other parts of the state. The comments of George Henry after he had worked in Prince George's County for a year were typical. The freedmen "are doing very well," he said, "and altogether [their] condition is much improved from what it was last year."[42]

III

As these reports demonstrated, Bureau agents' attempts to help freed Marylanders establish themselves as self-reliant farm laborers were serious. Nevertheless, there was much about the Bureau's program that was restricted in both operation and vision. First, it lacked sufficient authority in many parts of Maryland to enforce a universal or permanent contract settlement between white planters and freed slaves. In its advisory capacity the Bureau could influence both sides of labor agreements, but it could not institute rules or regulations enforceable by law. As Edgar Gregory explained, "all contracts between the white and colored population in this . . . [District] are regulated by mutual agreement between themselves without the approval of officers of the Bureau, our action in the matter being confined to the investigations of complaints made by colored persons against their employers."[43] As a presence, the Bureau helped in obtaining justice for black wage laborers, but even this lasted only two years, and once the Bureau departed it left no concrete legacy of protective laws or agencies.

Second, the Freedmen's Bureau in Maryland was woefully understaffed. The entire Eastern Shore where Gregory admitted in November 1866 "much bad feeling still exists against both the Freedmen and the Bureau," went without permanent field agents. The visits of touring officers helped the situation some but not enough. Even in the counties close to Washington where field agents were stationed in Annapolis, Rockville, Bladensburg, and St. Mary's County, Bureau personnel were spread thin. Despite their accomplishments, such agents as George Henry and R. G. Rutherford were hard-pressed to make them stand. All too often, local planters could subvert the efforts of a single officer or a handful of soldiers. "Intimidation and misrepresentation are resorted to," wrote Rutherford in October 1866, "to prevent Freedmen from bringing their complaints to this office, and where complaints have already been entered to prevent them from testifying."[44] With so little help at his disposal, there was not much a single agent could do to prohibit such white behavior or to encourage blacks to step forth with their complaints when no immediate protection was at hand.

Just as importantly, Bureau agents were restricted by their vision of blacks' future. Federal officers sought to establish freed people as self-reliant workers, but did not look much further. Rural blacks were agricultural laborers, they thought, and were essentially to stay that way. Even their acquisition of land did not constitute a basis for occupational mobility. Its purchase might mark the advance of a few black Marylanders to a new economic plateau, but was seen primarily as simply a supplement to a wage laborer's income that did not change his or her status.

Even when the Bureau had the opportunity to make land available to black Marylanders, it did so in such a fashion as to demonstrate the absence of any intention to make the experiment permanent. Between 1864 and 1866, the United States Army and the Bureau possessed more than 3,000 acres of excellent farm land on the Patuxent River in St. Mary's County. The "Government Farms," as they were called, had been abandoned by John H. Sothoron and Joseph Forrest, two Confederate sympathizers who had fled Maryland during the war.[45] On this land, the government placed five hundred black men, women, and children, most of whom were refugees (some of them wives of soldiers) who had gone first to Washington from the surrounding counties of Maryland and Virginia. With the assistance of the army and the Bureau, these people farmed the Sothoron and Forrest properties, selling the produce to defray costs. By most accounts, the farms were quite successful, but their existence was short lived. Within months of their start, the Bureau announced their imminent termination, and by 1866, the land was back in the hands of its original owners.[46]

The government farms offered an unusual opportunity to judge the capacity of freed slaves. Although most of the people involved worked as farm laborers under the general control of federal agents, a few actually leased land independently, and those who did not supervised much of the work themselves and participated in the making of important decisions. Workers served as overseers or gangsmen, helped enforce sanitation procedures and collaborated with army and Bureau officers in the planning of crops and work schedules.[47] According to one observer, such cooperation worked well. In August 1865, a correspondent to the *Baltimore American* wrote that the residents were "contented and happy and . . . fully satisfied with their lot."[48] Agents on the scene were even more enthusiastic. Seldon Clark claimed that "during a trip of 180 miles through St. Mary's and the adjoining counties, I saw no crops equal to those on the Government Farms." The people were in good condition, he said, and satisfied. "I talked with many of them and believe they concealed no complaint. . . . There was no lack of food. All were well-clad and tidy. The persons, clothing, and houses of the people were neat and clean."[49] In addition to clothing, housing, and food, each adult male farm laborer received between ten and fifteen dollars per month in wages and a small garden plot. Finally, two schools were provided for black children.[50]

Obviously, the federal government was genuinely interested in these farms and the people on them, and in the provision of guidance, food, equipment, and teachers, sought to run them as efficiently as possible. Moreover, in the caliber of personnel the Bureau chose to conduct farm operations, it did exceptionally well. For most of the period in question, Edward O'Brien served as commanding officer, with the assistance of Harry D. Bryon and Edward H. Gates. All three were determined friends of black progress who sought to demonstrate the ability of freed people to thrive under conditions conducive to their progress. The farms presented a "marked contrast" with what had preceded them in St. Mary's County, reported Bryon in January 1866, and showed "the difference between compensated labor and slavery."[51]

Still, the farms did not survive. By the end of 1866, the Freedmen's Bureau and all five hundred residents were out of business, the former having restored the land to its previous owners and the latter (both laborers and leaseholders) located wherever possible on private farms in southern Maryland or in Virginia. From the start, the whole project had the earmarks of a temporary expedient. During the war, military authorities in Washington were hard-pressed to care for thousands of "contrabands" and placing them on abandoned farms or confiscated lands provided an easy solution. With the end of hostilities and the assumption of responsibilities by the Freedmen's Bureau, the basic purpose of the farms did not change. Their sponsors still saw them as a means of assisting refugees in a time of emergency and not as permanent institutions. As early as May 1865, Oliver Otis Howard, commissioner of the Freedmen's Bureau, hinted at the imminent restoration of abandoned and confiscated land to private ownership, and in September, he announced that such action awaited only the presidential pardon of the individuals involved.[52] A month later, President Andrew Johnson extended such clemency to the Sothoron family and in the spring of 1866 to the Forrests.[53]

Other factors contributed to the farms' demise. Begun as refugee camps, they always contained too many dependents incapable of work. In fact, the task of issuing rations to indigent refugees soon became one of the farms' chief functions and denied them the chance of becoming truly self-sufficient. To make matters worse, returns from the sale of cash crops were never adequate to provide for even the able-bodied workers. Many rations went to farmhands who required extra food to meet family needs.[54] Added to the financial burden of providing rations was the expense of maintaining buildings and equipment. The Bureau reckoned that it had over $100,000 invested in implements and materials on the farms, some of it requiring costly upkeep.[55] Furthermore, the Bureau provided teachers, medical services, and military protection. None of these came cheaply, nor could their cost be offset by the sale of crops.[56]

Finally, there was one thing the Government Farms never did receive, and that was the support of rural white Marylanders and their conservative sympathizers. From the day the United States Army settled its first refugees on the banks of the Patuxent, the majority of white planters in the area objected vehemently. When it became apparent that early complaints were not about to budge the government, the *Baltimore Gazette* took up the cause of the dispossessed owners, branding the army's and the Bureau's occupation of the land as "one of the most wanton and shameful . . . outrages which have been perpetrated upon the people of Maryland within the past four years."[57] Days later, Governor Augustus W. Bradford wrote Howard in language less extreme but equally to the point. "Conditions [in St. Mary's County] ought to be altered as soon as possible," he said. "[I]f the government means to retain possession of these farms, immediate measures [should] be taken to turn them into money by confiscation and sale; or if not, they [should] be delivered to their former owners."[58]

Nor was it just the principle of land dispossession that disturbed white Marylanders. Planters near the government farms claimed that the latter were a nuisance and that the people living there were respon-

TABLE 2.1

MONTHLY REPORT OF THE GOVERNMENT FARMS, ST. MARY'S COUNTY,
MARYLAND, FOR MONTH ENDING AUGUST 31, 1865

Farm #1 [Sothoron], Name of Former Owner: John Sothoron
County: St. Mary's
Boundaries: North, Indian Creek; East, Patuxent River; West,
  land occupied by Dr. Shaw; South, Cat Creek.
How Held: Abandoned.
Cultivated Acres: 700
Cleared: 200
Woodland: 600
Buildings: 1 brick mansion, 10 barns, 1 dairy, 1 stable, 2 store houses and 10 log huts,
  1 new building 200 × 24 feet and 1 school house.
Remarks: There are engaged in the cultivation of the farm 58 women and 50 men, all
  self-supporting and 28 dependent women, 1 man and 28 children under 14.

Farm #2 [Sand Gates], Name of Former Owner: Joseph Forrest
County: St. Mary's
Boundaries: Patuxent River [None other given].
How Held: Abandoned.
Cultivated Acres: 200
Cleared: 140
Woodland: 785
Buildings: 2 brick houses, 1 frame building, 1 saw and grist mill, 1 wharf and 30 log
  huts.
Remarks: There are engaged in the cultivation of this farm 43 laboring men, 36 women
  self-supporting, also 52 dependent women and 120 children under 14 years of age.

Farm #3 [Coles Creek], Name of Former Owner: Joseph Forrest
County: St. Mary's
Boundaries: Patuxent River [None other given].
How Held: Abandoned.
Cultivated Acres: 200
Cleared: 140
Woodland: 360
Buildings: 2 wood houses, 1 stable and shed, 2 barns, 1 school house, and 14 huts.
Remarks: 27 laboring men and 23 women are self-supporting. Nine dependent women
  and 55 children under 14 years of age

Total of All Three Farms
Cultivated Acres: 1100
Cleared: 465
Woodland: 1745
Total: 3310

Source: Box Records, "Monthly Report of Lands," BRFAL, D.C., RG 105.

sible for untold neighborhood mischief. In September 1865, one such individual informed Bradford that:

> I am living directly between the two farms that was his [Forrest's] and are now occupied by the Government. I have been very much annoyed by them passing and repassing through my fields, trampling on my crops, leaving my fencing down and thus exposing my crops to stock and pilfering upon my fields. . . . There is on these two farms at times 4 or 5 hundred of these creatures so you may guess there is unpleasant living thus. Hundreds of those idle might be useful to themselves and the country if they could hire themselves out and work.[59]

That the Bureau could and did prove such allegations false or exaggerated did nothing to alter the fact that practically all white planters shared these opinions. They objected to the government's possession of the land, the presence of so many freed people in one place, and the tendency of the farms to encourage their "indolence" and "laziness."

Of course, the Freedmen's Bureau did not always pay close heed to the opinions and objections of white planters, even when backed by their state government. Indeed, in such matters as apprenticeship, civil rights, and contract abuse, its officers proved eager to combat conservative opinion, which had just as much authority behind it. Nevertheless, in the general area of land, labor, and the postwar reconciliation between planters and freedmen, the Bureau proved restrained by the limits of what it saw as a dual responsibility: one part devoted to the interests of freed people, the other to those of the planters. In the end, what it sought as much as anything else, was a harmonious relationship between ex-slaves and masters that satisfied the needs of *both* parties. Basically, the Bureau came to think in terms of an early restoration of the agrarian *status-quo ante bellum* with a well-treated but still restricted labor force taking the place of slaves.

It was this prospect that accounted partially for the Bureau's refusal to become too deeply involved in experiments in land tenure, or for that matter in contractual negotiations themselves between farm laborers and white planters. From the beginning, federal officers acceded to several contract stipulations designed by planters that lay at the core of the latter's attempts to reassert control over Maryland's black labor force. Of primary importance in this regard were the level of wages, the amount of work to be done, and the insistence upon a one-year contract that could be broken by the worker only with his employer's permission. Private and even Bureau-made contracts confirmed such ultimate authority of white employers, and although federal agents sought to assure blacks fair treatment and the regular receipt of "remunerative" wages, they did nothing to interfere with planters' power to determine blacks' economic status or geographic mobility.

IV

In part, the Bureau's failure to contribute more to greater black independence reflected the economic values of the time. As the Republican *Baltimore American* explained, hours of labor and rates of wages should be left to "the law of demand and supply."[60] But there was much more to it than that. Federal agents proved as genuinely determined to relate their policy to the needs of planters as to the aspirations of freedmen, and in so doing accorded them equal consideration. This included the automatic assumption that whites would remain planters and employers, and most black people laborers and employees. The Bureau's work, said Edward O'Brien, "is an honest effort to reestablish or re-organize the labor system, and is intended to be mutually beneficial to the employer and laborer."[61] Bureau agents were regularly instructed to explain "the duties and relations of whites and blacks *to each other*,"[62] and as John Eaton explained, "Great efforts have been made to reconcile the labor and capital thereabouts and induce the negroes to engage at industry with private parties."[63]

Like other white reformers, Bureau agents believed that freed slaves required a type of on-the-job tutelage that combined black aspirations for independence with planters' desire to have a reliable labor force at their disposal. In speaking to rural black audiences, Edgar Gregory often lectured them on the "duty of industry and scrupulous regard to the performance of contracts entered into."[64] He and his subordinates believed that only through such adherence to contractual responsibilities could blacks mature from childlike slaves to responsible adult workers. As a consequence, Bureau agents expressed repeated concern when black laborers violated such working stipulations as the one-year contract when no apparant ill treatment by planters was involved. "This habit of breaking contracts is an evil one," reported George Henry in July 1866, "as it often embarrasses the farmer, his men leaving him when he most needs their services."[65]

Nor was the government content with merely chiding workers who broke contracts. In a number of ways it pressed them to stay in place and at work just as it forced planters to honor their part of such agreements. In February 1866, C. H. Howard ordered agents in his district to deny support to families who "refused to accept situations . . . where they will be well treated."[66] In contracts drawn up by the Bureau, "each party was bound to perform faithfully, the freedmen agreeing that 25 per cent of their monthly wages may be retained in the hands of the employer until the expiration of their term of service."[67] On occasion the Bureau even blacklisted absconding laborers, taking out advertisements in local newspapers. "All persons are hereby cautioned against employing Henry Wilson," read one such entry in the *Port Tobacco Times,* "[he] having contracted to enter the service of Mr. Hamilton for and during the year 1866, and left such service without cause."[68]

Given the nature of Bureau sympathy with planter interests, it is not surprising that James Johnston could report in July 1866 that "now there is a feeling of confidence springing up among the white men in regard to the operations of the Bureau and the actions of its officers."[69] Obviously such confidence could not extend to the illegal withholding of wages or physical mistreatment of black laborers, but it remained true that the Bureau recognized the need of white planters to have a steady, available work force, and lent active assistance in maintaining it. White employers soon discovered that not all contract disputes adjudicated by the Bureau went in favor of the freedman. In June 1866, for example, Benjamin Haskins, a black laborer in Montgomery County, accused his employer James Higgins of withholding a portion of wages due him for services rendered since November 1865. After investigating the matter, R. G. Rutherford's decision was succinctly to the point. "Complaint dismissed," he wrote, "it appearing on examination, that Haskins had received all he could justly claim, having been unable to work a good part of the time and having violated an agreement in leaving without sufficient cause."[70]

Federal agents expressed the greatest satisfaction when freedmen under their charge were diligently at work in the fields abiding by their one-year contracts. Among many such observers, A. W. Bolenius in May 1866 praised "the good moral conduct of the colored community and their usefulness as laborers."[71] While touring the Eastern Shore in July of the same year, James Johnston reported that "The freedmen are industriously at work, and there is little, if any, idleness among them."[72]

Later that month, from Talbot County, Wells Bailey congratulated freed people on their progress and added that by their "uniform and general good conduct," they were "gaining the good opinion" of prospective employers.[73] And finally, according to R. G. Rutherford in October 1866, "The freedmen in this county . . . [are] an industrious and well disposed class of peoples. . . . [A]s a general thing [they] manifest a desire to avoid trouble with the white people."[74]

In siding so openly with the aspirations of white planters, Bureau agents did not see themselves as defenders of conservative traditions. The efforts they put forth to assist black workers were more than enough to convince them that the primary function of their work was to protect the rights of newly freed slaves.[75] Nevertheless, in trying to accomplish this goal within the context of a general agrarian restoration, "harmonious" or otherwise, federal agents assisted in the creation of a rural class structure almost as rigid as that of slavery. As the annual contract at planter-determined wages gradually took hold, black mobility, geographic or occupational, diminished. By the late 1860s, relative stability had returned to the Maryland tidewater (a fact that pleased Bureau agent and conservative planter alike for different, yet complementary reasons), but it had been achieved at considerable cost to the black community. By forcing freed slaves to find work that tied them to rural planters at wages supportive of self and family but little else, Bureau agents denied them whatever chance emancipation might have offered to escape their traditional economic status.

That they were party to such a denial did not occur to federal agents. Not only did they believe that steady contract labor was in black Marylanders' immediate best interest but they thought it ideally suited to their long-run economic freedom too. Hard work and contractual responsibility were to act ultimately as liberating, not restrictive, influences in helping them adjust from slavery to freedom. "There is no doubt," said Charles McDougall in May 1866, "that in a few years when they become accustomed to their new status, they will be greatly benefitted."[76] Later that year, George Henry added that in time black people would become "more conversant with the manner of doing business and better able to look out for their own interests."[77] It was, as Bureau Commissioner Oliver Otis Howard explained as the Bureau reduced its Maryland operations in October 1868, a question of their increased "general intelligence." They had become, he said, "more capable of securing their own rights in labor contracts and before the courts."[78]

In arguing in this fashion, Howard demonstrated the Bureau's concern for the rights of freed people, and that the effort, to use Eaton's words, to "reconcile" the interests of workers and planters represented something far more progressive than simply an attempt to reinstate white authority over freed slaves.[79] According to the Bureau, the purpose of its presence in Maryland was to enable blacks to stand on their own feet within the framework of a restructured agrarian system. "All visiting agents," ordered Howard in February 1866, "are enjoined to impress upon the colored people the necessity of self-support."[80]

The intent of enforced contracts was to do just that. Too much liberty for a people inadequately trained in the arts of self-help was, to the Bureau, counterproductive. Without contractual restraint, explained James Johnston, "It seems they cannot set a due value on their labor and are ever dissatisfied with their wages and rarely remain longer than a few days with one man but are constantly changing places."[81] Similarly, Bureau agents believed that lessons in contractual responsibility were much more efficacious than government-supported experiments in community land tenure. The former taught individual responsibility, the latter risked black dependency or even idleness. It was an honest sentiment, one that reflected nicely the laissez-faire economic ideology so prevalent among white reformers at the time.[82]

V

The Bureau wished to restrict its interference in Maryland to a minimum and to direct its essential actions toward the preparation of black self-reliance. In doing so, of course, it accomplished something closer to the opposite of self-reliance. Enforced contracts at subsistence wages handed ultimate control over tidewater economics back to white planters. The latter were not reformers and did not view diligent wage labor as an essentially liberating force. Throughout the Bureau's tenure in Maryland, conservative planters looked suspiciously upon its work, and although some were pleasantly surprised at the manner in which federal policy answered their own needs, most objected to the Bureau's presence. Since their state had never left the Union, rural whites felt qualified to look after freed people themselves and insisted on their right to do so. It was a compelling argument, one bolstered by such state officials as Augustus Bradford, who regarded the presence of the Bureau as an unwarranted intrusion into the affairs of loyal citizens destined to excite "extreme dissatisfaction."[83]

Under the control of white planters and in the face of such opinions, rural black Marylanders did not have much to build on. Steady work at sufficient pay to support a family and perhaps send a child to school or relieve a wife from labor in the fields was something (and indeed much appreciated), but it was insufficient to break the chains of economic subordination. To the extent that Bureau attitudes and policy contributed to that status, the federal government was responsible for the creation of a new second-class citizenship for black people. Despite their good intentions, Bureau agents failed to provide them with adequate leverage to translate self-reliance and hard work into genuine economic freedom.

NOTES

1. See chapter 4.
2. See chapter 8.
3. See chapter 5.
4. John W. Blassingame, "The Recruitment of Negro Troops in Maryland," *Maryland Historical Magazine* 58 (1963): 20–29; Fuke, "A School for Freed Labor"; Richard Paul Fuke, "Planters, Apprenticeship, and Forced Labor: The Black Family under Pressure in Postemancipation Maryland," *Agricultural History* 62 (fall 1988): 57–74.
5. Lewis ("Lew") Wallace was born in Indiana in 1827. He began to study law and then volunteered to fight in the Mexican War where he served as a first lieutenant. After the war he passed the bar and served in the Indiana legislature. During the Civil War he served as adjutant-general of Indiana, colonel of the 11th Indiana Volunteers, and brigadier and major general of volunteers. He commanded the 8th Army Corps of the Middle Department, headquarters Baltimore, and fought against Jubal Early at the Battle of Monocacy in July 1864 (*Dictionary of American Biography*, 19: 37–76; James Grant Wilson and John Fiske, eds., *Appleton's Cyclopedia of American Biography* [New York, 1898], Vol. 6, 334).
6. *The Statutes at Large of the United States of America*, Vol. 13, December 1863 to December 1865 (Boston, 1866), 507–8.
7. *Baltimore American*, October 3, 1865; E. M. Gregory to O. O. Howard, November 3, 1866, Volume 3 (Letters Sent, Assistant Commissioner, April 1, 1866–August 17, 1868), BRFAL, Md., RG 105.

8. *The Statutes at Large of the United States of America,* Vol. 14, December 1865 to March 1867 (Boston, 1868), 174.

9. *Baltimore American,* December 16, 1865.

10. "Summary Report of the District of Columbia, by Brevet Brigadier General John Eaton Jr., Assistant Commissioner [December 15, 1865]," *Senate Executive Documents for the First Session of the Thirty-Ninth Congress of the United States of America, 1865–1866* (Washington, 1866), 2:158.

11. *Chestertown Transcript,* April 7, 1866 [#1133]; Miscellaneous Contracts, Office of the Assistant Commissioner, BRFAL, D.C., RG 105.

12. E. F. O'Brien to J. S. Fullerton, December 30, 1865, Box 1 (LRAC, September, 1865–October 27, 1866), BRFAL, D.C., RG 105.

13. O. O. Howard to E. M. Gregory, January 24, 1867, Box 1 (LRAC, April 1, 1866–August 17, 1868), BRFAL, Md., RG 105; Circular No. 2, Assistant Commissioner, District of Columbia, February 20, 1866, Volumes 26, 27 (Special Orders and Circulars), BRFAL, D.C., RG 105.

14. "Summary Report of the District of Columbia [December 15, 1865]," 153.

15. *Chestertown Transcript,* April 7, 1866; Miscellaneous Contracts, Office of the Assistant Commissioner, BRFAL, D.C., RG 105. "Fine" is not quite the word. Employers were "bound" to a certain sum, usually a figure approximating the employee's yearly wages. I suppose this means they would have to forfeit this money if they failed to live up to the agreement in question. I have no evidence to suggest that this or any portion of it was "up front" money, nor do I know if anyone was forced to pay.

16. S. N. Clark to J. Eaton Jr., August 21, 1865, State Papers, Maryland State Archives; Special Order No. 8, Assistant Commissioner, District of Columbia, September 7, 1865, Volumes 26, 27 (Special Orders and Circulars), BRFAL, D.C., RG 105.

17. W. S. Bailey to J. F. Chur, July 16, 1866, Box 1 (LRAC, April 1, 1866–August 17, 1868), BRFAL, Md., RG 105; G. E. Henry to W. W. Rogers, October 22, 1866, Volume 50 (Register of Letters Sent, Bladensburg, June 4, 1866–September 18, 1867), BRFAL, Md., RG 105; R. G. Rutherford to C. H. Howard, October 27, 1866, Volume 53 (Register of Letters Sent, Rockville, June 5, 1866–October 20, 1867), BRFAL, Md., RG 105.

18. E. F. O'Brien to S. N. Clark, January 4, 1866, Box 1 (LRAC, September 1865–October 27, 1866), BRFAL, D.C., RG 105. "In looking over the contract," O'Brien added, "you will find the parties of the second part are not to have any parties in their houses only those mentioned in the contract thus virtually shutting off from each other members of the same family."

19. E. F. O'Brien to J. S. Fullerton, December 30, 1865, Box 1 (LRAC, September 1865–October 27, 1867), BRFAL, D.C., RG 105. It would appear that O'Brien encountered some difficulty because of his opinions and actions.

In his letter to Clark on January 4, 1866, he felt called upon to provide a "rebutting answer to the statements made that I do not allow freedmen to make their own contracts." This would suggest that even in St. Mary's County, where the Bureau was charged with finding work with private parties for the blacks on the Government Farms, its officers were not to take an initiatory role in making contracts. Interestingly, in May 1866, Seldon Clark was ordered to investigate possible "irregularities by Bureau officers in St. Mary's." This may have been in reference to O'Brien, but perhaps not, because he had been transferred more than a month earlier. Clark made no mention of O'Brien or "irregularities" in his report Special Order No. 38, Assistant Commissioner, District of Columbia, May 31, 1866, Volumes 26, 27 (Special Orders and Circulars), BRFAL, D.C., RG 105; S. N. Clark to C. H. Howard, June 16, 1866, Box 11 (Letters Received, Annapolis, July 20, 1866–September 11, 1868), BRFAL, Md., RG 105.

20. "Summary Report of the District of Columbia [December 15, 1865]," 158.

21. G. E. Henry to W. W. Rogers, July 19, 1867, Volume 50 (Register of Letters Sent, Bladensburg, June 4, 1866–September 18, 1867), BRFAL, Md., RG 105.

22. Browne and Smithers to C. H. Howard, March 1, 1867, Box 12 (Letters Received, Bladensburg, May 1866–December 1867) BRFAL, Md., RG 105.

23. A. K. Browne to C. H. Howard, May 17, 1867, Box 12 (Letters Received, Bladensburg, May 1866–December 1867), BRFAL, Md., RG 105.

24. W. F. Spurgin to W. W. Rogers, May 28, 1866, Box 12 (Letters Received, Rockville, May 19, 1866–September 30, 1867), BRFAL, Md., RG 105.

25. Volume 55 (Complaints, Rockville), BRFAL, Md., RG 105.

26. Volume 51 (Complaints, Bladensburg), BRFAL, Md., RG 105.

27. R. G. Rutherford to C. H. Howard, October 27, 1866, Volume 53 (Register of Letters Sent, Rockville, June 5, 1866–October 2, 1867), BRFAL, Md., RG 105.

28. Volume 17 (Complaints), BRFAL, Md., RG 105 [#M4–5]; *Baltimore American*, July 7, 1866; *Baltimore Sun*, July 7, 1866.

29. Volume 17 (Complaints), BRFAL, Md., RG 105; O. O. Howard to E. M. Gregory, January 24, 1867, Box 1 (LRAC, April 1, 1866–August 17, 1868), BRFAL, Md., RG 105; *Baltimore American*, July 7, 1866.

30. G. E. Henry to G. W. Gardener, October 9, 1866, Volume 50 (Register of Letters Sent, Bladensburg, June 4, 1866–September 18, 1867), BRFAL, Md., RG 105.

31. R. G. Rutherford to C. H. Howard, October 27, 1866, Volume 53 (Register of Letters Sent, Rockville, June 5, 1866–October 2, 1867), BRFAL, Md., RG 105.

32. G. E. Henry to W. W. Rogers, July 19, 1867, Volume 50 (Register of Letters Sent, Bladensburg, June 4, 1866–September 18, 1867), BRFAL, Md., RG 105.

33. E. M. Gregory to O. O. Howard, November 3, 1866, Volume 3 (Register of Letters Sent, Assistant Commissioner, April 1, 1866–August 17, 1868), BRFAL, Md., RG 105; E. M. Gregory to O. O. Howard, December 31, 1866, Box 10 (Reports), BRFAL, Md., RG 105; W. L. VanDerlip to W. W. Rogers, July 19, 1867, Volume 48 (Register of Letters Sent, Annapolis, June 28, 1866–March 13, 1868), BRFAL, Md., RG 105; G. E. Henry to W. W. Rogers, July 19, 1867, Volume 50 (Register of Letters Sent, Bladensburg, June 4, 1866–September 18, 1867), BRFAL, Md., RG 105.

34. "Letter of the Secretary of War . . . [Including] Reports of the Assistant Commissioners of Freedmen," *Executive Documents of the Senate of the United States, Second Session, Thirty-Ninth Congress, 1866–1867* (Washington, 1867), 2:42.

35. R. G. Rutherford to C. H. Howard, October 27, 1866, Volume 53 (Register of Letters Sent, Rockville, June 5, 1866–October 2, 1867), BRFAL, Md., RG 105.

36. *Baltimore American*, April 3, 1866.

37. Ibid., August 12, 1865.

38. S. N. Clark to J. Eaton Jr., August 21, 1865, State Papers [1865], Maryland State Archives. Emphasis added.

39. A. W. Bolenius to Baltimore H. Q., May 31, 1866, Box 1 (LRAC, April 1, 1866–August 17, 1868), BRFAL, Md., RG 105.

40. F. Von Shirach to Baltimore H. Q., June 8, 1866, ibid.

41. J. H. Johnston to J. F. Chur, July 19, 1866, ibid.

42. G. E. Henry to W. W. Rogers, September 18, 1867, Volume 50 (Register of Letters Sent, Bladensburg, June 4, 1866–September 18, 1867), BRFAL, Md., RG 105.

43. E. M. Gregory to O. O. Howard, November 3, 1866, Volume 3 (Register of Letters Sent, Assistant Commissioner, April 1, 1866–August 17, 1868), BRFAL, Md., RG 105.

44. R. G. Rutherford to C. H. Howard, October 27, 1866, Volume 53 (Register of Letters Sent, Rockville, June 5, 1866–October 2, 1867), BRFAL, Md., RG 105.

45. S. N. Clark to J. Eaton Jr., August 24, 1865, State Papers [1865], Maryland State Archives.

46. O. O. Howard to J. Eaton Jr., September 27, 1865, Box 1 (LRAC, September 1865–October 27, 1866). BRFAL, D.C., RG 105; Special Order No. 17, Assistant Commissioner, District of Columbia, March 8, 1866, Volumes 26, 27 (Special Orders and Circulars), BRFAL, D.C., RG 105.

47. *Baltimore American*, August 10, 1865; E. F. O'Brien to J. S. Fullerton,

December 30, 1865, Box 1 (LRAC, September 1865–October 27, 1866), BRFAL, D.C., RG 105.

48. *Baltimore American,* August 10, 1865.

49. S. N. Clark to J. Eaton Jr., August 24, 1865, State Papers [1865], Maryland State Archives.

50. *Baltimore American,* August 10, 1865.

51. Ibid., January 9, 1866.

52. Ibid., May 31, September 15, 1865.

53. See above, note 43.

54. Monthly Report of Lands, Office of the Assistant Commissioner, BRFAL, D.C., RG 105. See also C. Marchal Fuller, "Governmental Action to Aid Freedmen in Maryland, 1864–1869, with Special Emphasis on the Freedmen's Bureau" (M.A. thesis, Howard University, 1965).

55. S. N. Clark to J. Eaton Jr., August 24, 1865, State Papers [1865], Maryland State Archives.

56. Ibid.

57. *Baltimore Gazette,* August 30, October 12, 1865.

58. A. W. Bradford to O. O. Howard, October 4, 1865, State Papers [1865], Maryland State Archives.

59. H. Jones to A. W. Bradford, September 23, 1865, Ibid.

60. *Baltimore American,* April 3, 1866.

61. Ibid., December 16, 1865.

62. Special Order No. 8, Assistant Commissioner, District of Columbia, September 7, 1865, Volumes 26, 27 (Special Orders and Circulars), BRFAL, D.C., RG 105.

63. "Summary Report of the District of Columbia [December 15, 1865]," 153.

64. *Baltimore American,* August 5, 1867.

65. G. E. Henry to W. W. Rogers, July 14, 1866, Volume 50 (Register of Letters Sent, Bladensburg, June 4, 1866–September 18, 1867), BRFAL, Md., RG 105.

66. Circular No. 2, Assistant Commissioner, District of Columbia, February 20, 1866, Volumes 26, 27 (Special Orders and Circulars), BRFAL, D.C., RG 105.

67. *Chestertown Transcript,* April 7, 1866.

68. *Port Tobacco Times,* July 26, 1866. Quoted in *Baltimore American,* July 30, 1866.

69. J. Johnston to J. F. Chur, July 25, 1866, Box 1 (LRAC, April 1, 1866–August 17, 1868), BRFAL, Md., RG 105.

70. Volume 55 (Complaints, Rockville), BRFAL, Md., RG 105.

71. A. W. Bolenius to Baltimore H. Q., May 31, 1866, Ibid.

72. *Baltimore American,* July 7, 1866 [#1334]; *Baltimore Sun,* July 7, 1866.

73. W. Bailey to J. F. Chur, July 16, 1866, Box 1 (LRAC, April 1, 1866–August 17, 1868), BRFAL, Md., RG 105.

74. R. G. Rutherford to C. H. Howard, October 27, 1866, Volume 53 (Register of Letters Sent, Rockville, June 5, 1866–October 2, 1867), BRFAL, Md., RG 105.

75. See below, note 77.

76. C. McDougall to Baltimore H. Q., May 30, 1866, Box 1 (LRAC, April 1, 1866–August 17, 1868), BRFAL, Md., RG 105.

77. G. E. Henry to W. W. Rogers, October 22, 1866, Volume 50 (Register of Letters Sent, Bladensburg, June 4, 1866–September 18, 1867), BRFAL, Md., RG 105.

78. "Report of Major General O. O. Howard, Commissioner of the Bureau of Refugees, Freedmen, and Abandoned Lands . . . October 14, 1868," *Executive Documents, Printed by Order of the House of Representatives during the Third Session of the Fortieth Congress, 1868–69,* 14 Vols. (Washington, 1869), 3:1032.

79. Important recent works disagree with this assessment. William Mc-Feely and C. Peter Ripley, among others, see in the actions of the Bureau a pragmatic and even cynical policy designed to assist planter conservatives in controlling black labor. I would suggest that they and others unnecessarily belittle the reform impulse contained in mid-nineteenth-century ideas of individualism and laissez-faire. I agree that the Bureau's confidence in both was sadly misplaced, but to suggest that its policy was without progressive goals, without hope of making freedom for blacks fundamentally different from slavery, is simply incorrect. See William S. McFeely, *Yankee Stepfather: General O. O. Howard and the Freedmen* (New Haven, 1968) and C. Peter Ripley, *Slaves and Freedmen in Civil War Louisiana* (Baton Rouge, 1978).

80. Circular No. 2, Assistant Commissioner, District of Columbia, February 20, 1866, Volumes 26, 27 (Special Orders and Circulars), BRFAL, D.C., RG 105.

81. W. Johnston to J. F. Chur, July 19, 1866, Box 1 (LRAC, April 1, 1866–August 17, 1868), BRFAL, Md., RG 105.

82. For a thorough discussion of mid-nineteenth-century economic and political laissez-faire attitudes see Eric McKitrick, "Reconstruction's Ultraconservative Revolution," in *The Comparative Approach to American History,* ed. C. Vann Woodward (New York, 1968), 146–59; Michael Les Benedict, "Preserving the Constitution: The Conservative Basis of Radical Reconstruction," *Journal of American History* 61 (June 1974): 65–90; Donald G. Neiman, *To Set the Law in Motion: The Freedmen's Bureau and the Legal Rights of Blacks, 1865–1868* (Millwood, N. Y., 1979), xiii–xiv.

83. A. W. Bradford to O. O. Howard, October 4, 1865, State Papers [1865], Maryland State Archives.

3

A Few Acres of Land

I

SLAVES AND FREE BLACKS in tidewater Maryland had long sought access to at least some land as a way of resisting the dehumanization of bondage. Many slaves farmed garden plots that supplemented their diet and permitted minimal redirection of individual and family labor. Others assisted free relatives or neighbors in the cultivation of owned, rented, or sharecropped acres. Free laborers who actually owned land occupied the tip of a pre-emancipation pyramid that defined the autonomous possibilities within a tightly controlled system. By enhancing their capacity to employ land as the basis of a partially independent relationship with their employers, emancipation encouraged both the continuation and expansion of an important historical process.[1]

Such land was important, for although post-emancipation black proprietors in Maryland were few and their holdings small, the possession of even one or two acres helped enhance the options of their owners and those of the people around them. Through the individual and collective purchase of such land, black people could redirect a portion of their labor to personal, family, and community use. Alongside their struggle for fair contracts and the release of their children from enforced apprenticeship, access to even scattered pieces of land on which they might live, grow food, and build schools helped blunt the effect of otherwise tight control by whites over their daily lives and labor.

II

Access to land was particularly important in the slaveholding counties of the Eastern Shore, and—to a much lesser extent—in southern Maryland, where it fit a long-standing pattern of economic race relations based on a mixture of free and slave labor. At the time of general emancipation in November 1864, 36.5 percent of the black labor force in Maryland's fourteen Eastern Shore and southern counties was already free, enjoyed access to some land, and exercised partial control over the disposition of its labor.[2]

The presence of such a large free black community facilitated the exposure of newly freed slaves to the options hitherto enjoyed by their already free relatives and neighbors, including access to some land. Indeed, federal census data suggest that in many areas, post-1864 land acquisition represented something more than simply the continuation of past patterns. In Anne Arundel County in southern Maryland and in several counties on the Eastern Shore, enough new landowners appeared between 1860 and 1870 to indicate post-emancipation opportunities beyond those available to the pre-1864 black community. Moreover, insofar as many purchases served new, freedom-inspired community aspirations—especially collective purchases for the construction of schools—they improved blacks' prospects of controlling their own affairs in ways denied them before emancipation.

According to the population schedules of the United States Censuses of 1860 and 1870, the number of individual black Marylanders and groups (in the case of schools) who possessed land grew in each of the fourteen tidewater counties except one during the decade. In Anne Arundel it jumped from 80 to 137, in Kent from 201 to 340, in Queen Anne's from 74 to 271, and in Worcester, Somerset, and Wicomico combined, from 232 to 441. Altogether, the number of landowners recorded in the United States Census population schedules for these counties grew from 1,467 to 2,068.[3]

Of course, federal census data provide information for the years 1860 and 1870 and do not prove that such acquisition occurred exclusively or even primarily after 1864. Various other pieces of information, however, suggest that it did. Surviving deeds for Kent County, for example, indicate an appreciable increase in the purchase of land by blacks between 1864 and 1870. Altogether, 74 blacks are listed in the Kent County land transaction index as having acquired deeds during the decade, 58 of whom did so after emancipation.[4] Additional evidence appears in a tax assessment of Queen Anne's County taken in or around 1865 that lists 29 blacks who possessed $100 or more worth of real estate, a number approximating the 1860 federal population schedule figure of 21.[5] Significantly, by 1870 the number of such landowners listed in the census population schedule for the first and second election districts combined had grown to 167, a figure that may have included

as many as 88 from the second district alone.[6] Assessment records for
Somerset and Montgomery Counties appear to indicate similar increases in land acquisition after 1864.[7]

III

The mechanics of black land acquisition varied. In every county there
lived a few established free laborers who earned enough money from
land they already owned to purchase additional acres. The agricultural
schedule of the United States Census of 1870 lists a number of individuals with annual farm produce valued in excess of $100 who could
clearly afford to expand their holdings. In 1867, for example, Samuel
Derry, a black farmer near Chestertown, Kent County, purchased
eleven acres in Quaker's Neck for $458. In 1870, the census estimated
Derry's total holdings of twenty-eight acres to be worth $2,000. In
addition Derry owned two horses, two cows, and seven hogs. His 224
bushels of wheat, 600 bushels of corn, 10 bushels of Irish potatoes, 6
bushels of sweet potatoes, 100 pounds of butter, and livestock sold
and slaughtered earned him $1,100 in 1869–70. In 1866 another Kent
County black farmer, George Elias, purchased two acres of land and a
dwelling for $150. This property constituted but a part of a larger
eight-acre holding with an estimated value of $800 in 1870, which
yielded $700 worth of annual produce.[8] Less affluent blacks probably
scrimped and saved whatever money they could from their wages or
from accumulated Union Army enlistment bounties and back pay to
purchase smaller plots of land. More than 2,700 tidewater black
men—an astonishing number given the area's population base—
enlisted in the United States Army in 1863 and 1864. For these soldiers, most of whom returned after being mustered out in 1865,
bounties or back pay offered an unprecedented cash "windfall" that
undoubtedly permitted some of them to buy land for the first time in
their lives.[9]

Perhaps in some of these cases, and certainly in others, employers
facilitated such acquisition by selling their workers small pieces of land
cheaply or by giving them such plots free of charge in exchange for
services rendered. In September 1865, R. M. Smyth of Kent County
sold William Bradshaw a fourth of an acre for eleven dollars. In April
1866, George Hynson sold Mary Warrens an acre for a dollar.[10] Two

TABLE 3.1

NUMBERS OF BLACKS LISTED IN UNITED STATES CENSUS POPULATION
SCHEDULES AS OWNING $100 WORTH OR MORE OF LAND
IN FOURTEEN TIDEWATER COUNTIES

| | 1860 | | | | 1870 | |
County	Total Blacks	Slaves	Free Blacks	Land Owners	Total Blacks	Land Owners
Charles	10,721	9,653	1,068	14	9,318	42
St. Mary's	8,415	6,549	1,866	21	7,726	46
Anne Arundel	12,196	7,332	4,864	80	11,732	137
Calvert	6,450	4,609	1,841	24	5,533	137
Montgomery	6,983	5,431	1,552	48	7,434	116
Prince George's	13,695	12,497	1,198	38	9,780	40
Cecil	3,868	950	2,918	60	4,014	117
Kent	5,920	2,509	3,411	201	7,732	340
Queen Anne's	7,546	4,174	3,372	74	6,592	271
Caroline	3,525	739	2,786	85	3,758	128
Talbot	6,689	3,725	2,964	112	6,666	196
Dorchester*	8,807	4,123	4,684	478	7,556	158
Somerset/Worcester/ Wicomico	16,879	8,737	8,142	232	17,539	441
Total	111,694	71,010	40,684	1,467	105,380	2,068

Source: U.S. Bureau of the Census, Population of the United States in 1860, 214; U.S. Bureau of the Census, A Compendium of the Ninth Census, 56–57; Eighth Census of the United States, 1860, Schedule 1—Free Inhabitants; Ninth Census of the United States, Schedule 1—Inhabitants.
*There is no apparent reason for a decline in Dorchester County landowning. I suspect a problem with the census and the manner in which landowning was recorded by the Dorchester County census takers.

years later, J. C. Anderson, a Queen Anne's County employer, agreed to bestow a piece of land upon a black apprentice at the expiration of his service.[11] Whites employed a number of methods such as binding contracts, apprenticeship, and even support for schools to ensure the presence of black labor. Helping the latter acquire small pieces of land may have been part of the same strategy.[12] In the case of collective purchases for schools, black families joined together either independently or under the auspices of the Freedmen's Bureau to raise the money necessary to buy land. Black trustees or Bureau agents started subscription lists, and such fund-raising ventures as bake sales and fairs were popular. Once again, sympathetic employers often facilitated the process by selling land cheaply, and on occasion, black landowners donated property outright.[13]

IV

Relative to their white counterparts, the number of black landowners obviously remained small. The 340 Kent County proprietors in 1870 represented only a small proportion of the county's landowners, and their combined holdings a miniscule portion of its real estate. Furthermore, only a handful of individuals possessed sufficient acreage to become self-sufficient, the vast majority holding small plots of land while working as wage laborers. The 1870 United States Census population schedule lists practically all Kent County black landowners as "laborers," "farm laborers," or "farm hands." In the first election district, for example, only eight are identified as "farmers," each of whom possessed at least eight hundred dollars worth of land. The rest appear as "laborers."[14]

Post-emancipation Kent County purchases were typically small. An examination of available deeds shows that Alexander Benson bought "seven acres more or less . . . near the Head of Sassafras" in October 1865 for $100. In January 1866 Stephen Johnson acquired five acres near Bel Air for $130, and in June, George Martin purchased "7 acres plus" from R. H. Harris for $210.[15] With property selling at between $25 and $50 an acre, few could afford anything more. Of the 257 new Kent County landowners who appeared in the 1870 population schedules, only 48 possessed property valued in excess of $500, and indeed, throughout tidewater Maryland, small plots predominated.[16] Furthermore, many "new" post-emancipation landowners were not new at all but belonged to the small segment of the free black population that had previously owned land. According to the land index, of the 54 Kent County blacks who recorded deed transactions (purchases, sales, and mortgages) between 1865 and 1870, 15 were individuals with full names identical to those of previous landowners. The deeds themselves are often more precise. In June 1865, for example, John Blake sold five acres of land to Richard Smyth (white) for $300. Blake had originally purchased the property in 1853. In July of the same year, William and Susan Ford sold land that they had first obtained in 1855.

TABLE 3.2

CONCENTRATION OF BLACK LANDOWNERS ACCORDING TO VALUE OF
LAND IN EIGHT SELECTED TIDEWATER COUNTIES, 1870

$	An.A.	Chas.	Dort.	Kent.	Mont.	P.G.	Q.A.	St.M.
100–200	8	19	24	30	24	8	49	1
200–300	8	4	28	85	20	6	59	1
300–400	8	5	19	70	20	4	39	7
400–500	6	3	9	32	6	2	23	5
500–600	10	6	24	36	11	6	33	3
600–700	4	1	6	18	4	—	9	5
700–800	3	—	4	4	2	1	7	1
800–900	1	1	6	19	6	1	5	—
900–1000	13	3	8	21	12	2	11	4
1000–1100	1	—	—	—	—	—	1	—
1100–1200	1	—	—	—	—	—	1	—
1200–1300	—	—	—	1	2	—	—	—
1300–1400	2	1	—	1	1	—	—	—
1400–1500	1	—	—	6	—	—	—	—
1500–1600	3	3	2	—	1	2	7	3
1600–1700	—	—	—	—	—	—	2	—
1700–1800	1	—	—	—	—	—	1	—
1800–1900	—	—	1	1	—	—	—	—
1900–2000	—	—	—	—	—	—	—	—
2000–2100	7	—	2	2	2	2	7	3
2100–2200	—	—	—	—	—	—	—	—
2200–2300	—	—	1	1	1	—	1	—
2300–2400	—	—	—	—	1	—	—	—
2400–2500	—	—	—	—	—	—	—	—
2500–2600	—	—	3	1	—	—	4	—
2600–2700	2	—	—	—	—	—	—	—
2700–2800	—	—	—	—	—	—	—	—
2800–2900	—	—	—	—	—	—	—	—
2900–3000	—	—	—	—	—	—	—	—
3000–3100	2	2	1	1	—	1	4	1
3100–3200	—	—	—	—	—	—	—	—
3200–3300	—	—	—	—	—	—	—	—
3300–3400	—	—	—	—	—	—	—	—
3400–3500	—	—	—	—	—	—	—	—
3500–3600	2	—	—	—	—	—	1	—
3600–3700	—	—	—	1	—	—	—	—
3700–3800	—	—	—	—	—	—	—	—
3800–3900	—	—	—	—	1	—	—	—
3900–4000	—	—	—	—	—	—	—	—
Over 4000	9	—	1	6	1	3	6	5

Source: Ninth Census of the United States, 1870, Schedule 1. I have removed the
Annapolis figures from the Anne Arundel County column to maintain the rural nature
of this table.

In July 1866, George Elias bought two acres from William Clay (white) to add to property he already possessed, and in April 1866, Thomas and Louisa Horton borrowed $65 using land they had originally purchased in 1863 as collateral.[17]

Insofar as post-emancipation land purchases were indeed a part of a long-standing pattern of limited access to land by Kent County blacks who worked for subsistence wages, then such purchases represented, not a new form of independence, but a part of the process whereby post-emancipation labor-management relations took on the forms that characterized those of pre-1864 relations between white employers and free blacks.[18] Furthermore, the increase in black landholding between 1860 and 1870, and the total value of all black property, real *and* personal, remained a small part of Maryland's wealth. In Kent County, where black landowning was at its highest, the 1866 assessment of all property totalled $4,574,740.[19] Four years later, 321 blacks owned land valued at $100 or more. Their total of $271,655 worth of land and personal property represented only 5.2 percent of the 1866 assessment whereas their population constituted almost 50 percent of the county total.[20] In 1870, in Charles County, where black landowning was low, less than 2 percent of that county's 1866 assessment of $3,298,027. Blacks constituted 59 percent of Charles County's total population.[21]

V

Thus black landowners were few in number and generally possessed small holdings. Many of them had either owned land before emancipation or were related to someone who had. These facts, however, should not conceal the benefits of even scattered plots of land to individual owners and the larger black community. For one thing, rural landowning families averaged between five and six members in 1870, and thus proprietorship directly affected more than 10 percent of Maryland's total tidewater black population and as much as 15 to 20 percent in several Eastern Shore counties.[22]

Furthermore, extended family relationships and the cooperation of friends and neighbors with and without land connected even more people to its use. Clearly, those who could, bought land, often in the same neighborhood, and many of those who could not lived close to black relatives or neighbors with acres of their own. According to surviving

TABLE 3.3

CONTINUITY IN BLACK LAND TRANSACTIONS IN KENT COUNTY, 1842–1870

Name	Year of Post-Emancipation Transaction	Year of Earlier Transactions by Person with Identical Full Name
Benson, Alexander	1865	1848
Brown, Binah	1866	1851, 1858(3), 1862
Brown, Isaac	1866	
Brown, Sarah	1869	
Blake, John	1865, 1866	1843, 1850, 1853
Bond, James	1867	
Butcher, Robert	1869	
Bradshaw, William	1865	
Chambers, Perry	1870(2)	
Chambers, William	1866	
Calahan, Charles	1866	
Clark, James	1866	
Castle, Levi	1866	
Chatham, George	1866	
Cooper, Jacob	1865	
Dixon, Perry	1866, 1869	
Elias, George	1866	1851
Ford, William	1865	1855
Frisby, Hamilton	1867, 1868, 1869	
Gaddis, Daniel	1867, 1869	
Gilbert, Susan	1867, 1870	
Garrettson, William	1868	
Houston, Thomas	1866	1861, 1863
Hyland, Robert	1868	
Hyland, R.	1868	
Jones, Charles	1869	
Jones, William	1866(2)	
Johnson, S. H.	1866	
James, Isaac	1865, 1867	
Kennard, Levi	1868	
Kennard, William	1868	
Lias, George	1865, 1867	
Little, Joshua	1866(2)	1855, 1864
Martin, George	1866	
Neal, Frederick	1865	

Name	Year of Post-Emancipation Transaction	Year of Earlier Transactions by Person with Identical Full Name
Potts, William	1865	
Pearce, James	1868	1846, 1848
Pearce, Benjamin	1865(2), 1867	
Pearce, Lemuel	1866	
Perkins, William	1866	1849, 1855(2), 1856, 1858, 1860, 1861, 1864
Reed, P. R.	1866	
Reason, James	1867	
Shepard, David	1866	
Scott, George	1867	
Salter, Rachel	1867	
Toomy, Jacob	1866, 1868	1856, 1864
Wilson, Jacob C.	1867	
Wilson, John	1869	1852
Wilson, Jonathan	1866	1860(2)
Wilson, James	1869	
Wilson, Robert	1866(2)	1855, 1858, 1864
Wallis, Fred	1866	1859
Wilmer, Jacob	1867(2)	
Warrens, Mary	1866	

Source: Deeds, Office of the County Commissioner, Kent County, Index and Liber #JKH 5, pp. 29, 51, 211, 425, Maryland State Archives, Annapolis, Md.

Kent County deeds, the land sold by John Blake in 1865 was next to that of Sandy Bond, "f[ree] n[egro]." Land acquired by Stephen Johnson in 1866, "[a]djoins some land owned by W. H. Chambers (col.)." A particular district called the "Grange" contained the properties of several black landowners, both old and new, some related and some not.[23]

When not so clustered, landowning blacks might associate instead with their nonlandowning relatives and neighbors. An alphabetized 1866 Somerset County tax assessment shows spread throughout the county 305 black landowners whose immediate families alone included more than 1,000 people—almost 11 percent of the county's 1860 black population—and whose contact with others must easily have doubled that figure.[24] The 1865 Queen Anne's County second election district tax assessment, which listed owners of land and other property in geographic order, further reveals the proximity of landed and landless blacks and suggests the ongoing nature of their contact.[25]

In a fairly typical neighborhood, William Woodland, Jim Cooper, James Boon, David Hall, and the heirs of Richard Rochester lived close together (several of them in the same dwelling) and owned a variety of land, livestock, and private possessions. Woodland owned a small house and twenty acres of land with three horses, a cow, four hogs, some furniture, and implements. Rochester's heirs owned similar acreage and also possessed a house but had no livestock or tools. Cooper, Boon, and Hall owned no land but possessed horses, cattle, hogs, and farm implements. Rochester's heirs may have been too young to work; the others were likely wage laborers. What did David Hall do with his seventy-five-dollar horse and his farming equipment? In all likelihood, he was a wage laborer or sharecropper who spent most of his time

TABLE 3.4

THE NUMBER OF PEOPLE IN BLACK LANDOWNING FAMILIES IN
FOURTEEN TIDEWATER COUNTIES, 1870

County	Landowners	Number in Families	Average Family	% Total Black Population
Charles	42	264	6.3	3.0
St. Mary's	46	279	6.1	4.0
Anne Arundel	142	813	5.7	6.9
Calvert	36	203	5.8	3.6
Montgomery	116	661	5.7	6.9
Prince George's	40	200	5.0	2.0
Cecil	117	573	4.9	14.0
Kent	340	1,769	5.6	22.8
Queen Anne's	271	1,418	5.2	21.5
Caroline	128	631	4.9	16.7
Talbot	196	957	4.9	14.3
Dorchester	158	911	5.8	12.0
Somerset/Worcester/ Wicomico	441	2,323	5.5	16.8
Total	2,068	11,002	5.3	10.8

Source: Ninth Census of the United States, 1870, Schedule 1.

working a white planter's land. But he may also have helped William Woodland, who already owned three horses, or Richard Rochester's heirs, who owned none.[26]

Such cooperation was even more likely when neighboring pieces of land belonged to blacks in the same immediate or extended families. Although many "new" landowning families were not new at all, their enlarged holdings nonetheless further benefited their relatives through extending the opportunity for cooperative endeavor. According to the 1866 Somerset County tax assessment, twenty-nine blacks—five named Barkley; six Conway; nine Dashiell; and nine Nutter—owned land in the Tyaskin District alone.[27] Even if cooperation between owners of small pieces of land in tidewater Maryland and those who owned no property were confined to blacks who were related to each other, their numbers and efforts would still be significant.

The 1870 United States Census data permit a similarly detailed study of the relationship between landowning and landless blacks. At the enumeration or election district level, the population schedule not only identifies landowners but also shows their approximate relationship to whites and other blacks. The schedule fails to delineate the routes taken by census takers, thus making it difficult to reconstruct actual neighborhoods. Nonetheless, it offers clear evidence of the close proximity of blacks with and without property. Once they are identified by name and district in the population schedule, many black landowners—especially those with more than a few acres—can be located in the agricultural schedule. Here appears precise information regarding acreage, crops, livestock, and value of farm produce. Although census takers were supposed to confine their accounting to those individuals whose land produced $500 worth of produce or more, in fact they included many who possessed smaller plots of land with lower production totals.[28]

From such information, an assessment of the extent and nature of black landholding and its geographic relationship to and among black and white neighbors with or without land becomes possible. Most black landowners lived close to both the propertied planters for whom most of them worked, and other black and white laborers who owned either small pieces of land or none at all. Apart from a few pockets of all-white or all-black settlement, most rural areas featured a mixture of people and landholding patterns. Black landowners lived in the midst of a geographically interracial community made up of both landed and landless residents.[29]

TABLE 3.5

ASSESSMENT OF PROPERTY OWNED BY BLACKS IN THE SECOND
ELECTION DISTRICT OF QUEEN ANNE'S COUNTY, CA. 1865

Assessment Roll Number	Name	Value of Land	Value of Other Property
15	Anderson, Thomas	$100	$—
17	Moody, William	100	170
24	Anderson, Thomas	350	250
28	Wright, Jim	150	107
30	Wright, Tom	350	237
32	Richardson, William	600	315
49	Murray, Tom	—	150
50	Gibbs, Eliza J.	—	80
53	Martin heirs	75	30
54	Price, Fred	200	—
55	Ashley, Mary	75	20
56	Cooper, Jacob A. & John W.	408	228
56	Martin, Jim	100	10
56	Wright, John	120	28
56	Cooper, Jeff	—	105
58	Gafford, Ashley	70	10
58	Bordley, Joseph	50	30
59	Woodland, William	200	251
59	Rochester heirs	156	20
59	Cooper, Jim	—	180
59	Boon, James	—	170
60	Hall, David	—	155
67	Joseph, Norman	—	144
72	Harris, Samuel	100	200
72	Green, John	—	70
72	Harris, Toby	480	60
72	Harris, Nat	—	195
74	Sudler, Benjamin	—	70
74	Pierce, John	—	79
76	Thomas, William	—	270
80	Thomas, Edward	—	275
81	Potts, Thomas	—	50
83	Pritchard, Jonathan	150	20
84	Lewis, Anthony	600	20
84	Frisby, Joe	—	105

Assessment Roll Number	Name	Value of Land	Value of Other Property
84	Warwick, Jim	—	305
84	Mathews, Sam	—	160
85	Anthony, John	120	175
85	Bateman, Jane	60	—
86	Anthony, Charles	100	50
87	Sewel, Henry	100	190
89	Edward, Thomas	—	80
91	Thomas, Richard	—	355
95	Hutchards, Charles & William J.	650	—
97	Pinder, William	480	305
98	Cuff, William	—	55
99	Hall, Frederick	300	120
99	Brown, William	—	140
99	Coursey, Thomas	—	95
99	Thomas, Edward	—	54
103	Green, Gustavus	—	180
103	Turner, W. H.	—	135
104	Hutchens, Charles	—	255
108	Mason, Henry	150	100
109	Coursey, John	—	165
109	Wright, Samuel	—	85
109	Brown, Samuel	—	90
109	Benet, John	—	170

Source: "Assessor's Field Book," Queen Anne's County, 2nd District, ca. 1865, Office of the County Commissioner, Queen Anne's County, Md., Maryland State Archives. I assume that the assessment number refers to individual dwellings.

Essentially, the larger their holdings, the greater the similarity between the activities of black and white neighbors. Most black proprietors listed in the 1870 agricultural schedule—especially on the Eastern Shore—were identified as "farmers" (in the population schedule) and owned between twenty and eighty acres of cultivated land and concentrated on several basic crops, especially winter wheat, corn, and potatoes (Irish and sweet). On average, such owners possessed two or three horses, one or two milk cows, and several hogs. From their cows they produced butter, and some livestock were slaughtered annually. The

TABLE 3.6

DETAILED ASSESSMENT OF PROPERTY OWNED BY BLACKS IN A
REPRESENTATIVE NEIGHBORHOOD IN THE SECOND ELECTION DISTRICT
OF QUEEN ANNE'S COUNTY
CA. 1865

Assessment Roll Number	Name	Property
59	Woodland, William	20 acres land adjoining J. M. Sudler's with small house ($200), 3 horses ($150), 1 cow ($25), 1 yearling ($10), 4 hogs ($16), household furniture ($20), farming utensils ($30). Total: $451
59	Rochester heirs	26 acres land with small house adjoining T. N. Sudler's ($156), household furniture ($20). Total: $176
59	Cooper, Jim	2 old horses ($100), 5 hogs ($25), household furniture ($30), farming utensils ($25). Total: $180
59	Boon, James	1 horse ($30), 1 cow ($25), 1 yearling ($10), 3 hogs ($15), household furniture ($30), family utensils ($20), 1 carriage ($40). Total: $170
60	Hall, David	1 horse ($75), 1 cow ($25), 2 hogs ($10), 3 sheep ($15), household furniture ($20), farming utensils ($10). Total: $155

Source: "Assessor's Field Book," Queen Anne's County, 2nd District, ca. 1865, Office of the County Commissioner, Queen Anne's County, Maryland State Archives. I assume that the assessment roll number refers to individual dwellings.

agricultural schedule lists farm production values of several hundred dollars for most owners but does not differentiate between produce sold either on the market or to neighbors and that consumed by the families themselves or their livestock. It is possible, however, that some of the winter wheat was sold.[30]

Smaller proprietors appear far less often in the agricultural schedule, but a sufficient number exist to locate their lands and to compare their activities to those of their more affluent neighbors. For example, Joseph Singer, a Queen Anne's County black farmer, owned four acres of cultivated land in 1870 on which he grew fifty bushels of corn, fifty bushels of sweet potatoes, and twenty bushels of Irish potatoes. In addition, he possessed two horses and three hogs. Singer's property lay alongside that of William Johnson, another black farmer with five acres of land and similar quantities of corn, potatoes, and hogs.[31] As small proprietors, Singer and Johnson apparently concentrated on self-sufficiency. Neither planted wheat, the obvious cash crop in Queen Anne's County. Nearby, however, several black farmers with larger holdings did plant wheat, as did whites with even more substantial acreage and greater apparent commitment to cash crop production. Also living in the neighborhood were black and white landowners with holdings too small to appear on the agricultural schedule and wage laborers and sharecroppers of both races with no land at all. Clearly, most such people worked for whites, although petty landowners probably supplemented their incomes by growing corn and potatoes and raising a few hogs.[32]

Such geographic proximity of landed and landless blacks certainly permitted and probably encouraged their cooperation, a pattern of behavior confirmed by other evidence. From the start, blacks who rented or owned small pieces of land and houses opened their doors to less fortunate freedmen. Immediately after emancipation, thousands of indigent and dependent blacks, many of whom had been turned adrift by angry or uncaring masters, and even some able-bodied freed people looking for new places to work sought assistance from neighbors, friends, and relatives who possessed enough resources to help them through the winter. "[T]he free people, as far as they could," explained William Taylor in January 1867, "threw their doors open, took in those people, and did all they could to prevent them from starvation."[33]

Such mutual support is also implied in the manner in which black workers fulfilled their obligations to white employers. Many wage labor contracts and sharecropping agreements included more than one family in what appeared to be deliberate group arrangements. In a single contract in September 1865, William Davis, a Howard County planter, agreed to provide John Ellis, Joe Tucker, and Mary Tucker quarters and rations for the two families involved.[34] In December of the same year,

James Thomas of St. Mary's County contracted with John Dotson, Moses Jones, Alexander Jones, Peter Butler, Shedrie Smith, Peter Dorsey, Julia Dorsey, Rosie Dorsey, and Henrietta Dorsey to farm his land on shares.[35] Surely, the people involved in such contracts extended their joint efforts to include the cultivation of whatever land they might have possessed themselves. Indeed, the 1870 agricultural schedule suggests that some of this cooperation occurred on a more formal basis. Many black farmers actually hired labor to assist them in their operations, probably at harvest time. Such work was never enough to provide a living wage but was certainly sufficient to supplement the incomes of farm hands who worked primarily for white farmers.[36]

VI

Access to land obviously enhanced blacks' autonomy. This point was made eminently clear when parents linked land to the effort to free their children from enforced apprenticeship. "The man, Reese," explained a Kent County Provost Marshal in November 1864, "was in good circumstances, having at the time his children were seized, about 50 bushels of corn, 5 barrels of pork, 5 shoats, 1 barrel of meal and one of flour; he also owned a small tract of land and an oyster boat. . . . The boys were fine and healthy . . . and were wanted by many of the farmers in the neighborhood."[37] Blacks' determination to accomplish as much as they could by themselves reflected a general attitude that undoubtedly extended to the use of land. "They can and will take care of themselves," declared Joseph Hall, a white Calvert County merchant, "and want to be let alone."[38]

Ironically, white employers' own critique of black labor revealed similar evidence of the latter's determination to be as independent as possible and to gain access to land in the process. "The ambition of the negro as a race," complained the *Chestertown Transcript* on December 3, 1864, "does not rise above the meagre necessaries of life. . . . One fruitful source of idleness has been the ability to possess themselves of a hut and a few acres of poverty-stricken land, thereby enabling them to pursue the semblance of the means of living."[39] The *Transcript* touched a chord in a familiar refrain among planters in post-emancipation Maryland. Everywhere employers complained about freed blacks' "unreliability" and "demoralization" and made regular reference to their failure to respond to the needs of plantation agriculture. As a typical editorial in the *Maryland Farmer and Mechanic* explained in February, free black labor was "uncertain" and "untrustworthy."[40]

As inveterate foes of emancipation, planters could not be expected to look kindly upon free labor, and as outspoken proponents of black inferiority, their views on degradation and demoralization were well known. That rural whites proved unable to appreciate the true nature of black aspirations was hardly surprising. After all, their priorities were different. Once again, the *Baltimore Gazette* expressed a widely held point of view: "[T]he negro has imbibed ideas of freedom," it said, "that are utterly incompatible with that systematic labor which is essential to the proper management of a well-conducted farm, and upon which its successful culture mainly depends."[41]

Not everyone, however, was so critical of blacks' behavior. In the presence of United States Army officers, Freedmen's Bureau agents, and a few local whites, blacks found friends who understood their desire to exercise control over at least a part of their working lives. Sympathetic whites were quick to see energy and enthusiasm where conservatives saw sloth and indolence. Such applause was to be expected on the basis of the optimistic liberalism that supported postwar radical Unionism or Republicanism. "In proportion as . . . everyman feels his house to be his castle," proclaimed the *Easton Gazette* in February 1867, "in that proportion will their desire to remain be permanent and their labor cheerful." Moreover, prominent black Marylanders shared such sentiments. "[I]f you would be prosperous you must be industrious," advised Frederick Douglass in December 1864. Freedmen must "save up their funds and endeavor to buy lands." The Maryland Colored State Convention of 1865 exhorted rural blacks "[to] feel that you are free, and dependent upon yourselves for support . . . [to] purchase property and become men of wealth, owning the soil."[42]

VII

In this context, even the smallest plots of land served a vital individual and community function by providing rural blacks, not with prosperity or wealth, but with a modicum of autonomy amidst a generally discouraging environment. Land, even in one- or two-acre plots, provided an alternative to the close supervision of whites and permitted black families to dispose of some of their resources as they chose. Any expansion of their access to such an alternative was important for it enlarged their freedom of action and secured them at least partial independence from whites. Like slaves before them, post-emancipation black Marylanders pursued such independence whenever possible, especially on whatever pieces of land they might persuade whites to let them use or have. After November 1, 1864, slavery had gone, but the relationship between blacks, their employers, and the land remained in some ways the same. Access to small pieces of land, especially those that were owned, provided a measure of freedom within a system designed to restrict it. With only limited options at their disposal, blacks' pursuit of land was shaped essentially by what they found possible under the circumstances. In rural neighborhoods throughout Maryland's tidewater counties, post-emancipation black people related to the soil as they had for decades—in a basically practical fashion, buying what little they could from whites who more often than not were hostile to their aspirations.

Notes

1. Much has been written about the failure of the federal government to distribute land to freed slaves and the resistance of white planters to such a prospect, but relatively little attention has been paid to the ongoing acquisition of small pieces of land by blacks themselves—especially those purchased from whites. Most studies that do focus on black-acquired land tend to concentrate on all-black communities or on the efforts of blacks to change government policy. See, for example, Rose, 199ff.; Edward Magdol, 139–74; Janet S. Hermann (New York, 1981), 37ff.; Elizabeth R. Bethel (Philadelphia, 1981), 1–25; Leon F. Litwack (New York, 1979), 399–408. When dealing with blacks who did manage to acquire small pieces of land, recent scholars seem to minimize such accomplishment. Despite her appreciation of freed Marylanders' "peasant" priorities, Barbara Fields deemphasizes the importance of land in such a context. "Black people had to content themselves, by and large," she writes, "with a menial position in the developing landscape of rural Maryland. Few obtained land of their own at all, and those few generally in very modest amounts: the garden patch of slavery times carried over into freedom." While this was certainly true, Fields' own general interpretation of "peasant" priorities permits a more positive assessment of such acquisition (Fields, 175). For a general discussion of Southern slaves and their use of garden plots as a defense against the rigors of slavery, see Eugene D. Genovese (New York,

1974), 535–40. For treatment of the relationship between free blacks and slaves in Maryland, see Berlin, 218, 223–25; Wright, 149–73; Fields, 23–29.

2. U.S. Bureau of the Census, 214; Berlin, 213–25; Wright, 149–73.

3. U.S. Bureau of the Census, 214; U.S. Bureau of the Census, 56–57; U.S. Bureau of the Census, Eighth Census of the United States, 1860, Census Manuscripts, Schedule 1—Free Inhabitants and Ninth Census of the United States, 1870, Census Manuscripts, Schedule 1—Inhabitants, National Archives, Washington, D.C. Hereafter referred to as Eighth Census of the United States, 1860, Schedule 1, and Ninth Census of the United States, 1870, Schedule 1. The use of census data on landowning presents a problem in that the 1870 census takers in some parts of the South may have undercounted the rural black population and confused some owners with tenants. For a discussion of such possibilities see Roger L. Ransom and Richard Sutch, "The Impact of the Civil War and Emancipation," 12 (fall 1975): 6–11, and Weiner, 229–39. In the case of Maryland, the data appear to be accurate. Supporting evidence for the census statistics used in this paper can be found in corroborating deeds and tax assessment records. A good collection of deeds for Kent County, and relevant tax assessment records for Queen Anne's, Kent, Prince George's, Montgomery, and Somerset Counties support an increase in landowning similar to that recorded in the 1870 population schedule. Indeed, those for Somerset County suggest that it might have been higher. An 1866 tax assessment for Somerset lists more than 400 black landowners for that county alone. Available records that pertain to this discussion include, "Assessors Field Book, Queen Anne's County, 2nd District, c1865," Office of the County Commissioner, Queen Anne's County, MdHR 12701, Maryland State Archives; Deeds, Office of the County Commissioner, Kent County, Index and Liber #JKH 4–7, CR 6046, 6646, 6647, Maryland State Archives; "Assessment Ledgers [1867]," Office of the County Commissioner, Kent County, Court House, Chestertown, Md.; "Assessment Ledgers [1843–1876]," and "Assessment Book, 1866," Office of the County Commissioner, Somerset County, MdHR 13601–13619, and MdHR 20065–8 to 20065–22, Maryland State Archives; "Assessment Book, 1864," Office of the County Commissioner, Prince George's County, MdHR 11049, Maryland State Archives; Memorandum of Property assessed to the Colored People in Montgomery County, Box 12 (Letters Received, Rockville, May 1866–September 1867), BRFAL, Md., RG 105.

4. Deeds, Office of the County Commissioner, Kent County, Index and Liber #JKH 4–7, CR 6946, 6646, 6647, Maryland State Archives.

5. "Assessors Field Book, Queen Anne's County, 2nd District, c1865," Office of the County Commissioner, Queen Anne's County, MdHR 12701, Maryland State Archives; Eighth Census, 1860, Schedule 1.

6. Ninth Census, 1870, Schedule 1.

7. "Assessment Ledgers [1843–1876]," and "Assessment Book, 1866," Office of the County Commissioner, Somerset County, MdHR 13601–13619, and MdHR 20065–8 to 20065–22; "Assessment Books, 1864–1868," Office of the County Commissioner, Prince George's County, MdHR 11049–11054, Maryland State Archives; Memorandum of Property assessed to the Colored People in Montgomery County, Md., Box 12 (Letters Received, Rockville, May 1866–September 1867), BRFAL, Md., RG 105. The material for these counties is more difficult to assess. The Somerset County "Assessment Book, 1866" provides a richly detailed snapshot of black land-owning in 1866, but the "Assessment Ledgers [1843–1876]," although useful in detecting post-emancipation land transactions, do not appear to be as complete. The Prince George's County "Assessment Books" show a marked increase in black land acquisition between 1864 and 1867, but tax recorders may simply have been responding to the need to reorganize their books after a general reassessment in 1867. This fact may also skew the Queen Anne's County numbers, and the numbers that appear in the Freedmen's Bureau Memorandum for Montgomery County.

8. Deeds, Office of the County Commissioner, Kent County, Liber #JKH 6, p. 97, Liber #JKH 5, p. 211, Maryland State Archives; U.S. Bureau of the Census, Ninth Census of the United States, 1870, Schedule 3—Productions of Agriculture, Stack Location 3-47-9-11&12, Maryland State Archives. Hereafter referred to as Ninth Census of the United States, 1870, Schedule 3.

9. This is speculation on my part. I have no direct evidence of ex-soldiers using army back pay or bounties to purchase land. The figure of 2,700 soldiers comes from Adjutant General, Rolls of Md. Troops, U.S. Colored Troops, CR 5597, Maryland State Archives.

10. Deeds, Office of the County Commissioner, Kent County, Liber #JKH 5, p. 106, and #JKH 5, p. 386, Maryland State Archives.

11. J. C. Anderson to the Freedmen's Bureau, March 31, 1868, Box 3 (Letters Received by the Complaint Branch, 1866–1872), BRFAL, Md., RG 105.

12. Again, this is speculative and it runs against the grain of current scholarship. Roger L. Ransom and Richard Sutch, who agree that freed slaves could effect certain changes in their relationship with white employers, discount that possibility when it came to land because of "the extreme prejudice of the whites against land ownership on the part of blacks." (Richard Sutch and Roger L. Ransom, "The Ex-Slave in the Post-Bellum South: A Study of the Economic Impact of Racism in a Market Environment," 33 [March 1973]: 131–48). In a general sense, I am sure this statement applied to Maryland. Planters obviously did not wish to see widespread black landownership. Moreover, even though binding, year-long contracts and apprenticeship were clearly

intended to keep black labor in place, I have found no evidence of employers consciously selling blacks land for that purpose. Between 1865 and 1870, the leading journal of rural white opinion, the *Maryland Farmer and Mechanic* made no such suggestion, nor did any of the tidewater newspapers. This does not prove, however, that such practice was uncommon, at least at the one- or two-acre level. Prior to emancipation, many masters allowed slaves access to garden plots. After 1864 wage and sharecropping contracts made constant reference to similar arrangements. "I owe Robert Wilson, (colored) eighty-five dollars for wages for the year 1864," explained Thomas Ringgold of Kent County in a typical wage contract, "and have bargained to give him one hundred dollars, and a house for the ensuing year for his family to live in" (48). From evidence of garden plots and the renting of small pieces of land, it is tempting to speculate that planters treated the *sale* of such property in a similar fashion. As long as the land in question consisted of a few acres at most, its possession by blacks did nothing to threaten white economic hegemony and ensured its owners' continued presence and availability.

13. There are dozens of letters from Freedmen's Bureau officers regarding the purchase of land for schools to be found in BRFAL, Md., RG 105. The pertinent records are Volume 48 (Register of Letters Sent, Annapolis, June 28, 1866 to March 13, 1868); Volume 50 (Register of Letters Sent, Bladensburg, June 4, 1866 to September 18, 1867); and Volume 53 (Register of Letters Sent, Rockville, June 5, 1866 to October 2, 1867). See also *Third Annual Report of the Baltimore Association for the Moral and Educational Improvement of the Colored People* (Baltimore, 1867), 4. Rural whites' attitudes toward black schools varied greatly. Some were so opposed that they burned the buildings. Others simply refused their support. A handful of planters of Unionist or radical Republican sympathies offered enthusiastic assistance—some by giving land—and a few accorded grudging support when they realized that the presence of schools helped maintain an available labor force. See J. W. Alvord (Washington, D.C., 1868), 6.

14. Ninth Census, 1870, Schedule 1. According to this schedule, blacks in 1870 owned $271,655 worth of real and personal property in Kent County. This constituted 5.2 percent of the total value of such property in the county assessed in 1866. See "Annual Report of the Comptroller of the Treasury" (Annapolis: Henry A. Lucas, 1867), which appears as Document E in Maryland, General Assembly, House of Delegates (Annapolis, 1867).

15. Deeds, Office of the County Commissioner, Kent County, Liber #JKH 5, pp. 113, 273, 503, 580, 582, Maryland State Archives.

16. Ninth Census, 1870, Schedule 1. Land purchased by blacks during this period seems to have been in developed areas and was thus quite expensive. The range of $25–50 per acre (often including a house or cabin) is difficult to establish firmly but is based on a wide variety of sources. See especially No-

vember 17, 1864; 1 (July 1865): 116; R. G. Rutherford to W. W. Rogers, October 2, 1867, Volume 53 (Register of Letters Sent, Rockville, June 5, 1866–October 20, 1867), BRFAL, Md., RG 105; J. H. Butler to W. L. VanDerlip, October 12, 25, November 22, December 7, 1867, June 22, 1868, Box 11 (Letters Received, Annapolis, July 20, 1866–September 11, 1868), BRFAL, Md., RG 105; James Chreston to William VanDerlip, February 8, 1868, Ibid.; 5 (December 1868): 358–59; November 26, December 3, 1864, June 10, July 29, September 2, 16, October 7, November 11, December 9, 1865, June 23, 1866.

17. Deeds, Office of the County Commissioner, Kent County, Index and Liber #JKH 5, pp. 29, 51, 211, 425, Maryland State Archives.

Such continuity in black landowning in Kent County is clearly established in a combination of data provided by the United States Censuses of 1860 and 1870, surviving deeds from the period 1843 to 1884, and tax assessment records from 1867.

18. Eighth Census of the United States, 1860, Schedule 1, and Ninth Census of the United States, 1870, Schedule 1; Deeds, Office of the County Commissioner, Kent County; "Assessment Ledgers [1867]," Office of the County Commissioner, Kent County.

19. (Annapolis, 1867). This communication appears as Document E in Maryland, General Assembly, House of Delegates (Annapolis, 1867).

20. Ibid.; Ninth Census of the United States, 1870, Schedule 1.

21. Ibid.

22. Ninth Census of the United States, 1870, Schedule 1.

23. Deeds, Office of the County Commissioner, Kent County, Liber #JKH 5, pp. 29, 273ff., Maryland State Archives.

24. "Assessment Book, 1866," Office of the County Commissioner, Somerset County; Bureau of the Census, Ninth Census (Washington, D.C., 1872), 162.

25. "Assessors's Field Book," Queen Anne's County, 2nd District, c1865, Office of the County Commissioner, Queen Anne's County, Maryland State Archives. I assume the assessment roll numbers refer to individual dwellings.

26. Ibid.

27. "Assessment Book, 1866," Office of the County Commissioner, Somerset County, Maryland State Archives.

28. Ninth Census of the United States, 1870, Schedules 1 and 3.

29. Ibid.

30. Ibid.

31. Ibid.

32. Ibid.

33. Testimony of William F. Taylor, January 14, 16, 1867, Records of the House of Representatives, Testimony in Investigation of the Government of Maryland, 1867, Record Group 233, National Archives, Washington, D.C.

34. Miscellaneous Contracts, Office of the Assistant Commissioner, BRFAL, D.C. RG 105.

35. Copy of contract contained in Edward F. O'Brien to Seldon N. Clark, January 4, 1866, Box 1 (LRAC, September 1865 to October 27, 1866), BRFAL, D.C., RG 105.

36. Ninth Census of the United States, 1870, Schedule 3.

37. Ibid., 85.

38. Ibid., 63.

39. *Chestertown Transcript,* December 3, 1864.

40. *Maryland Farmer and Mechanic* 3, 1 (February 1866), 1.

41. *Baltimore Gazette,* November 3, 25, 1865.

42. *Easton Gazette,* February 25, 1865; *Baltimore American,* December 5, 1864; *Baltimore Sun,* January 1, 1866.

Baltimore Street between St. Paul and Calvert Streets, ca. 1870. *(Maryland Historical Society)*

Baltimore Street, ca. 1870. *(Maryland Historical Society)*

Judge Hugh Lennox Bond. *(Maryland Historical Society)*

Worcester County

In the Orphans' Court of Worcester County.

Margaret Ball a Negro *Girl* of the age of *Ten* years, the *First* day of *July* last past, comes into Court,—and it being represented to the Court that the said *Margaret* is not at service, or learning a Trade, or employed in the service of *her* parents, and that *she* is without means sufficient for *her* maintenance or support; and the Court being satisfied that said representation is true, and believing that it would greatly conduce to the good of the said child, that *she* should be put to learn some Trade or useful business:

The said *Margaret Ball* is, therefore, on this *Tenth* day of *November* in the year of our Lord one thousand eight hundred and sixty *four* BOUND AS AN APPRENTICE by *Wm A Merrill, Ino W Laws and James S Lecompte Justice* of the Orphans' Court for Worcester County, Maryland, to *Samuel T Ball* until *She* the said *Margaret* shall arrive to the age of *Eighteen* years—and the said *S T Ball* being here present in Court, agrees to take the said *Margaret* as an Apprentice, until *She* shall arrive to the said age; and the said *S T Ball* doth also, on his part, acknowledge himself bound, and by these presents doth contract, promise and agree to teach the said Apprentice the Trade of a *House Servant* and to supply *her* with suitable clothing and maintenance during *her* Apprenticeship—and when free to give *her a Suit of Clothing of the value of Fifteen dollars and Ten dollars in cash.*

IN WITNESS WHEREOF, the said *Justice* and *Ball* hereunto set their hands and affix their seals to this Indenture, this *Tenth* day of *November* in the year of our Lord one thousand eight hundred and sixty *four.*

Signed, sealed and delivered
in presence of

E. Stubbell

Wm A Merrill [SEAL]

John W Laws [SEAL]

James S Lecompt [SEAL]

Samuel T his Ball [SEAL]

Indenture papers, 1864. *(Maryland State Archives)*

Washington D.C.
Sept 26th 1865

Know all men by these presents that I, John F. Shortell of Millesville, Anne Arundle County State of Maryland, held and firmly bound to the United States of America in the Sum of 200 $. Two Hundred Dollars for the payment of which I bind myself my heirs Executors and Administrators firmly by these presents in this Contract. that I am to furnish the persons where names are subjoined (Two Labors) Quarters full Substantial and healthy Rations. And all necessary Supplies and attendance in Case of Sickness. And also to Raise a Hog and Poultry, +c. And the amount set opposite their Respective names per month. Monthly. less (25) twenty five per cent which Amount is to be retained until the termination of this Contract then to be paid to the Employees in full, also all cost of Transportation to my Residence from the City of Washington. This Contract to be broken only by mutual Consent.

Names	Age	Rate per month	Terms of Service	Remarks
Isaac Brown	35	$ 8.00	until 1 Jany 1866	And if they remain another
Washington Grosher	57	$ 8.00	until 1 Jany 1866	Year then this Contract to remain in full force —

John F. Shotell

We agree to work for John F. Shortell Esq of the Town County + State above mentioned for the time + Amount set opposite our names.

Isaac his × mark Brown
Washington his × mark Grosher

Witness
J. M. Vandenburgh
Chr of Int Office

Labor contract, 1865. (*National Archives*)

This Article of Agreement, made this *First* day of *January* 186*6*

between *William Anderson Freedman* of the first part, and
Benjaman F. Shreve of the second part,

WITNESSETH :

THAT for, and in consideration of the sum of *One hundred & Twenty* dollars, the
said *William Anderson* hereby agrees faithfully and diligently to
perform the duties of *Laborer* for the said
Benjaman F. Shreve at his place in *Montgomery* County, *&c*, or *Maryland*
such other place as he may direct, for the period of *Twelve* months, in consid-
eration of which services the party of the second part herewith agrees to pay the said party of the first part the sum of
Ten *10* dollars per month, with proper and suitable food and quarters. The said
parties hereby further agree that a sum equal to one month's pay shall be retained by the said party of the second part until
final settlement at the expiration of the said period *December 31st 1866*

And the said parties further unchangably agree that if this contract be violated by either party without legal cause, the
party so violating the same shall pay to the other, as liquidated damages, the sum of *Fifty Dollars*
50 dolla s.

And the said parties further agree that if it shall be mutually desirable to annul this contract before the expiration of
the term agreed upon, it shall be done only in the presence and with the concurrence of such officer of the FREEDMAN,S BU-
REAU as may have immediate jurisdiction in this matter in the district wherein the said parties reside.

Given at *Charlottestille* Va., on the day and date above written.

Benj F. Shreve {L. S.}

his
William X Anderson {L. S.}
mark

WITNESS :

Jno. M. Collins
Capt 58th Pa Vols
& Ast Supt Freedmans Bureau
Charlottesvill Va

Labor contract, 1866. *(National Archives)*

SIR:—Your attention is called to the Association formed in his City for the *Moral and Educational Improvement of the Colored People.*

The Address of the Association to the public is hereto appended, nd your aid and countenance in furtherance of its charitable object is earnestly requested.

Any amount of money you feel able to contribute may be haded to an member of the Finance Committee, and will aid the Association in their effort to ducate the Colored People.

ROOMS OF THE BALTIMORE ASSOCIATION FOR THE MORAL AND EDUCATIONAL IMPROVEMENT OF THE COLORED PEOPLE, ROOM NO. 3, BIBLE HOUSE.

Fellow Citizens:—Since the adoption of the New Constitution very grave issues are submitted for your consideration. That instrument, by its benevolent provisions, has added to the eighty thousand free colored people of our State eighty-seven thousand others, recently slaves.

These two classes constitute the greater portion of the labor of the State.

They are likely to remain among us, for they are attached to their homes, and no Government has ever consented to the violent removal of one-fourth of its population.

For the most part they are ignorant. The habits of their former industry have not been such as to teach them ideas of thrift, carefulness, or providence. Thrown upon their own resources, though their labor is in great demand, they cannot be expected to know the necessity of industry or how to seek at home permanent occupation and employment.

We are forced to think it the duty of every citizen of Maryland to seek to make this population most useful to the State, as it is the bounden duty of Christian men to seek their moral improvement.

There are but two courses to be pursued. The one is to leave these persons in the ignorance and moral destitution in which many of them now, unhappily, are, and the other to endeavor by education to improve their habits, instruct them in their industry, make diligent the idle, reform the vicious and stimulate the good, that they may rise in the scale of being, and be better fitted for the varied duties they are called on to perform.

The first course may at first seem the least troublesome and expensive, but ignorance is the mother of vice, and unless these people are taught their duties to the State, and their more important duty to God, and are not suffered to remain in the helpless state in which slavery has left them, the necessity for almshouses, jails and penitentiaries will teach the folly of such economy.

Educated labor produces more than uneducated labor. It is, therefore, the interest of the State that all labor should be instructed.

One of the hopes of the friends of Emancipation was that that measure would induce immigration into the State, raise the price of our lands, give demand for our labor in erecting mills and dwellings, and in manufacturing the various utensils necessary for the increased population of Maryland. But it cannot be expected that any number of the class of emigrants we desire will leave their homes to dwell in Maryland if they know they are to be surrounded by an illiterate, ignorant population, whose ignorance and vice are to be daily increased by withholding all instruction in the arts of labor, all educational improvement and every teaching of morality which would lead them to higher ideas of duty to God and to their neighbor.

To pursue this plan would deprive the State in the first place of the productive labor of one hundred and sixty thousand people, and would prevent desirable emigration into her borders, and oppress those of us now residents of the State with additional taxation to furnish what the expense of education would have entirely prevented.

Perhaps those of the colored people whose circumstances require daily toil for the support of their families can receive but little direct benefit atheir time of life from any effort now put forth, but we believe the influence of the education of their children will be felt upn the home an the household, that family respect will increae, that thrift au cleanliness will be promoted, and the same beneficent effets which education produces upon other popiations will be felt among the colored people.

They have been taxed or a long while for public schools, but have been allowed non. Their present condition, wen we consider what has been denied them, and how little means or opportunity they have had for self-improvement, is a stanting rebuke to those who think they are incapable of moral or mental culture.

They long for opportunity to show how readily they become a people no longer degraded by, but useful to, the State.

The Baltimore Association for the Moral and Educational Improvement of the Colored People, intends to do what it can to give them such opportunity. Its members will give their best efforts to this charitable purpose.

Those of our fellow-citizens who feel any interest in a people upon whom their vote has thrust the responsibilities of life, and those in whom Christianity prompts kindness and duty toward these people, are invited to give us their support in such manner as they may think the most useful, that we, if necessary, by private benevolence may do what long since ought to have been done, and we hope soon will be done, by the State, *i. e.*, provide means for the moral and educational improvement of one-fourth of our population.

We annex a list of the officers of the Association:

President—EVANS ROGERS.

Vice-Presidents—ARCHIBALD STIRLING, THOMAS KELSO, WILLIAM J. ALBERT, FRANCIS T. KING, JOHN W. RANDOLPH.

Recording Secretary—GEORGE A. POPE.

Corresponding Secretary—JOSEPH M. CUSHING.

Treasurer—JESSE TYSON.

Board of Managers.

REV. F. ISRAEL,	ASHUR CLARKE,
REV. WM. BRUCE,	JAMES CAREY,
REV. F. L. BRAUNS,	ALEX. M. CARTER,
REV. T. STORK, D.D.,	RICHARD M. JANNEY,
REV. J. F. W. WARE,	HENRY STOCKBRIDGE,
HON. H. L. BOND,	WM. DANIEL,
DR. C. C. COX,	JAS. CAREY COALE,
DR. R. W. PEASE,	A. STIRLING, JR.,
DR. J. C. THOMAS,	JNO. A. NEEDLES,
GALLOWAY CHESTON,	JNO. T. GRAHAM,
WILLIAM J. ALBERT,	E. STABLER, JR.,
WM. KENNEDY,	GEORGE B. COLE,
HAZLETT MCKIM,	ALEX. T. JOHNSON,
G. T. HOPKINS,	W. K. CARSON,
DANIEL HOLLIDAY,	JOHN S. GILMAN.

Finance Committee.

WM. J. ALBERT,	WASH. K. CARSON,
ARCHIBALD STIRLING, SR,	WM. DANIEL,
F. T. KING,	EDW. STABLER, JR.,
JOHN W. RANDOLPH,	ALEX. T. JOHNSON,
JAMES CAREY,	GEO. B. COLE.

Baltimore Association broadside. *(Maryland Historical Society)*

BALTIMORE ASSOCIATION FOR THE

Moral and Educational Improvement of the Colored People,

Baltimore, ... *186*

We have heard the colored people at   desire to have a school opened; if so, we will send them a teacher on the following terms :

They must provide a church or a room for the school,—must pay for the fuel and lights necessary, and pay the board and washing of the teacher.

The scholars will have to pay for their books, which the teacher will sell them at cost price.

On our part we will pay the salary of the teacher.

The people should meet and form a School Society, which every one should join. They should elect five of their best men for School Trustees, and send me their names. The first duty of the Trustees should be to get each man and woman to pledge themselves to pay a certain amount every month, towards paying the board, fuel, &c. I send you a paper to be signed. You will find some able to pay perhaps a dollar each month, and some not more than five or ten cents; but you must urge them to pay all they can spare. When you have sufficient on the paper to pay the expenses, send me a copy of it.

We must have the room for night as well as day school. The grown people must be educated, so that they can assist us in teaching the children.

We prefer sending a white or colored female teacher, it being very difficult to get good men.

When you answer this, state how many scholars you will probably have for the day school, and how many for the night.

In what house will the school be held, and what is its size?

With whom will the teacher board, and how far will it be from the school house?

What board will you have to pay?

What white persons in the neighborhood favor the school?

         Very respectfully,

....

                           Actuary.

Baltimore Association letter. *(Maryland Historical Society)*

Murder in Calvert County.

CALVERT COUNTY,
FRIENDSHIP, March 19, 1866.

Messrs. Editors Baltimore Gazette:

A few days ago two returned negro soldiers came to the residence of Dr. John Wilkinson, inquiring for certain gentlemen in the neighborhood who wanted labor. They spoke of them without using the Mr.; the Dr. called their attention to the fact; they at once used towards him the most abusive threats, and drew a revolver on him. He left them and got out a warrant for their arrest. This was put into the hands of officer Denton, who, with a *party comitatus*, proceeded to a negro meeting yesterday to arrest them As soon as the negroes discovered the officers, they drew their revolvers and commenced shooting. The officer's pistol missed fire, and one of the negroes drove a ball through the brain of one of our most estimable young men, Edwin Robinson, son of Mr. L. V. Robinson, of Salisbury, Maryland. He died last night. The negroes were arrested and taken to jail. The military has, to a very great extent, disarmed our people, and the negroes are armed to the teeth. Robbery is of nightly occurrence, and now murder is being accomplished. If some steps are not at once taken to check the negroes at once, God only knows what will come next.

PLEBS.

Baltimore Gazette, March 22, 1866.

Sharp Street Methodist Episcopal Church (Colored). *(Maryland Historical Society)*

A washerwoman and child. *(Maryland Historical Society)*

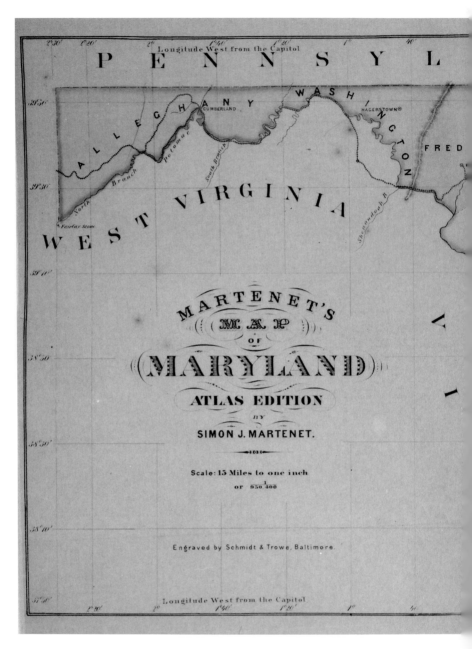

Maryland, 1865. *(Maryland State Archives)*

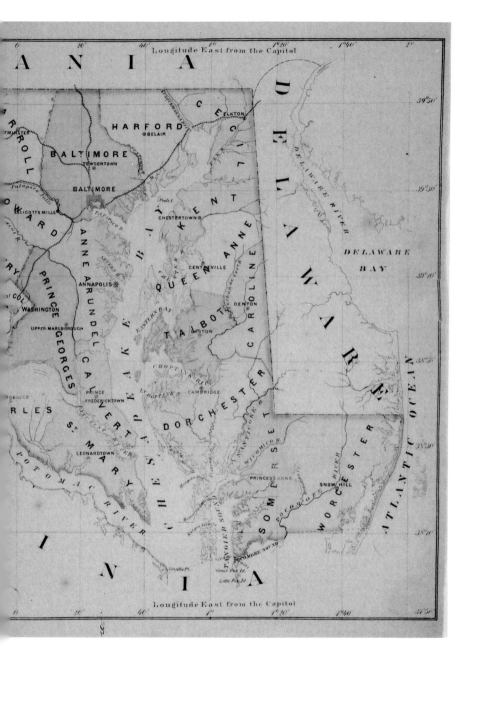

Governor Augustus W. Bradford. *(Maryland State Archives)*

Oden Bowie. *(Maryland Historical Society)*

On Steel by John Sartain. Phil.ᵃ

Archibald Stirling, Jr. *(Maryland Historical Society)*

John L. Thomas, Jr. *(Maryland Historical Society)*

Baltimore Street, ca. 1870. *(Maryland Historical Society)*

The Chesapeake Marine and Railway Drydock Company. (*Maryland Historical Society*)

The Douglass Institute. (*Maryland Historical Society*)

ARRIVAL OF FREEDMEN AND THEIR FAMILIES AT BALTIMORE, MARYLAND.—AN EVERY DAY SCENE.

Arrival of freedmen and their families at Baltimore. (*Maryland Historical Society*)

Slicing and canning fruit at Smith and Wick's Can Factory and Packing Houses. *(Maryland Historical Society)*

Fourth Regiment, United States Colored Troops. (*Library of Congress*)

Celebrating the Fifteenth Amendment, Baltimore, 1870. *(Maryland Historical Society)*

4

The Work of Children

I

WITHIN DAYS OF EMANCIPATION, Maryland planters and farmers seized the labor of some three thousand black minors under the provisions of an unrepealed section of the state's black code. Objecting vigorously, freed parents enlisted the support of the United States Army, the Freedmen's Bureau, and prominent Maryland radical politicians to win eventual control of their children. The integrity of their families served as one of black Marylanders' few defenses against white control and helped them carve as much autonomy as possible out of a system that otherwise dictated their subserviency.

Immediately after emancipation, parents exerted extraordinary efforts to maintain control of their families and the labor that they represented. "[T]hey wanted their children," explained Joseph Hall, "to help them make a living. . . . They want . . . the hiering [sic] of these children themselves and to draw the wages for them or to take them home to help their work if they choose."[1] Undeniably, the unity of the family stood by itself as a proud assertion of moral independence, but beyond that was the clear intention of freed men and women to use their families as the organizing agencies of total family labor. In the control of, provision for, and deployment of their children, freed parents sought to wrest this important aspect of rural economic control from the hands of whites. "It must be plain to the dullest," said the sympathetic *Easton Gazette*, "that in proportion as the laboring population are happy in their homes and families . . . in that proportion will their desire to remain be permanent and their labor cheerful."[2]

In their path stood the 1860 Maryland Code of Public General Laws, which authorized county orphans' courts to "summon before them the child of any free negro," and should it appear "better for the habits and comfort of said child," apprentice him or her to a white employer "to learn to labor."[3] Courts were expressly barred from apprenticing the children of parents who were capable of supporting them, but the judges, not parents, assessed such capacity. In addition, the code discriminated between black and white apprentices by relieving employers of the responsibility of educating black children and by permitting them to transfer the latter to other employers without parental consent. Emancipation changed nothing in the apprenticeship law. Whereas before its "Negro" provisions had applied only to the children of free black parents, they now covered all black minors in the state.[4]

Whites wasted little time putting apprenticeship to use in its new context. Hours after Governor Bradford's emancipation proclamation, Samuel Harrison of Talbot County reported that ex-masters "are having the . . . children bound to them, and the orphans' court has authorized such indentures." There were, he said, "very many applicants."[5] A few days later, George F. Curry, United States Army provost marshal in Annapolis, warned that apprenticeship was "being carried on here . . . to such an extent that it threatens to take every able-bodied negro boy without regard to age."[6] In Calvert County, eyewitnesses reported black children being brought to the court house in "ox-cart loads" and in "droves."[7] North of Baltimore, the story was the same. "The orphans' court has been engaged for some weeks," explained the *Towsontown American and Advocate*, "in binding negro children [and] in consequence of the great amount of business to be done . . . the judges have determined to continue their services each week."[8]

Within weeks of emancipation nearly one thousand children were indentured in Anne Arundel and Calvert Counties alone, and on the Eastern Shore, whites in Somerset, Worcester, Talbot, and Dorchester Counties claimed the labor of 1,600 children.[9] In Somerset, 765 were taken, approximately one-fourth of the newly freed minors in the county.[10] Local efforts to apprentice black children were at times even more intensive. On November 12, 1864, Sewell Hepbron of Still Pond, Kent County, reported, "I had twelve who were lately my slaves . . . bound to me a few days ago, six of them range from a small babe to eight years . . . the others from eleven to sixteen."[11] In December, General Henry H. Lockwood of the United States Army complained of "hundreds of abuses" in some areas of the Eastern Shore. A year later, William Taylor found it common that "the whites, the ex-masters of the slaves, had the children probably of about two thirds of the families of the freedmen."[12]

Tidewater whites were quick to defend their actions. As the *Kent*

News explained, apprenticeship was "prompted by feelings of humanity towards these unfortunate young ones."[13] According to William Bryan, sheriff of Anne Arundel County, "in most cases the parents agree to have their children bound out," because so many of them were "becoming suddenly free with a large number of children who they are unable to take care of or keep out of the almshouse."[14] Some children had "worthless parents," added W. Viers Bowie of Montgomery County, and others were "without parents and without the means of support." "To turn them loose," he concluded, "to roam at large without any restraint would be alike unwise and inhuman."[15]

Undoubtedly there was some truth in such assertions. In Talbot County, where nearly three hundred children were bound out, dozens of indentures bore the statements "no parents," or "parents cannot be found."[16] The complaints of Mathias Hammond of Ellicott City and James Gardener of St. Michaels were typical of many. "When the act of freedom went into operation," Hammond explained, "I was forced to have . . . [the child] bound out to me as there was no other person to take charge of her."[17] "A mother came to me," wrote Gardener, "with a little boy about two years old and begged and entreated me to take him. She had no home, no money, no friends and her husband was then in the Army."[18] Moreover, many black parents did agree to apprentice their children. Such action was entirely legal and could solve real problems for the individuals concerned. Nor were such arrangements entirely without recompense. In addition to room and board, indentures often included annual "wages" of ten to fifteen dollars.[19]

Nevertheless, planters' self-image of sacrificial concern was betrayed by their hurry to bind children and their preference for healthy youths of working age. "A good many of these children," reported Bartus Trew, a provost marshal in Kent County in November 1864, "are old enough to hire for good wages and can get plenty of labor."[20] A month later, from Salisbury, Somerset County, Henry Lockwood reported cases "where lads of sixteen and eighteen have been bound out."[21] In December 1866, the *Baltimore American* complained that "In many instances those apprenticed were over eighteen . . . and were actually hired out by their new masters, before they left the court room, for as much as eighty dollars a year. These youths who were able and eager to help support their younger brothers and sisters, and aged parents, were ruthlessly taken from them and they were left to face the winter as best they could."[22] As William Taylor explained, "The children who were able to support their families were the very ones they took away."[23]

Furthermore, the "voluntary" consent of many parents was clearly forced. On November 2, 1864, just a day after emancipation, Andrew Stafford, a United States Army provost marshal reported that Eastern Shore planters were "compelling the slaves to bind their children to them."[24] A Calvert County observer explained that "the persons who want children bound to them tell the parents . . . that the law compels them to be bound out and they know no better."[25] From Kent County came the same story. "The little Ethiopians were carried by the dearborn and wagonload," reported an anonymous correspondent to the *Baltimore American,* "for they were told they had to have their children bound out—'it was the law'—and thus, some of the most ignorant were opposed [*sic*] upon and willing consent obtained."[26] Some planters made their move as early as October 31, compelling parents to agree to the apprenticeship of their children just hours before freedom.[27]

Even when parents knew the truth, there was little they could do at first to stop the orphans' courts from apprenticing their children. The Talbot County court, for example, noted the presence of parents but seldom referred to their consent or lack of same.[28] If the account of Maria Nichols of Kent County is typical, it is evident courts felt no obligation to record protests. "[T]hey sent for me to come to the courthouse," she complained, "and i refused to go and they sent high sheriffs after me and taken [me] by force then after i got there they did not ask me anything but they taken him and bound him and they would not let me say a word."[29] Under such pressure, many parents were afraid to resist. As Fanny Thompson of Chestertown explained, "I could not help it, and any paper that I have signed has been done by threats against [my] will and consent."[30]

Many black women faced an additional obstacle in that they had to confront county orphans' courts in the absence of their husbands' or partners' support. According to Union Army muster rolls, 2,745 tidewater black men enlisted in the seventh, ninth, and nineteenth Regiments, United States Colored Troops in 1863 and 1864, leaving their families behind—by necessity—to cope as best they could.[31] In Somerset County alone, 500 men left for the war, in Worcester 482, and in Queen Anne's 425.[32] Such absence manifested itself starkly in orphans' court records. The Talbot County "Negro Docket" listed 221 children brought before the court between November 1 and 9, 1864, of whom

124 were accompanied only by their mothers, 42 were described as orphans, and 24 listed as having both parents absent.[33]

"My children were forced from me by constables," complained Linday Robbins of Worcester County, to a U.S. Army provost marshall in Snow Hill:

> and I proceeded to the Court House and protested against such an un-natural act but was put out of the court room, and would not even be allowed to speak. Now sir, if there is any way you can advise me to get my children, you will confer on me a great favor indeed. Colonel Birney told me at the time that my husband left should I be ill-treated at any time, to report to Head Quarters, although I have been ill-treated different times, I put up with it until now, but my children have been taken away from me and bound in slavery to my old mistress, I cannot rest until I know whether it is a lawful proceeding or not. I enclose a letter to my husband, which you will have the goodness to forward to him, his name and address is Charles Robbins, Co. B. 39th Reg't, U.S.C.T. Hoping that you will have the goodness to look into this matter.[34]

"Mr. Joshua C. Tolbert . . . [of] Baltimore County, has kept my three children and refused to give them up to me, as he says he has bound them in the Orphans' Court," complained Louisa Foster to a U.S. Army provost marshal in Baltimore:

> My husband is in the Union Army. Mr. Tolbert owes me a year's wages, which he refuses to pay me. He took the children directly after the adoption of the Free Constitution. I appeal to the General Commanding to enable me to procure the wages due me, and get back my children from Mr. Tolbert, who threatened to chain me down to the floor and whip me, if I asked him for my children any more.[35]

Nor was it only women who had difficulty reaching their partners. Soldiers themselves experienced similar frustrations. In a case that did not relate to apprenticeship but that illustrated the problems confronting men away from home, Mrs. William Jones of Baltimore complained to the Freedmen's Bureau in July 1866 "that her husband was transferred from the Army to the Navy, and is now attached to the U.S. Sloop of War St. Marys. That she is in destitute circumstances and cannot provide for herself and three children."[36] Mrs. Jones provided two letters from her husband to make her point:

> U.S. Ship St. Marys, February 22, 1866—My Dear Wife, I hope this few lines will find you and the children well as tha leve me. My dear what

is the reison you dont write to me this makes 3 letters i have wrought to you and i have not got a answer from you. My dear i think you think hard of me not sending you money but my dear you must not think hard of me not sending you any for my dear we have got one of the gratis olde raskells for a Captain you ever did see. he wont let no man in the ship have a cent of monney, so my dear whot can I do nothing, but at anny rate i think it won't be long now before I will be home with you and my dear little Children. So my dear, dont think hard of me but write offen and there is no doubt but we will get along yet, thoes lines leves me well and in good health, well my dear i will close these few lines hopen tha may find you and the children well as tha leve me, now my dear belve me ever your afectinate husband—Willam Jones to his wife Charity Jones.

U.S. Ship St. Marys, Panama Bay, March 3rd, 1866—My Dear wife, I take great pleasure in writeing these few lines to you hopeing this letter will find you all well as this leaves me here at present you must excuse me for not writeing sooner, but we have been so busy sailing about from one place to another that I have not had time to do anything so now we have arrived in Panama where I think we shall stop for eight or nine months you spoke for a money order in your letter that is a thing what we cannot get in this ship or else I would send it with all my heart and as for money we very seldom see a dollar but keep your heart up. I expect to be home very soon in about two months more. I hope I shall see you again give my kind love to the children. And if you can get any relief from any friend until i come home when i will make everything all right to them. Try if some of our friends won't lend you some money in advance they will oblige me very much so i must conclude with my most kind and Earnest love from your loving Husband—William Jones.[37]

The Bureau's response was succinct and to the point: nothing could be done to help:

Mrs. Charity Jones, 134 N. Eutaw St. —Received by Bureau, July 12, 1866 by R. Chandler, Act. Asst Comm—Baltimore—Forwarded to O. O. Howard—Referred to Major Fowler, July 18, 1866–August 9, 1866: "Respectfully returned to Bvt. Lt. Col. R, Chandler A. A. G. I know of no way by which Mrs. Jones can draw her husband's pay."[38]

Nonetheless, whenever possible, with or without their partners' help, parents of apprentices fought back. According to Joseph Hall, "in every case I could see or hear the parents positively objected to the binding."[39] Samuel Harrison recorded that many parents protested but "no atten-

tion whatever was paid to the objections . . . even though they manifested much feeling during the proceedings."[40] A lengthy list of black
complaints to United States Army provost marshals—including many
from women—supported this statement. On November 11, 1864,
Robert Wilson of Easton Neck, Kent County, made an affidavit to the
effect that his two children were apprenticed to Thomas R. Browne
without his "approbation" and "against the consent of his wife, the
mother of said children."[41] A week later, Lydia Dorsey of Baltimore
complained that a planter "has taken my grand-children to the Eastern
Shore . . . and has bound them against the will of their parents."[42]
On November 19, Frisbie Hinson, recently of Queen Anne's County,
reported that William H. Beck, the former owner of his three children,
"had them bound to him without my consent or wishes. . . . [H]e told
me I had nothing to do with the matter."[43] In December, Elizabeth
Kennard of Baltimore complained that "three of my children were
without my knowledge or consent, or that of my husband, taken into
Anne Arundel County, bound by the orphan's court . . . and have been
put to service beyond [our] control."[44]

Some parents parted with their children only under extreme duress.
Hester Anthony, an Eastern Shore freedwoman wrote, "I went to my
master after my children and he ordered me away; he told me if I did
not go he was going to shoot me; he says that before I shall have my
children he will blow their brains out; he says I must not step foot on
his farm again."[45] As late as January 1868, Thomas Groose of Calvert
County informed the Freedmen's Bureau that his apprenticed children
had escaped from their master only to be recaptured and whipped.
McDaniel also threatened Groose's wife with similar punishment
should she try to regain her children.[46] Such determination reached
right into the courtroom. The three children of Basil Croudy and his
wife were bound to Mrs. R. D. Sollars despite vigorous protests before
the judges of the Calvert County orphans' court. According to a Freedmen's Bureau agent, the Croudys obeyed the summons to appear "but
steadily refused to consent to the binding. The constable . . . finding
the mother obstinate, and deaf to reason, . . . struck her in the face
with his fist in the presence of the Judges."[47]

II

In filing their complaints with the United States Army and in attempting to register their opposition before county orphans' courts, black

parents made their economic motives clear. "The father of these children rents land," reported J. M. McCarter, a U.S. provost marshal in Caroline County, "[and] needs the help of his larger children for the purposes of farming and to help by their labor to support the younger."[48] "I have four children," explained a Talbot County freedwoman, "I can by their assistance maintain them."[49] "She has got homes for them of her own choice," said a Worcester County white of a neighboring black woman, "she could realize something for their hire to help her raise her younger children on, for she has six children to work for and her husband John Porter is in the Army."[50] A Somerset County observer stressed the same point.

> [T]hey can all get their own living if they have a fair chance. . . . [I]f they had their large children they could make [as] good [a] living as they got from their master, and much better. . . . Some of these children would bring into their mothers from 15 to 20 dollars per month, if they had them unto themselves. Many of the mothers have husbands in the armies of the United States and need the services of their children, with which they can make a good living.[51]

Elsewhere, others expressed the same needs and priorities. "Blacks here can take care of their own children," wrote Joseph Hall, "[A]ll or nearly all have children that they can get good wages for, which with their own labor they can get a decent support."[52] "I want my children back," explained Perry Riley of Kent County. "I can bring proof that I am able to support them. I can hire them out, one I can get twenty dollars for, and the other I can get victuals and clothes this year."[53] "The parents are very desirous," added James Johnston, "of having them returned to their keeping that they may have the benefit of their services."[54]

Black parents had obviously anticipated the assistance of their children and many had made provision for their labor only to have them apprenticed against their wishes. According to Henry Lockwood, "[M]any parents had rented small farms, expecting to have the labor of their children . . . [and also] many poor white tenants had made their arrangements to use this labor and are disappointed by the course pursued."[55] "The parents are very desirous of having them returned to their keeping," reported James Johnston in July 1866, "that they may have the benefit of their services."[56] To such observations by whites, blacks added their own. "I am very anxious to get him," said a Prince George's

County woman of her son, "for he would be of great help to me."[57] "I have four children," explained Emeline Woolford of Talbot County, "I can by their assistance maintain them."[58] "Would you be so kind to me and my son to ade us out of dence trubble," pleaded William Tilghman of Somerset County to the Freedmen's Bureau. "I had just got my son so that he was able to be of some help to me and then and not till then did the secesh take him away."[59]

Those parents who managed to resist or escape the apprenticeship of their offspring made their intentions plain. Their contractual arrangements with white employers made explicit reference to the participation of children in the earning process. "[H]e agreed to give me $100 a year for Charly," reported Francis Smallwood from Kent County, "he agreed to give me $20 for Emory and his clothes too."[60] Jordan Diggs of Prince George's County contracted with John Eamshaw to furnish eight working hands including several members of his family.[61] Less than a year later, Henna Howard of Worcester County explained, "I have four children one son nineteen and one daughter fourteen which I have hired out. . . . I have one girl eleven and one son nine at home with me my husban workes with his old master at ten dollars a month and he pays him and I do all the worke that I can and my husban and mee can support our children and them that is hired out can support themselves and help me."[62]

Other contracts contained similar provisions. "lucy going to school," wrote a Kent County freedwoman, "tomas employed at fifteen dollars a month."[63] William Nelson of Montgomery County signed a contract with Sarah Richards calling "for three of my sons helping."[64] Bristo Cheeks of Carroll County arranged to work for Joshua Shipley "for $160 per year . . . $10 per month for Bristo, his wife Sophia $5 per month and his daughter Aurelia $40 per year."[65] The contract of Peter Dorsey of St. Mary's County included provisions for Julia Dorsey, Rose Dorsey, and Henrietta Dorsey.[66]

III

In the face of so many obstacles, black Marylanders relied heavily on the support of their friends. In varying degrees, the army, the Bureau, and radical politicians helped freed parents win the release of their children. Members of all three groups recognized the desire of freed men and women to escape the master-slave relationship and shared their contention that a functioning black family would serve as a vital cornerstone of such self-reliance. According to Lew Wallace, commanding officer of the United States Army in Maryland at the time of emancipation, apprenticeship was a deliberate ploy by "evil disposed parties" intent on "obstructing the operation, and nullifying, as far as they can, the emancipation provision of the New Constitution."[67] Charles C. Fulton, editor of the *Baltimore American,* was equally forthright. "We object to refettering," he declared, "those who have been freed from the chains of slavery by a process which is regardless of the spirit and intent of the New Constitution."[68]

Furthermore, such "spirit and intent" included the right of freedmen and their families to seek self-reliant status. The *American* objected especially to county orphans' courts' refusal to consider black families' potential (as opposed to actual) capacity. The word "means" it complained, "was distorted into the sole sense of pecuniary ability, without any regard to that more comprehensive interpretation which includes the exertions of strong arms and the determination of willing hearts. Their daily labor like that of their fellow beings, forms their capital in trade and constitutes their 'means.'"[69] Judge Hugh Lennox Bond agreed. The consequence of apprenticeship, he argued, was "to destroy the family relation among a portion of the freedmen of the State; and to deprive by force the parents of the labor and comfort and society of their children."[70] "[T]he children taken," added John Eaton, "were the mainstay of the aged parents, whose best years had been spent in unrequited toil for their masters. The fruits of these abuses have not been alone the discouragement and hardship for the laborer, but uncultivated fields, short crops, and consequent pecuniary loss to the employer."[71]

Between 1864 and 1867, the United States Army, the Freedmen's Bureau, and prominent Unionist and Republican politicians joined black parents in attacking Maryland's apprenticeship law. On November 9, 1864, barely a week after emancipation, Wallace placed freed slaves under "special military protection," ordered county orphans' courts to stop apprenticing black children, and instructed his provost marshals to hear parents' complaints. Aware of the strength of the Union Army in the state, most judges chose to comply.[72] In May 1865, radical lawyers Henry Winter Davis, Henry Stockbridge, and Archibald Stirling, Jr., brought the cases of several black children before the

Baltimore Criminal Court. Judge Bond quickly remanded the children to the custody of their parents, declaring that "The present Constitution of Maryland . . . establishes a policy in favor of freedom and against the despotism of slavery."[73]

In fact, the actions of Wallace and Bond fell well short of their goal. The army's "special military protection" put an end to wholesale apprenticing by county orphans' courts but did nothing to free children already bound out. The decisions of the Baltimore Criminal Court obtained some releases but for so few children that their impact was minimal. Amidst such circumstances, black Marylanders continued to protest. In December 1865, a state convention of black leaders in Baltimore petitioned the Maryland General Assembly for a "removal of the disabilities under which . . . [we] labor."[74] In March 1866, several of these men addressed the same complaint to President Andrew Johnson:

> Because everywhere throughout the state our homes . . . [have been] invaded, and our little ones seized at the family fireside, and forcibly bound to masters who by law are expressly released from any obligations to educate them either in secular or religious knowledge; and because the legislature of Maryland would not by the repeal of this law, give us the right to a home or guarantee to us the safety of our children around the hearth while we are at labor, or their support in our old age.[75]

Parents, too, continued to complain. "Now sir," pleaded Hamilton Barclay of Somerset County in a letter to Judge Bond, "neither me nor my wife have bound my children or consented for them to be bound. I have been to the madgestraits and officiales in this place and they won't do anything for me. All I ask is that my . . . children may be restored to me again. And I pray your Honor will please take the matter in hand."[76]

The anti-apprenticeship campaign received a major boost in 1866, when the Freedmen's Bureau lent its full weight to the cause. With officers now in both southern Maryland and the Eastern Shore, the Bureau quickly made apprenticeship one of its chief concerns.[77] As early as July 1865, Oliver Otis Howard ordered that in Maryland:

> children . . . [must] not be bound without the consent of parents, or in the case of an orphan, not without the consent of an officer of this Bureau or a guardian approved by such an authority. . . . Consent must be obtained, otherwise the parent will have the right to the child.[78]

But just as Judge Bond found it difficult to accomplish his goals, so at first did the Freedmen's Bureau. No one cooperated with its agents in enforcing Howard's order, and whenever the possibility of federal force arose, Governor Bradford accused the Bureau of meddling in the affairs of a loyal state.[79]

Such remained the case until the passage of the federal Civil Rights Act of 1866. When Congress overrode Andrew Johnson's veto in April of that year, it opened new territory in Maryland for the opponents of apprenticeship which the Bureau, as an agent of the United States' government, was well poised to exploit. In fact, the relationship between apprenticeship and the Civil Rights Act became but one part of the Bureau's larger effort to win for blacks civil equality with whites under the aegis of the new statute. As such, apprenticeship assumed heightened importance and priority as part of the Bureau's general strategy for the state.

Black and radical white Marylanders were delighted and eager to join the federal attack. On July 28, 1866, radical lawyer William Daniel presented Bond and the Criminal Court with the first argument to incorporate the new act. "All oppressive bindings," Daniel maintained, "are abrogated by the Civil Rights Bill." The statute gave blacks "the equal benefit of all laws for the security of persons and property," and set aside "all laws and ordinances to the contrary." In that the sections of Article 6 of the Maryland apprenticeship law covering black children deprived the latter of education given whites, and permitted the reassignment of black (but not white) indentures, they were, therefore, unconstitutional.[80] Arguments such as Daniel's began to shape Bond's decisions. In deciding for the parents in an apprenticeship case in August 1866, the judge declared "[an] objection to these indentures arises from their opposition to the whole tenor and scope of the 'Civil Rights Bill' recently passed by Congress." Because of its provisions, "no distinction . . . [should] be made between white or black minors by the Orphans' Courts of the State. The requirements of the indentures must be equal . . . and not partial, unjust . . . [or] oppressive."[81]

For their part, Bureau agents identified offending planters, demanded that they release apprenticed children, and if that failed brought the former to trial before the Baltimore Criminal Court. Between July and November 1866, the Bureau confronted some twenty-five planters, all of whom, not unexpectedly, claimed that their apprentices had been indentured legally and that the whole affair was none of the Bureau's business.[82] But this time, planters had met their match. With its agents in the field, the Bureau could initiate many more cases than could a few radical lawyers. They were exposed to black complaints, had contacts in the rural community, and possessed the time and resources necessary to attack effectively.

Especially important were the efforts of William VanDerlip, agent for Anne Arundel and Calvert Counties. With the help of Joseph Hall, VanDerlip laid the groundwork for more than a dozen apprenticeship cases. Traveling to communities and neighborhoods in his district, he encouraged parents to come forward with their complaints and under his and Hall's guidance, to raise the funds to pay for sheriffs' fees. VanDerlip then correlated individual cases with Stockbridge's, Stirling's, and Daniel's schedules and with the docket of the Criminal Court. Gradually, such work began to pay off. Writs of habeas corpus reached into more areas of the state and brought a growing number of apprentices before the Baltimore Criminal Court. Here, Bond freed practically all of them on the ground that the Civil Rights Act rendered their indentures invalid.

By the summer of 1867, anti-apprenticeship forces were ready to take their campaign to the next level. Armed with briefs attacking every aspect of the system, Stockbridge, Stirling, and Daniel pushed to get a case before a federal court. In the fall of 1867, their persistence paid off when Salmon P. Chase, chief justice of the United States Supreme Court, agreed to hear while on circuit duty in Baltimore a petition for writ of habeas corpus from a black apprentice.

Chase heard the case of Elizabeth Turner of Talbot County on October 13, 1867, in the United States District Court in Baltimore. Stockbridge began with the contention that "the sort of apprenticeship adopted in Maryland is an evasion of the [13th] Amendment [to the United States Constitution]," but moved quickly to the substance of his argument: that the provisions of Sections 31 through 40 of Article 6 of the Maryland Code of Public General Laws were constitutionally irreconcilable with the Civil Rights Act of 1866. "Under the laws of Congress," Stockbridge declared, "there can be no distinctions between blacks and whites. . . . [Only] the law relating to white apprentices is applicable."[83]

The chief justice agreed. "Upon comparing the terms of this indenture with those required . . . for the apprenticeship of white persons," he declared, "the variance is manifest." The black minor, he pointed out, "is not entitled to any education; a white apprentice must be taught reading, writing, and arithmetic." Moreover, the black child was "liable to be assigned and transferred at the will of the master; . . . the white apprentice is not so liable." In short, argued Chase, "the indenture set forth in this [Turner's] return does not contain important provisions for the security and benefit of the apprentice which are required by the laws of Maryland in [the] indenture of white apprentices." It failed, therefore, to offer black children the protection guaranteed them by the first section of the Civil Rights Act.[84]

Armed with Chase's decision, the Bureau forced reluctant planters to release most of their apprentices by the summer of 1868.[85] It had been a long and difficult struggle. "We were delighted," exclaimed Lucy Lee of Baltimore, "when we heard that the Constitution set us all free, but God help us, our condition [was] bettered but little; free ourselves but deprived of our children, almost the only thing that would make us feel free and happy."[86] For the black families whose children were released, the end of apprenticeship constituted an important victory. With possession of their children, they were assured some of the autonomy that they so ardently sought. At the very least, they were guaranteed the right to call their families their own and to dictate some of the terms of their economic activities.

Like the purchase of land, blacks' struggle against the apprenticeship of their children provided a powerful example of their search for autonomy within a generally coercive system. Their battle for their children made one thing clear: Whatever they might accomplish in terms of family autonomy, it could be done only with the greatest of effort and with the determined assistance of white radicals and the Freedmen's Bureau. And at least on this question, such assistance was unreserved. In their struggle against apprenticeship, black Marylanders and white reformers functioned at their most effective level. Firmly believing that any reimposition of planters' control over black children threatened to resurrect slavery, they united in their condemnation of Article 6 of the Maryland Code of Public General Laws and mounted a successful attack against planter interests.

That same protest, however, revealed the limits of their success. The right to regulate the disposition of their families' labor was something for which black parents had to fight for more than four years and even at that, such regulation failed to shake either the determination of planters to maintain general control of black labor or the reluctance of white reformers to support more than minimal changes in basic labor-management relations. Whatever black Marylanders might accomplish in terms of family autonomy, their efforts remained confined by a white society determined to regulate them in other ways.

Notes

1. J. Hall to S. N. Clark, November 4, 1865, Box 1 (LRAC, September 1865 to October 27, 1866), BRFAL, D.C., RG 105.

2. *Easton Gazette*, February 25, 1865.

3. *Maryland Code of Public General Laws* (Annapolis, 1860), Article 6, "Apprentices," Sections 31–40, pp. 38–39.

4. Ibid.

5. Harrison Diary (MS 432.1), Maryland Historical Society.

6. *Communication from Major General Lew Wallace*, 13.

7. Ibid., 5–6.

8. *Towsontown American and Advocate*, as quoted in *Baltimore Sun*, December 3, 1864.

9. W. H. Gales to E. C. Knower, February 22, 1867, J. Goldsborough to E. C. Knower, February 27, 1867, G. N. Bishop to E. C. Knower, March 7, 1867, Box 2 (LRAC, April 1, 1866 to August 17, 1868), BRFAL, Md., RG 105; Talbot County Orphans' Court, Negro Docket (1855–1867), and Indentures (1853–1864 and 1864–1920), Worcester County, Orphans' Court Proceedings, 1863–1868, Kent County Register of Wills, Orphans' Court Minutes, 1864–1867, Maryland State Archives; Eighth Census of the United States, 1860, Schedule 1.

10. W. H. Gales to E. C. Knower, February 22, 1867, Box 2 (LRAC, April 1, 1866–August 17, 1868), BRFAL, Md., RG 105.

11. *Communication from Major General Lew Wallace*, 56–57.

12. *The War of the Rebellion: A Compilation of the Official Records of the Union and Confederate Armies*, Series 1, Vol. 43, Part 2 (Washington, 1893), 777; Testimony in Investigation of the Government of Maryland [1867], Records of the House of Representatives, Committee on the Judiciary, Record Group 233. It is difficult to determine the precise number of black children apprenticed in Maryland during the weeks following emancipation. Surviving county orphans' courts records are incomplete and contemporary Freedmen's Bureau and newspaper estimates varied widely. A conservative estimate might range between 3,000 and 4,000 children, although Barbara Fields suggests a figure as low as 2,519 (Fields, *Slavery and Freedom*, 153).

13. *Kent News*, December 17, 1864.

14. Testimony of William Bryan, January 11, 1867, Records of the House of Representatives, Committee on the Judiciary, Testimony in Investigation of the Government of Maryland [1867], Record Group 233.

15. W. V. Bowie to A. W. Bradford, November 16, 1864, State Papers [1864], Maryland State Archives.

16. Talbot County Orphans' Court, Negro Docket (1865–1867), and Indentures (1853–1864, and 1864–1920), Maryland State Archives.

17. M. Hammond to the Freedmen's Bureau, April 14, 1868, Volume 1 (LRAC, April 1, 1866 to August 17, 1868), BRFAL, Md., RG 105.

18. J. Gardener to the Freedmen's Bureau, May 4, 1868, Box 2 (LRAC, April 1, 1866–August 17, 1868), BRFAL, Md., RG 105.

19. Talbot County Orphans' Court, Indentures (1853–1864 and 1864–1920), Maryland State Archives.

20. *Communication from Major General Lew Wallace*, 40.

21. H. Lockwood to L. Wallace, December 10, 1864, *The War of the Rebellion: A Compilation of the Official Records of the Union and Confederate Armies*, Ser. 1, Vol. 43, Part 2, Correspondence, Etc. (Washington, 1893), 77.

22. *Baltimore American*, December 10, 1866.

23. Testimony of William F. Taylor, January 14, 16, 1867, Investigation of the Government of Maryland [1867], RG 233.

24. A. Stafford to H. H. Lockwood, November 2, 1864, Vol. 84 (Old Book 156), Endorsement Book No. 804, Records of the 8th Army Corps, Middle Department, United States Army, Continental Commands, 1821–1890, Record Group 393, National Archives.

25. *Communication from Major General Lew Wallace*, 75.

26. *Baltimore American*, December 13, 1864.

27. Ibid., November 22, 1864.

28. Talbot Court Orphans' Court, Indentures (1853–1864 and 1864–1920), Maryland State Archives. Significantly, the court did not record parental consent before 1864.

29. M. Nichols to O. O. Howard, October 11, 1866, Volume 1 (LRAC, April 1, 1866 to August 17, 1868), BRFAL, Md., RG 105.

30. *Communication from Major General Lew Wallace*, 72–73.

31. Adjutant General, Rolls of Md. Troops, U.S. Colored Troops [1863–1864], Maryland State Archives, Annapolis, Md.

32. Ibid.

33. Talbot County, Negro Docket, 1855–1867, Maryland State Archives, Annapolis, Md.

34. Affidavit contained in *Communication from Major General Lew Wallace*, 32–33.

35. Affidavit contained in ibid., 53.

36. Contained in Box 1 (LRAC, April 1, 1866–August 17, 1868), BRFAL, Md., RG 105.

37. Ibid.

38. Ibid.

39. J. Hall to S. N. Clark, November 4, 1865, Box 1 (LRAC, September 1865 to October 27, 1867), BRFAL, D.C., RG 105.

40. Harrison Diary (MS 432.1), Maryland Historical Society.

41. Affidavit contained in *Communication from Major General Lew Wallace*, 48.

42. Affidavit in ibid., 17.

43. Affidavit in ibid., 55.

44. Ibid., 66–67.

45. Ibid., 9.

46. T. Groose to W. L. VanDerlip, January 8, 1868, Volume 47 (Letters Received, Annapolis, July 20, 1866–September 11, 1868), BRFAL, Md., RG 105.

47. S. N. Clark to C. H. Howard, June 16, 1866, Box 11 (Letters Received, Annapolis, July 20, 1866–September 11, 1868), BRFAL, Md., RG 105.

48. *Communication from Major General Lew Wallace*, 36.

49. Affidavit in ibid., 78.

50. Ibid., 77.

51. Ibid., 61–62. Although it cannot be proved that the fathers of all these children served in the army, many—perhaps most—did. According to Union Army muster rolls, 288 Talbot County blacks enlisted in the United States Colored Troops between 1863 and 1864. (Adjutant General, Roll of Maryland Troops, U.S. Troops, Colored, Hall of Records, Maryland State Archives).

52. *Communication from Major General Lew Wallace*, 59.

53. Ibid., 73.

54. J. M. Johnston to J. F. Chur, July 25, 1866, Box 1 (LRAC, April 1, 1866–August 17, 1868), BRFAL, Md., RG 105.

55. H. H. Lockwood to S. B. Lawrence, December 15, 1864, Volume 85 (Old Book 161), Records of the 8th Army Corps, Middle Department, United States Army, Continental Commands, 1821–1890, RG 393, National Archives, Washington, D.C.

56. J. M. Johnston to J. F. Chur, July 25, 1866, Box 1 (LRAC, April 1, 1866–August 17, 1868), BRFAL, Md., RG 105.

57. Mrs. Moore to G. Henry, March 13, 1867, Box 12 (Letters Received, Bladensburg, May 1866–December 1867), BRFAL, Md., RG 105.

58. *Communication from Major General Lew Wallace*, 78.

59. W. Tilghman to O. O. Howard, October 30, 1865, Box 1 (LRAC, April 1, 1866–August 17, 1868), BRFAL, Md., RG 105.

60. *Communication from Major General Lew Wallace*, 35.

61. Miscellaneous Contract, Box 12 (Letters Received, Bladensburg, May 1866–December 1867), Md., RG 105.

62. H. Howard to A. Johnson, April 25, 1865, State Papers, Maryland State Archives.

63. S. Jackson to F. Bruen, June 1, 1868, Box 3 (Letters Received by Complaint Branch, 1866–1872), BRFAL, Md., RG 105.

64. W. F. Spurgin to W. W. Rogers, May 28, 1866, Box 12 (Letters Received, Rockville, May 1866–September 1867), BRFAL, Md., RG 105.

65. J. Shipley to Freedmen's Bureau, May 2, 1866, Box 1 (LRAC, April 1, 1866–August 17, 1868), BRFAL, Md., RG 105.

66. E. F. O'Brien to S. N. Clark, January 4, 1866, Box 1 (LRAC, September 1865–October 27, 1868), BRFAL, D.C., RG 105.

67. *Baltimore American,* November 10, 1864 [#181]; *Baltimore Sun,* November 10, 1864.

68. *Baltimore American,* January 18, 1865.

69. Ibid.

70. Ibid., May 29, 1865.

71. "Summary Report of the District of Columbia by Brevet Brigadier General, John Eaton, Jr., Assistant Commissioner, [December 15, 1865]," 158.

72. *Communication from Major General Lew Wallace;* Augustus W. Bradford to William Gooding et al., Judges of Orphan's Court, Kent County, November 16, 1864, Executive Letter Book, 1864–1866, Maryland State Archives; *Baltimore Sun,* November 18, 1864; *Baltimore American,* November 22, 24, 1864; *Christian Advocate,* November 24, 1864; Talbot County Orphans' Court, Indentures (1853–1864 and 1864–1920); Worcester County Orphans' Court, Proceedings (1863–1868), Maryland State Archives; Fields, *Slavery and Freedom,* 148–49.

73. *Baltimore American,* May 29, 1865. Henry Winter Davis was born in 1817. His father, Henry Lyon Davis, was president of St. John's College in Annapolis. Davis studied at Kenyon College in Ohio and the University of Virginia. He began practicing law in Alexandria, Va., in 1840, and in 1855 won a seat in the House of Representatives as a member of the American or "Know-Nothing" Party. A staunch Unionist from the beginning of the war, Davis allied himself early with Thaddeus Stevens and the radical wing of the Republican Party. Elected again to the House of Representatives in 1863, he cosponsored the Wade-Davis bill which would have committed the North to a more rigorous reconstruction of the South after the war. President Lincoln "pocket" vetoed the measure. Davis was clearly Maryland's leading radical, and his death in December 1865 robbed blacks of one of their most outspoken supporters (*Dictionary of American Biography.* 5:119–20; *Who Was Who in American History, Historical Volume, 1607–1896,* 138; *Harper's Weekly,* January 20, 1866. See also Gerald S. Henig, *Henry Winter Davis: Antebellum and Civil War Congressman from Maryland* (New York, 1973).

74. *Baltimore Sun*, December 29, 1865.

75. Andrew Johnson Papers, Manuscript Division, Library of Congress, Washington, D.C.

76. H. Barclay to H. L. Bond, September 1, 1866, Box 1 (LRAC, April 1, 1866–August 17, 1868), BRFAL, Md., RG 105.

77. *In re Turner*, 24 *Fed. Cas.* 337; No. 14,247 (1867); *Baltimore Sun*, October 15, 16, 17, 1867; *Baltimore Gazette*, October 16, 17, 1867; *Baltimore American*, October 17, 1867; *Nation*, October 24, 1867.

78. *Baltimore Sun*, July 24, 1865.

79. State Papers [1865], Maryland State Archives.

80. *Baltimore American*, July 31, 1866.

81. Ibid., August 14, 1866.

82. B. F. Beck to J. M. Johnston, July 29, 1866, Box 1 (LRAC, April 1, 1866–September 17, 1868), BRFAL, Md., RG 105.

83. *Baltimore Sun*, October 17, 1867; *Baltimore American*, October 17, 1867. Born in Massachusetts in 1822, Henry Stockbridge graduated from Amherst College in 1845. He then moved to Baltimore, where he was admitted to the bar in 1848. Originally a Whig, he became an early supporter of the Republican Party in 1856. Elected as a Unionist to the 1864 Maryland General Assembly, he was a vigorous supporter of emancipation and assumed a leading role in the state constitutional convention of that year which abolished slavery in the state (*Dictionary of American Biography*, 18:37; *Who Was Who in American History, Historical Volume, 1607–1896*, 508).

84. *In re Turner*, 24 Fed. Cas. 337; No. 14,267 (1867).

85. I rely on the statements of the Bureau itself in making this assertion. In September 1868, it estimated that only 200 black children remained in the hands of Maryland planters. (Volume 21, Apprenticeship Cases, Md., BRFAL, RG 105). According to Barbara Fields, some children were held much longer. (Fields, *Slavery and Freedom*, 153).

86. *Communication from Major General Lew Wallace*, 69.

5

Community Schools

I

THE FREEDMEN'S BUREAU and white radicals played a key role in the building of black schools, providing them with teachers, and shaping their educational objectives. Black Marylanders responded enthusiastically to the prospect of acquiring an education, were determined to send as many children to school as possible, and were committed to the same sort of liberal reform ideology that motivated the United States government and its educational program.[1] At the same time these schools represented something else: blacks' recognition of the necessity to sustain such schools themselves. As much as education was a part of a wider liberal venture in educational reform, it was also a part of the black community's search for as much local autonomy as possible amidst trying circumstances. Although such effort depended heavily on the support of the Freedmen's Bureau and northern freedmen's aid societies, it drew equally from forces within the black community itself.[2]

In November 1864, immediately after the state emancipation proclamation, a group of prominent white Baltimoreans—Quakers, businessmen, lawyers, and clergymen—met to commit themselves to black education.[3] The new state constitution of 1864 had for the first time provided a public education system in Maryland, but did nothing to compel local school boards to establish institutions for blacks.[4] Most of these men had been in the thick of the fight for emancipation and all belonged to or sympathized with the radical wing of the Unionist Party. To a man, they wanted more for blacks than a simple declaration of their freedom. On December 12, 1864, the Baltimore Association for the Moral and Educational Improvement of the Colored People defined its mission and petitioned the Baltimore City Council for financial support:

> The New Constitution [of Maryland] has added to the eighty thousand free colored people of our state, eighty-seven thousand others, recently

slaves. For the most part they are ignorant. . . . Thrown upon their own resources, they cannot be expected to know the necessity of industry, or how to seek permanent occupation and employment. We think it is the duty of every citizen of Maryland . . . to make this population most useful to the state, . . . [and to] instruct them in their industry . . . that they may rise in the scale of being, and be better fitted for the varied duties they are called upon to perform.[5]

On May 31, 1865, the Baltimore City Council allocated ten thousand dollars to the Association's school program within the city.[6] From Northern and European philanthropists the Association received an additional seven thousand dollars during its first year, and further contributions in 1866 and 1867.[7] In addition, Northern societies provided Maryland with teachers. Their sponsors, the New England Freedmen's Aid Society, the National Freedmen's Relief Association, the Pennsylvania Freedmen's Relief Association, and the American Missionary Association paid their transportation and a part of their salaries.[8] By the end of 1865, the Association had opened seven schools in Baltimore and eighteen in the rural counties of southern Maryland and the Eastern Shore.[9] A year later, in November 1866, it reported double that number of schools and an enrollment of more than six thousand students.[10]

Much of this expansion came about as a consequence of the Association's new partnership with the Freedmen's Bureau. On July 11, 1866, the Bureau sought a formal cooperative venture with the Association, which responded quickly with the request for "any aid you can afford us," and stressed especially the need for money and material to build new schoolhouses.[11] Expansion into Maryland's tidewater counties had exhausted most of the Association's money and all of the available space for schools in black churches and private dwellings. Despite its considerable backing, the Association had to allocate practically all of its funds to teachers' salaries and other operating expenses. Successful beyond even its most optimistic projections in attracting black interest in schools, the Association had clearly outstripped its resources.[12] In fact, it had been facing a building crisis since the end of 1865 when it found it impossible to construct new buildings.

It was into this breach that the Freedmen's Bureau moved, and in a short time it was actively engaged in providing lumber for schoolhouses. By the summer of 1866, the Bureau had commandeered empty buildings at Fort Marshall, Maryland, and Hicks United States Army

General Hospital in Baltimore.[13] Together, this material provided the essential lumber for more than sixty schoolhouses.[14] The Bureau also assumed the greater part of transportation costs, undertaking to get the lumber to its destinations free of charge to either local black leaders or the Baltimore Association.[15] The contribution of the Freedmen's Bureau in dollars and lumber constituted a significant measure of support for both the Baltimore Association and Maryland's black schools. After only six months of active participation, the Bureau had spent over five thousand dollars on lumber for county schools and had agreed to underwrite the rent of schools already established in Baltimore.[16] Moreover, the Bureau's assistance extended well beyond building materials and money. Throughout the tidewater counties, its agents worked closely with the Association and local black leaders in starting new school boards, canvassing for funds, buying land, and raising the actual buildings.[17]

II

"Being in almost daily receipt of requests from the colored people for schools," explained the Baltimore Association in its *First Annual Report* in November 1865, "[w]e have engaged to open schools at Cambridge, Dorchester County; Clearspring, Washington Co.; Centreville, Queen Anne's Co.; Denton and Preston, Caroline Co.; Uniontown, Carroll Co., and Long Green, Baltimore Co. We have also from 14 Counties, 38 applications for schools, which we anticipate having in operation before the first of January next."[18] In fact, the Association and Bureau were hard pressed to meet such demand. Between 1865 and 1867, both agencies were flooded by applications for lumber to build schools and teachers to teach in them. "[T]he colored people in every neighborhood [are] anxious for schools," explained the Baltimore Association in June 1865.[19] "They require school houses very much at present" reported the Bureau the following May, and in June, "The want of proper accommodation is severely felt. . . . Many applications are made from various localities for assistance in establishing schools."[20] By January 1, 1867, in response to such requests, the Association and Bureau had assisted black Marylanders in establishing more than sixty schools with a total enrollment of more than five thousand students.[21]

Behind such statistics lay the expressed enthusiasm of the black community. "You must build up your schools and educate your children," insisted Frederick Douglass in December 1864. "Hitherto you were wont to pride yourself on your muscles. . . . But you need something else now. You must have minds."[22] The Colored State Convention meeting in Baltimore a year later agreed: "We advise you to educate your children, give them trades and thereby qualify them for any position in life. For if ever we are raised to that elevated summit in life for which we are striving, it must be done by our individual exertion; no one can do it for us."[23] Indeed, "[t]he colored people of this State have settled down with the calm and firm resolution," explained Bureau agent Charles McDougall, "to make this work the one great and earnest effort of their life, thus demonstrating their manhood in the face of opposition and accumulated wrongs of many years."[24] As one freed woman put it, "I was a poor slave only a little time ago, and now when I tinks I can send my child to school it makes me so tankful that 'pears I mus do all I can for de school; we poor colored folk never seed anything like dis afore."[25] Nor was it just for the children. "I am determined to make the effort to learn to read my Bible before I die," explained an eighty-year-old woman, "and if I fail I will die on the way."[26]

Across the state, such enthusiasm translated into action as communities sought the assistance of the Bureau and Association. In August 1866, from Charles County, a Bureau officer reported that "[t]he freedmen manifest a strong desire to be educated and to educate their children."[27] "The colored people . . . are deeply interested in this building," explained a white observer in Potter's Landing, Caroline County, in May 1867, "and will do all they can toward putting it up."[28] By September of the same year, in Davidsonville, Calvert County, attendance had increased so rapidly "as to entirely fill the building now used and many have been turned away."[29] The message seemed clear. "The colored people," explained J. W. Alvord, Bureau Superintendent of Education, "are alive to the importance of the work, and feel that it is a vital point in their future welfare. They are doing all they can to help along *plans* for their education."[30]

Such grass roots involvement by the black community in this planning was of vital importance. From Kent County, William Perkins, a black merchant in Chestertown, provided eloquent testimony of this fact as he traveled the Eastern Shore as a field agent for the Bureau, visiting rural churches and talking to their congregations. "*Sir:* I went to Centreville yesterday according to your request. I met . . . a small congregation [at Spanish Neck Church], and found them anxious for a school. . . . I left Spanish Neck Church at 2 o'clock and went to Centreville, found a small congregation there still *more* anxious for a school and had been ready for the last six weeks. . . . I left Centreville at 5:30 P.M., arriving at Salem at 8 P.M., met a pretty large congregation there, [and] found them very anxious for a school."[31]

III

From the start, Baltimore Association and Freedmen's Bureau–supported schools occupied black churches or were constructed on black-owned land. Between 1866 and 1868 in the counties of southern Maryland alone, black school trustees purchased more than fifty pieces of such property—most costing between one hundred and three hundred dollars. The acquisition of this land represented a tremendous commitment of time, energy, and resources on the part of a rural community with little at its disposal. Alone, or with the assistance of Bureau officers or temporary field agents—some of them black—black parents met, organized committees, and raised the money for such property.

The results of such determination were impressive. In one of a series of reports on the work of John H. Butler, a black field agent hired by the Bureau to assist freedmen in Calvert and Anne Arundel Counties, William VanDerlip informed headquarters in February 1868, that: "I am informed by Mr. Butler that the lot at Swamp Dist is deeded to Colored Trustees exclusively for a school. I will endeavor to ascertain if it is recorded. . . . Land has been purchased at Mt. Zion but is not quite all paid for yet. Land has also been purchased at a point between Owensville and Birdsville about a mile north of Owensville. You can see the point on the map as there is a mill very near it. This with the Swamp school will serve better than the land at Chews Chapel. The money is ready to be paid. . . . We also expect very soon to have land at Tracey's Landing. Money is raised."[32]

The acquisition of land for schools was very much a cooperative affair, rooted in the activities of rural community life. Few individual blacks possessed or could afford to buy sufficient land on which to erect a school. With the assistance of the Freedmen's Bureau, blacks

instalment of money. Mr. Davidson was to give a deed to the Colored M. E. Church."[42]

For rural families, the church-school combination served as a highly visible center of community aspirations on land that they owned themselves. As such, its real and symbolic importance struck the white community with immediate force. As early as December 1864, arsonists in Newtown, Somerset County, burned a church in which black people were trying to start a school.[43] During the next few months, flames destroyed similar efforts in Cecil and Queen Anne's Counties.[44] In October and November of 1865, during a three-week period, whites destroyed black church-schools in Millington and Edesville, Kent County. In each case, it had been but a month since the school had opened its doors for the first time. Such attacks were aimed directly at the capacity of the black community to buy land and to organize schools. As Addie T. Howard, the teacher at Millington, reported to the Baltimore Association:

> I write in great haste to inform you of the calamity which befell us last night. Some malicious person or persons set fire to the church in which we have been holding our school. . . . The fire was set on the north side of the Church and was not discovered until it had made considerable headway. Of course, nothing could be done to save the building. It is a great loss to the people here, as they are very poor, and will not be able to build another, perhaps for years. . . . The people here now think it will be useless to hold a school here for some time, and perhaps for the rest of the year. They were trying to make preparations to put up a school house soon, but it would meet with the same ill luck.[45]

It was some time before the burning of churches and school houses had run its course. On November 11, 1865, whites burned a building in Baltimore County, and on March 11, 1866, the school in Spanish Neck, Queen Anne's County, went up in flames.[46] Several more were to follow. It was not until late that year, or even early in the next that the danger began to dissipate. By that time the determination of black trustees in rural Maryland and of the Baltimore Association and Freedmen's Bureau to build schools and to replace them where necessary was evident for all to see. Even the state government was compelled to recognize the legitimacy of such effort and to extend it some protection. After the Kent County fires, Governor Bradford offered a $500 reward for information leading to the arrest of the incendiaries.[47]

Opposition to or ambivalence toward the acquisition of land for school purposes was a part of a generally negative white attitude toward black land ownership of any sort. Small plots of land—whether purchased individually or by groups—contributed to the autonomy of black families who owned them and to those who shared in the process of cultivating them or raising churches or schools on them. Through the purchase of such land, they could redirect a portion of their labor to community use. Alongside their struggle for fair contracts and the release of their children from enforced apprenticeship, access to even scattered pieces of land on which they might build schools helped blunt the effect of whites' otherwise tight control over their daily lives and labor.[48]

IV

After buying the land, black Marylanders built their own schools. Again, with the assistance of the Baltimore Association, the Freedmen's Bureau, and with U.S. government–donated lumber from dismantled army barracks and hospitals, they erected several dozen buildings, each of them approximately thirty by forty feet and capable of accommodating forty to fifty students.[49] The Bureau shipped the lumber from Baltimore and Washington to points up and down the Potomac River and Chesapeake Bay where black workers unloaded it, hauled it, and combined it with local materials to construct school buildings. From time to time, the Bureau hired local carpenters, but most of the work was done by black field hands.

The process required detailed planning and coordination. "The work of building more school houses will be pushed forward as soon as the weather is of a character to justify operations," explained the *Baltimore American* on February 4, 1867. "During the bad weather which has prevailed for some time past the only thing that could be done was to transport lumber for school houses to such points as could be reached by railroad. The lumber now on hand, it is estimated, is sufficient to put up forty-five school houses of the size required."[50] By March 1, lumber from Baltimore had been sent to twenty-two locations from which blacks hauled it to the school sites.[51] "To get this lumber convenient [*sic*]," explained John Butler in August 1867, "it should be shipped to this place on board of the Plum Point Packet as she has conveniences to land it. . . . The people are very anxious to get a house here and say they will have [it] ready for use in four weeks after the Materials are landed. I have great confidence in these people doing what they say."[52]

Once the lumber was on the spot, black workers devoted whatever spare time and energy they could muster to the construction of the actual buildings. "[W]e wish you to send the lumber as soon as you can make it convenant [*sic*]," wrote David Williams, a school trustee in My Lady's Manor, Baltimore County, in June 1867. "[P]lease send me a letter in answar to this when you can seand the Lumber to Monkton Stasion we want to be thear to unlode it and make ore Reagements to have teams thear to take it away at the same time."[53] "I am here at this school house," reported John Butler from Nottingham, Prince George's County, in January 1868, "and the frame set up [is] a very substantial one. . . . I made an agreement with them [the workers] to go in the woods and get out the sleepers and perhaps the rafters and shingle the house and I would write to you for windows and sash and flooring and plank for the house. If we had . . . [these] I think the House could be finished in a few weeks."[54]

In Davidsonville, Calvert County, the black community committed its energy to a project even bigger than that originally called for. "They think a house less than 24 by 40 too small," reported Thomas Davidson, in September 1867. "[T]hey have now over 90 children enrolled and think that the number will be greatly increased next summer. They are willing to pledge themselves to furnish the sills, posts, braces, and plates for such a building, and commence at once. And if they should not be able to finish it this fall they will do so next spring."[55] "The . . . estimate [below] comprises the materials for the School house," explained Davidson:

	Lumber[56]			
2	Side Sills	8 × 10	40 ft. long	
1	Girder	8 × 10	40 " "	
2	End Sills	8 × 10	30 " "	
11	Posts	6 × 4	11 " "	
44	Rafters	3 × 4	15 " "	
20	Scantlin	3 × 4	12 " "	
20	Scantlin	3 × 4	24 " "	Collar beams
10	Sacantling	3 × 4	15 " "	

38	Sleepers	3×11 16 " "
1300	feet flooring	
5000	" weather boarding & Sheathing	
	Shingles fir 10 Square	
5	window frames & Sash	
12	lights	10×12
1	Door frame & folding door	
	Brick for underpinning & chimney	
	Laths, Lime & hair, Nails, Hinges &	
	Lock	

By necessity, such effort had to take into account the priorities of a working community. "The harvest which is commencing," explained a white observer in Prince George's County in July 1867, "will prevent their doing anything before that time."[57] "They are willing to do all they can to build the house," wrote John Butler from Calvert County a month later, "[and] will work as they can spare time."[58] In November, from Plum Point, Calvert County, Butler explained, "The people are getting their corn in now . . . and [will] complete as much of the work as possible by Christmas."[59] "I have been to look after the lumber," he said. "It has been landed and put neatly in a barn shed and will be hauled next week but those who will haul it have not yet finished sowing their corn and killing their hogs, but say next week all will be hauled up and house commenced if the weather is favorable."[60]

By early 1868, rural black workers had accomplished a remarkable feat. In less than two years they had constructed sixty such school houses at a pace that outstripped the Baltimore Association's capacity to supply them with teachers. "[O]ur Colored People have very willingly and very liberally helped on this cause in Maryland," reported the Association. "[T]hey have, from the lumber obtained by us . . . built at *their own unaided* expense *Sixty School Houses,* all of them good structures, and most of them very far surpassing the county school houses for whites."[61]

V

Once its own schools were built, the rural black community sustained them. The Baltimore Association provided teachers and paid their salaries, but beyond that, black trustees were on their own. The extent of local sustenance was considerable. Black families boarded their schools' teachers, maintained their buildings, effected necessary repairs, provided light and fuel, and paid cash for supplies that the schools could not provide themselves. Moreover, such support required organization. The boards of trustees that had purchased the land and facilitated the construction of the buildings had also to organize the community to maintain them once in operation.

In November 1865, after one year of operation, the Baltimore Association reckoned that black people had contributed $2,000 to its rural school program, 11 percent of its total expenditures.[62] "The colored people . . . have uniformly paid the board of teachers, besides the incidental expenses of the schools; thus contributing . . . some $6,000 or $7,000," reported the Freedmen's Bureau in July 1866, a figure that had grown to $9,000 by November, or 26 percent of the Association's budget.[63] A year later, in November 1867, these figures had grown to $21,000 and 36 percent.[64] Clearly, as one observer noted in October 1867, "The effort in Maryland . . . to make the schools partially self-sustaining has been a great success."[65] William J. Albert, president of the Baltimore Association, agreed. "It is a heavy tax upon them . . . but it shows that at no distant date their schools can be made almost self-supporting."[66]

To raise this money, the entire black community chipped in. "I am striving to get sufficient means," reported a teacher in Harford County. "During the holidays we had a fair in the church and raised one hundred and forty dollars."[67] "I am just now closing up a fair," wrote John Butler from Asbury, Calvert County. "I am glad to inform you that after working hard two days and nights in the rain we succeeded in raising one hundred and forty dollars. . . . I also intend to hold another fair Friday and Saturday next at Parkers Creek."[68] On another occasion, in yet another Calvert County village, Butler explained, "It is very hard to raise money here for anything; the colored people are cheated so badly they have not the money, but I have gathered the females together and we are about to hold fairs at different places and by doing so we expect to raise money enough."[69]

To sustain such effort, black leaders formed societies to raise money and to organize its expenditure. "The colored people are forming school societies," explained Joseph Hall in Calvert County, in September 1866. "In regard toward paying the board and washing of the teacher in my neighborhood the subscribers to the society number something over one hundred which pays something over twenty-five dollars."[70] "We the undersigned hereby pledge ourselves for the support of a school at Rockville," wrote a number of black men in Montgomery County in February 1867, "and agree to hold ourselves responsible for such sum as may be necessary to pay the board and washing of the teacher and to provide fuel and lights for the School-house":[71]

Feb 14/67	-William Kelley	signed
	-Louis Proctor	mark
	Reuben Hill	"
Feb 15/67	-Samuel Martin	"
	Solomon Williams	"
	Adam Baker	"
	Hilliary Powell	"
Feb 20/67	-William Baker	"
Feb 21/67	-Barney Lilles	"
Feb 22/67	-Henry Tyler	signed
Feb 27/67	-Henson Morris	"
	Alfred Rose	mark
Feb 28/67	-Hezekiah Williams	signed
	Richard Williams	mark
	Mason Martin	signed
Mar 2/67	-Henry Dove	mark
	Levi Hopkins	"
Mar 7/67	-Israel Butler	"
Mar 13/67	-George Blair	"
Mar 14/67	-Tilghman Graham	"

VI

However important money and organizational structure were, the bedrock of black community support for its schools came from the students—both children and adults—and the families who sustained them. Educational aspirations occupied a central place in the postemancipation agenda of the rural black community, and despite the many obstacles in their path, mothers, fathers, and children strove mightily to make their schools a success.

Teachers regularly reported on their students' eagerness and diligence. "My work in the school room is light," wrote M. S. Osbourne from Church Creek, Dorchester County, in October 1865. "I hardly realize that I have any governing to do. My pupils seem so eager to learn."[72] Later that month, Harrison T. Fletcher added, "I never saw scholars take so much pains to obey their teacher, and endeavor to learn. . . . I am confident they will make very rapid progress."[73] And from Matilda Anderson in Edesville, Kent County, "[their] artlessness of manner, the eagerness with which they seize upon their instruction, and their . . . affectionate manners are all subjects of deepest admiration."[74]

Tied to such enthusiasm was black students' obvious delight in attending their *own* schools. According to Osbourne, her children had "an unbounded love for and pride in their school. I never say 'this is your school' without bringing, if possible, a blacker hue to their eyes, and a happy color to their cheeks. I can't describe the emotions on their faces . . . . They show plainly they appreciate their school."[75] Phineas Waterhouse at Muirkirk, Prince George's County, commented that "[the] colored pupils manifest a good degree of interest in the school and all feel proud of the beautiful new school house."[76]

To send their children to school called for significant sacrifice from black parents. They had their work to think of first and usually required the help of their children simply to make a living. A child at class could not contribute as much to the support of his family as one who could work all day. This was particularly the case with older children. "Parents are taking their grown children away and hiring them out," explained a teacher in Burkettsville, in April 1866, "while they continue to send the younger [to school]."[77]

Indeed, in spite of all of their educational aspirations, the black community could ill afford to send more than a few of its children to school. In a typical election district of Anne Arundel County, for example, fewer than 10 percent of the children listed in the 1870 United States census had attended school during the previous year. A similar situation applied in the Chestertown area in Kent County. The first annual report of the Baltimore Association in 1866 recorded 82 students in the Chestertown school. The 1870 census listed 100 black children as having attended school in 1869, a number that represented 10 percent of the children in the area.[78] The fact was that most black children had to work to support their families.

Such sacrifice did nothing, however, to diminish the dedication of the black community to its schools or to its determination to educate as many people as possible. In a letter published in the *American Mis-*

sionary in February 1868, a teacher in Darlington, Harford County, described the level of such involvement and the profound impression it had upon her:

> There is an increasing interest among the people for education. We have more names on our register this term than ever before. A number of adults attend the day school, whose distance of residence forbids them from attending the night school. Several of them come four miles every day, and they learn with a rapidity which is truly astonishing. While the progress of the little ones acts as a stimulus for the older portion, the correct deportment of the latter has an influence for good on the former. So with all it is more of a benefit than a disadvantage for young and old to meet on a level, although it presents an odd appearance.
>
> It is interesting to look into our school; every nook and cranny is occupied, with all sizes and all ages. I think we have a fair representation of the four stages in life, for they rank from five years to sixty. Here and there a listless scholar, but mostly eager, anxious faces to greet you. As the school is Primary and Intermediate, seventy scholars keep me busily employed from nine o'clock in the morning until five in the afternoon, and at half past seven o'clock at night the school opens.[79]

And although many could not afford to attend school or to send their children, others somehow managed. Every rural school had its night classes for adults who attended after working a full day in the fields. Although weary, they struggled to absorb what they could. "It is truly encouraging," wrote Phineas Waterhouse, "to see these men and women, after working all day, come in and study so attentively. It is true their tired bodies . . . often say, silently if not in words, 'I am unfit for study'; and not infrequently the nodding head falls involuntarily on the desk before it . . . [but] I have not the heart to chide for such sleeping in school time . . . [for] those who attend do not spend their hours altogether in vain."[80]

Such dedication and determination expressed itself in a more public and dramatic fashion in a series of public educational meetings held throughout the state in 1867. Sponsored by the Baltimore Association and Freedmen's Bureau as a means to stir up both political and educational enthusiasm, these occasions turned out to be far bigger than expected and accomplished much more than originally intended. Where modest or moderate crowds were anticipated, hundreds or even thousands showed up in eloquent public testimony to the strength of their educational aspirations. At one such meeting in Dorchester

County in June, "a vast throng of people" gathered to hear speeches by General Edgar Gregory and Hugh Lennox Bond. "As the steamboat approached the wharf," reported the *Baltimore American,* "their greetings were loud and enthusiastic. At 3 o'clock P.M., after music from Smith's cornet band, of Cambridge, the meeting was organized. . . . There must have been three thousand people in front of the Court House."[81]

In late July, an estimated two to three thousand black spectators showed up at a similar meeting in Havre de Grace, Harford County, and a week later, another "eleven or twelve hundred" near Prince Frederick, Calvert County, and between one thousand and fifteen hundred in Centreville, Queen Anne's County.[82] At the latter, "The General, the Judge . . . and a few other gentlemen of this city took the morning boat and arrived at Queentown in good time," reported the *Centreville Citizen,* "and taking the conveyances provided, [they] started for Centreville . . . (six miles distant), and were met on the road about a mile from the latter place by a procession of about four or five hundred colored men, a hundred or more of whom had served in the Union army during the war. The greatest enthusiasm prevailed at the reception, and ranks were opened for the carriages to pass through and then closed up in the rear of the vehicles, making a procession somewhat imposing in its length and enthusiasm."[83] Similarly excited responses met the speakers at meetings in early September in Port Tobacco, Charles County, and Leonardtown, St. Mary's County, where over a thousand rural blacks turned out on each occasion.[84]

VII

Black participation in the establishment, organization, and support of post-emancipation rural schools constituted, in essence, a community grass roots educational movement of considerable force that by 1868 was responding to an annual enrollment of some several thousand students.[85] Clearly, none of this would have been possible without the encouragement and assistance of the Freedmen's Bureau and Baltimore Association. The government supplied lumber. Officers and agents helped find land, instructed rural black trustees in the fine arts of constituting committees, and provided public speakers. The Bureau offered whatever physical protection its scattered agents could, and the Association hired teachers and paid their salaries.

Once all of this is said, it is equally obvious that both agencies acted at best as facilitators of an educational movement shaped by the practical realities and priorities of the black community. In large part, rural black schools were what they were because rural black Marylanders had no alternatives. In the absence of sufficient money, manpower, and sympathy from the whites surrounding them, the schools became institutions built and maintained by black people on land purchased by the community. By necessity, these were local, cooperative enterprises and as such were similar to other activities that black Marylanders felt compelled to undertake for and by themselves.

Nothing demonstrated such necessity better than the general opposition by rural whites to the presence of black schools in their midst. The burning of a dozen buildings in 1865–66 provided simply the most dramatic evidence of such opposition. "[T]he school houses have all been rebuilt by the colored people themselves," reported the Baltimore Association in February 1867, "no assistance has been given by the white people in the neighborhood who sympathize in the outrages committed."[86] "In their present condition they have no encouragement," explained a white observer in Calvert County in June.[87] "The owners of land are so much opposed to schools down in these counties," added John Butler, also from Calvert County, in October.[88]

Teachers and students also felt the brunt of such opposition. On October 18, 1865, M. S. Osbourne reported—with some sarcasm—from Church Creek, Dorchester County, that:

> Last week there was considerable agitation about my work, and a meeting was held in which it was decided that I should leave the town. A committee of five was appointed to wait on me, and a letter written to inform me of the good feeling of the people of Church Creek in regard to me. The committee thus far has failed to do their duty, and I very much fear that I shall not have an opportunity of seeing what "Southern chivalry" is. Excuse me if I haven't much respect for this peculiar characteristic of Southern rebels. I cannot refrain from comparing 1860 with 1865; *then* one Southern boy could whip five Yankee men; *now* five Southern men, if they dared, would visit one Yankee girl to force her to leave a legal pursuit. "How the mighty have fallen!"[89]

Later that month, Martha Hoy, a teacher in Trappe, Talbot County, reported that "On arriving at my school house last Wednesday morning, I found that one of the window shutters had been forced open and all the lower panes of glass broken in. . . . The school house is located in such a lonely place, and it seems to me that the whites are so wicked here that they would, if they got the opportunity, injure us badly."[90] Nor did it get any better. On November 25, she described the nature of white opposition to her school in detail:

> Men, apparently intoxicated, would come and rush to my school-house door and frighten the children in such a manner that the parents of my scholars would not send them to school. . . . When my scholars would be returning from school, the whites would take their slates away from them and rub out the copies that I had set for them, and return the slates when they felt disposed to do so; at other times they would have a rope laid to trip them and beat them with, or else they would chase them. In the morning when I would be going to school, they would lay hoops and other impediments in my way to trip me; in the afternoons or on return-ing home, they would push me off the walk, throw dirt on me, and stone me; they have threatened my life, and they said they would kill me any way, if I attempted to teach at night. They also threatened to burn the school.[91]

And it could get worse. From Spanish Neck in Queen Anne's County, J. W. Cromwell, a male teacher, reported in March 1866:

> The crisis of affairs has at last arrived. Last night returning from school I met on the road five men posted four on one side in the opening to a bypath and one on the other side, "*at a charge bayonet.*" It was so very dark that I was in their grasp before I beheld them. . . . One advanced, placing his muzzle near my breast and said, Halt! Halt! You d——b——k s—— of b—— halt! I clung to one who accompanied me, then, turned and ran across the road, they all immediately fired, balls went whizzing all around me but the crooked road, dark night, and dense woods alone protected me and rendered their firing uncertain, so I barely escaped with my life.[92]

With so few agents at their disposal, there was little either the Freed-men's Bureau or the Baltimore Association could do to protect schools, teachers, and students, other than rely on good fortune and the assis-tance of the few rural whites who supported black educational aspira-tions. Such support, however, did not normally amount to much. According to Martha Hoy, a magistrate who was supposedly sympa-thetic toward the black community told her "that he could not advise me what to do in such a case . . . and that they did not allow colored people to have any say against a white person in their State."[93]

Under the circumstances the black community was compelled to fend for itself much of the time. Essentially they had no choice but to do so. It was not, after all, that they *wanted* their schools to occupy a place within the defensive strategies of an oppressed community. Rural black Marylanders shared with the agents of the Freedmen's Bureau and Baltimore Association an enduring faith in the essentially liberating potential of the Northern educational ideology. There was, however, no escaping the fact that although both the United States government and black Marylanders aspired to an educational system and curriculum similar to that offered whites, the mechanics of the situation compelled blacks to operate within drastically different and reduced circumstances.

NOTES

1. W. A. Low, "The Freedmen's Bureau and Education in Maryland," *Maryland Historical Magazine* 47 (1952): 29–39; Ronald E. Butchart, *Northern Schools, Southern Blacks, and Reconstruction: Freedmen's Education, 1862–1865* (Westport, Conn., 1980), 97–168; Robert C. Morris, *Reading, 'Riting, and Reconstruction: The Education of Freedmen in the South, 1861–1870* (Chicago, 1976), 149–212; Jacqueline Jones, *Soldiers of Light and Love: Northern Teachers and Georgia Blacks* (Chapel Hill, 1980); James D. Anderson, *The Education of Blacks in the South, 1860–1935* (Chapel Hill, 1988), 4–32. See also, Roberta Sue Alexander, "Hostility and Hope: Black Education in North Carolina during Reconstruction, 1865–1867," *North Carolina Historical Review* 53 (January 1976): 113–32; James Smallwood, "Black Education in Reconstruction Texas: The Contributions of the Freedmen's Bureau and Benevolent Societies," *East Texas Historical Journal* 19 (spring 1981): 17–40; Kenneth B. White, "The Alabama Freedmen's Bureau and Black Education: The Myth of Opportunity," *Alabama Review* 34 (April 1981): 107–24; Paul A. Cimbala, "Making Good Yankees: The Freedmen's Bureau and Education in Reconstruction Georgia, 1865–1870," *Atlanta Historical Journal* 29 (fall 1985): 5–18.

2. See also, Joseph L. Browne, " 'The Expenses Are Borne by Parents,' Freedmen's Schools in Southern Maryland, 1865–1870," *Maryland Historical Magazine* 86 (winter 1991): 407–19.

3. Baltimore Normal School Account Book (MS 94), Maryland Historical Society; Baltimore Yearly Meeting, Religious Society of Friends, Orthodox, "Meeting for Sufferings, 1828–1877," Quaker Records, Maryland State

Archives; Richard Paul Fuke, "The Baltimore Association for the Moral and Educational Improvement of the Colored People, 1864–1870," *Maryland Historical Magazine* 66 (winter 1971): 369–404.

4. Francis N. Thorpe, comp., *The Federal and State Constitutions, Colonial Charters, and Other Organic Laws of the States, Territories, and Colonies . . .*, 7 vols. (Washington, 1909), Vol. 3, 1772–1773; *Laws of the State of Maryland . . . 1865* (Annapolis, 1865), 269.

5. Baltimore Normal School Account Book (MS 94), Maryland Historical Society; Bond-McCulloch Family Papers (MS 1159), Maryland Historical Society; *Baltimore American,* December 12, 1864.

6. City Council, Reports and Resolutions, RG 16 S1, WPA 1865, Document 605, Baltimore City Archives, Baltimore, Md; *Journal of Proceedings of the First Branch City Council of Baltimore at the Sessions of 1864 and 1865* (Baltimore, 1865), 572; *The Ordinances of the Mayor and City Council of Baltimore, Passed at the Sessions of 1864 and 1865* (Baltimore, 1865), 100.

7. *First Annual Report of the Baltimore Association of the Moral and Educational Improvement of the Colored People* (Baltimore, 1866), 8; *Second Annual Report of the Baltimore Association for the Moral and Educational Improvement of the Colored People* (Baltimore, 1866), 7; *Third Annual Report of the Baltimore Association for the Moral and Educational Improvement of the Colored People* (Baltimore, 1868), 8.

8. *First Annual Report of the Baltimore Association,* 8; *Freedmen's Record,* 1, no. 7 (July 1865), 119 and 11 (November 1865), 119; *National Freedman,* 1, no. 9 (October 15, 1865), 310–11; *American Missionary,* 9, no. 10 (October 1865), 217.

9. *First Annual Report of the Baltimore Association,* 4, 7.

10. *Second Annual Report of the Baltimore Association,* 14–16.

11. F. Israel to J. Kimball, July 11, 1866, Box 12 (Letters Received, Bladensburg, May 1866 to December 1867), BRFAL, Md., RG 105.

12. Ibid.

13. G. W. Bradley to E. M. Gregory, June 27, 1866, Volume 1 (LRAC, April 1, 1866 to August 17, 1868), BRFAL, Md., RG 105; R. Chandler to [?] Ketchum, July 14, 1866, Volume 3 (Register of Letters Sent, Assistant Commissioner, April 1, 1866–August 17, 1868), BRFAL, Md., RG 105; R. M. Janney to E. M. Gregory, August 31, 1866, Box 1 (LRAC, April 1, 1866–August 17, 1868), BRFAL, Md., RG 105; *Baltimore American,* October 15, 1866.

14. *Third Annual Report of the Baltimore Association,* 6; *Baltimore American,* October 15, 1866.

15. E. M. Gregory to O. O. Howard, November 3, 1866, Volume 3 (Register of Letters Sent, Assistant Commissioner, April 1, 1866–August 17, 1868), BRFAL, Md., RG 105; F. Von Shirach to A. C. Knower, March 31,

1867, Box 11 (Letters Received, Annapolis, July 20, 1866–September 11, 1868), BRFAL, Md., RG 105.

16. E. M. Gregory to O. O. Howard, October 13, 1866, Volume 3 (Register of Letters Sent, Assistant Commissioner, April 1, 1866–August 17, 1868), BRFAL, Md., RG 105; J. W. Alvord, *Fourth Semi-Annual Report on Schools for Freedmen, July 1, 1867* (Washington, D.C., 1868), 4; F. Von Shirach to A. C. Knower, March 31, 1867, Box 11 (Letters Received, Annapolis, June 28, 1866–September 11, 1868), BRFAL, Md., RG 105.

17. C. H. Howard to J. Kimball, May 31, 1866, RG 105, Vols. 26, 27 (Special Orders and Circulars, Assistant Commissioner), BRFAL, D.C., RG 105; G. E. Henry to W. W. Rogers, June 4, 1866, Volume 50 (Register of Letters Sent, Bladensburg, June 4, 1866 to September 18, 1867), BRFAL, Md., RG 105.

18. *First Annual Report of the Baltimore Association*, 9, 18.

19. *Freedmen's Record*, 1, no. 7 (July 1865), 116.

20. A. W. Bolenius to Freedmen's Bureau, May 26, 1866, Box 1 (LRAC, April 1, 1866–August 17, 1868), BRFAL, Md., RG 105; G. Stannard to O. O. Howard, June 5, 1866, Volume 3 (Register of Letters Sent, Assistant Commissioner, April 1, 1866–August 17, 1868), BRFAL, Md., RG 105.

21. J. W. Alvord, *Third Semi-Annual Report on Schools for Freedmen, January 1, 1867* (Washington, D.C., 1868), 6–7.

22. *Baltimore American*, December 5, 1864.

23. *Baltimore Sun*, January 1, 1866.

24. Alvord, *Third Semi-Annual Report*, 6.

25. M. S. Osbourne to J. T. Graham, October 31, 1865, contained in *First Annual Report of the Baltimore Association*, 23.

26. Alvord, *Third Semi-Annual Report*, 6.

27. J. C. Brubaker to W. W. Rogers, August 26, 1866, Volume 1 (Letters Received, Assistant Commissioner, September 1865 to October 27, 1866), BRFAL, D.C., RG 105.

28. C. B. Boynton to E. M. Gregory, May 23, 1867, Box 2 (Letters Received, Assistant Commissioner, April 1866–August 1868), BRFAL, Md., RG 105.

29. W. L. VanDerlip to W. W. Rogers, September 28, 1867, Box 11 (Letters Received, Annapolis, July 20, 1866–September 11, 1868), BRFAL, Md., RG 105.

30. Alvord, *Second Semi-Annual Report on Schools and Finances of Freedmen*, 11.

31. W. Perkins to J. T. Graham, November 1, 1865, contained in *First Annual Report of the Baltimore Association*, 28–29.

32. W. L. VanDerlip to J. Kimball, February 18, 1868, Volume 48 (Register of Letters Sent, Annapolis, June 28, 1866 to March 13, 1868), BRFAL, Md., RG 105.

33. R. G. Rutherford to Freedmen's Bureau, July 23, 1867, Volume 53 (Register of Letters Sent, Rockville, June 5, 1866–October 20, 1867), BRFAL, Md., RG 105.

34. D. Williams to E. M. Gregory, June 12, 1867, Box 10 (Reports & Schools Miscellaneous), BRFAL, Md., RG 105.

35. R. G. Rutherford to W. W. Rogers, October 2, 1867, Volume 53 (Register of Letters Sent, Rockville, June 5, 1866–October 20, 1867), BRFAL, Md., RG 105.

36. C. B. Boynton to E. M. Gregory, May 23, 1867, Volume 1 (LRAC, April 1, 1866–August 17, 1868), BRFAL, Md., RG 105.

37. J. H. Butler to W. L. VanDerlip, June 22, 1868, Box 11 (Letters Received, Annapolis, July 20, 1866–September 11, 1868), BRFAL, Md., RG 105.

38. J. H. Butler to W. L. VanDerlip, August 22, 1867, Volume 47 (Letters Received, Annapolis, July 20, 1866–September 11, 1866), BRFAL, Md., RG 105.

39. *First Annual Report of the Baltimore Association*, 5.

40. G. J. Stannard to O. O. Howard, June 5, 1866, Volume 3 (Register of Letters Sent, Assistant Commissioner, April 1, 1866–August 17, 1868), BRFAL, Md., RG 105.

41. S. Hughes to E. M. Gregory, December 24, 1866, Volume 1 (LRAC, April 1, 1866–August 17, 1868), BRFAL, Md., RG 105.

42. W. L. VanDerlip to W. W. Rogers (two letters), September 23, 1867, Volume 48 (Register of Letters Sent, Annapolis, June 28, 1866–March 13, 1868), BRFAL, Md., RG 105.

43. *Baltimore Clipper*, December 9, 1864.

44. *First Annual Report of the Baltimore Association*, 29.

45. Records of the House of Representatives, Committee on the Judiciary, Testimony in Investigation of the Government of Maryland, 1867, Record Group 233.

46. C. A. Watkins to O. O. Howard, March 13, 1866, Box 1 (LRAC, September 1865–October 27, 1866), BRFAL, D.C., RG 105.

47. "Proceedings of the Governor of the State of Maryland [1861–1869]," State Papers, Maryland State Archives.

48. Ibid.

49. R. M. Janney to Freedmen's Bureau, August 31, 1866, and F. J. Israel to E. M. Stanton, September 28, 1866, Box 1 (LRAC, April 1, 1866–August 17, 1868), BRFAL, Md., RG 105; *Baltimore American*, October 15, 1866.

50. *Baltimore American*, February 4, 1867.

51. R. M. Janney to Freedmen's Bureau, March 1, 1867, Box 2 (LRAC, April 1, 1866–August 17, 1868), BRFAL, Md., RG 105.

52. J. H. Butler to W. L. VanDerlip, August 28, 1867, Volume 47 (Letters

Received, Annapolis, July 20, 1866–September 11, 1866), BRFAL, Md., RG 105.

53. D. Williams to E. M. Gregory, June 12, 1867, Box 10 (Reports, School Miscellaneous), BRFAL, Md., RG 105.

54. J. H. Butler to W. L. VanDerlip, January 4, 1868, Volume 47 (Letters Received, Annapolis, July 20, 1866–September 11, 1868), BRFAL, Md., RG 105.

55. T. Davidson to J. Kimball, September 13, 1867, Box 11 (Letters Received, Annapolis, July 20, 1866–September 11, 1868), BRFAL, Md., RG 105.

56. T. Davidson to W. L. VanDerlip, August 18, 1867, Volume 47 (Letters Received, Annapolis, July 20, 1866–September 11, 1867), BRFAL, Md., RG 105.

57. S. J. Alsop to G. E. Henry, July 2, 1867, Box 12 (Letters Received Bladensburg, May 1866–December 1867), BRFAL, Md., RG 105.

58. J. H. Butler to W. L. VanDerlip, August 22, 1867, Volume 47 (Letters Received, Annapolis, July 20, 1866–September 11, 1867), BRFAL, Md., RG 105.

59. J. H. Butler to W. L. VanDerlip, November 18, 1867, Box 11 (Letters Received, Annapolis, July 20, 1866–September 11, 1868), BRFAL, Md., RG 105.

60. J. H. Butler to W. L. VanDerlip, November 10, 1867, ibid.

61. *Third Annual Report of the Baltimore Association,* 6.

62. *First Annual Report of the Baltimore Association,* 8.

63. *Second Annual Report of the Baltimore Association,* 7.

64. *Third Annual Report of the Baltimore Association,* 6.

65. Baltimore Yearly Meeting, Religious Society of Friends, Orthodox, Records Deposited at Homewood Meeting House, "Minutes, Meetings for Sufferings, 1829–1877," M 781, p. 311, Maryland State Archives.

66. W. J. Albert to American Freedmen's Union Commission, March 21, 1868, Baltimore Normal School Minute Books (MS 95), Maryland Historical Society.

67. *American Missionary,* 12, no. 5 (May 1868): 101.

68. J. H. Butler to W. L. VanDerlip, November 29, 1867, Box 11 (Letters Received, Annapolis, July 20, 1866–September 11, 1868), BRFAL, Md., RG 105.

69. J. H. Butler to W. L. VanDerlip, November 18, 1867, ibid.

70. J. Hall to W. L. VanDerlip, September 4, 1866, ibid.

71. Subscription list, Box 12 (Letters Received, Rockville, May 1866–September 1867), BRFAL, Md., RG 105.

72. *Freedmen's Record,* 1, no. 12 (December 1865): 194.

73. *First Annual Report of the Baltimore Association,* 19.

74. Ibid., 22.

75. Ibid., 24.

76. *Freedmen's Record,* 3, no. 4 (April 1867): 62–63.

77. *National Freedman,* 2, no. 5 (May 1866): 148–49.

78. Ninth Census of the United States, 1870, Schedule 1; *First Annual Report of the Baltimore Association,* 7.

79. *American Missionary,* 12, no. 5 (May 1868): 101.

80. *Freedmen's Record,* 3, no. 4 (April 1867): 62–63.

81. *Baltimore American,* July 1, 1867.

82. Ibid., July 30, August 3, 12, 1867.

83. Ibid., August 5, 1867.

84. Ibid., September 5, 1867.

85. *Third Annual Report of the Baltimore Association,* 4.

86. Testimony in Investigation of the Government of Maryland, 1867, Records of the House of Representatives, Committee on the Judiciary, Record Group 233.

87. J. Hall to W. L. VanDerlip, June 18, 1867, Box 11 (Letters Received, Annapolis, July 20, 1866–September 11, 1868), BRFAL, Md., RG 105.

88. J. H. Butler to W. L. VanDerlip, October 31, 1867, ibid.

89. *Freedmen's Record,* 1, no. 12 (December 1865): 194.

90. *First Annual Report of the Baltimore Association,* 20.

91. *Baltimore American,* December 4, 1865.

92. Testimony in Investigation of the Government of Maryland, 1867, Records of the House of Representatives, Committee on the Judiciary, Record Group 233.

93. *Baltimore American,* December 4, 1865.

6

Baltimore

I

BETWEEN 1860 AND 1870, the United States Census reported a 42 percent growth in Baltimore's black population from 27,898 to 39,558.[1] Of the city's 54,936 new arrivals during the decade, 11,660, or 21 percent, were black, an influx that raised the black percentage of the entire city population from 13 to 15. During the same period, the census reported a decline in the black population of all but one of the six rural counties in southern Maryland and in four of eight on the Eastern Shore.[2] Contemporary observers estimated Baltimore's black population to be even higher than what the census figures indicate. In December 1866, a Freedmen's Bureau officer claimed that blacks constituted 20 percent of the city's residents, and in July 1867, the *Baltimore American* placed the total at 44,400.[3]

As to exactly when these people came to Baltimore, the census did not say, but contemporaries clearly placed their arrival after emancipation in November 1864. A week after the Governor's proclamation, the Friends Association in Aid of Freedmen observed that "[t]he faces of the newly-freed population are naturally turned toward the City of Baltimore."[4] In January 1866, the city Trustees of the Poor reported that "[a] large mass of colored persons . . . have been thrown from the several counties of the State upon the City of Baltimore."[5] In June of that year, the *Baltimore Gazette* referred to "the great influx of negroes in the city since the emancipation," and in July 1867, the *Baltimore American* confirmed that "this class of our population has largely increased since the close of the war."[6]

Compelling statistical evidence of the post-emancipation surge in black migration to Baltimore appeared in W. H. Woods's annual *City Directories*. Between 1864 and 1871, the number of black householders listed in the *Woods' City Directory* tripled from 4,000 to 12,000.[7] The 1867 directory recorded an increase of 3,400 black householders in one year alone.[8] Some of Woods's figures seem high compared to those of the United States Census, but his estimates compared favorably to other sources. The 1871 directory calculated Baltimore's population to be approximately 300,000, a number higher than the census's 267,354, but equal to many other assessments at the time. Similarly, its estimate of the number of black people in the city agreed with those of the Freedmen's Bureau and the Baltimore media.[9]

Black migrants came to Baltimore for a variety of reasons. Some saw the city as a source of higher income, many sought to join family members, and others had no choice. At first, whatever their motives, they had reason to be optimistic. "The field of employment is broad," claimed the *Baltimore American* in November 1864, "and laborers are

TABLE 6.1

BLACK POPULATION OF BALTIMORE

	1860			1870	
Ward	*Whites*	*Blacks*	*Ward*	*Whites*	*Blacks*
1st	14,545	487	1st	16,815	448
2nd	8,666	674	2nd	13,458	1,063
3rd	13,478	1,865	3rd	13,188	2,247
4th	6,553	457	4th	8,677	753
5th	4,416	944	5th	9,880	3,499
6th	7,916	1,972	6th	12,880	2,249
7th	10,984	1,421	7th	15,379	836
8th	13,575	812	8th	11,061	1,355
9th	2,864	280	9th	6,820	1,455
10th	3,712	603	10th	8,514	2,545
11th	7,829	2,742	11th	8,641	3,580
12th	7,793	2,078	12th	8,684	1,892
13th	3,691	788	13th	8,562	1,825
14th	5,744	1,318	14th	9,982	1,656
15th	10,101	2,960	15th	10,645	3,209
16th	6,675	1,562	16th	13,454	3,235
17th	12,784	2,171	17th	11,047	357
18th	19,837	1,494	18th	16,236	2,661
19th	11,944	1,113	19th	11,372	1,889
20th	11,413	2,163	20th	12,463	2,804
Total	184,520	27,898		227,794	39,558

Source: U.S. Bureau of the Census, *Population of the United States in 1870,* 163.

TABLE 6.2

POPULATION SHIFT IN TIDEWATER MARYLAND

Southern Maryland County	1860	1870
Anne Arundel	12,196	11,732
Calvert	6,450	5,533
Charles	10,721	9,318
Montgomery	6,973	7,434
Prince George's	13,677	9,780
St. Mary's	8,415	7,726

Eastern Shore County	1860	1870
Caroline	3,525	3,758
Cecil	3,868	4,014
Dorchester	8,807	7,556
Kent	5,920	7,732
Queen Anne's	7,546	6,592
Somerset	9,660	9,477
Talbot	6,689	6,666
Worcester	7,219	8,072
Wicomico		4,050

Source: U.S. Bureau of the Census, *A Compendium of the Ninth Census,* 10–11; U.S. Bureau of the Census, *Population of the United States in 1870,* 163–65.

needed." A year later, the *American* boasted "[t]hey have, or can have constant employment, for there is no lack of demand for the kind of labor which for the most part they perform."[10] Experts claimed that the city had done well during the war and postwar years, extending its commerce, industry, and population. An 1867 description of Baltimore spoke enthusiastically of its

> European lines of steamships keeping up constant communication with all the chief ports of our Union;—with its Railroads opening speedy and direct communication with every portion of the [country], conveying to them all the fabric and material of domestic manufacture and foreign commerce, and receiving in return the agricultural and mineral wealth of the whole [nation].[11]

The relative ease with which at least some migrants found work was typified by the experiences of two freed slaves, Annie Young Henson and Richard Macks. "I came to Baltimore [in 1864] and have never been back since," explained Henson. "I think I was about 17 or 18 years old when I came away. I worked for Mr. Marshall, a flour merchant." Richard Macks arrived in 1868, and "worked in a livery stable for three years, three years with Dr. Owens as a waiter and coachman, [and] 3 years with Mr. Thomas Winans on Baltimore Street as a butler."[12] Baltimore possessed unquestioned appeal, a fact that worried Frederick Douglass. "I believe that $150 in the country is better than $400 in the city. . . . If the colored people of Maryland flock to this city, crowding the alleys and streets, woe betide them, sad indeed will be their fate."[13]

Douglass was mainly concerned with migrants' moral well-being, but his warning of crowded alleys was equally pertinent. For despite the success of some, the arrival of so many rural black people in such a short period of time severely challenged and almost overwhelmed Baltimore's capacity to absorb them. Within a month of emancipation, the Friends Association reported "many calls from women with children . . . who have neither food nor shelter."[14] "We find more suffering than we are able to alleviate," it added in January 1865, "They [are in] want of the most necessary food and clothing, and have crowded into alleys and cellars."[15]

These conditions attracted the attention of many but not always with the Friends' sympathy. "The great influx of negroes in the city since the emancipation has become a nuisance," complained the *Baltimore Gazette* in June 1866. "[S]o great has become the evil that the Marshal of Police has been constrained to cry out against it. . . . They come to the city without the means of support and . . . depend on what they can pick up to satisfy the demands of hunger, and seek shelter at night in the police stations."[16] The *Baltimore Sun* was equally alarmed. "Many freedmen . . . are now loafing about the wharfs acquiring vicious habits, or obtaining the means of a precarious existence only by the few jobs they procure."[17]

Many rural migrants came to Baltimore because they had no choice, and that made matters even worse. "Thousands of women and children (many of the women who are soldiers wives) have been thrown out of homes and are now very destitute," reported the Friends Association in January 1865.[18] "The objects of sympathy," explained the *Baltimore American*, are mostly old women and young children recently released from Slavery and cast out upon the world by their unpitying and inhuman masters, at the most inclement season of the year, utterly unprovided for and help-less. In most cases their natural protectors are in the army, and up to this time, they have been left without assistance.[19]

Nor was Baltimore the only destination for such dislocated people. From the counties of southern Maryland, many sought refuge in nearby Washington. "Yesterday afternoon," related a Washington correspondent on November 19, 1864, "the stage which arrived from Charles County let out an old colored woman of over 60 years at the corner of 11th and G streets (Navy Yard) named Charity Ann Canton. She had no place to go to in this city. . . . She states that she belonged to a Mr. Dement who put her on the stage telling her she would be taken care of."[20]

II

Under these circumstances, Baltimore proved woefully ill-equipped to handle so many people. Without enough immediately available jobs or homes to offer black migrants, and in the absence of municipal services designed to find them, city officials were caught by surprise. At the behest of the police, the city council's first reaction was to petition the state legislature to pass a law compelling rural counties to keep and care for their unemployed freedmen and women.[21] When that failed, the council was forced to cope with new arrivals as best it could. The City Trustees for the Poor distributed limited relief to an ever growing number of blacks but such resources fell far short of what was needed, and from the start, officials had to consign indigent migrants to an already crowded city almshouse.

The problem, explained Mayor John Lee Chapman in January 1865, was self-evident. It reflected plainly "the increase in principally colored persons, who are daily admitted from the several counties of the State."[22] A year later the overseer of the almshouse reported, "The class of inmates received during the year, who have presented themselves for admittance, have been received in a most miserable condition. . . . The large mass of colored persons who have been thrown from the several counties of the State upon the city of Baltimore for support . . . calls loudly for legislation, so that the interests of the city should be properly guarded."[23] The City Trustees of the Poor expressed similar alarm. Try as they might to respond to the needs of "all worthy persons without distinction of nation or color," there were simply too many people to help.[24] "The wants of the poor are pressing, and have been more numerous than at any former period," explained the trustees in February 1866.[25] A year later, things were no better as the trustees complained of being "entirely exhausted, having expended for the month of January for groceries and fuel $7,150.31 for the relief of 2,698 families embracing 8,407 persons of these 1,161 were Americans, 1,063 foreigners, and 474 colored persons."[26]

In the face of limited municipal resources, and in the absence of any help from the state, blacks—not surprisingly—turned to the United States government. Immediately after emancipation, Lew Wallace and the 8th Army Corps tried to set up a "Freedman's Bureau," to help destitute blacks, but despite his plans to commandeer a Baltimore building known as the "Maryland Club" and to assess contributions from known "rebel sympathizers," nothing much came of it. In the end, the army restricted its efforts to investigating rural apprenticeship and to only modest assistance for poor city blacks.[27]

Its successor, the Freedmen's Bureau, did not do much better. In 1866 the Bureau established a district headquarters in Baltimore, but for all its impressive accomplishments in the city and the rest of the state, relief for indigent migrants was not high among its priorities.[28] Officers responded to black workers' complaints of nonpayment of wages and other job-related abuses, but specifically denied them government rations.[29] Indeed, in the face of the obvious difficulties confronting rural arrivals, the Bureau deliberately resisted a charitable approach. Although sympathetic to the plight of black migrants, the Bureau had its problems with charity. "Governments . . . may, to save themselves from the violence of the mob, temporarily nurse multitudes into beggary," warned John Eaton:

> But republics, dependent on the labor, integrity, and intelligence of the individual, cannot for a moment afford to empty their treasuries, or degrade the self-respect of any of their individual members, by any such disbursement of supplies as will encourage beggary, or foster idleness, or other crime. . . . The negro has never been a beggar among us; he should not be made such now, as he drops his chains, and while he accepts his manhood as a ward of the government . . .[30]

Even black migrants' most outspoken supporters had their doubts about too much philanthropy. "[W]e say to our colored people in all kindliness as well as in earnestness," admonished the *Baltimore American*, "[that] they should depend mainly upon their own exertions, and not upon extraneous aid."[31] Despite evidence to the contrary, the *American* seemed convinced that every migrant who was willing to work hard could get a job. "[I]f he is of little account he will meet with proportionally small encouragement; if his services are *indispensable* to his fellow men, he will be universally sought after."[32]

In fact, apart from the city Trustees of the Poor, only the Friends Association in Aid of Freedmen responded directly to the plight of black migrants. Baltimore Quakers were already very much involved in the establishment of black schools in the city, and their efforts on behalf of indigent arrivals constituted the second of what was an ambitious two-part effort to assist the black community. The principal purpose of the Association was "to provide homes and employment for them [migrants] not only in town, but in the country, as fast as they come in, when they cannot get places through their own exertions." In addition, the Friends hoped "to aid these helpless children of toil in entering upon their new life of freedom, to counsel them, to assist in their instruction, and to do everything else that good Samaritans ought always be ready to do for the suffering and troubled."[33]

The Association served essentially as an employment agency, listing jobs in both Baltimore and nearby rural counties and placing people in those positions whenever possible. "Those who want servants are earnestly requested to address [us] . . . at once," explained the Association, "stating what kind of help they want, whether cooks, waiters, house servants, or otherwise, male or female and whether they will take mothers with children, and if so, how many, accompanying their proposals with the price of labor per month."[34] "Agreable to arrangements made with you and Friend James Baynes when you was last in Baltimore respecting the procuring of homes for the surplus collored population," wrote Association agent Andrew Muirhead, "I have to inform you that we have advertised in the city papers and can now dispose of a considerable number of good farm hands and teamsters [?] also females who can cook in country homesteads."[35]

The Association sought also to meet migrants' more immediate needs. "We are greatly in need of pecuniary aid," it explained. "Efforts are being made to increase the funds of the Association and in securing as many needed supplies as possible to those who apply for aid."[36] To accomplish this, "[T]he charitable everywhere are solicited for donations, either in money, clothing or goods for making into apparel."[37] The Association was quick to recognize the extent of the emergency it faced and unlike others, refrained from preaching to its constituency. "[W]hile it is believed that the greater portion of these people are capable of self support," it argued, "it is also true that many are unfitted to assume at once the cares and responsibilities which freedom brings. A large portion are infirm, and a large portion helpless, and for the present all need protecting care and guidance in their new relations."[38]

With the limited resources at its disposal, the Association did the best it could. By January 1865, it had placed 107 domestic servants in the city, received 29 requests for farmhands in adjoining counties, and provided food and clothing for 102 migrants, "mostly women and small children."[39] In its annual report in December, the Association reported that $2,888 had been spent during the year, that employment had been found for 416 migrants, and that 988 people had been provided direct relief, included in which were 1,100 pieces of clothing and 100 pairs of shoes.[40] In all 1,660 people had benefited directly from the Association in one fashion or another.[41] "There is no scheme of practical benevolence that appeals more forcibly to the philanthropist than that of aiding the recently emancipated Bondsmen," concluded the annual report, "[e]mployment must be found for those able to work, and food and clothing for those not able to support themselves."[42]

III

But the efforts of the Friends Association, even when added to those of the city and federal governments, were still insufficient to meet the demands of so many people at once. In the end, these needs either went unmet, as migrants spent their nights on the street or in police station houses, or migrants were provided for by the black community itself. Ultimately, the latter had to assume primary responsibility for the city's indigent population. To the extent that Baltimore eventually absorbed so many black migrants without even greater disruption or dislocation, it depended on the generosity—especially for relief and housing—of its twenty-five thousand free black residents.

For decades, free blacks had constituted a substantial portion of Baltimore's total population and a major part of Baltimore's unskilled and semiskilled labor force. Most black men worked as day laborers, waiters, porters, draymen, and oyster shuckers. Women labored as domestic servants, laundresses, and cooks. Some men held jobs as semiskilled hod carriers and brickmakers, and among the most skilled were ship caulkers. A few served both the white and black community as barbers and caterers, and a small professional and business elite taught school, preached the gospel, and ran businesses within the black community.[43]

The Civil War sustained the black urban economy, especially at the unskilled level, and the prospect of employment at relatively high wages constituted an important part of the post-emancipation attraction of city life. Generally, urban employment paid more than farm work—often three or four times as much—although rent and food were seldom included. From a yearly wage of $300 to $400, a steadily employed black laborer might count on $200 or $250 after room and board, a figure substantially higher than the net pay of a tidewater farmhand.[44]

Although the crush of post-emancipation migration quickly diminished the allure of city life, the vast majority of those who came to Baltimore eventually found their way into its black economy and community. The steady climb in the city's total population, its growing number of black residents, and the increased number of black householders in the city directories between 1864 and 1871 testified to the long-run success of most in finding homes and work. By 1868, the *Woods' City Directory* counted 8,000 employed black heads of households, a 100 percent increase from four years earlier.[45] More specifically, the number of day laborers grew from 883 to 1,880, laundresses from 616 to 1,431, waiters from 350 to 662, porters from 294 to 421, draymen from 288 to 371, and cooks from 176 to 325.[46] By 1870, the ranks of black male day laborers had swelled to 2,644, laundresses to 2,206, waiters to 798, cooks to 565, porters to 474, and draymen to 423.[47]

Many other employed blacks, especially women and children, were not listed in the directories. With their exclusive focus on householders, the latter omitted thousands who worked with and for their families in a number of different occupations—especially housekeeping—or who lived with whites as servants, cooks, chambermaids, nurses, butlers, and the like. Unlike the directories, the United States Census identified these people and indicated a substantial growth in their numbers between 1860 and 1870.[48] This was particularly the case with female domestic servants. The 1860s witnessed a dramatic increase in the number of black women working as domestic servants, laundresses, cooks, and chambermaids.[49]

Clearly, like most of the twenty-five thousand free blacks before them, rural migrants found jobs in Baltimore by swelling the ranks of the city's unskilled labor force. That they managed to do so may have reflected in part a healthy postwar economy, but the nature of their absorption also indicated change and cost to the black community in the process. In the 1864 *Woods' City Directory*, unskilled men and women represented 81.6 percent of Baltimore's black householders. By 1871, that figure had grown to 87.5 percent.[50] Census statistics demonstrated the same development in the entire black community.[51] Specifically, migration contributed to substantially increased numbers of women working as domestic servants and laundresses and men as day laborers, while at the same time, the percentage of semiskilled, skilled, and professional blacks declined.[52]

With respect to housing, a similar situation prevailed. A large number of female servants found homes with whites, but others had to find theirs within or alongside already existing black neighborhoods next to or mixed together with white. Increasingly, blacks crowded into cellars and laneway apartments of already occupied buildings, and although the number of actual black dwellings listed by the United States Census increased between 1860 and 1870, the availability of new housing clearly did not keep pace. From time to time the substandard condition of much of that housing attracted the attention of city authorities.[53] During the cholera outbreak of October 1866, for example, city health officials reported that several dwellings on Elbow Lane "are in a state of indescribable filth, there being as many as eighty persons in one and no adequate means of ventilation or cleanliness."[54]

In addition to absorbing migrants into its work force and neighborhoods—factors over which it exerted little control—Baltimore's black community responded generously to the plight of its indigent people. Like city officials and white managers of the Friends Association in Aid of Freedmen, black leaders were initially hard-pressed to meet the needs of so many at once. In time, however, their institutions assumed responsibility for many who were unable to care for themselves. A *New York Independent* reporter expressed it well, his sarcastic wit notwithstanding. "We were invited 'to see something of what was being done for the freedmen [in Baltimore],' " he wrote in February 1865, "and

TABLE 6.3

OCCUPATIONS OF BLACK HOUSEHOLDERS IN BALTIMORE LISTED
IN WOODS' CITY DIRECTORIES

Occupation	1864	1868	1871
Laborer	883	1,880	2,644
Laundress [and Washerwoman]	690	1,531	2,206
Waiter [and Waitress]	350	666	798
Cook	176	325	565
Porter	294	421	474
Drayman	288	371	423
Shucker [and Oyster Shucker]	61	0	368
Mariner	185	216	347
Brickmaker	212	207	226
Driver	13	54	219
Hod Carrier	64	109	214
Barber	106	158	198
Seamstress	44	122	169
Whitewasher	130	148	130
Coachman	69	107	127
Servant	1	39	115
Stevedore	63	72	110
Sawyer [and Woodsawyer]	93	126	106
Caulker	117	123	98
Carter	101	112	97
Grain Measurer	75	52	88
Hostler	38	62	86
Chambermaid	19	20	75
Dressmaker	14	32	67
Huckster [and Huckstress]	59	54	65
Shoemaker	18	36	63
Nurse	16	16	53
Wagoner	37	66	48
Minister	4	12	44
Carpenter	13	32	34
Grain Runner	35	16	33
Steward	29	35	32
Teacher	14	28	30
Grocery	1	31	29
Oysters	6	10	27
Blacksmith	26	32	25

Occupation	1864	1868	1871
Musician	8	17	24
Cooper	20	32	23
Fireman	34	33	23
Butcher	23	22	22
Engineer	9	14	22
Sailor	18	88	20
Farmer	24	35	19
Hackman	22	28	19
Janitor	0	5	17
Tavern	0	0	17

Source: *Woods' Baltimore City Directory, Ending Year 1864* (Baltimore, 1865), 443–84; *Woods' Baltimore City Directory, 1867–1868* (Baltimore, 1868), 564–626; *Woods's Baltimore City Directory, 1871* (Baltimore, 1871), 667–757. See Note 53.

thereupon were put through such a series of negro meetings, from the committee on starving infants and ragged women to the board of education for promising colored youth, as we venture to say Boston never saw in the palmiest days of the abolition agitation, certainly not in one afternoon and evening."[55]

The *Independent* correspondent certainly knew of which he spoke. Many such black organizations devoted tremendous energy to charitable programs. Bethel African Methodist Episcopal Church, Sharp Street Methodist Episcopal Church, the Lincoln Zouaves (a military regiment), the Colored Ladies Union Association, the State Fair Association (Colored), the First Colored Christian Commission of Baltimore, the St. Francis Orphan Asylum, the Oblate Sisters of Providence, the Shelter for Orphans of Colored Soldiers and Friendless Colored Children, and the Gregory Aged Women's Home, were but several prominent black institutions and organizations that responded energetically to the needs of the poor, homeless, and orphaned in Baltimore.[56]

Such work served as a clarion call to action on the part of the black community. "Frederick Douglass Will Lecture—before the Union State Fair Association [Colored] in Bethel Church, Saratoga Street, on Thursday evening, November 17th, 1864 at 8 o'clock," proclaimed an advertisement in the *Baltimore American*. "The proceeds will go to aid the association in getting up a fair . . . to relieve the wants of the sick

TABLE 6.4

BLACK OCCUPATIONS IN BALTIMORE LISTED
IN THE UNITED STATES CENSUS

Occupation	1860	1870
Servant [Domestic/Hotel]	4,141	5,726
Keeping House	0	4,299
Laborer [Day Laborer]	1,341	3,269
Washerwoman [Laundress]	2,084	2,531
Waiter [Private, Hotel/Rest]	616	1,045
Cook [Hotel]	264	682
Drayman [Drives a Dray]	369	518
Mariner [Seaman, Sailor]	374	513
Porter [in Store]	334	431
Brickmaker [Moul/Mas/App]	518	418
Seamstress [Dressmaker]	155	322
Hod Carrier	35	283
Works in Brickyard	0	212
Carter	155	210
Barber [App]	142	208
Whitewasher	174	188
Wagoner [Wagon Driver]	30	185
Stevedore	60	174
Nurse	40	158
Coachman	71	157
Oysters [Shuck/Works at]	14	150
Woodsawyer [Sawyer]	89	122
Hostler [Ostler/Groom/Stab]	52	117
Huckster	57	108
Ship Caulker [Caulker]	158	99
Chambermaid	45	97
Farm Hands	11	70
Works in Pickling House	0	69
Grain Measurer	60	63
Driver [Carriage Driver]	54	58
Shoemaker	24	55
Carpenter	17	51
Works Out	0	44
School Teacher	17	43
Butcher	24	40
Blacksmith	27	38

Occupation	1860	1870
Steward	23	35
Minister	12	33
Gardener	12	32
Hackman [Hack Driver]	38	30
Works in Lumber Yard	8	29
Musician	19	29
Works in Store	0	25
Cooper [Journeymen]	26	25
Grain Runner	4	23
Fireman on Steamboat	11	22

Source: Eighth Census of the United States, 1860, Schedule 1, Ninth Census of the United States, 1870, Schedule 1.

and wounded soldiers."[57] The response was gratifying. "The State Fair Association return their sincere thanks to the generous public," read another *American* entry in January 1865, "for their liberality in behalf of the Fair for money and articles received, and beg leave to report $1,827.34 received."[58] Similar energy accompanied Bethel A.M.E. Church's "Fair for the Benefit of the Poor," which commenced on Christmas Day, 1865. As the managers explained, "This fair will continue during the week and will close on New Year's night with a grand festival. All kinds of fancy articles will be offered for sale on reasonable terms. Refreshments at moderate prices. Admission 10 cents, children half the price. Come one, come all."[59]

On occasion the entire community gathered to raise funds. In July 1867, for three successive days, several thousand people paid their way onto the grounds of the Gregory Aged Women's Home to watch the maneuvers of several black military regiments and to hear martial music and popular radical speakers. The affair was a huge success, attracting the attention of the general public with banner headlines in the city's several daily newspapers, and raising thousands of dollars.[60] The Gregory Aged Women's Home event typified a close relationship between black community affairs and charitable objectives. Between 1865 and 1870, black military encampments, fraternal lodge parades, political rallies, and religious camp meetings all served as means to raise money for those in need.[61]

The extent of black community self-help in Baltimore attracted widespread attention from white observers who heralded the importance of such efforts in addressing black homelessness and joblessness. "There are over thirty thousand colored people in Baltimore," explained the *American,* on October 9, 1865, "We always take pleasure in recording any evidences of thought or enterprise on their part."[62] A year later, the *American* added:

> We doubt whether, among the same number of our citizens similarly situated . . . and dependent upon employment as common laborers for subsistence, there will be found more activity and successful industry and less absolute pauperism, mendicity and want. . . . We do not believe that the statistics show a material over proportion of crime or disease, and death among them. Certainly their efforts to improve themselves . . . deserves the highest commendation, and must surprise everyone acquainted with the facts.[63]

Others said the same. "I want this fact to be known," announced J. F. W. Ware, a prominent white Republican in December 1867, "as a stimulus to others, and as a proof that the negro does not only understand and appreciate his advantages, but is willing to help his race."[64]

In fact, white supporters exaggerated the capacity of the black community to solve the problems caused by the influx of rural migrants into the city. Throughout the several-year period following emancipation, unemployment—or at best underemployment—remained chronic for many blacks, housing was still inadequate, crowded, and hard to find, the police station houses full of temporary lodgers, and the almshouse too frequently a destination of last resort.[65] Clearly, black Baltimoreans did the best they could under difficult circumstances. Equally clearly, they did so without a lot of help from the white community.

Indeed whites tended in the end to consign responsibility for social problems to those most affected by them—blacks themselves. In October 1865, the *American* called to black Baltimoreans' attention "the necessity of taking care of the fatherless of their race. Many of those who have been thrown upon public charity by the circumstances of the past few years," it pointed out, "need assistance." The *American* continued:

> We wish to see them still further vindicate the confidence reposed in them by their friends by establishing an Orphan Asylum for the colored children. A collection in each of the African churches on a Sunday, to be paid and given out before hand would be a good way of starting an

interest in the subject, and result in accumulating at least sufficient means for a nest egg.[66]

The advice was sound enough as far as it went. In 1865, a group of concerned whites organized an orphanage for the children of black Civil War veterans and acquired a building from the Freedmen's Bureau to be their home.[67] Blacks supported the institution, as the *American* had suggested, through church and other donations.[68] Yet, it was hardly sufficient. On several occasions, the Baltimore City Council refused to assist the orphanage and it remained small as a consequence. As usual, it was left to others to pick up the slack. In November 1866, St. Francis Colored Catholic Church opened an orphan asylum "for the reception of colored children of all denominations."[69] A year later, the Oblate Sisters recounted their experience.

> To rescue from want and misery many young children left helpless by the ravages of war and poverty, we in the year 1866 opened an Orphan Asylum. In this home [black] children are received from infancy to the age of 16. . . . The building and furnishing of the house cost $3,300. We have depended upon the charitable collections of the colored people for the maintenance and clothing of these orphans.[70]

IV

There was too much for blacks to cope with on their own and in the absence of greater support from the city, state, or federal governments, the long-term absorption of so many people imposed additional social costs not only on the black community but on the entire city. These costs were reflected in patterns of crime and arrests and in the reaction to both, especially by city newspapers and the Baltimore police force. Beginning immediately after emancipation, black Baltimoreans fell afoul of the law in unprecedented numbers, a fact that exacerbated tensions both within the black community and between it and neighboring whites.

Between 1864 and 1870, a growing number of blacks were charged with petty theft, assault, and disorderly conduct.[71] The picture that emerged from the records of justice of the peace, the Baltimore Criminal Court, and the city jail was clearly that of a class of people chronically at odds with the police and the justice system. Such was particularly the case with female servants charged by their employers with theft, intoxicated men and women accused of disorderly conduct or assault, and juveniles, particularly boys—whose presence on the city's streets expanded dramatically during these years—arrested for a litany of petty offenses.[72]

Unable to cope with the increased case load, and hard-pressed to find additional jail cells, city officials dismissed many such charges, especially those against minors, and accepted them as an unavoidable consequence of black migration and the shortage of incarceration space.[73] In 1867, in a poignant reflection on the problem, the grand jury of the criminal court commented on the occupants of the city jail. "We have found confined," it said, "quite a number of young negroes of both sexes between the ages of ten and fifteen years:

> Most of them are committed by magistrates upon trivial charges, and after an imprisonment of ten to thirty days are discharged. . . . [O]f this class many are discharged, not from the want of legal evidence of guilt, but from a belief in the minds of the jurors that from their youth and ignorance of right from wrong, they are not morally accountable to the law for their actions. But imprisonment in idleness, and contact with older prisoners hardens them in guilt and gives new lessons in the school for crime.[74]

Such practice, however, alarmed everyone and led to impassioned discussion in the city press. The conservative *Baltimore Gazette* was quick to attribute the relationship between the black migrant and crime to the former's inherent shortcomings. "His habits are generally shiftless and desultory," the *Gazette* explained in November 1865,

> and nothing short of subjecting him to a certain measure of control, through the influence of just laws . . . can prevent him from becoming a burthen and an annoyance to the community in which he resides in consequence of his idle ways and of those habits of petty larceny to which so many of the race seem naturally addicted.[75]

More than a year later, the *Baltimore Sun* offered much the same opinion.

> Here, then, lies the precise cause of the present difficulty—the vast number of idle or unemployed blacks, who have been thrown upon the public by the events of the past two or three years and the application to them of a penal code made for a different order of society. The crime of larceny is one, under the unfortunate circumstances which surround them, into which that class of persons is most prone to fall, and at the same time

their ignorance of the proper relations of things is such that there will be no diminution of crime effected by the severity of the punishment.[76]

The radical *Baltimore American* shared the *Gazette*'s and *Sun*'s concern about black people's characteristics but believed they were habits imposed by slavery. "Complaints of theft and worthlessness are frequently urged against our free colored population," it argued in November 1864. "This is the inevitable consequence of social degradation and this degradation is an offspring or reflex of Slavery."[77]

Indeed, most radicals shared conservative fears of black behavioral tendencies but argued that education, opportunity, and just treatment under the law would reform recently freed slaves into productive citizens. "If . . . the colored people are left in hopeless ignorance and without education," argued Hugh Lennox Bond, "[they will] grow more vicious till their presence is intolerable and requires ten times the pecuniary expense in police regulations that their education would require."[78] It was, explained John Ware of the Baltimore Association for the Moral and Educational Improvement of the Colored People:

incumbent upon us to educate them beyond the temptations of vagabondism, vice, and criminality to which they are liable, and by which they are beset so long, as they are in a condition of mental inferiority and moral darkness. . . . The slave a dangerous element as a slave before is a more dangerous element as a free man now. . . . He is without the wonted restraint. He is ignorant, he may become vagabond, and then vicious, and then—why, danger—new laws, new jails, new police, the cumbersome, costly, superficial, tardy, uncertain cure. . . . Neglect this *now*, this golden opportunity, . . . and the curse will come. The horde of ignorant, unrestrained men, women, and children will be upon you. —Your city will be the charnel house of vagabondism and vice and crime. . . . Already they come. . . . They must be met by prisons and punishments, or by *education*.[79]

On at least one subject, the proliferation of juvenile arrests and what to do about it, almost everyone agreed. In May 1868, the grand jury of the Baltimore Criminal Court reported:

We have been compelled time after time to forego presenting especially juvenile colored thieves for punishment because neither state authority nor private beneficence has yet provided any house of correction for this class—they are multiplying rapidly and becoming criminals of a larger growth. We have to look helplessly on while the negro boys attain their growth in vice and stature finally to be sent to the state Penitentiary to herd there with hundreds in a single room unemployed and with every opportunity to become worse and worse merely because no adequate provision has been made to punish or correct them at an earlier age.[80]

Baltimore lacked an equivalent for black youths to the House of Refuge, a correctional institution for white minors. Such a facility for "offending colored youth," argued the *Baltimore Sun*, would be of "incalculable value to the future peace and morals of this community."[81] The *American* agreed. "Whilst the establishment of a House of Refuge for the reformation of white offenders has had the tendency to diminish crime among that portion of the population," it argued, "the absence of such an institution for the colored youth of the State has had the contrary effect."[82]

The degree and intensity of public attention to migration, poverty, and crime and whites' explanation of the relationship of each to the other made it difficult for blacks to defend themselves. Nor was it made any easier when the city's main law enforcement agency—the police— operated on the basis of such assumptions. From the start, the police were quick to call attention to the presence of rural migrants, to seek their removal to the counties from whence they came, and—when that failed—to keep a close eye on their behavior.[83] Such vigilance led to constant police scrutiny of the black community and the instant deployment of armed squads whenever blacks participated in public occasions either on their own or with whites.[84]

In short, the actions of the police served as a constant reminder of white Baltimoreans' perception of not only blacks' place in the community, but also of the connection between it and civil disorder. "The negro population of Baltimore have lately become . . . 'irrepressible,'" complained the *Baltimore Gazette* in November 1865, "and collisions between them and the whites are quite frequent."[85] Two months earlier, the *Gazette* had gone so far as to celebrate the police roundup of "twenty-seven darkies, who were standing on the pavement in front of the Orchard St. African Church, and . . . [who] were lodged in the Station house. Justice Dryden imposed a fine of one dollar and costs upon each of them for obstructing the footway." Blocking the streets outside their churches was, the *Gazette* explained, "a habit indulged in by negroes," something which "the police intend to abate."[86]

The conservative *Gazette* was quick to notice such things and provided a virtual running commentary on blacks and their run-ins with the police.[87] Although its tabloid approach to black-police relations, and its approval of prompt police action articulated only a portion of the white community's response, the *Gazette*'s obvious concern resonated with many, including those with quite opposite opinions. Blacks and white radicals were equally disturbed at the occurrence of such confrontations but blamed the police for much of the tension behind them. In the aftermath of the fatal police shooting of Eliza Taylor, a black woman, in September 1867, the *Baltimore American* responded critically. "A colored woman was killed," it said, "under circumstances which show the spirit of hate and oppression cherished toward that portion of the population by many of the police."[88] Upon the acquittal of the police officer on charges of murder, a convention of black leaders in Baltimore said much the same thing. As reported by the *American*:

> The President [George A. Hackett] stated the object of the meeting, quoting the Declaration of Independence in proof of the fact that "all men were created free and equal." He referred to the fact that the colored people have no friends in Baltimore in the Governor or the police, and cited the action of the Grand Jury in discharging the Policeman Frey, charged with the murder of the colored woman, Eliza Taylor, as a specimen of the justice which is meted out to colored people in this city.[89]

V

Unskilled workers and their families were not the only ones to suffer from the problems associated with post-emancipation migration into the city. Hitherto, both the black professional and business elite and semiskilled and skilled workers had enjoyed a protected status of sorts assured by the need for their services and a recognition of their "place" in the static labor market of Maryland's strictly controlled slave and free black economy.[90] Such protection disappeared after emancipation. In the volatile atmosphere of the city's wartime and postwar economy and race relations, blacks could no longer be sure of such "place," and confronted a new level of competition with whites.

Black workers in a number of occupations found themselves under particular pressure from whites after emancipation. Historically, whenever white Baltimoreans had feared black competition, they tried to restrict it. This had been the case especially with black stevedores and ship caulkers who had waged bitter struggles with white workers in Baltimore's dockyards on a number of occasions before the Civil War.[91] Moreover, emancipation did nothing to diminish whites' antagonism to blacks in such occupations. Indeed it contributed to its intensification as the arrival of so many rural migrants raised the specter of even greater competition.

As early as November 14, 1864, representatives of several black labor organizations predicted trouble. In an open letter to the *Baltimore American*, they expressed:

> an indefinable apprehension of an antagonism on the part of white working men. [We believe] . . . it likely to lead not only to the repression of [our] efforts towards an honest maintenance, but to render our social position so uncomfortable as to result ultimately in driving us beyond the boundaries of our state.[92]

A case in point were the city's black oyster shuckers. On two occasions, the first in December 1864, and the second a year later, what the *Baltimore American* described as "an association of oyster shuckers, consisting entirely of colored men," struck several city restaurants for higher wages. In both instances they attracted widespread publicity and in fact reclaimed their jobs despite the efforts of proprietors to hire replacements, but in neither case did they achieve their goals.[93] Black brickmakers encountered similar difficulties. When several yard owners threatened to reduce wages, they went on strike and in the end were compelled to start their own company, the First Colored Brickyard Association, selling shares to the black community at five dollars each.[94]

All too often, violence accompanied such competition. When the black oyster shuckers returned to reclaim their work, a riot ensued.[95] In November 1865, whites attacked black stevedores at work on the South Street Wharf, and badly injured several.[96] In February 1866, white workers at the Union Dock prevented blacks from unloading ships and police officers had to intervene.[97] A month later, at Locust Point, black stevedores were again forced off the job, and in July 1867, black brickmakers at Ely and Company Brickyard were fired upon by whites intent on driving them off the grounds.[98]

Blacks protested such violence as best they could. An eyewitness to the November 1865 attack on the South Street Wharf stevedores addressed an impassioned plea to the *Baltimore American* asking, "Is there no protection for the inoffensive colored men when they are pursuing the most humble walks of life [and seeking] a living for themselves and families?"[99] The platform of the State Colored Convention in December 1865 demanded that black Baltimoreans receive the "protection of the law" when pursuing their occupations.[100] Neither protest accomplished much. Within months of emancipation, white antagonism toward black workers in certain trades had become an established part of the Baltimore economy.

The most serious dispute between white and black labor involved ship caulkers and other dockyard workers in the autumn and winter of 1865–66. On September 26, at the instigation of white caulkers at the Federal Hill Yards, white carpenters, joiners, and painters in East Baltimore struck to force the firm of John J. Abrahams and Son to fire its seventy-five black caulkers. The white workers timed their demand to coincide with the company's last-minute efforts to complete repairs to the *Worcester* and *Somerset*, the twin flagships of the new Liverpool Steamship Line.[101]

Initial response to the strike was hostile. On September 28, the *Baltimore American* declared the question to be "whether the employers have a right to engage such persons . . . as they may think proper without respect to color, or whether they shall discharge . . . [black workers] at the bidding of others."[102] The usually Negrophobic *Baltimore Gazette* was equally firm. "It seems to us," it said, "that this effort to drive out the negro caulkers is wholly unjustified and indefensible. It is very hard that they should be compelled to abandon their work in deference to the wishes of white men who have chosen to follow the same calling."[103]

Nor did the black caulkers remain silent. Determined to retain their positions in the East Baltimore yards, and to protect their right to a fair share of the labor market, they remained on the job at Abrahams, working alone under police protection. Then, on October 2, the Colored Caulkers' Association assumed the offensive in a public attempt to counter the strikers' action. In an appeal that appeared that day in every Baltimore newspaper, blacks made it clear they would speak out in defense of their jobs. "From the earliest period of shipbuilding in Baltimore," they said,

> it has been our privilege to successfully conduct that branch of mechanics known the world over as "caulking." Our qualifications have given us an

enviable reputation; our workmanship challenges competition with the world. . . . And now, whilst quietly and diligently trying to make an honest living . . . an unjust cry is raised: Away with Negro caulkers! Extermination! Annihilation! —and for what? Because God chose to make our skins dark. . . . Why should white organizations . . . suspend work, paralyse business [and] arrest the progress of commerce because a few colored men in this little corner of creation have a little business to themselves. . . . We ask to be "left alone." Let us work for those who will employ us. . . . [Let] us make an honest livelihood for the support of our families.[104]

The East Baltimore shipyard owners maintained their lockout until mid-October but they were losing money daily and the strikers were as determined as ever. To make matters worse, some of the latter had found new jobs in the South Baltimore shipyards, and a few had established an independent operation in Canton with a number of lucrative contracts.[105] Finally, on October 25, the owners yielded to the strikers' demands, abandoning their previous position and agreeing to phase out all black caulkers by the spring of 1866. Henceforth they were to be hired only if there were no whites available.[106]

A week later, black caulkers from all the East Baltimore yards walked off the job, and on November 7, met with black workers from every trade in the city. Together they expressed their disgust with Baltimore's white laborers. Laying the entire blame for the shipyard dispute at their feet, they declared:

> There do exist in the city of Baltimore certain organizations having for their object the extermination of colored labor. . . . We believe said organization[s] to be repugnant to the fundamental principles of a democratical government and a flagrant outrage upon the common rights guaranteed . . . to all American citizens. . . . Said organizations are based on prejudice on account of color and the desire to monopolize and control the labor market. . . . We believe that the right to labor is sanctioned by all laws human and divine.[107]

It was a bitter defeat that angered black Baltimoreans and soured race relations in the city for years to come. The settlement, explained the *Baltimore American*, gave white workers "all or nearly all that they contended for."[108] Beyond the promise of some winter employment, black caulkers received nothing. As the *American* added later, "The days of Negro caulking are virtually over."[109] But the damage was more widespread than that. According to one estimate, the widening strike had cost over 1,000 black workers their jobs, only 200–300 of whom were actually caulkers.[110] After its reporter interviewed several black leaders, the *New York Tribune* explained that "extermination of [all] colored mechanics was openly declared to be the aim of their white rivals. . . . Very soon the strike threatened to become general . . . [and] the violence threatened to be extended even to hotel workers of the proscribed race."[111]

Under the circumstances, blacks had little choice but to act independently. Certain they could compete in the marketplace, they purchased their own marine railway and drydock company in February 1866. John H. Smith and Company, as this venture was first called, was nothing short of a triumph for the entire black community. Under the leadership of Isaac Myers, himself a ship caulker, the company raised the first installment of the $40,000 purchase price between November 1865 and February 1866. As the *Tribune* described it:

> [T]he leading colored caulkers, carpenters, and mechanics, seeing what the crusade meant, determined on a vigorous . . . effort. Their conclusion was reached in the organization of the Maryland Joint Mutual Stock Railway Company, whose capital was to consist of $10,000 . . . [in] shares at $50 each. About 2,000 shares were taken within a few days, and about $10,000 subscribed, 100 shares the largest amount being taken by any one person. Most of the shares were taken in ones, twos, and threes, by mechanics, caulkers, laborers, even the barbers and washerwomen being represented.[112]

The new company was in full operation by mid-February 1866, employing sixty-two workers. At first, the owners provided their men with four days of work a week at $3.00 a day.[113] Over time, the company attracted more contracts, and by January 1867, had handled $60,000 worth of business with a profit of $15,000.[114] Profits climbed during 1867–68 and more men were employed. In 1868, the company was incorporated under a new name, the Chesapeake Marine Railway and Drydock Company, and by 1870, profits had grown sufficiently to employ three hundred men and to permit final payments for land and equipment.[115]

VI

But black Baltimoreans paid dearly for such an accomplishment. Although the Chesapeake Marine Railway and Drydock Company represented a triumph of community initiative and determination, it served also as a reminder of blacks' failure to open the greater Baltimore economy to their participation on an equal basis with whites. By 1870, the city's skilled trades employed few blacks. Most—especially rural migrants—remained unskilled, and their life, like that of their rural counterparts, was essentially a struggle to maintain subsistence. Most urban blacks found work but remained assigned to the bottom of the city's economic ladder. All of this transpired within what was, by all accounts, a growing urban economy. According to observers, Baltimore did well during the war and postwar years, expanding its commerce, its industry, and its population. By 1870, Baltimore had completed its transformation from cotton entrepot to eastern terminus of the Baltimore and Ohio Railroad and the influence of Northern industrialism was beginning to appear.[116]

To the extent that Baltimore's economy had room for several thousand additional unskilled and semiskilled jobs, rural black migrants shared in such growth. But they did not enjoy what the *Baltimore American* identified as the progress "commensurate with the demands of our rapidly increasing business."[117] If anything, blacks' menial role as Frederick Douglass's "hewers of wood and drawers of water" was more starkly defined in 1870 than it had been six years earlier.[118] Far from opening opportunities to blacks at all levels, the post-emancipation years witnessed a flattening of their participatory profile in the greater Baltimore economy.

Such conditions provided the essential backdrop for interracial violence. Competition for jobs often led directly to physical confrontation, but more importantly, the broad demographic and economic changes that shaped post-emancipation Baltimore, and the attitudes they engendered among whites, created a gulf of misunderstanding and hence tension between blacks and whites. Insofar as most of the latter attributed blacks' economic plight to characteristics inherent among freed people it was perhaps inevitable that white Baltimoreans should respond awkwardly and inappropriately to such tension. Too often they saw it in terms of blacks' "demoralized" state and attributed poverty and crime to the character flaws of an idle and degenerated people. As such, the actions of urban blacks threatened the peace and good order of the community and called for appropriate legislation and vigilant police protection.

Clearly, the level of racial antagonism in post-emancipation Baltimore engendered a set of attitudes or assumptions that served to widen the distance between the black and white communities. The appearance of so many rural ex-slaves in their midst, and the confrontations that accompanied them frightened white Baltimoreans into thinking that the peace and stability of their city stood imperiled by a new class of residents that respected neither the value of labor nor the necessity for law and order. Steeped in mid-nineteenth-century beliefs about hard work and upward mobility, whites were shocked by the unemployment and poverty found within the black community and were quick to ascribe such conditions to the moral shortcomings of its residents.

Such thinking hindered white Baltimoreans' capacity to assess the problems of urban race relations objectively or realistically. Long accustomed to the presence of a stable free black population within the larger context of slavery, they were ill-equipped to recognize the implications of emancipation for both the city's traditional black community and rural blacks who were suddenly free to move in. What had developed over time into a carefully crafted and defined relationship between free blacks and whites suddenly became disrupted in both theory and fact. Emancipation thus removed the restraints of slavery which had not only controlled the movement of the rural black population, but also, in the minds of whites, served to define the relationship between free blacks and urban society.

NOTES

1. U.S. Bureau of the Census, *Population of the United States in 1870*, 163.

2. U.S. Bureau of the Census, *A Compendium of the Ninth Census, June 1, 1870*, 10–11; U.S. Bureau of the Census, *Population of the United States in 1870*; 163–65.

3. Report by W. R. DeWitt, December 20, 1866, Box 1 (LRAC, April 1, 1866–August 17, 1868), BRFAL, Md., RG 105; *Baltimore American*, July 31, 1867.

4. *Baltimore American*, November 10, 1864.

5. Report of the Trustees of the Poor, January 1866. Contained in *Ordinances of the Mayor and City Council of Baltimore, Passed at the Session of 1866*,

To Which is Annexed the Mayor's Communication, Reports of City Officers, and a List of the Members of the City Council, and Officers of the Corporation (Baltimore, 1866), 329.

6. *Baltimore Gazette,* June 2, 1866; *Baltimore American,* July 31, 1867.

7. *Woods' Baltimore City Directory, Ending Year 1864* (Baltimore, 1865), 443–84; *Woods' Baltimore City Directory, 1871* (Baltimore, 1871), 667–757.

8. *Baltimore American,* July 31, 1867; *Baltimore Sun,* August 1, 1867.

9. *Woods' Baltimore City Directory, 1871,* Preface; *Baltimore Sun,* June 18, 1866, July 25, 1867; *Baltimore American,* July 31, 1867, January 15, 1868; *New York Tribune,* September 1, 1870.

10. *Baltimore American,* November 7, 1864, October 9, 1865.

11. James Higgins, "A Succinct Exposition of the Industrial Resources and Agricultural Advantages of the State of Maryland" (Annapolis, 1867), 90–91, which appears as Document DD in *Journal of the Proceedings of the House of Delegates, January Session, 1867.* For a discussion of the state of the Baltimore economy in the 1870s, see Fields, *Slavery and Freedom,* 169, 200–202.

12. George P. Rawick, ed., *The American Slave: A Composite Autobiography,* Vol. 16, "Kansas, Kentucky, Maryland, Ohio, Virginia, and Tennessee Narratives" (Westport, Conn., 1972), Vol. 8, "Maryland Narratives," 26, 51.

13. *Baltimore American,* November 23, December 5, 1864.

14. *Communication from Major General Lew Wallace,* 66.

15. Ibid., 80; *Baltimore American,* February 7, 1865.

16. *Baltimore Gazette,* June 2, 1866.

17. *Baltimore Sun,* August 9, 1865.

18. *Communication from Major General Lew Wallace,* 80.

19. *Baltimore American,* February 7, 1865.

20. Ibid., November 19, 1864.

21. Message of John Lee Chapman, Mayor, to the Members of the First and Second Branches of the City Council, January 3, 1865, contained in *Ordinances of the Mayor and City Council of Baltimore, Passed at the Sessions of 1864 and 1865, to Which Is Annexed the Mayor's Communication, Reports of City Officers, and a List of the Members of the City Council, and Officers of the Corporation* (Baltimore, 1865), 11; *Journal of Proceedings of the First Branch of the City Council of Baltimore At the Sessions of 1864 and 1865* (Baltimore, 1865), 57; *Baltimore American,* January 3, 1865; *Baltimore Gazette,* January 3, 1865.

22. Message of John Lee Chapman, Mayor, January 3, 1865, 11.

The following table is taken from the Report of the Trustees of the Poor, attached to the mayor's message.

Table F

SHOWING THE MONTHLY AVERAGE OF PERSONS IN THE ALMSHOUSE FROM
JANUARY 1, 1864, TO DECEMBER 31, 1864, INCLUSIVE

	White				Colored			
Date	M	W	C	TotalW	M	W	C	TotalC
Jan	214	247	111	572	40	59	13	112
Feb	208	254	109	571	35	60	20	115
Mar	181	240	103	524	29	63	15	107
Apr	159	234	101	494	34	76	20	130
May	160	242	106	508	37	72	20	129
Jun	169	242	102	513	37	70	18	125
Jul	175	236	108	519	39	71	18	128
Aug	199	223	110	532	34	83	20	137
Sep	206	225	112	543	32	78	19	129
Oct	200	233	118	551	37	71	22	130
Nov	215	252	120	587	41	80	23	144
Dec	240	281	126	647	46	91	27	164

23. Report of the Trustees of the Poor to the Mayor and City Council of Baltimore, as found in *The Ordinances of the Mayor and City Council of Baltimore, 1866*. The following table is taken from the Report.

Table F

SHOWING THE MONTHLY AVERAGE OF PERSONS IN THE ALMSHOUSE FROM
JANUARY 1, 1865, TO DECEMBER 31, 1865, INCLUSIVE

	White				Colored			
Date	M	W	C	TotalW	M	W	C	TotalC
Jan	249	277	134	660	54	95	31	180
Feb	237	271	136	644	56	100	32	188
Mar	223	262	136	621	57	91	31	179
Apr	210	267	131	608	57	89	26	172
May	211	272	128	611	51	86	32	169
Jun	221	270	132	623	49	77	27	153
Jul	223	267	134	624	46	68	25	139
Aug	215	264	135	614	38	58	26	122
Sep	225	254	128	607	41	58	30	129
Oct	200	260	129	589	46	51	26	123
Nov	217	254	129	600	47	58	26	131
Dec	225	259	119	603	43	66	27	136

24. Petition to Baltimore City Council, February 20, 1866, City Council, Petitions and Memorials, RG 16, S1, WPA 1866, Vol. 1, Book 6, Document No. 1045, Baltimore City Archives, Baltimore, Md.

25. Ibid.

26. Petition to the Baltimore City Council, February 18, 1867, City Council, Petitions and Memorials, RG 16, S1, WPA 1867, Vol. 1, Book 6, Document No. 879, Baltimore City Archives.

27. *Communication from Major General Lew Wallace*, 4–5; *Baltimore Sun*, November 10, 1864; *Baltimore American*, November 10, 1864.

28. *The Statutes at Large of the United States of America*, Vol. 14: December 1865 to March 1867 (Boston, 1868), 174; E. M. Gregory to O. O. Howard, November 3, 1866, Volume 3 (Register of Letters Sent, Assistant Commissioner, April 1, 1866 to August 17, 1868), BRFAL, Md., RG 105.

29. Circular No. 2, February 20, 1866, Volumes 26 & 27 (Special Orders and Circulars), BRFAL, D.C., RG 105; *Baltimore American*, February 20, April 2, 1866; *Baltimore Sun*, April 2, 1866.

30. United States Documents and Reports, *Senate Executive Documents for the First Session of the Thirty-Ninth Congress of the United States of America, 1865–1866*, Vol. 2 (Washington, 1866), Serial No. 1238, Senate Executive Document No. 27, "Message from the President of the United States, Communicating in Compliance with a Resolution of the Senate of February last, A Communication from the Secretary of War, together with Reports of the Assistant Commissioners of the Freedmen's Bureau made since December 1, 1865," 153–54.

31. *Baltimore American*, November 11, 1864.

32. Ibid., emphasis in original.

33. Ibid., November 10, 1864.

34. Ibid.

35. A. Muirhead to C. H. Howard, February 12, 1866, Box 1 (LRAC, September 1865–October 27, 1866), BRFAL, D.C., RG 105.

36. *Baltimore American*, February 7, 1865.

37. Ibid., November 10, 1864.

38. Ibid., November 24, 1864.

39. Ibid., February 7, 1865.

40. Ibid., December 19, 1865; *Baltimore Sun*, December 20, 1865.

41. *Baltimore American*, December 28, 1865.

42. Ibid.

43. Wright, *The Free Negro in Maryland*, 149–74; Berlin, *Slaves Without Masters*, 217–50; Richard Paul Fuke, "Black Marylanders, 1864–1868" (Ph.D. diss., University of Chicago, 1973), chapter 6.

44. Fuke, "Black Marylanders," chapter 6.

45. *Woods' Baltimore City Directory, 1864*, 443–84; *Woods' Baltimore City Directory, 1867–1868*, 564–626.

46. *Woods' Baltimore City Directory, 1867–1868*, 564–626.

47. *Woods' Baltimore City Directory, 1864*, 443–84; *Woods' Baltimore City Directory*, 564–626; *Woods's Baltimore City Directory, 1871*, 667–757.

48. Eighth Census of the United States, 1860, Schedule 1; Ninth Census of the United States, 1870, Schedule 1.

49. Ibid.

50. *Woods' Baltimore City Directory, 1864*, 443–84; *Woods's Baltimore City Directory, 1871*, 667–757.

51. Eighth Census of the United States, 1860, Schedule 1; Ninth Census of the United States, 1870, Schedule 1.

52. Ibid.

53. Ibid.

54. *Baltimore Sun*, October 15, 1866.

55. As quoted in *Baltimore American*, February 17, 1865.

56. *Baltimore American*, November 16, 18, 26, 1864, January 28, August 24, December 14, 1865, November 20, 1866, February 16, July 21, 1867; *Baltimore Sun*, December 22, 1865; *Christian Advocate*, March 27, 1867; Oblate Sisters to W. H. Day, October 22, 1867, Box 2 (LRAC, April 1, 1866– August 17, 1868) BRFAL, Md., RG 105.

57. *Baltimore American*, November 16, 1864.

58. Ibid., January 7, 1865.

59. *Baltimore Sun*, December 22, 1865.

60. *Baltimore American*, July 9, September 3, 4, 5, 6, 1867.

61. Ibid., October 7, December 14, 15, 1865, May 10, September 1, 1866, May 15, 29, July 30, September 2, 3, 1867; *Baltimore Sun*, October 7, 1865; *Baltimore Gazette*, October 7, 1865.

62. *Baltimore American*, October 18, 1865.

63. Ibid., November 19, 1866.

64. Ibid., December 27, 1867.

65. Reports of the Trustees of the Poor, January 1, 1865–1872, and Reports of the Police Commissioner, January 1, 1865–1872, as found in *The Ordinances of the City Council of Baltimore* (Baltimore, 1865–1872).

TABLE F

SHOWING THE MONTHLY AVERAGE OF PERSONS IN THE ALMSHOUSE FROM JANUARY 1, 1866, TO DECEMBER 31, 1866, INCLUSIVE

	White				Colored			
Date	M	W	C	*TotalW*	M	W	C	*TotalC*
Jan	202	230	122	554	52	74	29	155
Feb	190	207	125	522	58	80	36	174

Mar	183	209	127	519	49	70	37	156
Apr	182	198	131	511	51	79	36	166
May	138	136	88	362	40	46	30	116
Jun	124	129	60	313	30	40	29	99
Jul	132	137	61	330	40	43	32	115
Aug	129	144	68	341	47	51	39	137
Sep	141	146	69	356	48	53	41	142
Oct	142	148	91	381	71	75	63	209
Nov	165	150	95	410	75	81	67	223
Dec	216	240	96	552	58	55	42	155

STATEMENT F

The following figures will show the number of lodgers and those discharged without trial in the several station houses during the year 1866.

White Males 11,258
White Females 1,575
_____
12,833

Colored Males 2,187
Colored Females 383
_____
2,570

TABLE F

SHOWING THE MONTHLY AVERAGE OF PERSONS IN THE ALMSHOUSE FROM JANUARY 1, 1867, TO DECEMBER 31, 1867, INCLUSIVE

Date	*White*				*Colored*			
	M	W	C	TotalW	M	W	C	TotalC
Jan	316	245	36	597	69	64	17	150
Feb	315	240	33	588	82	70	22	174
Mar	288	256	34	578	80	62	22	164
Apr	239	257	35	531	55	67	16	138
May	237	251	31	519	54	56	13	123
Jun	231	250	37	518	47	62	16	125
Jul	224	237	40	501	45	68	10	132
Aug	246	244	36	526	50	69	17	136
Sep	240	241	27	508	41	71	14	126
Oct	260	242	34	536	42	70	15	127
Nov	279	251	31	561	45	75	12	142
Dec	322	256	38	616	63	83	23	169

STATEMENT D

The following figures will show the number of lodgers and those discharged without trial in the several Station Houses during the present year [1867]:

White—Males	7,203
Females	1,390
	8,593
Colored—Males	1,258
Females	389
	1,647

TABLE F

SHOWING THE MONTHLY AVERAGE OF PERSONS IN THE ALMSHOUSE FROM JANUARY 1, 1868, TO DECEMBER 31, 1868, INCLUSIVE

	White				Colored			
Date	M	W	C	TotalW	M	W	C	TotalC
Jan	356	273	33	662	71	86	19	176
Feb	377	272	39	688	80	83	25	188
Mar	293	261	41	595	65	82	25	172
Apr	271	261	37	569	57	74	28	159
May	260	250	32	542	61	76	26	163
Jun	239	227	30	496	47	77	28	152
Jul	251	218	28	497	48	72	19	139
Aug	244	226	29	499	52	77	25	154
Sep	243	243	26	512	47	81	26	154
Oct	263	239	33	535	61	71	25	157
Nov	286	249	25	560	64	88	29	181
Dec	322	261	26	609	78	97	36	211

TABLE F

SHOWING THE MONTHLY AVERAGE OF PERSONS IN THE ALMSHOUSE FROM JANUARY 1, 1869, TO DECEMBER 31, 1869, INCLUSIVE

	White				Colored			
Date	M	W	C	TotalW	M	W	C	TotalC
Jan	340	270	32	642	80	94	34	208
Feb	328	257	34	619	80	99	32	211
Mar	277	246	33	556	81	90	32	203

Apr	244	236	23	503	69	85	23	177
May	216	233	23	472	68	67	17	153
Jun	231	243	21	495	65	65	29	159
Jul	228	245	16	489	61	55	13	129
Aug	220	231	17	468	61	59	13	133
Sep	233	243	22	498	61	62	13	136
Oct	262	249	22	533	69	66	11	146
Nov	288	252	21	561	80	72	16	168
Dec	315	260	32	607	88	80	20	188

TABLE F

SHOWING THE MONTHLY AVERAGE OF PERSONS IN THE ALMSHOUSE FROM
JANUARY 1, 1870, TO DECEMBER 31, 1870, INCLUSIVE

| | White | | | | Colored | | | |
Date	M	W	C	TotalW	M	W	C	TotalC
Jan	310	261	25	596	69	89	22	180
Feb	312	253	26	591	58	83	21	162
Mar	241	258	20	519	46	93	24	163
Apr	220	269	23	512	41	89	23	153
May	197	257	21	475	38	79	18	135
Jun	187	252	27	466	42	76	20	138
Jul	182	246	25	453	40	80	14	134
Aug	204	253	27	484	45	72	10	127
Sep	205	265	34	504	41	82	8	131
Oct	210	242	22	474	40	90	11	141
Nov	210	240	21	561	39	85	14	138
Dec	233	237	24	494	56	81	18	155

STATEMENT F

The following Figures show the Number of Persons Accommodated with
Lodgings in the several Station Houses during the Year 1870.

Month	WM	WF	WT	CM	CF	CT
Jan	1,592	269	1,861	170	17	187
Feb	1,299	184	1,483	193	29	222
Mar	1,142	169	1,211	179	34	213
Apr	1,025	287	1,312	85	24	109
May	705	198	903	114	16	130
Jun	441	146	587	118	16	134

Jul	317	124	441	54	21	75
Aug	326	110	436	58	23	81
Sep	361	122	483	63	22	85
Oct	536	243	779	67	16	83
Nov	951	233	1,184	80	31	111
Dec	1,397	242	1,638	172	34	206
	10,092	2,327	12,419	1,353	283	1,636

66. *Baltimore American,* October 18, 1865.

67. Petitions to Baltimore City Council, February 7, 1866, March 20, 1867, City Council, Petitions and Memorials, RG 16, S1, WPA 1866, Vol. 1, Book 6, Document No. 1022 and WPA 1867, Vol. 1, Book 6, Documents, Nos. 470 and 1513, Baltimore City Archives; *Baltimore Gazette,* February 9, 1866; *Baltimore American,* April 13, 30, 1866, February 16, March 21, 1867; *Baltimore Sun,* October 2, 1866, April 23, 1867; J. S. Norris to Freedmen's Bureau, April 20, 1867, Box 1 (LRAC, April 1, 1866–August 17, 1868), BRFAL, Md., RG 105; *Journal of Proceedings of the First Branch City Council of Baltimore at the Sessions of 1866 and 1867* (Baltimore, 1867), 687.

68. *Baltimore American,* October 18, 1865, February 16, December 27, 1867.

69. Ibid., November 20, 1866.

70. Oblate Sisters to W. H. Day, October 22, 1867, Box 2 (LRAC, April 1, 1866–August 17, 1868), BRFAL, Md., RG 105.

71. Reports of the Visitors to the Baltimore City Jail, January 1, 1865–1871, as found in *The Ordinances of the Mayor and City Council of Baltimore [1865–1871]* (Baltimore, 1865–1872).

72. Ibid.

73. Report of the Police Commissioners, January 1867, as found in *Ordinances of the Mayor and City Council of Baltimore [1867]*; Baltimore City, Criminal Court, Minutes, September 1867, Transer 483, 1857–1871, Volume 2, Stack Location: 3-30-11-9, Baltimore City Archives.

74. "Memorial of the Grand Jury of Baltimore City Praying that a Place of Punishment May be Provided for Minor Colored Children" (Annapolis, 1867), which appears as Document X in *Journal of Proceedings of the House of Delegates, January Session, 1867* (Annapolis, 1867); *Baltimore American,* February 16, 1867; *Baltimore Sun,* February 18, 1867.

75. *Baltimore Gazette,* November 3, 1865.

76. *Baltimore Sun,* February 18, 1867.

77. *Baltimore American,* November 14, 1864.

78. *Easton Gazette,* January 7, 1865.

79. *Baltimore American,* March 15, 1865.

80. Baltimore City, Criminal Court, Minutes, May Term 1868, p. 445, Transer 483, 1857–1871, Volume 2, Stack Location: 3-30-11-9, Baltimore City Archives.

81. *Baltimore Sun*, March 13, 1867.

82. *Baltimore American*, January 8, 1868.

83. *Journal of Proceedings of the First Branch City Council of Baltimore At the Session of 1866* (Baltimore, 1866), 646; *Baltimore Gazette*, June 2, 1866.

84. See chapter 9 for a broader discussion of white efforts to impose social control upon blacks.

85. *Baltimore Gazette*, November 2, 1865.

86. Ibid., September 22, 1865.

87. See for example, ibid., December 29, 1864, May 15, 27, June 13, July 20, August 5, November 1, 2, 3, 27, 1865.

88. *Baltimore American*, September 23, 1867.

89. Ibid., October 8, 1867.

90. Wright, *The Free Negro in Maryland*, 149–74.

91. Ibid. See also Ray M. Della, Jr., "The Problems of Negro Labor in the 1850's," *Maryland Historical Magazine* 66 (spring 1971): 14–32.

92. *Baltimore American*, November 14, 1864.

93. Ibid., December 28, 1864; *Baltimore Gazette*, December 29, 1864.

94. Jeffrey R. Brackett, *Progress of the Colored People since the War* (Baltimore, 1890), 29, 37; Signature Book 713, Records of the Freedmen's Savings and Trust Company, Record Group 101, National Archives, Washington, D.C.

95. *Baltimore American*, December 29, 1864; *Baltimore Gazette*, December 29, 1864.

96. *Baltimore American*, November 23, 1865.

97. Ibid., February 5, 1866.

98. *Baltimore Sun*, April 2, 1866, July 30, 1867; *Baltimore American*, August 1, 1867.

99. *Baltimore American*, November 23, 1865.

100. Ibid., December 29, 1865; *Baltimore Sun*, December 29, 1865.

101. *Baltimore Gazette*, September 27, 1865; *Baltimore Sun*, September 27, 1865; *Baltimore American*, September 27, 1865.

102. *Baltimore American*, September 28, 1865.

103. *Baltimore Gazette*, September 28, 1865.

104. *Baltimore Sun*, October 2, 1865.

105. Ibid., October 25, 1865.

106. *Baltimore American*, October 27, 28, 1865; *Baltimore Gazette*, October 28, 1865.

107. *Baltimore American*, November 8, 1865.

108. Ibid., October 28, 1865.

109. Ibid., November 6, 1865.

110. *New York Tribune,* September 1, 1870.

111. Ibid.

112. Ibid. See also Bettye C. Thomas, "A Nineteenth Century Black Operated Shipyard, 1866–1884: Reflections upon Its Inception and Ownership," *Journal of Negro History* 59 (January 1974): 1–12. Born in Baltimore in 1835, Isaac Myers became a ship caulker at the age of sixteen. In 1860 he was employed by Woods, Bridges, & Company, a wholesale grocery, as chief porter and shipping clerk. In 1865 he returned to ship caulking. Prominent in the organization of the caulkers association and the Chesapeake Marine Railway and Drydock Company, he also represented black Baltimoreans. In 1869 and 1870, Myers was active in the organization of the National Labor Congress and the National Colored Labor Union (George F. Bragg, *Men of Maryland* [Baltimore, 1925], 94–98; Leroy Graham, *Baltimore: The Nineteenth Century Black Capital* [Washington, D.C., 1982], 198–251).

113. *New York Tribune,* September 1, 1870.

114. Ibid.

115. Ibid.

116. Higgins, *A Succinct Exposition,* 90–91; Fields, *Slavery and Freedom,* 169, 200–202.

117. *Baltimore American,* October 18, 1865.

118. *Baltimore American,* November 23, 1864.

7

Suffrage

I

DESPITE THE FAILURE of white Baltimoreans to respond more effectively to the challenge of black migration, the city provided the principal arena for black and radical leaders' most ambitious reform effort: universal manhood suffrage. The ballot stood as the one right above all others; the most important benchmark of citizenship. As the epitome of liberal ideology, universal manhood suffrage earned the unalloyed enmity of white conservatives, and tested the limits of radical support. On the one hand it represented the high-water mark of blacks' and radical Unionists and Republicans' reform alliance. On the other, it created practical divisions among the very people most dedicated to its achievement and revealed political limits beyond which few whites or even blacks were prepared to go.

The campaign for universal suffrage began in November 1864, when Frederick Douglass stirred a black audience in Baltimore with the claim "if the negro is called upon to take his share of the toils and danger of warfare . . . he should also have the privileges of elective franchise."[1] For almost a year after emancipation, however, black aspirations for political equality won little sympathy from whites. Even radicals shied away from a measure they considered too extreme. The subject failed to surface in the 1864 state constitutional convention, and several petitions from blacks seeking the vote received scant consideration from either house of the General Assembly.[2]

Predictably, the most vigorous opposition to universal suffrage came from conservative Unionists and Democrats. In April 1864 Thomas Swann announced that he was "utterly opposed [to] any attempt to force negro suffrage upon the State of Maryland." He believed that it "could end in nothing but negro equality."[3] In an editorial on July 3, 1865, the *Baltimore Gazette* proved equally categorical. Since social amalgamation was "out of the question," it explained, so was black political participation. Enfranchised blacks could not help but "form a separate class in the social system . . . [and] act with special reference to their own race." The end result would be a war of the races—a war "tenfold as bloody and relentless as that which has just closed."[4]

Opposition was almost as strong among white radicals. Most who championed the repeal of the black code and who fought against apprenticeship and for education were no more inclined initially to grant universal suffrage than their conservative opponents. As late as June 6, 1865, the *Baltimore American* claimed that black Marylanders were as yet ill-prepared to exercise such a heavy responsibility. "No true friend of the negro," it argued, "will ask for the indiscriminate concession of the right of suffrage. . . . To say that all negroes who have just escaped the ignorance and stupidity engendered by slavery are prepared to vote intelligently would be transparently absurd." The *American* maintained further that:

> They need instructions; they require preliminary training, just as foreigners do who are ignorant of our institutions. At the present time, it is of quite as much importance to them to be trained in the duties of citizenship as to exercise its rights. That the time will come that they will be properly fitted for the enjoyment of such rights, and that the privileges of citizenship will be properly conceded to them, we do not doubt.[5]

Prominent radicals supported this stand. Later in June, James Valliant of Talbot County warned that black suffrage must be approached with "great caution." He admitted that blacks had "a right to have some say in the making of laws by which they shall be governed," but held that "at this time [they] cannot be other than incompetent voters."[6]

II

Not all radicals shared this view. Several, including Henry Winter Davis, Hugh Lennox Bond, and Archibald Stirling, Jr., believed that blacks were ready to vote and committed themselves to universal suffrage at an early date. "Negroes are as integral a part of this state as whites," said Davis on May 27, 1865. "Both are citizens. Neither can speak in the name of the state for the other [and] it is the equal right of both to be heard and represented."[7] That same month, before the New England Freedmen's Aid Society, Bond referred to the ballot as the "fundamental power of the citizen," and branded as "erroneous" the notion that society must have "a test or limitation on the right to vote." In words that were to become familiar in his many speeches he maintained, "There is no safety . . . [for him] if the black man is not given . . . the elective franchise."[8]

The arguments of Davis and Bond naturally won blacks' approval and in fact coincided auspiciously with the latter's most vocal expression of post-emancipation political aspirations to date: the resolutions of the Colored State Convention of December 1865. Led by such black Baltimoreans as Benjamin T. Tanner, Isaac Myers, and William E. Matthews, 153 delegates from every county in Maryland met in Baltimore in the Douglass Institute to call for the repeal of discriminatory legislation affecting apprenticeship, testimony, and education. In addition, the convention petitioned the General Assembly to extend to blacks "those manhood rights which are enjoyed by the white citizens of the state, viz: the right of suffrage."[9] Such a right, explained convention leaders, was essential if blacks were to enjoy "the protection necessary to make them . . . valuable citizens."[10] Although the Colored State Convention adjourned on December 29, its enthusiasm carried into early 1866. On January 12, black Baltimoreans assembled for a mass meeting in the Nazarite Assembly Hall on Clay Street. A week later, they met again with representatives from the rural counties for the first session of the State Colored League, an organization authorized by the State Convention. At both of these meetings, blacks reaffirmed their demand for the ballot.[11]

Although the efforts of blacks and their white supporters made little immediate headway, their views gradually acquired momentum. In January 1866, Radical Republicans in Congress raised the question of black voting in the District of Columbia, an issue that took them more than a year to settle, but that indicated the strength of universal suffrage as a major element in national Republican thinking.[12] Of even greater importance were the results of the 1866 split in Maryland's Union Party which left the pro-suffrage radical forces in a relatively powerful position.

In May and June of that year, Thomas Swann and his fellow conservatives bolted the ranks of the Union Party. Disturbed over radical Unionists' efforts to extend the rights of blacks, the governor and his followers—almost half the Union party—threw in their lot with tidewater planters and joined the Democratic Party.[13] This division left antisuffrage "moderates" in control of those Unionists who remained, but in a badly deteriorated position. Hitherto, as proponents of a middle ground between conservative and extreme views, they had benefited from their party's need to compromise. With Swann and the conservatives gone, their status became increasingly untenable and they were forced to confront directly Bond and other pro-suffrage extremists who were now allied with the Radical wing of the national Republican Party.

Such a task proved difficult. As it became apparent that both white southerners and Marylanders would refuse to accept the spirit of the Civil Rights Act, such moderates on the suffrage question as John A. J. Creswell and Charles C. Fulton felt compelled to support its strengthening by incorporating its provisions into the Fourteenth Amendment of the United States Constitution. At the same time, they accepted the latter's stipulation reducing Congressional representation of states that restricted suffrage.[14] In doing so, moderates insisted they did not endorse the right of blacks to vote, arguing somewhat disengenuously that the amendment protected the latter's civil rights while at the same time *avoiding* such an extreme step. As Creswell explained, "This amendment [is] conceded on all hands to be a *waiver* of negro suffrage. . . . It [is believed] by everyone in Congress . . . that it leaves the question of suffrage to the states. So much it means and nothing more."[15]

But he was playing a dangerous game. Supporting the Fourteenth Amendment while disclaiming universal suffrage placed him in a vulnerable position, and when Charles Sumner and Thaddeus Stevens backed the amendment as a way of encouraging black voting, Maryland moderates found it difficult to avoid guilt by association with their attitudes. On July 3, 1866, the *Baltimore Sun* reminded its readers that radicals had already moved from a first Freedmen's Bureau bill to a second, and from the Civil Rights Act to the Fourteenth Amendment, and said there was little reason to believe they would hesitate from going further. "It is not an extravagant or vain fear," the *Sun* warned, "that the power will be asserted to give the negro . . . all the political privileges as well as the civil rights which belong to citizens in any part of the country."[16]

The debate intensified in September 1866, when moderates engaged in an open quarrel with their extremist colleagues at the Southern Loyalists Convention in Philadelphia. When delegates from several gulf states advocated black suffrage as the only way to achieve Republican ascendancy in their region, most border state representatives, including the majority of the Maryland delegation, objected to such a measure. They not only opposed universal suffrage in principle at this stage, but feared that concurrence with the gulf states would jeopardize Republican prospects in 1866 state elections in all the border states.[17] Bond and several other Maryland extremists disagreed. On September 4, the judge rose to support the gulf states and to link universal suffrage firmly to the Fourteenth Amendment. He resolved:

> That this convention urge the loyal men of the North to support the Congress of the United States in demanding of the Southern States the wise guarantee of the [Fourteenth] . . . amendment, . . . and that as we believe the justice we mete out shall be the measure of our safety, . . . in our opinion there can be no permanent peace or Security for loyal men in the South without . . . negro suffrage.[18]

In the end, border state moderates resisted both Bond's and the gulf states' efforts to pass a measure in favor of universal suffrage. Nevertheless, the debate within their delegation exposed the tensions among Maryland Unionists—now Republicans—and left them in an unenviable situation. Democrats, knowing that a majority of voters in the state opposed universal suffrage, could now capitalize on their opponents' dispute by driving a wedge between them. In a letter to the *Baltimore American,* on May 12, 1866, an anonymous correspondent claimed that the question at stake in the November election would be black voting and nothing else. "[T]he issue on this subject," he predicted, "[is] well made."[19] Later in May, a Democratic mass meeting in Baltimore accused Republicans of "designedly looking . . . to negro suffrage," and on June 21, Governor Swann denounced his Republican foes, saying, "They have fraternized almost exclusively with negro suffrage radicals."[20]

Until the November election, moderates tried their best to convince Maryland voters that the Republican Party did not stand for all of which it was accused. On May 14, John L. Thomas explained to a Washington County meeting that:

> Efforts are being made by our opponents . . . to say that . . . [we are] in favor of negro suffrage. I denounce it as a lie unqualifiedly. . . . I am not in favour of negro suffrage and neither are . . . [my Republican colleagues]. It is a delusion and an attempt of the . . . Democratic party and

silly men . . . who are afflicted with negrophobia to deceive well-intentioned Union [voters] who want to stand up for the right but who are frightened by this bugbear of negro suffrage.[21]

On May 15, the *Baltimore American* called the whole issue a "false ghost," claiming that "*No body in Maryland asks for negro suffrage and no party desires it.*"[22] In June, it labeled opposition charges as "the Conservative Bugaboo," and said that "all discerning men can see this is only an attempt to . . . mislead the thoughtless and unreflecting."[23] That same month, the *Frederick Examiner* branded Democratic allegations as "gross misrepresentations and political jugglery." It argued that "No sensible man is likely to give credence to the charge that the Union Party favors Negro suffrage. . . . All this talk . . . is a rebel trick gotten up for the purpose of dividing the Union Party."[24]

Yet moderates found it difficult to make their case stick. Continued statements by Bond and other pro-suffrage extremists exacted a deadly toll, and to make matters worse, an unexpected about-face by none other than the *Baltimore American* sealed their fate. As the summer of 1866 progressed and the Southern states began to reject the Fourteenth Amendment, the *American* decided to reconsider its course. Throughout September and October, it maintained a generally antisuffrage stand, but in the aftermath of the Southern Loyalists Convention, it examined the extremists' position in a different light. On September 11, the *American* attacked Bond's support of the gulf states as ill-timed and quixotic, but awarded that support a degree of respect for the first time. The newspaper conceded the debate over black suffrage was "one of the most important events of the time," and admitted "It is possible that it may be a turning point in our affairs."[25] The *American* could not have chosen a less opportune time to equivocate. The Republican Party was divided enough without such last-minute second thoughts. By election day on November 6, few voters believed moderates could withstand the pressure of the universal suffrage advocates. Combined with the split of the Union Party in the spring and the votes of thousands of hitherto disfranchised whites, fear of black suffrage was more than sufficient to assure victory for the Democrats. The latter won fifty-three of eighty seats in the House of Delegates and solidifed planters' traditional grip on the state Senate.[26] For the first time since 1861, the friends of black progress, the supporters of emancipation, the Freedmen's Bureau Bill, and the Civil Rights Act, were out of office.

III

As an issue, however, universal suffrage by no means disappeared from the scene. Ironically, the election defeat accomplished what victory might never have obtained: it cleared the way for the pro-suffrage forces to seize Republican Party leadership and led directly to the adoption of black political equality as the salient feature of its platform. The 1866 election dealt moderates a severe blow. Disheartened and discredited, they retreated, permitting Bond and his allies to come to the fore. The latter emerged from the election as convinced as ever in the merits of universal suffrage and called upon moderates to join them.[27]

Most of the latter did so. Disappointment with defeat was sufficient to force their accommodation, and the fight for civil rights alone no longer seemed adequate in the face of Democratic electoral strength. If blacks were to receive the protection necessary for the enjoyment of these rights, the ballot must be theirs. On March 1, 1867, the *Baltimore American* attacked the "prejudices and passions . . . which sustain the abuses by which the negro is now oppressed." It praised the leaders of the universal suffrage movement and argued that "justice and humanity compel us to respond to the call." The opposition to black suffrage, it concluded, "remains alone of the formidable antagonisms which resist . . . efforts to unfetter the slave."[28]

Additional pressure came from blacks themselves, who continued to force the issue. On January 8, 1867, delegates from several Northern states, including Maryland, met in Philadelphia at the Colored Soldiers and Sailors Convention to appeal to Congress for the elective franchise.[29] A few days later, delegates from both North and South gathered for the same purpose at the Colored Peoples Convention in Washington, D.C.[30] In Philadelphia, black Marylanders made their wishes clear when A. Ward Handy of Baltimore, a convention vice president, declared:

Our appeal is to the heart of the great American people for sympathy and for those rights which [should] have been ours since the foundation of the Republic. . . . A black man who can tell a loyal man from a traitor is entitled to vote. He is as fully competent to vote a traitor down as to shoot him down. The [black] men who fought for the flag of America did not do so for pay but because they could boast of American birth.

. . . They should enjoy the envied right to put a small piece of paper in the ballot box.[31]

Throughout 1867, blacks persisted in their demands. "We intend to stand up for our rights," declared Handy in May, "and demand of the Maryland Union Party that they will stand by their colored brethren . . . and allow us the protection and enjoyment of these privileges."[32] In a mass meeting in June, blacks in Frederick County resolved: "It is the ballot we have started for, it is the ballot we ask, it is the ballot we demand."[33]

Responding to both these demands and the realities of their political situation, Maryland Republicans moved promptly to establish their position. Universal suffrage became official party policy on February 27, 1867, when five hundred party delegates from across the state convened in Baltimore. Here they resolved unanimously that "the principle of [universal] manhood suffrage is the only basis for reconstruction," and that "the time has come when its adoption by every state is demanded by every consideration of right and justice."[34] A month later, Republicans underlined the nature of this new platform when they met a second time and chose longtime radical Archibald Stirling, Jr. as their principal speaker. Stirling told a cheering audience that "while we recognize the right of our state within reasonable limits to fix [the nature of] the elective franchise, we do not recognize [its] right to exclude [a portion of our] population . . . on account of color." "Any State Constitution," he argued, "which deprives one fourth of its whole population of the right of the franchise . . . is an oligarchy and anti-republican."[35]

Next, Maryland Republicans turned their attention to no less a task than overturning the results of the 1866 election. To most party members, moderate or radical, the return to power of politicians sympathetic to the conservative cause constituted a throwback to the dark days of slavery and an undoing of some of the Union Party's great work of emancipation and reform. Republicans were especially upset with the Swann-appointed registrars who had ignored the provisions of the 1865 Registration Act in permitting previously disfranchised Marylanders to vote in 1866, and the Democratic General Assembly of 1867, which called for a new state constitutional convention. As the *Baltimore American* explained in an editorial that contrasted Maryland's condition with that of the ex-Confederate states:

Congress can reconstruct the ten rebellious states upon the basis of loyalty and manhood suffrage [but] Maryland and [the other border states]
have passed into the hands of Rebels. . . . When the work of reconstruction is complete, when the Union men shall have obtained the mastery
of the ten Rebel States, as they now have the mastery of the Northern
States, there will be a small belt running through the middle of the
country, given over to the darkness of secession and pro-slavery.[36]

Soon after the legislature's call for a new constitutional convention,
Maryland Republicans appealed to Congress for help. With the House
of Representatives and Senate Judiciary Committees already studying
Maryland's testimony and apprenticeship, Republicans asked Congress
to include an investigation of the 1866 election and the 1867 proposal
for the new constitutional convention. They hoped that Congress, in
its power to ensure each state "a republican form of government,"
would overturn the results of the fall election and somehow reinstate a
"loyal" administration.[37]

It was in this appeal to Congress that Republicans pressed their
stand on universal suffrage into practical service. How could Maryland's Democratic government be "republican," they asked, as long as
it denied the franchise to one-fourth of its population? How could it
function constitutionally when its black and Republican opposition
made up a majority of the state's potential voters? Surely, under these
circumstances, any attempt to conduct such vital business as the calling
of a new constitutional convention was an illegal usurpation of power.
"No change in our existing constitution," claimed the Republican state
convention on February 22, 1867, "ought to be recognized . . . which
is not made by impartial manhood suffrage, without regard to color."
Furthermore, "no state government without [such] suffrage ought to
be considered republican."[38] To this, the Grand Union League of
Maryland added the request that Congress "as far as is practicable"
extend to Maryland the provisions of the military reconstruction law
and "secure [for] all loyal citizens in the state the right of suffrage."[39]
Next, the Republican caucus of the General Assembly demanded "a
republican form of government on the . . . basis of right, truth, . . .
peace [and] impartial suffrage without respect to race or color," and
the Republican members of the Baltimore City Council insisted "as a
matter of right and justice," that the franchise "be given to all males
over the age of twenty-one years without regard to race or color."[40]

Finally, in encouraging Congress to act, Maryland Republicans did their utmost to prove themselves more worthy or "republican" than their Conservative-Democratic counterparts by inviting blacks to participate in party affairs, specifically in a statewide convention scheduled for May 1867. It was a daring move, one that pleased black Marylanders greatly. On March 27, in a letter to the *Baltimore American*, "Bethel Church" (probably Benjamin Tanner), celebrated the call by asking:

> Will not the loyal men of the state unite—white men and black men? Let the only test of Union be loyalty—not caste, not color. As a negro I plead not . . . altogether for the sake of my race; for both classes of the great loyal party are mutually dependent upon each other: the black loyalist of Maryland needs his white compatriot to go ahead—to lead on; the white loyalist needs his black compatriots to stand at his back and maintain him. If the two unite they will succeed; if they remain apart they will both be defeated. . . . We call upon the white loyalist in Maryland to accept the negro. Spurn him no more for you will need him. His vote must be counted.[41]

Across the state, blacks reacted with equal enthusiasm. Between April 17 and the convention a month later, they met with white Republicans in every county and in all twenty Baltimore wards to elect delegates to Maryland's first interracial political convention. In stressing the new nature of Republican politics, an advertisement in the *Baltimore American* was typical:

> To All The Republicans of Baltimore City
> All Loyal Citizens of Baltimore
> Without regard to past political differences, race or color, who are in favor of the principles of the Republican Union Party are invited to meet in the various wards . . .[42]

In rural areas, black laborers crowded into mass meetings. From Denton, Caroline County, a correspondent described the gathering there saying, "Today has been a '*big thing*' here. . . . The colored citizens were out in strength. So great was [their] interest that the Court House could not hold them. Quite a number stood outside in the rain and listened to the speakers."[43] From Baltimore County came the word that blacks there were just as enthusiastic. Before the ninth election district primary meeting, the *Baltimore County Free Press* announced that "those from the vicinity of Towsontown will march down the pike in a body with flags and music, and those from near the city will come in the same manner."[44]

In addition to attending primary meetings, blacks took stock of their potential political power. At the encouragement of the Republican State Central Committee, their leaders in several counties established Republican clubs and began registering adult males of voting age. Instructions from the Central Committee read:

INSTRUCTIONS FOR THE ORGANIZATION OF REPUBLICAN
CLUBS AMONG THE COLORED PEOPLE

In accordance with the resolutions of the State Convention of the Republican Party, the colored people of [all] the counties are requested to organize as follows:

1. They will cause to be made as early as possible an accurate list of the names of every colored man above the age of 21 in each Election District in the county.

2. In order that the full colored vote of the county may be polled at any election that may hereafter be held for delegates to a state convention, they are requested to organize at once at such places as may be most convenient, a Republican club to be composed of only colored men over the age of 21 years.

3. In order that the work of these clubs may be thorough, they are requested to choose a chairman and a secretary and keep a correct minute of all their proceedings.

4. They are requested to keep their proceedings STRICTLY PRIVATE— not to admit to their meetings any person under 21 years of age, and especially no females. They should talk of their proceedings only among the men.

5. They are requested to suffer no delay in organizing—to make it early and complete, so that when an election shall be held, every colored man shall be at the polls, . . .

6. And when the lists of any district are finished, they should be returned without delay . . . to the Central Committee.[45]

In Caroline County, a Republican club was in place by April 27, complete with a list of almost eight hundred voters.[46] On May 4, in Dorchester County, eighty blacks gathered at Church Creek to start a club and to collect names. They established registries for the election districts of Cambridge, Church Creek, and New Market.[47] On May 14, 1867, when the statewide Republican convention finally met in Baltimore, 181 black delegates from the city and twelve counties presented their credentials. Sixty-seven blacks came from Baltimore alone, more than a third of the city's total delegation. Other large black contingents came from Frederick County, which sent 29 members; Cecil with 20; and Baltimore County with 18. Of the smaller delegations,

Prince George's County led the way with 9, Caroline had 8, and Talbot, 7.[48] During the convention, blacks played a prominent role. Two served as delegation chairmen, five as convention vice presidents, and three on the resolutions committee. Of the convention's ten major speakers, four were black. In the morning session, William Sanders addressed the assembly at length and in the afternoon, A. Ward Handy, Henry J. Brown, and Henry C. Hawkins did the same.[49] Each stressed the significance of the Republicans' interracial experiment and called upon their white colleagues to maintain the struggle for universal suffrage.[50] "We are meeting today on the broad platform of manhood equality," declared Handy, "[but] I trust for the better time when we shall meet at the ballot box on the platform of manhood suffrage."[51]

Republicans, both black and white, were immensely pleased with the May 14 convention. For one thing, the final resolutions were radical enough to suit even the most extreme delegates. The first and key resolution stated unequivocally:

> That we affirm our demand, heretofore made, for the recognition by law ... of the entire equality of all American citizens in all civil and political rights without regard to color.

And to achieve this goal, the convention further resolved that:

> We call upon Congress ... to carry out the principles of the Declaration of Independence ... to abolish all legal distinction on account of color, and to give the suffrage to the colored [people] of this and all other states.[52]

Republicans were equally pleased with the interracial aspect of the convention. The *Baltimore American* claimed that "A new epoch has dawned in [Maryland] politics. For the first time, our citizens have assembled in a convention founded on the principle of equal rights, and called without distinction of color." The significance of this event lay not only in its resolutions calling for universal suffrage, but also in the fact that "whites and blacks have met upon a common ground [to] discuss ... the future welfare of both races and the destiny of the state." Nor did the *American* lose sight of the convention's political potential. "We claim to have formed," it said, "the strong nucleus of a party which will, whenever manhood suffrage is granted, control the State."[53]

No sooner had the convention adjourned than Republicans sought to capitalize on this spirit. In response to the demands of both white and black party members, the State Central Committee agreed to include blacks in its ranks. On May 31, 1867, John Creswell, state chairman, announced the appointment of five black Baltimoreans, headed by Isaac Myers and William Sanders, to the committee.[54] Next, Republicans formed a new wing of the party: black Union Leagues. The latter appeared in Baltimore as early as March 1867, and their number soon spread throughout the city and rural counties. In July, the *Baltimore County Free Press* reported that Leagues were starting in several places in its area, and the *Salisbury New Era* announced the formation in Worcester County of a League with more than one hundred members. "Like organizations," it added, "exist throughout the county."[55]

In addition to black participation in the Republican State Central Committee and the establishment of Union Leagues, the enthusiasm of the May 14 convention led promptly to the idea of a second such interracial gathering. On May 31, 1867, the Central Committee called on not only black and white Marylanders to meet again in Baltimore in September, but also invited Republicans "regardless of color" from several border states to join them.[56] The Border State Convention, as this meeting was called, attracted a large delegation of black Marylanders, including thirty-two from Baltimore alone. Called to "advance the interests and cause of manhood suffrage," the convention petitioned Congress "to secure to the [border] states . . . a republican form of government," by amending the United States Constitution to read "that no State shall disfranchise any citizen because of race or color."[57] As convention speakers, black delegates pursued the same theme. "I can stand here as a citizen of the United States," said Henry J. Brown, "but I am not a citizen of Maryland until I am clothed with the right of the ballot."[58] William E. Matthews asked the convention, "Are you in earnest?" He wanted to know if Maryland were to be redeemed and demanded universal suffrage "not as a favor, but as an inherent right."[59]

The Border State Convention marked the climax of Republican efforts in 1867 to include blacks in party affairs. Along with the state convention in May and the formation of ward associations and Union Leagues, the September 12 gathering represented the culmination of this major revolution in the structure and emphasis of the Maryland Republican Party. From this point on, black participation was an established fact, and the call for universal suffrage the salient feature of the Republican platform. In October, the party gave a ringing endorsement to this practice and policy by nominating the leading advocate of both—Judge Hugh Lennox Bond—as Republican gubernatorial candidate for the state election of that year.[60]

IV

Unfortunately for Maryland Republicans, however, neither interracial cooperation, a universal suffrage platform, nor Hugh Lennox Bond, were sufficient to rescue their party from inevitable political disaster. Despite their intensive efforts to court its assistance, Congress refused to interfere in the affairs of a state that had never left the Union. Neither the Senate nor House of Representatives Committee on the Judiciary moved beyond its brief investigation of black Marylanders' civil rights, thus leaving the election results of 1866 and the Democratic call for a new state constitutional convention intact.[61] Without outside help, Republicans faced a desperate situation. Tainted in the eyes of most voters by their extreme stand on black political equality, they were virtually obliterated in the November 1867 election. Republicans failed to win a single seat in the House of Delegates, saw their influence in the Senate almost disappear, and suffered the worst gubernatorial defeat of any party in the history of the state. To Democrat Oden Bowie's more than 70,000 votes, Hugh Lennox Bond could muster barely 20,000.[62]

The immediate and hardly surprising result of this electoral catastrophe was a renewal of the split between white Republicans over the wisdom of retaining a strong universal suffrage platform. This time, both moderates and extremists agreed that black voting was a noble principle eminently worth striving for, but the former now argued that the issue should be softened and subordinated to broader considerations. "Are we now," asked Creswell, "to endanger everything by a [continued] attempt to convert [our people] by a simple command to negro suffrage? . . . We might as well be plain, if such counsels prevail, we shall be beaten."[63] Creswell and others pointed to the 1867 defeat of not only the Maryland Republican Party but also of several universal suffrage referenda in other Northern states. In 1868, with the presidential election imminent, many were prepared to sacrifice principle in the short run to achieve it in the long. Arguing that any hope for universal suffrage lay ultimately in the supremacy of the national Republican Party, they sought a platform as broad and as inoffensive as possible.

In an editorial on May 11, 1868, the *Baltimore American* explained that as far as universal suffrage was concerned:

> We are powerless. We can accomplish nothing. We can agitate and keep the principle alive, but farther than this we cannot go. We must have assistance from abroad. This we can obtain only from Congress. If we fail to have a majority there we are [lost].[64]

Most Republicans accepted this assessment of their situation. Even blacks counseled moderation. On May 14, a large mass meeting of black Baltimoreans endorsed Creswell and the *American*. The opinion of the assembly was expressed best by William Taylor who said, "The steps of the colored people should be well-measured. . . . Be discreet, be cautious. . . . [We] are not voting yet. . . . If things go wrong . . . this question would be put back a long way."[65]

But not everyone agreed. A minority of both blacks and whites, led once again by Bond, insisted that unequivocal support of universal suffrage should remain a "cardinal principle" and that its abandonment or even diminution in importance represented a betrayal of Republican goals. Bond and his followers rejected the notion that retreat offered the best chance of ultimate success and argued that Republicans everywhere should "adhere to impartial manhood suffrage . . . [and] advocate it both in theory and principle throughout the Union."[66]

The renewed debate over black suffrage came to a climax when the Maryland Republican Party began the process of selecting delegates for the 1868 national convention in Chicago. The one faction, represented by Bond, insisted on delegates committed wholeheartedly to a strong pro-suffrage platform. The other, led by Creswell, advocated a more flexible approach.[67] In addition, the Bond forces demanded that the party abandon a policy established in 1867 that restricted participation at the nominating level to whites. Combining principle and expediency, the extremists called for broadened black participation in what was shaping up to be a bitter contest.[68] Predictably, moderates objected, arguing that the party should not endanger its image or survival by allowing nonvoters to share in the selection of delegates.[69]

The struggle began on February 16, 1868, when the Baltimore City Executive Committee published its call for ward primaries to a February 27 citywide convention. The convention was to select Baltimore's delegation to the state nominating convention scheduled for March 6, which was, in turn, to choose delegates for Chicago. Samuel Hatch, president of the City Executive Committee, and most of his fellow-members supported Judge Bond. Seeking to force the participation issue by bringing blacks into city ward meetings, Hatch specified in his call that "all Republicans" should attend. In his attempt to assure pro-suffrage strength, Hatch deliberately omitted the customary restriction to "Republican voters."[70]

Moderates reacted angrily. The *Baltimore American* condemned the "glaring impropriety" of the City Executive Committee's action. The newspaper attached itself firmly to the moderate stand and did its best to convince Bond's people of their folly. In addition, the *American* issued a firm warning to black Republicans telling them to avoid association with Hatch and his fellow committee members. "We think we have the right to advise the colored people of Baltimore," it said on February 27, "and we urge them not to allow themselves to be thrust into a contest that [will] alienate them from the sympathies of . . . their most earnest political friends."[71] Most blacks heeded the *American*'s advice and stayed clear of entanglement with Bond and the extremists. Nevertheless, when city ward meetings met on February 26, it became apparent that some were no longer content with a restricted role in party affairs. Blacks turned up at several meetings and in three wards, the eleventh, fifteenth, and sixteenth, their numbers were sufficient to split pro- and antisuffrage supporters into warring camps. In each case, moderates withdrew to hold meetings of their own and proceeded to nominate delegates to the city convention. In all three wards, the white extremists and blacks who remained behind selected contesting slates.[72]

On February 27, Baltimore Republicans met for their city convention. Moderates dominated both organization and deliberations and the credentials committee rejected the extremist delegations from the eleventh, fifteenth, and sixteenth wards.[73] In response, twenty-eight extremists who had been elected from other wards through normal channels, including Bond, bolted the convention.[74] In a letter to the *Baltimore American* on February 29, these men defended the right of blacks to take part in nominating meetings. According to them, the defeated delegations represented the voice of the true and regular Republican Party. In addition, the bolters described what they believed to be the basic cause of the dispute. They accused moderates of taking every step possible to eliminate extremists because the latter were "determined to maintain the loyalty of the Republican Party to manhood suffrage, and . . . [would insist] that the Chicago convention avow its adherence to that principle."[75]

The Bond faction then decided to hold a city convention of its own. To build up its numbers and enhance its legitimacy, it called for new primary meetings to be held in all wards not represented by the original twenty-eight bolters. Blacks were invited to attend and take full part.[76] The convention met on March 3, at the Douglass Institute. Over one hundred delegates attended and every ward but one was represented.[77] Samuel Hatch was chosen president and the convention passed resolutions asserting its legitimacy and calling upon the Republican Party to adhere firmly to the black suffrage platform. It then nominated twenty-one delegates to contest those chosen by the regular city convention to attend the state nominating convention. Among those selected were Bond, Stirling, and Hatch. Many blacks attended the Douglass Institute meeting but none served as ward representatives or as delegates to the state convention.[78]

The state convention met on March 6. Again, organization and deliberations were in moderates' hands. Delegates approved a flexible platform on universal suffrage and threw out Bond and his contesting city delegation.[79] Rebuffed now by two conventions, one city and one state, the judge and his followers resolved to continue their bolting politics by calling a second statewide convention to contest the results of the first. Gathering a dozen or so county delegates in addition to his twenty-one disappointed Baltimoreans, Bond rallied his forces in the Douglass Institute just hours after their rejection and set May 6 as the date for a counter state convention.[80]

In preparing for this new meeting, Bond continued to solicit blacks' support. In a letter to the *New York Tribune* he defended black participation at the nominating level and accused moderates of nothing less than an attempt "to thrust the colored people out of the party."[81] Accordingly, on April 14, the call went out once again for Republicans "without regard to race or color" to meet in ward primaries in preparation for yet another city convention to choose delegates for May 6. In response, a number of blacks attended ward meetings, two of which took place in black churches, the Sharp Street Methodist Episcopal Church and the "Colored Peoples' Church" on Madison Avenue between Park and Cathedral.[82]

On April 16, the extremists' third city convention of the year met in the Front Street Theatre. Two hundred persons attended, half of whom were delegates. According to the *Baltimore American,* about a third of the onlookers were black.[83] The meeting moved through the now customary resolutions claiming its legitimacy and endorsing a strong universal suffrage platform, and featured an address by Robert Sorrell, a black delegate from the thirteenth ward.[84] In all, four blacks, including Sorrell, answered the roll call as delegates. Their presence marked the first occasion in which blacks had served in this capacity at a nominating convention.[85]

But by this stage, the strength of the bolting movement was beginning to ebb. Content with the fact they had made their point, even Bond's closest advisers began counseling restraint. Few extremists possessed the courage or temerity to push a contesting delegation all the way to Chicago, especially when the majority of Maryland Republicans opposed them. Moreover, such opposition included most blacks. Although some continued to support Bond to the bitter end, black Republicans generally sided with Creswell and other moderates even on the subject of participation in nominating conventions. "I am just as much for [this] advancement as any gentleman," explained William Taylor, "[but] we are not voting yet."[86] "We have not yet the right," added Isaac Myers, "to nominate or vote for candidates."[87]

In March and April, when the Bond faction tried its hardest to seize control of the Republican Party, most black leaders remained aloof. Of the prominent blacks who had participated in the two 1867 interracial state conventions, only Henry J. Brown lent his name to the extremist cause. At no time did such other men as Samuel Chase, Benjamin Tanner, William Matthews, or Isaac Myers cooperate with Bond and the bolting Republicans.

The May 6 convention reflected the absence of such support. Although Baltimore and most of the counties were represented, few delegations had more than two or three members. Blacks attended in respectable numbers, but apart from Henry Brown, no one of prominence participated. Indeed, many black delegates had been brought up from the Eastern Shore and southern Maryland in a deliberate attempt to pack the convention. By this time, the presence of blacks at such gatherings no longer indicated extremists' strength, but represented something new—the "forced Africanization," as its opponents called it, of the bolters' movement. As each step in their revolt grew more extreme, Bond and his followers were forced to rely on an increasing number of fringe politicians, both black and white.[88]

Still, the speeches were fiery, and the selection of delegates to contest Maryland's seats in Chicago proceeded as scheduled. Bond was there of course, as were Archibald Stirling, Jr., Francis Thomas, and Samuel Hatch. True as ever to the principles of universal suffrage and black participation in party affairs, the bolters nominated four blacks to the Chicago slate, one, Robert Sorrell, as a full delegate and three as alternates.[89] But by this time their fate was sealed and somewhat anticlimactic. With no support from the Maryland Republican Party, Sorrell and his colleagues stood little chance of winning their seats at the Republican national convention. And if rejected there, the Bond faction would have no other place to turn. Consequently, on June 14, 1868, the bolting Republicans finally consulted their better judgment and withdrew from the contest.[90] "[We] will urge the adoption of our views upon the party at every suitable opportunity," said Bond, but in the meantime, "we will cordially unite in the support of our national ticket . . . [and] urge . . . a vigorous campaign throughout the state."[91]

V

The Republican debate over universal manhood suffrage demonstrated both the strengths and weaknesses of the alliance between white and black reformers. Clearly, the issue provided an area of basically common agreement that combined the aspirations of whites and blacks alike in an articulate and powerful statement of principle. As in the case of apprenticeship, civil rights, and education, whites and blacks stood on ideologically common ground that transcended the differences dividing them racially, socially, and economically. Moreover, even the caution of moderate Republicans in 1868 proved politically astute. By postponing immediate action on the suffrage question and by affirming their essential devotion to the *principles* of "justice and manhood suffrage," Creswell and the majority of Maryland Republicans helped defuse a potentially difficult situation and assured the victory of their national party in the federal election in November.[92] The following year, Congress initiated proceedings toward the Fifteenth Amendment to the United States Constitution, which prohibited states from restricting suffrage according to race.[93]

Nevertheless, that same caution revealed the inability of blacks' and whites' reform alliance to make any headway within the state. Universal

manhood suffrage, more than any other issue, consolidated the opposition of Maryland conservatives against black progress, isolated radicals'
support, and drove Republicans out of office. In seeking to obtain the
ballot for black Marylanders, Republicans put forth their strongest,
most articulate arguments and came closest to surmounting the inherent limitations of their own racial philosophy. Yet in 1865 and 1866
most held back, and again in 1868 only Hugh Lennox Bond was prepared to persevere. As was the case with so many other issues, caution
ultimately prevailed.

NOTES

1. *Baltimore American,* November 23, 1864.
2. Maryland, General Assembly, House of Delegates, *Journal of Proceedings, January Session, 1866* (Annapolis, 1866); Senate, *Journal of Proceedings,
January Session, 1866* (Annapolis, 1866), 177; *Baltimore American,* February 6,
1866; *Baltimore Sun,* February 6, 1866.
3. *Baltimore American,* November 4, 1864.
4. *Baltimore Gazette,* July 3, 1865.
5. *Baltimore American,* June 6, 1865.
6. Ibid., June 22, 1865.
7. Ibid., March 19, 1866. This quotation is from a letter written by Davis
in May 1865, but not released by Mrs. Davis until March 1866.
8. Ibid., June 9, 1865. As a delegate from Maryland, Bond had joined
even earlier with the members of the American Freedmen's aid union in declaring on May 9, 1865, "the right of suffrage is not only due to the fidelity of
the colored man but is the only sure basis for a permanent and righteous
reconstruction of the union" (*Freedmen's Record,* 1 [June 1865], 1).
9. *Baltimore Sun,* December 29, 1865.
10. Ibid.
11. *Baltimore American,* January 17, 1866.
12. *Congressional Globe,* 39 Cong., 2 Sess., 261–64.
13. See Richard Paul Fuke, "The Break-Up of the Maryland Union Party,
1866," M.A. thesis, University of Maryland, 1965.
14. Amendment XIV [1868], Section 2, "when the right to vote at any
election . . . is denied to any of the male inhabitants . . . being twenty-one
years of age, . . . the basis of representation . . . shall be reduced in the proportion which the number of such male citizens shall be to the whole number of
male citizens twenty-one years of age." John A. J. Creswell was born in Port
Deposit, Md., in 1828. He studied at Dickinson College and was admitted to

the bar in Maryland in 1850. A Whig in the 1850s, Creswell became a strong Republican during the war. He served in the Maryland House of Delegates and between 1863 and 1865, in the House of Representatives. In March 1865, he was appointed to the United States Senate to finish Thomas Hicks's term. In 1869, President Ulysses Grant appointed Creswell head of the Post Office Department (*Dictionary of American Biography*, 4:541; *Who Was Who in America, Historical Volume, 1607–1896*, 127).

15. *Baltimore American*, October 5, 1866, emphasis added.

16. *Baltimore Sun*, July 3, 1866.

17. Ibid., September 5, 1866.

18. Ibid.

19. Ibid., May 12, 1866.

20. Ibid., May 25, June 22, 1866.

21. Ibid., May 15, 1866.

22. Ibid. Obviously, for the sake of effect, the *American* was stretching the truth. It knew full well that Bond and others supported universal suffrage.

23. Ibid., June 5, 1866.

24. *Frederick Examiner*, June 27, 1866.

25. *Baltimore American*, September 11, 1866.

26. Ibid., November 7, 1866; *Baltimore Sun*, November 7, 1866. Although the Union Party's defeat can be attributed largely to the defection of the conservatives, Governor Swann's disregard of state law also played an important role. In the spring of 1865 the unionist-dominated General Assembly passed a Registration Act designed to disfranchise Southern sympathizers. Had this act been enforced strictly, Marylanders who had been disqualified during the Civil War because of their inability to swear to a rigidly defined loyalty oath would have remained disfranchised after 1865. The appointment of voter registrars, however, was in the hands of the governor. Intent on having the conservative Unionists and Democrats win the election of 1866, Swann appointed registrars sympathetic to his cause and instructed them to permit wide open registration (Richard P. Fuke, "The Break-Up of the Maryland Union Party, 1866," 46–59).

27. See below.

28. *Baltimore American*, March 1, 1867.

29. Ibid., January 10, 1867.

30. *Baltimore Sun*, January 11, 1867.

31. *Baltimore American*, January 10, 1867.

32. Ibid., May 15, 1867.

33. Ibid., June 19, 1867.

34. *Baltimore Sun*, February 28, 1867.

35. *Baltimore American*, March 28, 1867.

36. *Baltimore American*, July 9, 1867.

37. United States Congress, House of Representatives, *The Miscellaneous Documents of the House of Representatives for the First Session of the Fortieth Congress, 1867* (Washington, 1868), Vol. 1, Document No. 32, "Affairs in Maryland: Resolutions of the Republican State Convention of Maryland, March 27, 1867."

38. Ibid.

39. Ibid., Document No. 28, "Affairs in Maryland: Resolutions adopted by the Grand Union League of Maryland, March 20, 1867."

40. Ibid., Document No. 27, "Affairs in Maryland: Memorial from the Members of the General Assembly of Maryland Asking the Immediate Consideration by Congress of the Condition of Public Affairs in that State, March 27, 1867"; Document No. 34, "Affairs in Maryland: Memorial from the Mayor and Members of City Council of Baltimore Asking Congress to Assist the people of Maryland to Form a State Government, Republican in Form, and in Unison with the Spirit of the Age, Order Printed, March 30, 1867."

41. *Baltimore American*, March 27, 1867.

42. Ibid., April 25, 1867.

43. Ibid., May 10, 1867, emphasis in original.

44. *Baltimore County Free Press*, n.d., quoted in *Baltimore American*, May 9, 1867.

45. *Baltimore Gazette*, May 11, 1867.

46. *Baltimore American*, April 27, 1867.

47. *Cambridge Intelligencer*, n.d., quoted in *Baltimore American*, May 13, 1867.

48. *Baltimore American*, May 15, 1867; *Baltimore Sun*, May 15, 1867; *Baltimore Gazette*, May 15, 1867.

49. Dr. Henry J. Brown was one of Baltimore's most active black civic leaders during the post-emancipation period. By profession a phrenologist, he spoke frequently in Baltimore about his work and "affairs of the day." In April of 1865, the United States Army placed him under special military protection as he went about his business. In May of that year a reporter to the *Easton Gazette* called him "a well-organized, educated, able lecturer. His mission is to benefit his race." In 1867, Brown delivered major addresses to the Republican State Convention in May, and the Republican Border State Convention in September (*Cecil Whig*, January 28, 1865; Vol. 36 [Old Book 40], p. 383, Records of the 8th Army Corps, Middle Department, United States Continental Commands, 1821–1890, Record Group 393, National Archives; *Easton Gazette*, May 13, 1865); see also below.

50. Henry Hawkins paid for his temerity. The *Baltimore American* of May 18, 1867, carried the following:

"Petty Revenge on a Colored Delegate—Henry C. Hawkins, one of the colored delegates who addressed the Republican Convention on Tuesday last, was at the time the employee of a business firm on West Baltimore Street. On Wednesday morning, the day after the Convention, while Hawkins was sweeping out the store, he was accosted by one of the members of the firm with the remarks, 'I don't want any negro politicians here; anyone who makes a speech like yours should be sent to the penitentiary for life!' The man was discharged for differing with his employers. To the honor of the Democracy we will state that the men who were guilty of this petty spite are what we call 'Conservatives.' We have heard of several cases where colored men have been threatened with discharge from employment if they join any of the Union Leagues or Republican Associations."

51. Ibid. A. Ward Handy served in the Union Army in the 4th United States Colored Troops where he rose to the rank of sergeant and was an active participant in Republican Party affairs in 1867 and 1868 (Leroy Graham, *Baltimore: The Nineteenth Century Black Capital*, 153, 161, 181ff., 259).

52. *Baltimore American*, May 15, 1867.

53. Ibid.

54. Ibid., May 31, 1867.

55. *Baltimore County Free Press*, n.d., quoted in *Baltimore American*, July 6, 1867; *Salisbury New Era*, n.d., quoted in *Baltimore Gazette*, July 24, 1867.

56. *Baltimore American*, May 31, 1867.

57. Ibid., September 13, 1867.

58. Ibid.

59. Ibid.

60. Ibid., October 8, 11, 1867.

61. Testimony in Investigation of the Government of Maryland, United States Congress, House of Representatives, Committee on the Judiciary, Record Group 233.

62. *Baltimore American*, November 5, 6, 7, 8, 9, 11, 1867.

63. Ibid., March 7, 12, 1868.

64. Ibid., May 11, 1868.

65. Ibid., May 15, 1868.

66. *New York Tribune*, March 12, 1868.

67. The debate between the two Republican factions received detailed coverage in the press between February and July of 1868. See especially *Baltimore American*, February 17, 18, 25, 26, 28, 29, March 2, 4, 6, 7, 12, April 9, 14, 15, 16, 17, 22, 27, 30, May 4, 7, 8, 9, 11, 14, 15, 18, 21, June 30, July 8, 1868.

68. Ibid.

69. Ibid. Democrats accused Bond and his supporters also of trying to swing the Maryland Republican Party to the presidential candidacy of Salmon P. Chase. The judge's detractors maintained that he was not at all interested in blacks' welfare and that he was using them to pursue purely political ends. Throughout the campaign, Bond denied these charges. He claimed to be a

firm supporter of Ulysses S. Grant and said that his efforts to include blacks in party affairs were aimed solely at obtaining a firm Republican commitment to universal suffrage (*Baltimore American*, March 7, 12, 1868).

70. *Baltimore American*, February 17, 1868.

71. Ibid.

72. Ibid., February 27, March 6, 1868.

73. Ibid., February 28, 29, 1868.

74. Ibid., February 29, 1868.

75. Ibid.

76. Ibid.

77. Ibid., March 4, 1868.

78. Ibid.

79. Ibid., March 7, 1868.

80. Ibid.

81. *New York Tribune*, n.d., quoted in *Baltimore American*, March 12, 1868.

82. *Baltimore American*, April 16, 1868.

83. Ibid., April 17, 1868.

84. Ibid.

85. Ibid.

86. Ibid., May 15, 1868.

87. Ibid., October 8, 1867.

88. Ibid., May 7, 1868.

89. Ibid.

90. Ibid., June 30, 1868.

91. Ibid.

92. Ibid.

93. Amendment XV [1870], Section I, "The right of citizens of the United States to vote shall not be denied or abridged by the United States or by any State on account of race, color, or previous condition of servitude."

8

Black Society

I

On November 17, 1864, Frederick Douglass addressed an "immense audience" in "Big Bethel" A.M.E. Church. A few days later, he addressed an overflow crowd at the Baptist Church at the corner of Saratoga and Calvert Streets. The next night he spoke to a similar gathering in the Temperance Temple on North Gay Street, on the twenty-fifth, he lectured at the Dallas Street Methodist Episcopal Church, and in early December he traveled to Havre de Grace in Harford County. Pausing only briefly, he spoke again at Bethel Church on February 22, 1865, on March 1, at Sharp Street Methodist Episcopal Church, and on June 14, at Madison Street Presbyterian Church.[1] Everywhere the message was the same: "I return to you with freedom in my hand. . . . The billows of slavery are rolling back to leave the land blooming again in the purer air of liberty and justice."[2]

Emancipation accelerated such celebration. Freedom alone proved sufficient cause for spontaneous public occasion and in a deeper sense it empowered blacks with a new capacity to define the contours of both their personal and collective lives.[3] The effect of these emancipation celebrations was marked. The excitement and enthusiasm they engendered served to make them exceptionally popular forms of expression and entertainment. Between 1864 and 1868, dozens of public meetings across the state attracted thousands of spectators. Particularly successful were the rallies sponsored by the Freedmen's Bureau and the Baltimore Association for the Moral and Educational Improvement of the Colored People. In 1866 and 1867, the Bureau and the Association sponsored more than twenty such meetings in the rural counties alone. Featuring speeches by Edgar Gregory, Hugh Lennox Bond, and other prominent radicals, these occasions often drew more than a thousand people.[4]

In addition to white-sponsored activities, blacks organized celebrations of their own. Almost all of Frederick Douglass's appearances during the winter of 1864–65 were sponsored by the black community. With the end of the war, blacks conducted parades, fairs, and ceremonial sword presentations to welcome local regiments of United States Colored Troops.[5] In April 1865, black regiments paraded as part of the escort for the remains of Abraham Lincoln.[6] All of these occasions drew crowds of spectators onto the streets in celebration of emancipation and the end of the war, or in commemoration of the dead president, and as the next few years passed, the anniversaries of the events occasioned renewed festivity and ceremony.

As was the case with public addresses, black-organized celebrations and ceremonial occasions in Baltimore became a vital part of blacks' social life. Between 1864 and 1868, city blacks attended a wide variety of special public events that included the opening of the Douglass Institute in September 1865, a celebration of Lincoln's emancipation proclamation in October 1865, the Semi-Centenary Celebration of the African Methodist Episcopal Church in April 1866, and, in July 1867, a grand parade in honor of Schuyler Colfax and Thaddeus Stevens.[7] In addition to these citywide events, there were numerous smaller ones sponsored by individual clubs and societies. Intended principally for the benefit of smaller numbers of people, the combined effect of these events contributed significantly to what had become an active social environment.[8]

Nor were rural blacks left behind in celebrating their own events. In June 1865, in Chestertown, Kent County, in Easton, Talbot County, and in other communities on the Eastern Shore and in southern Maryland, hundreds of black farm laborers gathered for the traditional Whitsuntide holiday. In August of that year, an estimated three thousand blacks in Frederick County met to celebrate emancipation, and on several occasions in 1866 and 1867, blacks from counties close to Washington visited the capital to participate in parades and anniversary celebrations.[9] In the years immediately following emancipation, blacks in the rural areas of the state also held numerous community parades, picnics, fairs, and other social gatherings that, along with more formal religious and educational activities, competed for a large portion of what little leisure time they could afford.[10]

II

Although many of these events in both Baltimore and the tidewater counties sprang from such special occasions as emancipation and the end of the war, others grew from the regular programs of black churches, benevolent and fraternal societies, social clubs, and military regiments. Some of these organizations had been in existence for years, others began after emancipation, but old or new, all played a vital role in the lives of their rural and city members. The excitement over freedom might provide the catalyst for celebration, but it was the organizational strength of black associations and societies that translated specific enthusiasm into new and lasting social patterns.

Of special importance in this regard were churches. Traditionally the chief source of solace, spiritual fulfillment, and entertainment, black religious institutions offered the best facilities, the most educated leaders, and the greatest experience of any black organizations. In both Baltimore and the rural counties, churches stood as one of the few social institutions that brought blacks together regularly in significant numbers. As such they were well positioned to assume a leading role in the post-emancipation black community.

Religious worship had long served as an emotional support for slaves and free blacks alike. Enthusiastic preaching, singing, and congregational participation had played an integral part in the lives of black Marylanders for more than a century, and in this fashion had provided them a buffer against the more brutal aspects of slavery and plantation labor. Certainly this function of black churches continued after emancipation. Indeed, freedom lent even greater intensity to what was already a highly emotional experience. As legal restrictions were repealed, revivals, church dedicatory ceremonies, and especially rural camp meetings provided blacks with renewed opportunities to express their religious fervor.[11]

But churches provided blacks with more than religious worship, joyous as it might be. In their vital position in Baltimore and rural communities, churches were also well situated to serve the general social life of their parishioners. Possessing such physical requirements for community activities as buildings and rooms, and having the experience of long association and connection with almost every person in their neighborhoods, churches and their pastors stood as logical leaders in black Marylanders' search for a richer and more active social life.

In 1864, the great majority of blacks in Maryland were Methodists, most of whom belonged to either the independent, all-black African

Methodist Episcopal Church or to the black conferences of the Methodist Episcopal Church (North). The oldest of the two institutions in terms of independent black control was the A.M.E. Church. Founded in Philadelphia as a black offshoot from white Methodism, it expanded rapidly into neighboring states. By 1864, the Baltimore Conference of the A.M.E. Church, with congregations in Baltimore, Washington, and rural Maryland, boasted a membership of over six thousand parishioners.[12] Its leading Maryland churches were those in Baltimore. "Big Bethel," at the corner of Saratoga and Gay Streets, was the center of A.M.E. activity in the city, with smaller congregations at Ebeneezer Church on Montgomery Street east of Hanover, Union Bethel on Wolfe Street south of Pratt, and Waters Chapel on Spring Street between Jefferson and McElderry.[13]

In the years immediately following emancipation, A.M.E. leadership in Baltimore was second to none in promoting black religious, social, and political life. In 1864, Alexander W. Wayman, pastor of "Big Bethel," became a bishop in the church, adding prominence to Baltimore's A.M.E. community.[14] Benjamin Tanner, Wayman's successor at Bethel, became one of black Baltimore's most active leaders. Prominent in church work, politics, and literary circles, Tanner served regularly as secretary of the Baltimore Conference, played an active role in Republican state conventions and, in 1867, wrote a book entitled *An Apology for African Methodism*.[15] Other prominent A.M.E. officials and church members were the Reverend William H. G. Brown, William Matthews, and the Reverend James A. Handy.[16]

Alongside the accomplishments of its pastors and leading members, Bethel Church itself—the building—contributed greatly to black Baltimoreans' religious and social life. It competed with the Douglass Institute as the most popular meeting place for public lectures, fairs, celebrations, and ceremonial occasions. Between 1864 and 1868, under the direction of pastors Benjamin T. Tanner and Savage L. Hammond, Bethel Church opened its doors not only to the religious activities of thousands of black Baltimoreans but also to functions that catered to their entertainment, education, and political interests. In the winter of 1864–1865, overflow audiences filled the building at several times to hear public speakers, and on two occasions to attend fund-raising fairs for the benefit of the poor.[17] During the next two years, Bethel Church remained at the center of community activities:

Bethel Church, 1865–1867

August 24, 1865	—Mass meeting "to consider the condition and wants of the freed people of the South." Speaker: Rev. James Lynch.
February 4, 1866	—Lecture by Rev. Bishop Daniel A. Payne (A.M.E. Church) on behalf of the Baltimore Association for the Moral and Educational Improvement of the Colored People.
February 9, 1866	—Lecture by Frederick Douglass. Subject: "Reconstruction."
March 8, 1866	—Temperance Lecture by "THE BLACK JOHN B. GOUGH." Subject: "The Drunkard's Son."
April 8–16, 1866	—Semi-Centenary Celebration of the African Methodist Episcopal Church.
December 13, 1866	—Mass meeting sponsored by the Baltimore Association for the Moral and Educational Improvement of the Colored People.
December 25, 1866	—Fund raising fair under auspices of Women's Colored State Union Fair Association.
March 13, 1867	—Public Lecture by Rev. Bishop A. W. Wayman (A.M.E. Church) on return from tour of South.
July 9, 1867	—Public Lecture by William Howard Day, for benefit of Widows' Home.
August 26, 1867	— Public Lecture by John M. Langston of the Freedmen's Bureau. Subject: Education.[18]

In rural counties, A.M.E. churches served similar functions. In Hagerstown and Cumberland, for example, black groups and societies made regular use of these buildings. On June 27, 1867, the black Masonic Order of Hagerstown concluded a day of parades, music, and celebration with closing exercises and speeches in the rooms of the A.M.E. church. A week later in Cumberland, over three hundred people filled the A.M.E. church to hear representatives from the Baltimore Association and to inaugurate plans for a new school.[19] Between 1864 and 1868, similar events occurred in many other rural communities. A.M.E. churches served as places of worship, schools, meeting houses, and concert halls. To its numerous parishioners as well as to blacks of other religious denominations, the African Methodist Episcopal Church offered encouragement and facilities for a wide variety of black Marylanders' social and community activities.

Of equal stature to the A.M.E. Church in Maryland were the black conferences of the Methodist Episcopal Church (North). The M. E. Church comprised the largest single body of Methodists in the United States and its membership was primarily white. Prior to 1864, Maryland's Methodist churches belonged to either the Baltimore, East Baltimore, or Philadelphia Conferences. All three had black church members, some who attended white services and others with congregations of their own.[20]

In 1864, at the M. E. General Conference that year in Philadelphia, black delegates successfully petitioned for the establishment of two all-black conferences to cover the Maryland area. Beginning on October 31, 1864, black Methodist churches in Washington, D.C., and all of Maryland except the Eastern Shore, constituted the Washington Conference, and those on the Eastern Shore a part of the Delaware Conference of the Methodist Episcopal Church.[21] With this step, black congregations won complete autonomy from white churches in the state, answering only to the General Conference.

The fact that black Methodists' independence occurred just a day before Governor Bradford's emancipation proclamation did much to heighten the significance of the two new conferences. It was as if freedom and the new church structure had approached their realization hand in hand, and that black M. E. churches were destined to lead black Marylanders into the post-emancipation world. On October 31, 1864, while presiding over the first annual meeting of the Washington Conference, Bishop Levi Scott (white) told his listeners, "there is [much] in the fact that the day on which [this] first Conference closes, is the day on which the dominion of slavery ceases."[22]

But the importance of the black Methodist Episcopal conferences stemmed from more than their auspicious beginnings. It grew also from the size of their membership. In 1864, the new Washington Conference included seventeen churches and 7,877 parishioners. Five of the largest congregations were in Baltimore. Sharp Street, Asbury, Orchard Street, Dallas Street, and John Wesley M. E. churches accounted for more than 3,600 members.[23] In addition to these, there were Washington Conference churches in Anne Arundel, Frederick, Allegany, Calvert, and Prince George's Counties.[24]

The Maryland churches in the Delaware Conference were all on the Eastern Shore. With a combined membership of five thousand parishioners (including churches in parts of Delaware and Pennsylvania) the conference included churches or traveling circuits in almost every Eastern Shore county. These were organized under two major divisions, the Eastern District and the Choptank District. Several of the one-minister travelling circuits had as many members as the large Methodist churches in Baltimore. Pocomoke Circuit (Worcester County) in the Choptank District, for example, had six hundred members, and the Manoken Circuit in neighboring Somerset County—also a part of Choptank—had four hundred.[25]

Like the African Methodist Episcopal Church, the Washington and Delaware M. E. Conferences proved to be of vital importance to the religious, educational, and social life of the black community. Such men as James H. Harper, Stephen Tascoe, and Perry G. Walker, all Baltimore pastors, provided both religious and secular leadership. Their churches and those of their colleagues in the tidewater counties offered places for worship, schools, and public meetings. Sharp Street Church in Baltimore vied with the Douglass Institute and "Big Bethel" as a favored location for public lectures, celebrations, and ceremonies. Throughout Maryland, M. E. churches were pressed into service by the Baltimore Association and the Freedmen's Bureau for their mass educational and political meetings. On the Eastern Shore particularly, where black farm workers had no other place they could call their own, churches provided the focal point of much of their nonworking lives.[26]

No other religious denomination had a black membership as large as the A.M.E. or M. E. Churches. The Baptist, Presbyterian, Catholic, Protestant Episcopal, and A.M.E. Zion Churches all had black parishioners but their total number, in each case, was relatively small. During the first four years after emancipation, there were three Baptist congregations in Baltimore, one Protestant Episcopal, one Presbyterian, one Catholic, and one A.M.E. Zion.[27] The largest of these denominations, the Baptists, had a total membership in the city of slightly over three hundred and no members or churches at all in the rural counties.[28] The Saint James 1st African Protestant Episcopal Church at the corner of North and Saratoga Streets had a congregation of fewer than a hundred, as did also the Madison Street Presbyterian (Colored) Church on Madison Street near Park, the Roman Catholic St. Francis Xavier Chapel at the corner of Calvert and Pleasant Streets, and the A.M.E. Zion Church at South Howard and Montgomery.[29] In the rural counties, all of these denominations tried to encourage black membership but only the Protestant Episcopal Church (P. E.) enjoyed much success. Even here, the figures were small. Between 1864 and 1868, annual black membership in all P. E. churches amounted to little more than two hundred people.[30]

Nevertheless, since smaller city and rural churches—like their larger counterparts—could offer space for schools, lectures, meetings, and other activities, their contribution to the black community was substantial. Many of the leaders of these institutions provided energetic leadership out of proportion to the relatively small sizes of their congregation. Harrison H. Webb, pastor of St. James P. E. Church in Baltimore, and Noah Davis, of Saratoga Street Baptist Church in the same city, were but two such men who made their churches centers of not only religious worship but also education, entertainment, and community activism.[31] From these beginnings grew social, religious, and benevolent societies that were as effective as those of bigger churches, and to the participants equally important.[32]

III

The connection between emancipation and religion was undeniably strong but freedom offered more than the chance to celebrate or worship in churches and encouraged wider community activity than that provided by institutions primarily concerned with religious matters. Often, the only connection between churches and blacks' social activities during these years was the physical space that the former provided for meetings, lectures, and classes. In fact, most black associations, clubs, or societies were distinctly separate from churches. In both Baltimore and the tidewater counties, numerous independent secular groups sought deliberately to provide a type of entertainment, instruction, or security that could not be found in any religious institution. Some of these organizations, especially those in Baltimore, were new and direct reflections of post-emancipation life. All of them played a vital role in the social life of black Marylanders.

Of the older, traditional groups, "social" clubs and fraternal and benevolent societies stood out. A majority of blacks in the city of Baltimore belonged to at least one of these types of organizations and many to all three. In the rural areas of the state these societies were fewer, but in several locations black clubs flourished, especially in county villages and towns.[33] Of the three associations, benevolent societies were the most common. Comprised of anywhere from a dozen to more than a hundred members, they sought specifically to provide blacks with a modicum of financial security. Benevolent societies offered blacks the chance to meet with others, collect general funds, and pay for such items as funeral expenses or hospital costs. A few doubled as social clubs, with meeting halls and regular schedules of events. Several benevolent societies were incorporated under acts of the state legislature.[34]

Because of its large population of blacks, many of whom had been free for some time, Baltimore possessed the great majority of Maryland's black benevolent societies. Some stemmed from particular trades or occupations, some from specific religious groups, and others simply from local neighborhoods. Their names revealed the nature of both membership and intent. In 1867, the Freedmen's Savings and Trust Company listed nineteen such societies as depositors:

Musicians Social and Beneficial Association
First Young Men's Lincoln Beneficial Association
Union Aid Beneficial Society
The Mary Small Beneficial Society
The Rising Star Beneficial Society
The Old Women's Relief Society
First Carthaginian Beneficial Society
The First Baltimore Colored Barbers' Beneficial Society
Good Intent Beneficial Society
Friendship Beneficial Society
Phillip Lee's Double Beneficial Society
Evening Star Benevolent Society
Coachmen's Harmonious Aid Society
1st Laborers' Beneficial Association
National Relief Association
Preachers' Aid Society
United Female Beneficial Society
Union Musicians' Practical Beneficial Society[35]

In the rural counties, benevolent societies were active in such centers as Chestertown, Annapolis, Frederick, Cumberland, and Hagerstown. In 1866, the General Assembly passed an act incorporating the Colored Peoples' Beneficial Society of Hagerstown. The next year it did the same for the Beneficial Society of the Laboring Sons of Frederick City (Colored).[36] In April 1867, the Colored Soldiers Protective Association of Annapolis paraded with other Maryland groups in Washing-

ton in celebration of the anniversary of emancipation in the District of
Columbia. In June of that year, the Brown Benevolent Association of
Michaelsville, Harford County, sponsored a celebration with music, a
parade, and several public speeches. A year later, five black benevolent
societies in Chestertown, Kent County, did the same.[37]

The makeup or constitution of these organizations was straightfor-
ward. The Act of 1866 that incorporated the Hagerstown society stated
simply:

> Be it enacted . . . That Henry Darks, Charles Reeder, Jacob Wheeton,
> Jeremiah Farmer, Lloyd Morgan, Samuel Lake, Cornelius Green and
> the officers and members of the Colored Laboring Sons and Daughters
> Beneficial Society of Hagerstown . . . be and they are hereby declared a
> body politic for the objects and intentions of said society which are
> hereby declared to be for mutual aid and assistance and benevolent pur-
> poses generally.[38]

To effect their "objects and intentions," the members of the Hagerstown society were permitted to "require such dues and fines as may be
necessary; . . . receive donations, invest their funds in stocks, personal
or real estate, or in such manner as they or a majority of them, may
deem best."[39]

But the financial side of these groups' activities was only one way in
which they contributed to the betterment of black Marylanders. Of
greater importance in terms of blacks' purely social lives were benevolent societies' numerous parades, celebrations, and ceremonial occasions. Like churches, these organizations provided members in both
Baltimore and the rural counties with numerous opportunities for
group or community activities. Close association in financial affairs led
to similar relationships in other areas, and since fund-raising projects
were of special importance, benevolent societies often reached out to
the entire black community.[40]

Some society-sponsored events were quite elaborate. In August
1867, the *Cumberland Civilian* described one such occasion in its city,
saying:

> Last Thursday the anniversary of the Emancipation Proclamation was
> generally observed by our colored citizens as a holiday. The members of
> the colored beneficial societies . . . marched through our streets in a
> long procession, clothed in their regalia, attended by martial music and
> carrying the national colors. They then repaired to [a] farm . . . where
> they spent the day in joy and amusement.[41]

On June 6, 1868, the *Chestertown Transcript* described a similar event:

> The procession headed by the Society of "Sons and Daughters" moved from William Perkins Hall through the main street to the colored M. E. Church. In the line were the following societies: "Sisters of Love and Friendship," "Mount Vernon Society," "Brothers of Love and Charity No. 3," and the "Society of Rising Youth." Reaching the church at about 3 o'clock P.M., the societies were addressed by Rev. Thomas J. Murray. . . . At 8 P.M., the societies were again addressed by the Rev. Mr. Stubbs. The contributions received upon the occasion amount to about $125.[42]

Nor was the purpose of such occasions necessarily purely social. Often, benevolent society celebrations doubled as political or educational mass meetings. Dr. C. H. Ohr, a white radical, addressed the August 1867 meeting in Cumberland. William Perkins, a black leader prominent in Republican Party, Baltimore Association, and Freedmen's Bureau work, was a manager of the June 1868 celebration in Chestertown. In June 1867, a Harford County benevolent society gathering featured the presence of black politicians A. Ward Handy and George Hackett. Hackett delivered "a stirring Radical speech," and Handy "addressed the audience appropriately on the great questions of the day."[43] Sometimes, the process reversed itself. When the Baltimore Association and Freedmen's Bureau called an educational-political meeting for a certain area, black benevolent societies often used such an event as a pretext for a meeting or procession of their own.

Similar in some of their functions to benevolent societies, although fewer and much larger, were black fraternal associations. Two principal ones stood out: the United Order of Odd Fellows and the Masons. Each of these orders boasted lodges in Baltimore and in several rural counties with combined memberships of over a thousand men. Understandably, Baltimore possessed the largest and most active groups, but several county towns had sizable organizations as well. Black Masons in Easton, Talbot County, were sufficiently organized to have their own lodge and school buildings. Masonic chapters in Havre de Grace, Harford County, and Salisbury, Somerset County, were similarly well off. Annapolis had an active Odd Fellows lodge that between 1864 and 1868 conducted several excursions, parades, and celebrations.[44]

Black fraternal associations operated in the same fashion as benevolent societies, providing financial security for members as well as serving as community organizations to promote various forms of entertainment. In this capacity, Masons and Odd Fellows were particularly active. On October 6, 1865, the Baltimore lodges of the United Order of Odd Fellows sponsored what was by all accounts the biggest black parade the city had ever seen. Called to celebrate the seventeenth anniversary of the black Odd Fellow organization, the parade included members of eight Baltimore lodges and representatives from Washington, D.C.; Alexandria, Virginia; Wilmington, Delaware; and Norristown and Philadelphia, Pennsylvania. Also in the procession were three brass bands, an honor guard with the ark and emblems of the order, and an eight-horse dray carrying orphan children under the charge of the Grand Lodge. In all, over six hundred people participated in the parade. When the marchers completed their route, which had taken them along the principal streets of the city, they gathered amidst a huge throng of spectators at Monument Square to hear speeches and muster out. The *Baltimore American* thought the celebration was hugely successful and was particularly impressed with "rich regalia" and "beautiful banners of costly silk."[45]

The Masons or Odd Fellows offered black Marylanders a taste of social life normally enjoyed by whites only. When the October 1865 Odd Fellows parade terminated its route in Baltimore's Monument Square, one of the speakers, black politician James H. Jordan, remarked on the "quiet and peaceful enjoyment of their new privileges," and referred to the "great change" brought by emancipation. Blacks engaged in things now, he said, that before November 1, 1864, would have been impossible. "In former years," Jordan reminded his listeners, "such display as that made [today] would have provoked violent reaction."[46] The Odd Fellows' parade with all of its regalia and banners thus signified something new. As the *Baltimore Gazette* pointed out, "Monument Square had packed into it the largest collection of blacks ever assembled since Maryland joined herself with the original colonies."[47]

Such a large and open display of black Marylanders' new social freedom as that presented by the Baltimore Odd Fellows extended far beyond the capacity of small benevolent associations to organize. On occasion the latter might band together for parades and ceremonies, but at no time between 1864 and 1870 could they muster the numbers of the large fraternal orders. As vehicles for expressing the independent spirit attached to emancipation, the Odd Fellows and Masons were particularly successful. Well established and organized, they possessed the leadership, experience, and financial resources necessary to make blacks' new independence visible on a wide-scale basis.

In addition, high posts in fraternal orders attracted some of Maryland's leading black citizens. George A. Hackett, a Baltimore coal dealer and Republican politician, held an important rank in the United Order of Odd Fellows, and for parades and other celebrations he served as its Grand Marshal.[48] W. H. Wood, another black Republican, was a Grand Inspector in one of Baltimore's several Masonic Lodges. Also prominent in the City's Odd Fellow or Masonic organizations were the Reverends James Handy and William Brown of the African Methodist Episcopal Church, and Samuel W. Chase, Jr., a fifteenth Ward cabinetmaker and politician.[49] The presence of these men served to tie fraternal orders closely to such other major areas of black interest and concern as religion, politics, and education, and thus further strengthened the orders' role as representatives of black Marylanders' social progress.

In addition to Odd Fellows and Masons, other smaller fraternal orders in both Baltimore and the rural counties carried such biblical and historical names as the Sons and Daughters of Mount Tabor, Hannibal Lodge No. 1, and Union Bethel Lodge. These groups attracted small memberships and usually confined their activities to a specific neighborhood or rural community. Many of them combined benevolent functions with their fraternal structure, and some purely social clubs offered weekly dances or "balls" to supplement the activities of their more formal associations. Alone, the contribution of each of these smaller groups was minimal, but in combination with that of larger groups, it became a vital part of blacks' social life. Along with Masons and Odd Fellows, small societies played a key role in providing blacks with activities they otherwise might not have enjoyed.[50]

IV

None of these social institutions, churches, benevolent associations, clubs, or fraternal orders were new in 1864. They enjoyed, certainly, a tremendous rejuvenation after emancipation, and they assumed the lead in celebrating the fact of freedom, but in each case their organization, or at least their type of organization dated well back into the nineteenth century. Particularly in Baltimore, where thousands of blacks had been free for years, all of these societies and organizations were common well before 1864, although they were certainly not as visible.[51]

One vital new institution did, however, develop from the forces of war and emancipation: the black military club or militia. Beginning in 1865, United States Colored Troop veterans in Baltimore organized several completely equipped military regiments. Within months of their inception, these associations had become major factors in the social and political life of the black community. Since 1863, more than ten thousand black Marylanders had fought in the United States Army and Navy. Most of these men had enlisted or had been conscripted into the fourth, seventh, or thirty-ninth Regiments of the United States Colored Troops. In 1865 and 1866, these regiments were mustered out in Baltimore.[52] In addition to these soldiers there were a few companies of Negro militia that General Lew Wallace had raised in 1864 in response to the state's refusal to admit blacks into the regular Maryland militia.[53]

In April 1865, black Marylanders tried to gain admittance to the state militia, but were rejected. The door to participation in the all-white official militia was closed and it would remain so. Between 1865 and 1870, the question of black militia enlistment came up several times in the state legislature, but lawmakers did nothing to reverse their decision of 1864.[54] In the face of this rejection, black soldiers in Baltimore decided to start their own organizations. Building on the framework of Lew Wallace's wartime precedent and the equipment—including muskets—that they had purchased from the United States Army at a minimal fee, they gathered together as many volunteers as they could find, and established several regiments of black troops. These organizations used the Douglass Institute, Mount Vernon Hall, and any other available space for their armories, and soon after their formation, paraded along Baltimore's streets in new uniforms made by their wives or friends and with the firearms they had acquired from the United States government.[55]

The first black militia unit to appear on the scene was the Lincoln Zouaves, Corps d'Afrique, which on December 14, 1865, served as an honor guard at a reception in the Douglass Institute for the recently mustered out thirty-ninth Regiment, United States Colored Troops.[56] Several months later, they turned out at a similar occasion in honor of the fourth Regiment, U.S.C.T. After the soldiers' arrival in Baltimore on May 9, 1866, the Lincoln Zouaves escorted them through the city's streets. The next day, black citizens held a reception for the regiment at the Douglass Institute. Again, the Zouaves took part, escorting the troops from their barracks into the center of the city.[57]

Other black regiments in Baltimore formed soon after the Lincoln Zouaves. In April 1867, the Oakland Invincible Guards marched in Washington, D.C., in the grand emancipation celebration on the sixteenth of that month. On June 24, 1867, the Hugh Lennox Bond Militia held its first drill in Mount Vernon Hall, the Lincoln Zouaves' armory at the corner of Howard and Franklin Streets. On August 2, the Henry Winter Davis Guards held their first parade with five full companies and a brass band. Three weeks later, the Butler Guards of South Baltimore made their appearance as the honor guard for a public lecture at Bethel A.M.E. Church.[58]

Among the black community, these regiments were immensely popular. By 1867, both the Lincoln Zouaves and the Henry Winter Davis Guards boasted a membership of more than a thousand men, and the smaller units counted at least two hundred in each.[59] This popularity extended also to black Baltimoreans who were not militia members. Crowds of spectators lined city streets to see these regiments on parade and to celebrate the martial air of brass bands and brilliant uniforms. The Lincoln Zouaves and Oakland Invincibles, for example, put on particularly colorful displays. The uniform of the Zouaves featured a light blue tunic trimmed with orange and white, and baggy white leggings. The Invincible outfits were equally resplendent with yellow and dark blue predominating.[60] To black citizens, the sight of such brightly clothed black soldiers marching freely with firearms along Baltimore's principal streets was an occasion of great pride. Such an exhibition offered even more joyous proof of their freedom than did Odd Fellows' or Masons' parades.

In blacks' pride at the sight of black military regiments lay much of the reason for the latter's widespread appeal. But it was not simply a question of brass bands and bright uniforms. Color and ceremony were important, but they represented something far deeper. Essentially, military activities of any sort symbolized equality with whites in a manner that no other organization or institution could. Combined in the weekly drills of black militiamen were the pride and stature that came from their service in the United States Army and the hope that such could be extended into their post-emancipation lives. On September 3,

1867, Archibald Stirling, Jr. told a mass encampment of black regiments:

> The question of [equality] was settled when the soldiers, black and white, marched against the common enemy, laid down their lives and souls and ascended to the same God. The significance of our being here today is that it shows that colored men are ready to bear the duties of [full] citizenship.[61]

In their capacity as symbolic leaders of blacks' search for equality, military associations played a key role in most of black Marylanders' important community activities. After 1866, Baltimore's most popular parades were those of black regiments. At almost every black ceremony or celebration in the city, the Lincoln Zouaves or some other regiment served as the honor guard. Nor was Baltimore the only location for such activities. Black militia companies flourished in several tidewater counties, and their armories, as well as those in the city, became institutions that competed with the church and lodge as places for relaxation, entertainment, and community meetings. Companies drilled two or three times a week, held public lectures, and sponsored dances, promenades, picnics, and fund-raising fairs.[62]

In fact, the Lincoln Zouaves of Baltimore sponsored one of the largest single black social events of the period 1864 to 1868. Starting on September 2, 1867, the regiment staged a "grand encampment" on the grounds of the Gregory Aged Women's Home at the west end of Townsend Street in Baltimore. The event extended over three days, featuring parades to and from the grounds, military drills and exhibitions, public addresses, band music, and fireworks. Every day, close to two thousand black Baltimoreans came to view the festivities. The *Baltimore American* complimented the Zouaves on their "familiarity with martial evolutions" and had high praise for the "*corps d'esprit* [sic] of the command." It was also impressed by the "brilliant illumination and the recreations and amusements . . . so numerous and [so] varied."[63]

Typically, the emphasis of the Zouave encampment was not purely social. Just as the churches, Odd Fellows, Masons, and other smaller beneficial and fraternal societies combined pleasure with community concern, so too did military regiments. Present at the Zouave encampment were black leaders—one of them, George A. Hackett, was a captain in the Butler Guards—white radical politicians, and officers of the

Freedmen's Bureau. Edgar Gregory, Archibald Stirling, Jr., and Captain M. H. Maroney, of the United States Army delivered major addresses. Speeches focused on black Marylanders' economic, political, and educational concerns. The remarks of General Gregory were perhaps the most forceful. "The sufferings endured by the Union soldiers during the rebellion," he said, "were not intended to save the life of the nation, but were [to ensure] that four million people for whom Christ died might be set at liberty for ever." Gregory went on to stress the value of education, and as a conclusion to the assistant commissioner's remarks, Archibald Stirling, Jr. added a clarion call for universal suffrage. "The time is not too far distant," he declared, "when you and I can rally around the same ballot box and there plant our tickets."[64]

Through such activities as the Zouave encampment, black military regiments reflected the factors present in black Marylanders' search for a meaningful post-emancipation life. The parades, uniforms, and muskets combined blacks' desire for an active social life and the determination to devote their nonworking hours to the educational, economic, and political betterment of their community. In their various functions, black military regiments epitomized pursuits common to all black social institutions. Together with churches, benevolent associations, and fraternal orders, they sought to combine enjoyment with progress.

V

The years 1864 to 1870 witnessed in Maryland an active, indeed dynamic, black social revival. Emancipation and the repeal of black-code restrictions provided the means, but blacks' longing for a better society in which to live supplied the movement its real force. So much of this longing, of course, was for a share of activities hitherto available only to whites, but if black social activity during this period had any one theme, it was the celebration of new possibilities and the hope for happiness that only freedom—and full equality—could bring.

Perhaps no other institution expressed such new possibilities more forcefully than did the Douglass Institute. In 1865, a group of black leaders purchased a building on the north side of Lexington Street between Davis and North. The structure, formerly the Newton University, and occupied during the war by a United States Army hospital, cost $16,000 plus $5,000 for renovations.[65] When completed, it housed a lecture hall, library, music department, and several classrooms. The Institute served as a multipurpose center for lectures, conventions, mass meetings, and other community functions.

On September 29, 1865, Frederick Douglass visited Baltimore to dedicate the Institute, thereby opening what was to become the center of blacks' intellectual and cultural life for years to come. "This occasion is one of no ordinary character," he said.

> The establishment of such an Institute . . . is the indication of the rise of a people . . . bound in the chains of ignorance to a freer and higher plane of life, manhood, usefulness, and civilization. . . . It implies that the colored people of Baltimore not only have the higher qualities attributed to the white race, but that they are awaking to a healthy consciousness of those qualities in themselves, and that they are beginning to see, as the dark cloud of slavery rolls away, the necessity of bringing those qualities into vigorous exercise. It implies an increased knowledge of the requirements of a high civilization, and a determination to comply with them. This Institute, in character and design, . . . represents the abilities and possibilities of our race.[66]

NOTES

1. *Baltimore American*, November 21, 23, 24, 26, 1864, February 18, 21, June 14, 1865; *Liberator*, November 25, 1864; J. Lockwood to S. B. Lawrence, November 28, 1864, RG 393, Middle Department, Volume 85, Letter Book, March 24, 1864–December 31, 1864.

2. *Baltimore American*, November 19, 1864.

3. *The Maryland Code of Public General Laws [1860]* (Baltimore, 1860), 450–68; *Journal of Proceedings of the House of Delegates, January Session 1865* (Annapolis, 1865), 752; *Journal of Proceedings of the Senate of Maryland, January Session 1865* (Annapolis, 1865), 385–86; *Laws of the State of Maryland [1865]* (Annapolis, 1865), 305–7.

4. *Annapolis Gazette*, April 26, 1866; *Baltimore American*, May 22, 1866, July 6, 30, August 24, September 5, 1867; *Baltimore Gazette*, September 7, 9, 1867; *Baltimore Sun*, September 10, 1867; Special Order 125, RG 105, D.C., Book Records, Special Orders, Assistant Commissioner, 1867.

5. *Baltimore American*, November 21, 23, 1864, December 14, 15, 1865, May 10, 11, 1866; *Baltimore Sun*, December 15, 16, 1865, May 10, 1866; *Baltimore Gazette*, May 10, 1866; *Liberator*, November 25, 1864. Some of Douglass' sponsors were the Sharp Street Methodist Episcopal Church, The

Unions State Fair Association (Colored), Temperance Temple, Dallas Street Methodist Episcopal Church, and the Colored Ladies Union [State Fair] Association.

6. *Baltimore American,* April 21, 22, 1865.

7. *Baltimore American,* September 28, 29, 1865, April 6, 14, 1866, July 3, 4, 1867; *Baltimore Gazette,* September 29, 30, October 6, 1865, July 3, 1867; *Baltimore Sun,* September 30, 1865, July 3, 1867.

8. See below.

9. *Frederick Examiner,* August 30, 1865; *Chestertown Transcript,* June 10, 1865; *Baltimore Sun,* June 8, 12, 1865, April 16, 17, 1867; *Baltimore American,* June 20, 1865, April 5, 17, 1867.

10. *Annapolis Gazette,* August 9, 1866, August 1, 1867; *Baltimore American,* May 9, June 20, 27, 28, July 30, August 1, 3, 5, 6, 10, September 3, 1867, June 8, 1868; *Baltimore Sun,* May 9, July 30, August 3, 6, 29, 31, 1867; *Baltimore Gazette,* July 30, August 3, 6, 9, 24, 1867; *Frederick Examiner,* August 7, 21, 28, 1867; *Chestertown Transcript,* June 6, 1868; G. E. Henry to W. W. Rogers, May 13, 1867, Volume 50 (Register of Letters Sent, Bladensburg, June 4, 1866–September 18, 1867), BRFAL, Md., RG 105.

11. W. L. VanDerlip to J. Kimball, October 2, 1866, February 7, 1868, Volume 48 (Register of Letters Sent, Annapolis, June 28, 1866–March 13, 1868), and Box 1 (LRAC, April 1, 1866–August 17, 1868), BRFAL, Md., RG 105; *Baltimore Sun,* July 18, 25, 31, August 3, 1865, August 14, 24, September 1, 3, 5, 8, 15, 1866, August 22, 23, 31, 1867; *Baltimore Gazette,* July 31, 1865; *Baltimore American,* August 25, 26, September 6, 1865, August 8, 1866, September 1, 3, 5, 6, 8, 11, 12, 1866, August 15, 17, 22, 27, 1867; *Annapolis Gazette,* August 9, 30, 1866.

12. Daniel A. Payne, *History of the African Methodist Episcopal Church* (Nashville, 1891), 415; *Baltimore American,* April 11, 1868.

13. *Woods' Baltimore City Directory, 1865–1866* (Baltimore, 1866), 616.

14. Alexander W. Wayman was born a free man in Caroline County in 1821. Moving to Baltimore in 1840, he became an exhorter in the A.M.E. Church, and after education in New Jersey, was ordained a deacon in 1845. From 1848 to 1864 he served as pastor in several parishes in Washington and Maryland and at "Big Bethel" Church in Baltimore. He was chosen bishop at the General Conference of the A.M.E. Church in 1864 (*Dictionary of American Biography,* 19:561–62; *Who Was Who in America, Historical Volume, 1607–1896,* 567; George F. Bragg, *Men of Maryland,* 119–20; Benjamin T. Tanner, *An Apology for African Methodism* [Baltimore, 1867], 151–57; *Appleton's Cyclopedia of American Biography,* 398).

15. Benjamin T. Tanner was born in Pittsburgh, Pa., in 1835. He attended Avery College and in 1856 became a "licensed preacher" in the African Methodist Episcopal Church. In 1860, after attending the Western Theological

Seminary, he was ordained a deacon and elder. In 1866 he became pastor of "Big Bethel" A.M.E. Church in Baltimore, and in 1868, secretary of the A.M.E. Church general conference, and editor of its journal, the *Christian Recorder* (*Dictionary of American Biography*, 18:296).

16. Alexander W. Wayman, *My Recollections of African M. E. Ministers* (Philadelphia, 1881), 95–104; Tanner, *An Apology for African Methodism*, 151–57, 207–53. William E. Matthews was born in Baltimore in 1843. A prominent leader of "Big Bethel's" lay community, he lived for a while in Washington, D.C., where he established a bank. According to George F. Bragg, "since his sixteenth year, [Matthews] has been . . . identified with all the public movements in his birth city." Between 1865 and 1870, he worked at the forefront of black Baltimoreans' political, social, and educational efforts (Bragg, *Men of Maryland*, 99–102; Tanner, *An Apology for African Methodism*). James A. Handy was born in Baltimore in 1826, his father a slave and his mother a free person. He joined the A.M.E. Church in 1852 and was ordained deacon in 1864 and elder in 1865 (Richard R. Wright, ed., *Centennial Encyclopedia of the African Methodist Episcopal Church* [Philadelphia, 1916], 105; Bragg, *Men of Maryland*, 72–73; Tanner, *An Apology for African Methodism*, 222–26).

17. *Baltimore American*, November 18, 19, December 3, 1864, January 18, February 21, 1865. Savage L. Hammond was born in Virginia in 1814. He moved to Baltimore and then to Philadelphia where he studied under the Reverend Daniel Payne. He then followed Payne back to Baltimore when the latter became pastor at Bethel A.M.E. Church (Tanner, *An Apology for African Methodism*, 215–18).

18. *Baltimore American*, August 24, 1865, February 3, 9, April 6, December 17, 25, 31, 1866, March 13, July 9, 20, 22, August 27, 1867; *Baltimore Sun*, February 9, March 8, 1866, March 13, July 22, August 27, 1867; *Baltimore Gazette*, July 22, 1867.

19. *Baltimore American*, June 27, July 6, 1867.

20. *Journal of the General Conference of the Methodist Episcopal Church [North], 1864* (New York, 1864), 217, 224; *Minutes of the Annual Conferences of the Methodist Episcopal Church [North], 1864* (New York, 1864), 129–30, 235–36.

21. *Journal of the General Conference of the Methodist Episcopal Church [North], 1864*, 217–24.

22. "Journal of Proceedings, Washington Annual Conference, Methodist Episcopal Church, Session October 27–31, 1864," Methodist Historical Society, Lovely Lane Museum, Baltimore, Md.

23. Ibid.

24. Ibid.

25. *Minutes of the Annual Conferences of the Methodist Episcopal Church [North], 1864*, 129–30.

26. *First Annual Report of the Baltimore Association*, 4.

27. *Woods' Baltimore City Directory, 1865–1866* (Baltimore, 1866), 616; *Houston's Baltimore City Directory [1867]* (Baltimore, 1867), 108; *Woods' Baltimore City Directory, 1867–1868*, 758.

28. Davis, *A Narrative*, 2; A. Briscoe Koger, *Negro Baptists of Maryland* (Baltimore, 1946), 8. The three Baptist churches were: Union, on Lewis near Orleans, First Colored, on Thompson near Forrest, and Saratoga Street, on corner of Saratoga and Calvert.

29. *Journal of the Eighty-Second Annual Convention of the Protestant Episcopal Church in Maryland* (Baltimore, 1865); *Woods' Baltimore City Directory, 1865–1866*, 614–15.

30. *Journal of the Eighty-Fourth Annual Convention of the Protestant Episcopal Church in Maryland* (Baltimore, 1867).

31. Harrison H. Webb was born in Pennsylvania. In 1843 he joined St. James First African Church in Baltimore and in 1854 he was ordained as a minister in the Protestant Episcopal Church. A few years later he became rector of St. James Church (Bragg, *Men of Maryland*, 129–30). Noah Davis was born in Virginia. His book *Narrative of a Colored Man* is a well-known first-person account of slavery in that state. In 1843 he established what was then the second black Baptist Church in Baltimore (Union Baptist was the first). Davis died in 1867 (A. Briscoe Koger, *Negro Baptists of Maryland* [Baltimore, 1946], 42).

32. George F. Bragg, *History of the Afro-American Group of the Episcopal Church* (Baltimore, 1922), 90–192; Davis, *Narrative*, 83–100; Grace Hill Jacobs, "The Negro in Baltimore, 1860–1900" (M.A. thesis, Howard University, Washington, D.C., 1945), 54.

33. *Baltimore American*, January 12, 1866, April 5, 17, June 28, August 10, 1867, March 18, June 1, 1868; *Baltimore Sun*, February 22, April 16, 17, 1867; *Chestertown Transcript*, June 6, 1868.

34. *Journal of Proceedings of the House of Delegates, Extra Session, 1866* (Annapolis, 1866), 20; *Journal of Proceedings of the Senate of Maryland, Extra Session, 1866* (Annapolis, 1866), 78; *Laws of the State of Maryland [1866]* (Annapolis, 1866), Chapter 116, p. 187; *Laws of the State of Maryland [1868]* (Annapolis, 1868), Chapter 178, pp. 313–14; *Baltimore American*, January 13, 1866, March 18, 1868; *Baltimore Sun*, February 22, 1867.

35. Signature Books 334, 664, 668, 698, 701, 769, 793, 931, 806, 888, 901, 836, 963, 1068, Records of the Freedmen's Savings and Trust Company, Baltimore, RG 101, National Archives, Washington, D.C.

36. *Laws of the State of Maryland [1866]*, Chapter 116, p. 187; *Baltimore Sun*, February 22, 1867.

37. *Baltimore American*, April 5, 17, June 29, 1867, June 8, 1868; *Baltimore Sun*, April 16, 17, 1867; *Chestertown Transcript*, June 6, 1868.

38. *Laws of the State of Maryland [1866]*, Chapter 116, p. 187.

39. Ibid.

40. *Cumberland Civilian*, n.d., quoted in *Baltimore American*, August 10, 1867; *Chestertown Transcript*, June 6, 1868.

41. *Cumberland Civilian*, n.d., quoted in *Baltimore American*, August 10, 1867.

42. *Chestertown Transcript*, June 6, 1868.

43. Ibid.; *Baltimore American*, June 29, 1867.

44. *Easton Gazette*, November 11, 1865; *Annapolis Gazette*, August 23, 1867; *Baltimore Gazette*, October 7, 1865; *Baltimore Sun*, October 7, 1865; *Baltimore American*, October 7, 1865, December 30, 1867. Masonic lodges under the Grand Lodge of Maryland were: Friendship Lodge, Baltimore; St. John's Lodge, Baltimore; St. Paul's Lodge, Baltimore; Henry Freeman Lodge, Baltimore; King David Lodge, Havre de Grace; Lewis B. Wells Lodge, Baltimore; Unity Lodge, Baltimore; Lincoln Lodge, Alexandria, Va.; Warren Lodge, Washington, D.C.; Celestial Lodge, Baltimore; Lamech Lodge, Salisbury; St. John's Lodge, Washington, D.C. Odd Fellow Lodges in Baltimore were: Nemiah Lodge No. 1216; Manassah Lodge No. 1214; King David Lodge; Mount Lebanon Lodge; Zerrubable Lodge; Crystal Fount Lodge; Olive Lodge; Eden Lodge.

45. *Baltimore American*, October 7, 1865; *Baltimore Sun*, October 7, 1865; *Baltimore Gazette*, October 7, 1865.

46. Ibid.

47. *Baltimore Gazette*, October 7, 1865.

48. George A. Hackett was one of Baltimore's leading black citizens of this period. He was born in 1806, perhaps in Jamaica, perhaps in Maryland. As a young man he served as a steward aboard the U.S.S. *Constitution*. In the 1830s he owned a livery stable in Baltimore. Later he acquired a coal yard, with its office in the Douglass Institute. In April 1865 he served as the chief marshal of the various "colored associations" gathered at Camden Station to honor the remains of Abraham Lincoln. He was a prominent official of the Grand Lodge of the United Order of Odd Fellows, and a captain of the Henry Winter Davis Guards, a black military regiment. He was active in Republican Party politics, and was a founding officer of the Chesapeake Marine Railway and Drydock Company (Leroy Graham, *Baltimore: The Nineteenth Century Black Capital*, 147ff.; *Baltimore American*, April 22, October 7, 1865, August 5, 1867; Thomas, "A Nineteenth Century Black-Operated Shipyard," 40).

49. *Baltimore American*, October 7, 1865, December 30, 1867; *Baltimore Sun*, October 7, 1865; *Baltimore Gazette*, October 7, 1865.

50. Index, Deposit Ledger A, Records of Freedmen's Savings and Trust Company, Baltimore, RG 101.

51. Wright, *Free Negro in Maryland*, 239–61.

52. *Baltimore American,* December 14, 15, 1865, May 10, 1866.

53. Lew Wallace to C. A. Dana, August 30, 1864, *War of the Rebellion: A Compilation of the Official Records of the Union and Confederate Armies,* Series 1, Volume 43, Part 1—"Reports, Correspondence, Etc.," Serial 90 (Washington, 1893), 969–70.

54. *Baltimore American,* January 21, 1865, February 20, 21, October 21, 1867.

55. Ibid., December 14, 15, 1865, April 5, 17, 18, August 3, 5, 26, 1867; *Baltimore Sun,* December 15, 16, 1865, April 16, 17, August 3, 1867.

56. *Baltimore American,* December 14, 15, 1865; *Baltimore Sun,* December 15, 16, 1865.

57. *Baltimore American,* May 10, 11, 1866; *Baltimore Sun,* May 10, 1866; *Baltimore Gazette,* May 10, 1866.

58. *Baltimore American,* April 5, 17, 18, June 24, August 3, 5, 27, 1867; *Baltimore Sun,* April 16, 17, August 27, 1867.

59. *Baltimore American,* August 5, 26, 28, 31, September 2, 4, 5, 1867; *Baltimore Sun,* September 2, 3, 5, 1867; *Baltimore Gazette,* September 3, 5, 6, 1867.

60. *Baltimore American,* July 3, August 26, September 3, October 18, 1867; *Baltimore Gazette,* July 3, September 3, 1867; *Baltimore Sun,* July 3, September 2, 3, 5, 1867.

61. *Baltimore American,* September 4, 1867.

62. Ibid., May 13, July 30, August 28, 31, September 2, 3, 4, 5, 6, 1867; *Annapolis Gazette,* August 1, 1867; *Baltimore Gazette,* July 29, September 3, 5, 6, 1867; *Baltimore Sun,* July 30, September 2, 3, 5, 1867.

63. *Baltimore American,* August 28, 31, September 2, 3, 4, 5, 6, 1867; *Baltimore Gazette,* September 3, 5, 6, 1867; *Baltimore Sun,* September 2, 3, 5, 1867.

64. *Baltimore American,* September 4, 1867.

65. *Baltimore Sun,* September 30, 1865; *Baltimore Gazette,* September 30, 1865; *Baltimore American,* September 29, 1865; Leroy Graham, *Baltimore,* 136–37.

66. *Baltimore American,* September 30, 1865.

9

Separate and Not Equal

I

FEW BLACKS had much contact with whites other than at work in post-emancipation Maryland. Even radical politicians and federal agents confined their social exchanges with blacks to attendance at lectures, public meetings, and the occasional contact on an individual basis. No blacks lived, worshipped, studied, or entertained on a regular basis with whites. Clubs, beneficial societies, and military organizations remained strictly segregated as did schools of all kinds. In almost no significant manner did blacks' economic, legal, or political progress disrupt the strength of racial division in society. Indeed, in several key areas, emancipation and the subsequent enlargement of black privileges exacerbated interracial tensions in such a way as to encourage whites to call for greater separation from blacks.

As was the case in almost every aspect of post-emancipation society, conservative whites led the way. That people who opposed legal, political, and economic progress for black Marylanders should resist close interracial contact was not surprising. That radical proponents of such progress should share in the construction of a separated society was less predictable. Nonetheless, given the carefully circumscribed nature of radical ideology, the reluctance of blacks' friends to countenance "social equality" was ultimately understandable. Just as blacks had to earn the right to own land and to vote, interracial contact had to be approached slowly and cautiously.

Blacks themselves faced a dilemma. As much as they might wish to destroy segregation, they lacked the means by which to do so. Confronted by rigid and often violent resistance to any thought of integration, and faced with a choice between separate institutions or no institutions at all, they usually opted for the former. In the context of Maryland's post-emancipation race relations, there was really no choice. The freedom offered blacks after 1864 included no room for an integrated society.

II

The most visible indication of a divided society was the physical separation of white and black residential areas. In both urban and rural areas of the state, the races lived apart. Although no written statutes required blacks to reside in certain sections of cities or rural communities, unwritten law and diverse forms of social and economic pressure made certain they did. Even where neighborhoods contained a racially mixed population, as was the case in most rural areas and many sections of Baltimore, black residents commonly occupied houses behind white homes or on separate streets and alleys. Such neighborhoods, both urban and rural, established dividing lines within themselves.[1]

In addition, in Baltimore, the presence of businesses and places of manufacture that hired black laborers in some quantity encouraged the growth of all black districts. After emancipation, migrating blacks were naturally attracted to areas of likely employment. Incipient ghettos expanded around brick manufacturers, shipyards, and oyster-packing firms.[2] Some of these new districts were grafted upon older black sections of the city that had been centers of black service trades for years and where grocery stores, restaurants, churches, mortuaries, and taverns had existed to serve Baltimore's long-standing free black community.[3]

Most black Marylanders lived on streets and alleys behind white thoroughfares, on parts of plantations designated as workers' quarters, or on small plots of land that they sharecropped, rented, or owned. In Baltimore, almost every ward possessed its all-black section, usually comprised of two or three streets in close proximity or several alleys alternating with white streets. In the fifth ward, for example, blacks were concentrated on Chesnut Street, with minor pockets on Douglass and McElderry. In the twentieth, Orchard and Little Monument Streets were virtually all black. South Dallas and South Bethel Streets in the second and third wards (close to the East Baltimore shipyards) were also almost totally black.[4] Similarly, but on a smaller scale, Annapolis had its predominantly black section, as did Chestertown, Cambridge, Salisbury, and other rural centers. Away from urban development, almost entirely black districts containing pre-emancipation free laborers were located in parts of St. Mary's, Charles, and Calvert Counties, with lesser equivalents elsewhere.[5]

The precise extent of such concentration was particularly evident in

Baltimore. Assessment and city directory records from 1866 and 1867 show that the bulk of the 1,455 blacks listed in the 1870 United States Census as living in the ninth ward were confined to two small blocks, one on Bethel Court in the shadow of the Phoenix Iron Foundry, and the other on Davis between Pleasant and Franklin.[6] The ninth was a business, manufacturing, and shipping ward and did not contain the residences of many blacks or whites, but its pattern of close black concentration typified several parts of the city. In the thirteenth ward, a residential district, blacks lived on Pierce and Sarah Anne Streets and almost nowhere else.[7] In the sixteenth, in southwest Baltimore, they occupied every second street (most were narrow alleys), between Pratt and Lee.[8] One, Elbow Lane, was referred to by the *Baltimore Sun* in October 1866 as "a narrow street . . . densely inhabited by colored oyster shuckers and other families."[9] Orchard Street in the twentieth ward provided better homes but featured similar concentration. Seeking to sell her home on Orchard in late 1867, a white resident complained that the "character of the neighborhood has been changed; it now being almost entirely inhabited by negroes, there being scarcely a white family living in the square in which said house is situated."[10]

Black residences in both Baltimore and the tidewater counties were smaller and by necessity housed more people than their white counterparts. Again, such crowding was particularly evident in the city. In the south and southwest wards especially—where many newly arrived blacks lived and worked—hundreds of laborers and their families found quarters near the harbor in small dwellings that housed many more occupants than was considered safe or sanitary. Conditions were most acute during the winter of 1864–65 when so many black migrants entered the city. In February 1865, the Friends Association in Aid of Freedmen reported that refugees were "crowded into alleys and cellars where their destitution [causes] extreme misery."[11] Nor did the situation change quickly. In early 1867, officials of the Marine Hospital warned of the health hazards associated with "densely crowded lanes and alleys" in black neighborhoods.[12]

In letters sent north to the *Freedmen's Record*, teachers working in black schools in Baltimore offered a detailed glimpse of living accommodations at all levels. In December 1866, Fannie Ellis reported that:

> During the month, . . . [I have] visited forty-seven families, mostly Orchard and Calvert Street districts. These calls have introduced us to all

classes of our colored citizens. We have been to the house where the presence of the piano, of books worth reading, of pictures worth looking at, tell of the civilizing and elevating influence of Freedom and education, and of the ambition and industry of its occupants. We have climbed to the attic and descended to the cellar, where less of thrift, or sickness, or other misfortune, or, mayhap, vice, has brought its attendant discomforts.[13]

In January 1868, Charlotte McKay described the situation favorably:

we have visited sixty-five families during the month. I find them all in comfortable circumstances, with an appearance of industry and thrift very gratifying to their well-wishers. In no house that I have entered since Christmas have I found the Christmas tree wanting; decorated according to the means of the inmates, always with a degree of taste, and sometimes heavily loaded and looking quite beautiful. One family, father, mother, and eight children, came from Virginia since the close of the war, where they had been living in slavery. They hire a house for fifteen dollars per month, let enough to pay half the rent, the remainder making them a good home. The older children are at service. The combined efforts of father and mother maintain the others very comfortably. They, too, had their Christmas tree. The father is anxious to have his children go to school and learn to read. . . . I believe him and his family to be good specimens of what the freedmen will do in the way of self-help, if they have a fair chance.[14]

But not everyone could manage so successfully. In March 1868, McKay visited the home of a black laundress:

we reached No. 3, X Alley, and climbed up the narrow rickety stairway, into the little room whither he had summoned me. It was one of the coldest days of the season, but there was no fire in the room, "Miss Downs" having taken her family to a neighbor's to save the few bits of fire wood which were lying behind the stove, and all she had. She soon came in, however, and kindled a little fire. Her family consists of two little orphan girls, left to her care by the death of her only daughter, and a little three year old boy, the *chance child,* of a young woman who is at service and pays her three dollars a month for his board. On inquiring into her means of living, I found that she had an income of a dollar and a quarter every week from her washing and ironing, and a friend hires a corner of her little room, enough for a bed and standing room, for which she pays her one dollar per month. This added to three dollars for her boarder, makes nine dollars a month out of which she pays two dollars rent, leaving a net income of seven dollars per month with which to keep up her boarding establishment, and run her laundry and orphan asylum. A part of this has to be expended in medicines for one of the little orphans, who is dropsical, her head and neck swelled to an unnatural size, and her arms and legs slender as pipe stems. Yet she is bright and cheery, says she has "never been without *any mouthful*," thanking the Lord and me too for the little assistance I gave her.[15]

In the final analysis, the location of even the best black districts left much to be desired. In the tidewater counties, blacks continued to reside in quarters once used by slaves, close to the fields where they worked.[16] In Baltimore, conditions facing or surrounding black homes were equally unfavorable. Confronting much of the fifth ward from across Jones Falls were a string of factories, breweries, and slaughterhouses which poured liquid waste into the waterway. Low-lying homes along the Falls also contributed to what was a generally foul atmosphere, especially in the summer. Most possessed outdoor toilet facilities (called "sinks") which added additional pollution to the water.[17] Conditions in other black sections of the city were just as unattractive. Near brickyards in South Baltimore, large pools of water lay unattended, the cause, according to the *Baltimore American*, of attacks of chills and fever as one of the "regular penalties of residence south of Baltimore Street."[18] Many of these pools were in the fifteenth and sixteenth wards, the home in 1870 of more than six thousand black people.[19]

III

Of course, much more marked the separation of black and white Marylanders than the location and quality of their homes. In almost everything they did, the two races functioned separately. Since the majority of blacks worked for whites, daily contact was unavoidable but confined to economic essentials. As much as blacks may have wished to share their nonworking lives with whites, the latter refused to permit it. Few white associations opened their doors to black participation, and those that did—almost all of them churches or freedmen's aid associations—relegated blacks to separate subcategories, or when together with whites, separate seating areas. Such practices were common to all churches and organizations and represented the extent to which even the most reform-minded whites were willing to go in associating with black people.[20]

As far as public aid was concerned, black Marylanders enjoyed reasonably free access to it. But in an age when most tax-supported institutions were of a purely charitable nature, serving the needs of only the desperately poor, this hardly represented open access to the institutions of the white community. The Bay View Asylum in Baltimore, the most important case in point, might boast that "admittance is granted to all irrespective of color, no discrimination being made in the treatment," but the number of blacks in its facility remained disproportionately high compared to whites, and most of the latter were in desperate circumstances.[21] The City or "Marine" Hospital operated along the same lines as did the Bay View Asylum and public almshouses in the tidewater counties. Blacks were accepted in these institutions on an equal basis with whites who could not afford private—and better—care. The hospital and county almshouses were, like such other public medical facilities as the several dispensaries located throughout Baltimore, charitable services designed to meet the needs of the state's indigent. To the extent that blacks were poor—and most of them were—they enjoyed equal access to available facilities of this sort.[22] James S. Snow of Worcester County put it quite well when he explained in April 1867, "This county has a public 'Alms House' where unfortunate colored residents of the County, and *even unfortunate whites* are received, and provided for at the expense of the County."[23]

Whenever public agencies did serve a wider sector of Maryland's population, black access to these facilities was curtailed. Of key importance were Baltimore's City Passenger Railway, a public corporation, and several railroads, including the Baltimore and Ohio, private companies that provided the only public transportation between Baltimore and neighboring cities. Although blacks were permitted to travel on these lines, they were barred from sitting in the same cars with whites. The horse-drawn street cars of the City Passenger Railway limited black seating to women who were nursing white children. All other blacks were forced to ride on platforms to the front and rear of the cars.[24] The various railroads provided seating for all blacks but only in the cars designed for white men who either were unescorted by women or wished to smoke.[25] Similarly, steamships servicing Baltimore and the Chesapeake counties confined black passengers to separate—and usually lower—sleeping accommodations.[26] Other private companies that depended on public patronage maintained the same type of restrictions. The Holliday and Front Street Theaters in Baltimore, for example, forced blacks to sit in specific areas for all forms of public entertainment and public lecturers.[27]

Belonging to a separate category of public agency that provided—theoretically—for everyone regardless of their race, were the Baltimore City Jail and Maryland State Penitentiary. Here, as was the case with the Bay View Asylum, Marine Hospital, and county almshouses, blacks were admitted on an equal basis with whites. Once inside either the jail or penitentiary, however, they were housed separately in cell accommodations inferior to those assigned white prisoners.[28] During the entire period 1864–70, the penitentiary was overcrowded and housed a disproportionate number of blacks, especially from the rural counties. State regulations called for separate accommodations for each convict, but this proved impossible. Officials found it necessary to house many people together, and invariably blacks were the first to be so grouped.[29] To make matters worse, neither the state nor city made any provision for black juvenile offenders. Convicted white minors served terms in the House of Refuge, a facility that barred its doors to blacks. Despite pleas from a wide sector of both the white and black community, the state refused to build a separate accommodation for black youths and in 1870, such offenders were still housed in the penitentiary proper along with adult prisoners.[30]

IV

The stiffest white opposition to close interracial contact occurred in the area of personal relations. Conservative opposition to and radical ambivalence toward "social equality" kept blacks and whites thoroughly apart when educating or entertaining themselves except under specially arranged circumstances. As the radical *Frederick Examiner* explained, it was "a question of ethics and not of politics. . . . Socially, the whites and blacks cannot intermingle."[31] Such separation characterized not only churches but also lodges, clubs, associations, and all forms of casual communication. Standard procedure dictated that blacks and whites deal with each other as groups, not individuals, and the establishment of the all-black conference of the Methodist Episcopal Church typified the division of Maryland society into parallel racial structures. There were white Masons and black Masons; white Oddfellows and black Oddfellows. Whites formed their own benevolent associations, so did blacks.[32] On occasions these organizations might meet, but the nature of such contact remained stiff, formal, and cautious.

Nor was any of this new. Segregation in social matters was a long-standing tradition. For decades, Maryland's free black community had recognized the need to create its own network of social institutions.[33] Significantly, emancipation effected little change. The level of formal contact between black and white *reformers* rose substantially but the latter constituted only a tiny minority of the total white population, and their activities could make few inroads into a society generally opposed to contact with blacks.

Of course, no one could expect patterns of racial separation to change overnight. There was nothing in the Emancipation Proclamation that provided for the immediate installation of a fully integrated society. Indeed, taken literally, it did not say anything about integration, nor, for that matter, did the federal Civil Rights Act of 1866. Both dealt with the establishment of minimal rights and assiduously avoided any mention of "social equality." Even blacks and radical Unionists and Republicans approached the question of social contact cautiously.[34]

Nonetheless, emancipation did change the nature and content of black expectations. Suddenly the presence and purpose of separate institutions assumed new meaning, some of it positive, but some of it fraught with dissatisfaction and frustration. Blacks proved willing, indeed eager, to form their own institutions and societies—especially in areas barred to them under slavery—but sought through them to gain eventual access to the community at large.[35] Such a dual thrust created a level of tension between blacks and whites and among blacks themselves that charged the atmosphere of interracial relations for the entire period in question. "I once flattered myself," said Frederick Douglass, "that the day had happily gone by when it would be necessary for colored people . . . to act together as a separate class. . . . [But] the latent contempt and prejudice towards our race . . . make it eminently necessary."[36] In some areas the tension remained well below the surface. Separate churches and purely social groups such as lodges and benevolent associations seemed generally to meet with the approval of both races without causing much conflict. In other areas—those of particular symbolic importance to black aspirations and white fears—activities no matter how separate led to bitter confrontation. Black participation in certain activities, even when segregated, clearly represented a claim to racial equality, one that everyone recognized.

Nowhere was this more evident than in education. Although all but the most extreme white racists agreed that some sort of schooling was necessary for Maryland's black population, most whites remained troubled by the deeper implications of such change. Prior to 1872, when the State of Maryland finally assumed control of black schools, only the City of Baltimore participated directly in their management.[37] Elsewhere whites proved disinclined to offer positive assistance. Throughout rural Maryland, only the Baltimore Association for the Moral and Educational Improvement of the Colored People and the Freedmen's Bureau offered real help.[38] Indeed, in many parts of the state the lack of white enthusiasm took on the shape of outright hostility. Just as the classroom became rural blacks' symbol of hope, it stood for some whites as a target for their own frustration and rage.[39]

In other areas of the economy and society, such resistance stood out almost as vigorously. Despite its separate or segregated status, the postemancipation participation of blacks in certain, even customary activities aroused sustained opposition from whites who defined it as a threat to the status quo. A clear case in point were the white workers in the East Baltimore shipyards who went on strike against the firm of John J. Abrahams and Son in the winter of 1865–66. No longer were whites in the shipyards willing to compete with black labor or even countenance its existence. "All we ask of our employers," explained the White Journeymen Shipwrights, "is that they will give the white man the preference."[40] On October 3, 1865, white workers from a number of city trades paraded through Baltimore's streets. Huge crowds turned out to cheer banners and transparencies that disparaged the work of black caulkers. One such emblem bore the likeness of a black man's head with the sarcastic inscription: "The White Man's Superior!" Another portrayed a sinking ship with the title: "Caulked by Negroes!"[41] The situation, declared a retired white shipwright, was simple. "White labor must . . . have the precedence."[42]

Less basic perhaps than problems with education and employment but equally volatile were the efforts of blacks to constitute their own military regiments.[43] To blacks militia membership represented the capacity to extend the pride with which they had served in the United States Army, and to reinforce the statement of racial equality that such service had so eloquently expressed. And that was precisely the point. Although blacks had fought in the army and, under General Lew Wallace's orders, served in the wartime militia, white Marylanders insisted that such participation cease with the end of hostilities.[44] Given the immediacy of the war and the importance attributed by blacks and whites to military service, such exclusion occasioned no surprise. That white conservatives should reject the idea of black participation in the militia, even on a segregated basis, was fully in line with their general principles.

Blacks' subsequent constitution of their own regiments aroused white Marylanders' immediate opposition. Uniforms and guns represented highly visible symbols of racial equality, the possession of which placed the black man on the same footing as the white. To make matters worse, blacks did not hesitate to display both uniforms and weapons in open daylight, especially on the streets of Baltimore. Of the various regimental activities, none were more popular with their participants than full dress parades through the central core of the city. Nothing, however, could be better calculated to anger whites. Hardly a parade took place without some sort of altercation between marchers and spectators, and as time went on, such outbreaks became increasingly violent. In 1866, black regiments clashed in open fist fights with whites on three separate occasions, during one of which shots were fired from both sides.[45] In 1867, both the Lincoln Zouaves and Henry Winter Davis Guards encountered bricks and pistol shots during several parades and at least once they responded in kind.[46] And in October 1867, the escalation of such violence reached its peak when the rear rank of the Butler Guards wheeled and fired into the crowd killing a white man.[47]

Both whites and blacks expressed their dismay at such an outcome, but predictably the former placed most of the blame upon black militia regiments. Public pressure was sufficient to secure a ban upon all their parades, and city police confiscated as many regimental firearms as they could get their hands on.[48] Although they were not declared illegal, black regiments were now hard-pressed to function effectively and were certainly no closer to winning admission to the state militia. The entire experience had the opposite effect, making whites more determined than ever that blacks should not share in this part of community responsibilities. "Drilling with loaded muskets," proclaimed the *Balti-*

more Gazette, "is a special privilege which should not be allowed negroes."[49]

V

The violent reaction of the white community that greeted black attempts to acquire an education, work in the East Baltimore shipyards, or enlist in the militia did not confine itself solely to such highly visible issues. Indeed, white Marylanders resorted to violence against blacks as a regular, everyday means of protecting racial separation. Blacks in post-emancipation Maryland were to learn their place just as they had under slavery, and whites of all walks of life—especially in the tidewater counties—were quick to employ force when "necessary." Such behavior, either overt or condoned, served as an effective disciplinary device and as such worked to keep separate the lives of the two races.

Under the circumstances, not only were blacks forced to mind their own business, but had to do so within a strictly defined sphere of acceptable behavior every bit as confining as that of slavery. Moreover, apart from scattered agents of the Freedmen's Bureau, blacks could count on no white protection from violence unless they deported themselves cautiously. As the *Baltimore American* explained in July 1867, "For years the relationship between the two races has been that of master and slave. . . . It was something that came naturally with slavery but ought to pass away. . . . Yet the rebels now demand the same fawning, servile, and subservient mein as of old."[50]

Blacks who failed to read the message accurately suffered predictable consequences. It seemed that whenever they sought to break free from the prescribed mold (or seemed to be doing so in the eyes of whites), they encountered violent opposition. The litany of white attacks on black activities between 1864 and 1870 was a long one and it was all designed to teach black people their place. During the first three months after emancipation, whites broke up black public meetings in Dorchester County and burned black churches in St. Mary's and Somerset Counties.[51] In June 1865, whites assaulted blacks who had gathered to celebrate Whitsuntide in Chestertown.[52] Two weeks later, a group of returned Confederate soldiers attacked a black camp meeting near Spark's Switch, in Anne Arundel County.[53] On July 23, an excursion of black Baltimoreans heading for another camp meeting in the same county met with similar trouble in the neighborhood of Rock Creek.[54] In August, whites attacked Isaac Graig, a Charles County farmhand who raised his hat and cheered upon hearing the word "emancipation" at a public meeting.[55] In November, at the foot of Baltimore's South Street Wharf, a party of white excursionists attacked several black dock workers. Through it all, the assailants cheered lustily for ex-Confederate President Jefferson Davis while dozens of other whites stood by doing nothing.[56]

Events in 1866 and 1867 followed the same pattern. Whenever blacks, either individually or in groups, engaged in assertive activities that caught whites' attention, they paid a price for their temerity. In August 1866, a band of white men attacked black worshippers at an interracial (segregated) Methodist camp meeting at Hanover Switch in Anne Arundel County. Pistol shots rang out from both sides and the entire meeting ground became the scene of fistfighting and shooting that did not cease until late in the evening.[57] On August 1, 1867, in Centreville, Queen Anne's County, a riot disrupted an educational meeting sponsored by the Freedmen's Bureau and the Baltimore Association. What began as a scuffle between two or three whites and blacks soon escalated into a running street battle involving dozens of people. Several blacks sustained severe injuries but no whites were arrested.[58] Tension in both Hanover Switch and Centreville obviously focused upon the meetings themselves, their purpose, and the fact that at Centreville several hundred blacks had gathered in one place to hear Hugh Lennox Bond and Edgar Gregory. The combination of all of these things provided an open invitation to whites intent on curtailing such displays of black assertiveness.

Especially vulnerable to such attacks were uniformed and armed blacks returning to rural Maryland after service in the United States Army. Several thousand men from the Eastern Shore alone had enlisted in 1863 and 1864, and their return—often with muskets—attracted considerable attention, especially from ex-Confederate soldiers. In February 1866, a band of ex-Confederates attacked two black veterans, William Mills and Essex Barbour, at Chaptico, St. Mary's County. Mills later told Edward O'Brien of the Freedmen's Bureau that he could think of no reason for the attack except "the antipathy of a certain class of whites towards black men who had served in the army."[59] Barbour added that Kepley Tibbet, one of his assailants, was an ex-Confederate who "makes it his business to injure colored people, more especially colored soldiers . . . at all times and places."[60] In March of the same year, a Queen Anne's County veteran told Oliver Otis Howard that "returned colored soldiers are in many cases beaten, and their guns taken from them. We dare not walk out in the evenings. If we do and are met by some of these rowdies that were in the rebel army, they beat us badly and some times shoot us."[61] In July, William VanDerlip reported from Calvert County that "There are large numbers of young men . . . in [this area] who have served in the rebel army . . . [and who] threaten Negroes and any who may come here with a helping hand."[62]

Judging by the relative ease and impunity with which whites could attack blacks, one can readily conclude that blacks could count on little protection from civil authorities. County courts seldom found whites at fault in cases of assault and rarely arrested any of them after riots or other civil disturbances. After the 1866 camp meeting riot at Hanover Switch, only blacks were detained, despite plenty of evidence that clearly implicated whites.[63] The only arrests to follow the Centreville outbreak in 1867 were those of two blacks.[64] Arrests ensuing the Butler Guards shooting in Baltimore in the same year were similarly confined to blacks.[65] Furthermore, county law enforcement officers themselves often became directly involved in the perpetration of violence. In an incident in Dorchester County in early 1865, the leading assailant turned out to be William H. Neild, the local constable.[66]

From time to time, county courts enlisted the aid of the very people most interested in restricting blacks' freedom. Often, the bands of young white men who made life miserable for rural blacks acted under the tacit approval or express authority of a county court or a justice of the peace. For real or alleged crimes it was a simple matter to obtain a warrant for the arrest of a black person, and an even easier task to round up a group of men to assist in its delivery. Dr. John Wilkinson, the assailant of John Shannon, a black veteran in Anne Arundel County, obtained an arrest warrant on the grounds that Shannon had "insulted" him. The men who assisted Wilkinson in tracking Shannon down were constituted by the county authorities as an official *posse comitatus*.[67] Similarly, Isaac Craig's attackers turned themselves into a posse the moment magistrate Dent issued an order for his arrest.[68]

Nor did the rural white community have any difficulty justifying such action. Whether it was in the form of a band of ex-Confederate soldiers or a *posse comitatus*, planters approved of the idea that whites should discipline "unruly" blacks. "Let . . . [the court] appoint as many active young men in each district of the county as may be necessary," advised the *St. Mary's Gazette* in August 1865, "to enable the regular officers of the law . . . to execute the process of our magistrates."[69] Not everyone advocated so extreme a measure but approval of or acquiescence in overt violence towards blacks was widespread even among the most respectable elements in society. After witnessing a brutal attack upon a black man in Talbot County, Samuel Harrison observed that "Not one of . . . [many onlookers] attempted to interfere in the Negro's behalf. . . . There were more men present who would have risked personal harm in saving a dog . . . than were willing to save this poor . . . [victim]."[70] From that same county in August 1865, James Valliant wrote that "the negro though free, is yet a degraded being. . . . By the policy of the white man towards him . . . [he] is demoralized and brutalized."[71]

Even if local whites wanted to speak up in defense of mistreated blacks it took tremendous courage to do so. "It is one of the saddest signs of these sad times," wrote one such friend in December 1864, "that popular feeling and local prejudice break out in such licentiousness. . . . [Those whites] who dare favor [Negroes] are branded with scorn and threatened by ruthless mobs. . . . We are still practically surrounded with a rebel reign of terror."[72] That same month from Somerset County, William Daniel observed that he had "never witnessed such a state of feeling against the negro and everyone . . . who favors him in any way."[73]

VI

The principal shaping force of white opposition—both violent and nonviolent—to black assertiveness was Maryland's predominantly conservative philosophy. Basically, most whites believed that traditional social distinctions had served society well and that everyone—especially blacks—should abide by them even though slavery had ceased to exist. Few whites applauded brutality, but many defined its cause within the context of forced social change. Conservatives saw violence as an unfortunate but inevitable response to the threat posed to their traditions and institutions by the aspirations of newly freed blacks. Opposed to anything but the most gradual acquisition of social rights and privileges by blacks, conservatives saw the latter's agitation (fuelled by white radicals) for more rapid change as the essential cause of conflict. Consequently, conservatives maintained that blacks should not seek sudden change in their traditional social status; that they should avoid activities that threatened the status quo and be content with modest gains within the context of white paternalism and the traditionally separated society. Such a relationship, conservatives promised, would restore social harmony—to say nothing of economic prosperity—and save blacks from violent treatment.

Thus, in its editorial of July 26, 1865, the *Baltimore Sun* could insist—contrary to the evidence surrounding it—that "our late owners of slaves, as well as our people generally, have by instinct and education, as kindly a feeling for the colored race, and as genuine and humane [a] concern for individual suffering among them as any others on the face of the earth."[74] This may have been so, but clearly within a carefully defined set of limitations. "The relations at present between white and colored races," explained another conservative, Governor Augustus Bradford, in October 1865, "require judicious and delicate management. . . . The Master is still irritated . . . that he was deprived . . . of all his slave labor, . . . his late Slave, with his freedom suddenly . . . acquired [is] inflated with exaggerated and erroneous notions of its character."[75] Such a combination, Bradford suggested, made some conflict inevitable, but modest deportment by blacks and prompt and judicious reaction by city and county authorities to incidents of racial conflict would prove the most efficacious way of maintaining order. At all costs, Bradford argued, such outsiders as the Freedmen's Bureau should be kept at bay. With respect to interracial violence within his state, Bradford complained, "Unfortunately it too often happens that some third party . . . by his interposition and agitation, very unseasonably aggravates prejudices, and is by far the greatest mischief maker."[76]

Reverdy Johnson, Maryland's conservative United States senator, agreed. A black person was "as safe in Maryland as he is in Massachusetts," he claimed, so long as planters and their ideas prevailed.[77] On the floor of the Senate in January 1866, Johnson supported his claim by quoting John T. B. McMasters and Levin S. Waters, two Eastern Shore state legislators. "In justice to the people of the Eastern Shore," they began, "we must say that . . . negroes as a class have as large a liberty and are as humanely treated . . . as in any section of the United States *where social equality and amalgamation does not prevail.*"[78] The message was clear. Blacks were safe in Maryland as long as they ceased to aspire toward either "social equality" or "amalgamation," and were content to endure a separate and restricted existence. Maryland was, after all, as conservative Governor Thomas Swann often explained, "a white man's society," and equal access to the privileges enjoyed by whites should be denied "a race wholly and entirely distinct . . . from our own."[79] Or, as a conservative correspondent to the *Baltimore American* put it, whites and blacks "were never intended for each other's society, and so . . . have been kept separate."[80]

Of course, not all whites in Maryland were conservatives. Within the minority radical faction, views on segregation and the violence that accompanied it differed substantially from those of Swann, Bradford, and Johnson. Such men as Hugh Lennox Bond, John Creswell, and Edgar Gregory talked incessantly of the right of blacks to testify, vote, go to school, join the militia, and share public transportation facilities with whites. In defense of black military regiments, Bond asserted "it has always, in every declaration of rights, in every constitution in every free State, been declared that the right of the citizen to bear arms shall not be infringed."[81] Put simply, white radicals did not share conservatives' fear of social change.[82]

Radicals were convinced that the violence that sustained separation served only as a tool of the intransigent—for those planters and their henchmen who refused to accept the meaning of emancipation. Rather than offer protection to only those blacks who assumed a servile role, radicals sought to discredit all such brutal treatment as an outmoded relic of slavery. As the *Baltimore American* said of school burning, "These incendiary acts could disgrace the dark ages."[83] The radical *Cambridge Intelligencer* joined in such sentiment lamenting the "cowardly and barbarous proceedings . . . [which] are deeply rooted in the hearts of the people." On the Eastern Shore, it said, "Freedom is as yet of too recent birth to effectually roll back the tide of fanaticism and intolerance."[84] On April 12, 1866, the *American* took dead aim on an excerpt of a Thomas Swann speech when it asked:

> We are told that negroes have all the protection which the "requirements of the *social order* demand." What social order? That which holds that the world was made especially for white men; that for them alone the sun shines and the stars give their light? That which is prejudice and selfishness? For that system and those who believe in it, that protection

may be ample. But it is not sufficient for those who love justice for itself,
. . . Justice, simple justice, is all we seek.[85]

With this in mind, radicals tried in a number of ways to break down
the barriers to racial interaction. The Freedmen's Bureau and Baltimore Association encouraged mixed participation at public meetings
and leading white radicals attended important events in the black community. Bond, Gregory, Archibald Stirling, Jr., and John L. Thomas
made many such appearances, calling upon members of both races to
cooperate in building a better Maryland.[86] More specifically, the Freedmen's Bureau on at least one occasion challenged segregation directly.
In May 1866, after the passage of the federal Civil Rights Act, it supported the suit before the Baltimore Criminal Court of Mary J. C.
Anderson and Ellen J. Jackson, black school teachers who had been
forcibly removed from a "whites only" waiting room of the Baltimore
and Ohio Railroad. The Bureau obtained the necessary writs and the
case got a hearing that, according to the *Baltimore Sun*, attracted "quite
a number of the friends of the [Civil Rights] Act recently adopted
by Congress."[87] Bond himself waged personal battle upon conservative
custom by inviting a black friend to sit beside him at church. It was his
right, Bond argued, to "introduce any person white or black who
wanted to hear the Gospel into the pew."[88]

Nevertheless, radicals, too, had their problems with the concept of a
truly integrated society. Unlike conservatives, they welcomed widened
contact with blacks, but like them, they placed limitations upon such
interaction and spoke of the mistake of forcing "social equality."[89] Bond
and others believed that racial distinctions might one day disappear
when society found them outmoded and anachronistic, but argued that
until such time their presence constituted an inescapable fact of life.
There was, explained the *Baltimore American* on August 7, 1865, a
"natural antipathy towards amalgamation [that] acts as a barrier against
homogeneity."[90] Consequently, radicals did relatively little to challenge
racial segregation in Maryland. Between 1864 and 1870, practically all
their major battles for black progress left the separate society un-
touched. Repeal of the black code, apprenticeship, testimony, education, and suffrage commanded tremendous energies but none
necessitated full racial integration. Instead, each permitted radicals to
concentrate on defending the rights of blacks in engaging in the same
activities as whites in their own, separate, organizations.

Such a limited approach to reform—a sort of "progress within prejudice"—characterized radicals' reaction to the separate society in all its forms. It seemed that blacks' friends shared with conservatives the idea that blacks were still a special or peculiar people who by definition required their own "place" in society. Just as economically radicals believed that blacks should come to terms with the ex-master class as soon as possible, socially they argued along similar lines. For all the improvement that radicals sought for blacks, they still regarded them as fit subjects for a special, subordinate relationship to whites. As one radical explained, "The duty of watching over . . . [the Negro] is imposed upon us by a wisdom higher than ours, and we cannot shirk it."[91] Of course, radicals did not interpret such duty in the same fashion as conservatives. Duty to radicals permitted ample room for the development of a more progressive society, one marked by widened freedom of action for blacks. Nevertheless, such freedom still bore its limitations, one of which was the continuation of a segregated society.

Notes

1. Eighth Census of the United States, 1860, Schedule 1; Ninth Census of the United States, 1870, Schedule 1; *Woods' Baltimore City Directory, Ending Year 1864*, 443–84; *Woods' Baltimore City Directory, 1867–1868*, 564–626; *Woods's Baltimore City Directory, 1871*, 667–757.

2. Ibid.

3. Ibid.

4. Ibid.

5. Eighth Census of the United States, 1860, Schedule 1; Ninth Census of the United States, 1870, Schedule 1.

6. Field Assessors' Books, 1866, 9th Ward, Vols. 1–5, Record Group 4, Series 3, Field Assessors' Work Books, 1837–1898, Baltimore City Archives; *Woods' Baltimore City Directory, Ending Year 1864*, 443–84; *Woods' Baltimore City Directory, 1867–1868*, 564–626; *Woods's Baltimore City Directory, 1871*, 667–757.

7. Field Assessors' Book, 1866, 13th Ward, Record Group 4, Series 3, Field Assessors' Books, 1837–1898, Baltimore City Archives; *Woods' Baltimore City Directory, Ending Year 1864*, 443–84; *Woods' Baltimore City Directory, 1867–1868*, 564–626; *Woods's Baltimore City Directory, 1871*, 667–757.

8. *Woods' Baltimore City Directory, Ending Year 1864*, 443–84; *Woods' Baltimore City Directory, 1867–1868*, 564–626; *Woods's Baltimore City Directory, 1871*, 667–757.

9. *Baltimore Sun,* October 15, 1866.

10. *Baltimore American,* December 14, 1867.

11. Ibid., February 7, 1865.

12. Message of John Lee Chapman, Mayor, to the Members of the First and Second Branches of the City Council, as found in the *Ordinances of the Mayor and City Council of Baltimore, Passed at the Sessions of 1866–1867 . . .* (Baltimore, 1867), 26.

13. *Freedmen's Record,* 3, no. 3 (March 1867): 35–36.

14. *Freedmen's Record,* 4, no. 2 (February 1868): 26–27.

15. *Freedmen's Record,* 4, no. 5 (May 1868): 79–80.

16. Eighth Census of the United States, 1860, Schedule 1; Ninth Census of the United States, 1870, Schedule 1.

17. *Baltimore American,* March 12, 1867; Report of the Board of Health to the Mayor and City Council of Baltimore, as found in the *Ordinances of the Mayor and City Council of Baltimore, Passed at the Session of 1866,* 296; Message of John Lee Chapman, Mayor, to Members of the First and Second Branches of the City Council, January 1st, 1866, as found in ibid., 37.

18. *Baltimore American,* June 24, 1867.

19. U.S. Bureau of the Census, *Population of the United States in 1870,* 163.

20. *Frederick Examiner,* August 1, 1866; H. L. Bond to K. Bond, February 17, 1867, Bond-McCulloch Family Papers (MS 1159), Maryland Historical Society; *Journal of the Eighty-Second Annual Convention of the Protestant Episcopal Church in Maryland* (Baltimore, 1865), 19–50.

21. Report by W. R. DeWitt, December 20, 1866, Box 1 (LRAC, April 1, 1866–August 17, 1868), BRFAL, Md., RG 105; *Baltimore American,* July 31, 1867. See also chapter 6.

22. *Baltimore American,* October 16, 1866; Message of John Lee Chapman, Mayor, to the Members of the First and Second Branches of the City Council, as found in the *Ordinances of the Mayor and City Council of Baltimore, Passed at the Sessions of 1866–1867,* 27; Testimony of William Bryan, January 11, 1867, Testimony in Investigation of the Government of Maryland, 1867, Record Group 233; W. Stewart to Freedmen's Bureau, March 29, 1867, J. S. Jones to Freedmen's Bureau, April 5, 1867, J. B. Nock to Freedmen's Bureau, April 10, 1867, W. H. Zeigler to Freedmen's Bureau, April 6, 1867, J. A. Perkins to Freedmen's Bureau, April 24, 1867, J. Turner to Freedmen's Bureau, May 1, 1867, Box 1 (LRAC, April 1, 1866–August 17, 1868), BRFAL, Md., RG 105.

23. J. S. Snow to Freedmen's Bureau, April 5, 1867, Box 1 (Letters Received Assistant Commissioner, April 1, 1866–August 17, 1868), BRFAL, Md., RG 105, emphasis in original.

24. *Baltimore American,* May 23, 25, June 1, August 13, 1866; *Baltimore Gazette,* May 23, July 9, 1866; *Baltimore Sun,* May 24, 25, July 10, 1866.

25. *Baltimore American,* April 16, May 23, 1866, January 10, February 13, 1868; *Baltimore Sun,* May 17, 23, 1866; *Baltimore Gazette,* April 18, May 17, 1866; E. G. Jackson to Freedmen's Bureau, May 8, 1866, Box 1 (LRAC, April 1, 1866–August 17, 1868), BRFAL, Md., RG 105.

26. *Baltimore Gazette,* October 7, 11, 1867.

27. *Baltimore Gazette,* April 18, 1866; *Baltimore American,* April 16, 1866, February 9, 1867; *Freedmen's Record,* 2, no. 11 (November 1866): 194–95.

28. "Annual Report of the President and Directors of the Maryland Penitentiary, January 1866" (Annapolis, 1866), 6, which appears as Document F in *Journal of Proceedings of the House of Delegates, Extra Session, 1866* (Annapolis, 1866); "Report of the Select Committee on the Penitentiary" (Annapolis, 1867), 4–9, which appears as Document AA in *Journal of Proceedings of the House of Delegates, January 1867* (Annapolis, 1867); *Baltimore American,* February 19, 1867; *Baltimore Sun,* February 21, May 13, 1867; *Baltimore Gazette,* May 13, 1867.

29. Ibid.

30. See chapter 6.

31. *Frederick Examiner,* May 22, 1867.

32. *Baltimore American,* April 21, 22, October 7, 1865, April 2, June 27, November 12, December 30, 1867; *Easton Gazette,* November 11, 1865, November 21, 1866; *Baltimore Sun,* October 7, November 25, 1865, May 1, 1866, February 13, July 31, 1867; *Baltimore Gazette,* October 7, 1865; Signature Books, 334, 664, 668, 698, 701, 769, 793, 806, 836, 888, 901, 931, 963, 1068, Records of the Freedmen's Savings and Trust Company [Baltimore], RG 101.

33. Wright, *The Free Negro in Maryland,* 209–61.

34. *Frederick Examiner,* May 22, 1867; H. L. Bond to K. Bond, n.d., Bond-McCulloch Family Papers (MS 1159), Maryland Historical Society; *Baltimore American,* June 1, 1866; *Baltimore American,* September 30, 1865, May 15, 1866; *Debates of the Constitutional Convention of the State of Maryland,* 3 vols. (Annapolis, 1864), 3:1590.

35. *Baltimore American,* September 30, 1865.

36. Ibid.

37. *Baltimore American,* June 5, 8, 26, 1867; *Baltimore Gazette,* June 6, 1867; *Baltimore Sun,* June 5, 8, 26, 1867; *The Ordinances of the Mayor and City Council of Baltimore, Passed at the Sessions of 1866–1867,* 45; *Journal of Proceedings of the First Branch City Council of Baltimore At the Sessions of 1866 and 1867,* 905–06, 928–29.

38. Fuke, "The Baltimore Association for the Moral and Educational Improvement of the Colored People, 1864–1870," 369–404. See also chapter 5.

39. Ibid.

40. *Baltimore American,* October 4, 1865.

41. Ibid.

42. Ibid., October 3, 1865.

43. *Baltimore American,* January 21, 1865, February 20, 21, 1867.

44. Ibid.; L. Wallace to C. A. Dana, August 30, 1864, *War of the Rebellion: A Compilation of the Official Records of the Union and Confederate Armies,* Series 1, Volume 43, Part 1—"Reports, Correspondence, Etc.," Serial 90 (Washington, 1893), 969–70.

45. *Baltimore Gazette,* May 10, August 18, 1866; *Baltimore Sun,* May 10, 1866; *Baltimore American,* August 18, 1866.

46. *Baltimore American,* July 3, 4, August 5, September 5, 1867; *Baltimore Gazette,* July 3, 1867; *Baltimore Sun,* July 3, 1867.

47. *Baltimore American,* October 18, 19, 21, 22, 23, 29, 1867; *Baltimore Sun,* October 18, 19, 21, 22, 26, 29, November 15, 1867; *Baltimore Gazette,* October 18, 19, 21, 12, 26, November 8, 1867.

48. *Baltimore American,* October 18, 19, 21, 22, 23, 29, 1867; *Baltimore Sun,* October 18, 19, 21, 22, 26, 29, November 15, 1867; *Baltimore Gazette,* October 18, 19, 21, 22, 26, November 8, 1867.

49. *Baltimore Gazette,* October 18, 1867.

50. *Baltimore American,* July 9, 1867.

51. *Baltimore Sun,* January 30, 1865; *Christian Advocate,* November 3, 1864; *Baltimore Clipper,* December 9, 1864.

52. *Chestertown Transcript,* June 10, 1865; *Baltimore Sun,* June 12, 1865; *Baltimore American,* June 20, 1865.

53. *Baltimore Sun,* July 18, 1865.

54. Ibid., July 25, 31, 1865; *Baltimore Gazette,* July 31, 1865.

55. S. N. Clark to J. Eaton Jr., August 21, 1865, State Papers [1865], Maryland State Archives.

56. *Baltimore American,* November 23, 1865.

57. *Baltimore Sun,* September 1, 3, 5, 8, 15, 18, 23, 25, October 20, 1866; *Baltimore American,* September 1, 3, 5, 6, 8, 11, 12, 17, 18, 19, 21, 24, October 19, 20, December 24, 1866; *Baltimore Gazette,* September 3, 14, 18, 26, 1866; *Annapolis Gazette,* September 6, 20, October 25, 1866.

58. *Baltimore Gazette,* August 3, 6, 9, 1867; *Baltimore American,* August 3, 5, 6, 1867; *Baltimore Sun,* August 3, 6, 1867.

59. *Baltimore American,* February 9, 1866.

60. Statement of Essex Barbour, contained in E. F. O'Brien to S. N. Clark, February 7, 1866, Box 1 (LRAC, September 1865–October 27, 1866), BRFAL, D.C., RG 105.

61. C. A. Watkins to C. H. Howard, March 13, 1866, Box 1 (LRAC, September 1865–October 27, 1866), BRFAL, D.C., RG 105.

62. W. L. VanDerlip to W. W. Rogers, July 11, 1866, Box 11 (Letters Received, Annapolis, July 20, 1866–September 11, 1868), BRFAL, Md., RG 105.

63. H. P. Jordan to E. M. Gregory, December 4, 1866, Volume 47 (Letters Received, Annapolis, July 20, 1866–September 11, 1868), BRFAL, Md., RG 105; W. L. VanDerlip to W. W. Rogers, December 18, 1866, Volume 48 (Register of Letters Sent, Annapolis, June 28, 1866–March 13, 1868), BRFAL, Md., RG 105; E. M. Gregory to O. O. Howard, December 31, 1866, Box 10 (Reports), BRFAL, Md., RG 105; *Baltimore American*, January 12, 16, 1867; Testimony of R. G. Lanahan, John W. Start, J. S. Perry, William H. Downs, James Kelly, O. P. Burnside, Rev. N. J. B. Morgan, George T. Warfield, George E. Shipley, L. Baldwin, Rev. George B. Leech, January 14–February 1, 1867, Testimony in Investigation of the Government of Maryland, 1867, Records of the House of Representatives, Committee on the Judiciary, RG 233.

64. *Baltimore Gazette*, August 3, 6, 9, 1867; *Baltimore American*, August 3, 5, 6, 1867; *Baltimore Sun*, August 3, 6, 1867.

65. *Baltimore American*, October 29, November 18, 1867; *Baltimore Gazette*, November 8, 1867; *Baltimore Sun*, November 15, 1867; F. Von Shirrach to D. G. Swain, October 10, 1868, Volume 4 (Maryland and Delaware, Assistant and Sub-Assistant Commissioner, Letters Sent, July 23, 1868–December 29, 1868), BRFAL, Md., RG 105.

66. *Baltimore Sun*, January 30, 1865.

67. *Baltimore Gazette*, March 22, 1866; H. P. Jordan to H. L. Bond, May 21, 1866, Box 1 (LRAC, April 1, 1866–August 17, 1868), BRFAL, Md., RG 105; W. L. VanDerlip to W. W. Rogers, July 22, 1866, Volume 48 (Register of Letters Sent, Annapolis, June 28, 1866–March 13, 1868), BRFAL, Md., RG 105; H. P. Jordan to O. O. Howard, August 24, 1866, Volume 47 (Letters Received, Annapolis, July 20, 1866–September 11, 1866), BRFAL, Md., RG 105.

68. S. N. Clark to J. Eaton Jr., August 21, 1865, State Papers [1865], Maryland State Archives.

69. *St. Mary's Gazette*, August 7, 1865, as quoted in ibid.

70. Harrison Diary (MS 432.1), Maryland Historical Society.

71. *Baltimore American*, August 31, 1865.

72. *Baltimore Clipper*, December 9, 1864.

73. W. Daniel to W. A. Bradford, December 9, 1864, State Papers [1864], Maryland State Archives.

74. *Baltimore Sun*, July 26, 1865.

75. A. W. Bradford to O. O. Howard, October 4, 1865, State Papers [1865], Maryland State Archives.

76. Ibid.

77. *Baltimore Sun*, January 24, 1866; *Congressional Globe*, 39:1, January 23, 1866, 373–74. Born in Annapolis in 1796, Reverdy Johnson graduated from St. John's College in 1811. He was admitted to the Maryland bar in 1815 and

moved to Baltimore two years later. A Whig for much of his political career, he became a conservative Unionist during the Civil War and allied with the Democrats after. He was elected to the Maryland House of Delegates in 1861 and to the United States Senate in 1863. He opposed Lincoln's Emancipation Proclamation and supported George McClellan's 1864 presidential bid (*Dictionary of American Biography*, 10:114; *Who Was Who in America, Historical Volume, 1607–1896* [Chicago, 1963], 281; Dan Morris and Inez Morris, eds., *Who Was Who in American Politics* [New York, 1974], 344).

78. *Baltimore American*, February 13, 1866; *Baltimore Gazette*, February 9, 1866; emphasis added.

79. *Baltimore Sun*, June 21, 1866. See also *Baltimore American*, April 6, 1864; "Message of Governor Swann to the General Assembly of Maryland" (Annapolis, 1866) appears as Document A in *Journal of the Proceedings of the House of Delegates, Extra Session, 1866*; "Message of Governor Swann to the General Assembly of Maryland" (Annapolis, 1867) appears as Document A in *Journal of the Proceedings of the House of Delegates, January Session 1867*.

80. *Baltimore American*, September 5, 1865.

81. Ibid., July 30, 1867.

82. See chapter 10.

83. *Baltimore American*, November 14, 1865.

84. *Cambridge Intelligencer*, December 9, 1865.

85. *Baltimore American*, April 12, 1866, emphasis in original.

86. Ibid., July 1, 30, August 3, 5, 12, September 5, 1867.

87. *Baltimore Sun*, May 17, 21, 1866; *Baltimore Gazette*, May 16, 1866; *Baltimore American*, May 16, 1866; E. G. Jackson to Freedmen's Bureau, May 8, 1866, Box 1 (LRAC, April 1, 1866–August 17, 1868), BRFAL, Md., RG 105.

88. H. L. Bond to K. Bond, February 17, 1867, Bond-McCulloch Family Papers (MS 1159), Maryland Historical Society.

89. *Baltimore American*, August 14, 1866; See also chapter 10.

90. *Baltimore American*, August 7, 1865.

91. Ibid., April 4, 1866.

10

The Confines of White Racial Attitudes

I

THEORETICALLY, emancipation possessed the power to destroy traditional patterns of behavior and to offer black Marylanders significantly new alternatives, but without accompanying white attitudinal changes that transcended the assumptions of slavery, such prospects were endangered from the start. As previous chapters in this study have shown, not everyone opposed change. Blacks and a vocal minority of radical politicians and federal officials not only sought a genuinely new status for Maryland's freed slaves, but did much to ensure that a large part of their dream became reality. Against such progress, however, were marshaled the opinions of virtually the entire planting class as well as many prominent Baltimoreans who had consistently opposed emancipation or accepted it reluctantly as a necessary evil that did not commit them to further black "elevation." Moreover, while white radicals believed honestly and optimistically in a better society for both blacks and whites, they shared with conservatives several ideological assumptions that restricted such belief. Under the circumstances, blacks themselves had difficulty formulating public attitudes. They naturally opposed the pejorative assumptions of both conservatives and radicals but were loath to force an issue that might cost them valuable white support.

Clearly, the starkest element of this philosophical combination was planter conservatism. As has been seen, few Marylanders who had owned slaves were prepared to countenance any alteration in blacks' subordinate relationship with whites. Rural conservatives, with powerful urban support, maintained that blacks were inherently incapable of functioning on the same social or economic plane as whites. As a consequence of such inferiority they believed the denial of equal rights of any sort to blacks justified, and they viewed attempts to force the "intermingling" or "amalgamation" of such unequals with extreme distaste. Theirs was a white man's society, stressed planter conservatives; one that must be protected from all debilitating influences if its strength and integrity were to prevail.

Understandably, there were many prominent individuals in Maryland who espoused the conservative point of view. The state's three governors between 1864 and 1870 all spoke of the need to maintain white control over blacks. Augustus Bradford defended Maryland's apprenticeship laws and opposed the presence of the Freedmen's Bureau.[1] Thomas Swann assumed the role of his state's leading defender of the separated society, and Oden Bowie believed that blacks had been thoroughly and permanently demoralized by emancipation.[2] Supporting these state leaders were two influential federal politicians from Maryland, United States Senator Reverdy Johnson and Representative Benjamin Harris. Unlike most conservatives, Johnson professed confidence in blacks' capacity for self-improvement but like his colleagues, objected vigorously to social or political equality and to the attempt by radicals to obtain black elevation through legislation or the efforts of the Freedmen's Bureau. Harris believed that blacks were inherently inferior to whites and in need of constant supervision by their ex-masters.[3]

Other important conservatives at the state level were Daniel Clarke, Richard Edelen, Eli Henkle, William Purnell, and Isaac Jones, who along with a dozen or more supporters constituted an outspoken minority at the 1864 Maryland constitutional convention opposed to protective measures for blacks beyond their simple emancipation. Many of these men went on to serve as conservative state legislators, delegates to the Democratic-dominated state constitutional convention of 1867, or as appointed officials; Isaac D. Jones, for example, becoming state attorney general in 1867. Most of these men represented rural counties, but conservatives could also count on the backing of two of Baltimore's daily newspapers, the moderate *Sun* and the Negrophobic *Gazette*. Several county journals, especially the *Chestertown Transcript*, added considerable weight to the conservative cause. The influential *Maryland Farmer and Mechanic* also represented the planter point of view.

"The negro and the white man belong to two distinct races," explained the *Baltimore Gazette*. "Providence, for some wise purpose has so determined it."[4] "History furnishes . . . no record of a successful intermingling," added the *Sun*, "between the great divisions of mankind."[5] In a letter to the radical *Baltimore American* in September 1865 a conservative correspondent argued, "There is a natural antipathy between the white man and the black which neither time nor association can remove."[6] As the *Gazette* reiterated:

> Between the blacks and the whites in this country the differences—moral, mental, and physical—are far more strongly marked than between those of any two . . . nations. . . . They are of such a character as to forever preclude such a blending of the Caucasian and the negro on this Continent. . . . Nature has her laws and man must bond to their inexorable dictates.[7]

Moreover, to the conservative there was no question as to which of the two races was superior. In a statement atypical only in its language, Montgomery Peters, an Eastern Shore delegate to the constitutional convention of 1867, insisted:

> [The black man] has acquired no character . . . He huddles together in small houses abandoned mostly by the whites and there he indulges his brutal appetites in the most brutal way. None of the signs of order, none of the insignia of genteel social regulation, none of the emblems of morality, none of the marks of the Christian man, with reverence for his God and with respect for his fellow-man are found in his houses or in his deportment outside. He is a savage with the bacchanalian orgies of his strange savage nature.[8]

Not everyone chose words so intemperate but Peters's view, or something like it, was shared generally by all conservatives. "Does anyone profess," asked William Purnell, "that the negro will ever occupy the status of the white man? The idea is preposterous."[9]

Because of blacks' obvious inferiority, conservatives opposed the status of unabridged freedom for them. Without the benevolent control of the planter class, they argued, ex-slaves were doomed to an inevitable process of demoralization. "The natural inclinations of the negro are to idleness, dissipation, and vice," explained one planter, "and where . . . they are suffered to follow their natural inclinations, they will lapse into barbarism and even idolatry."[10] "They are degraded in point of intellect," added a second, and the consequence of their freedom would be "further degradation, the perpetuation of further crime, and every sort of vice." If left to their own resources, blacks were destined to suffer "the same fate that has awaited the red man upon our border, final extirpation as a nuisance intolerable in any community of which white men are members.[11] Conservatives were quick to point out that the rapid degeneration of free black populations was a well-established historical phenomenon. Where emancipated in the West Indian Islands, claimed Isaac Jones, "the negro is fast relapsing into his original African savagism."[12] A correspondent to the *Maryland Farmer and Mechanic* in December 1865 agreed. "[L]eft to his own fitful and desultory exertions," he explained, the negro in Jamaica had become "a tax and burden upon the State." "[N]o amount of legislation," he concluded, "can impart to him, the brains, the energies and aspirations of the white race."[13]

Freed blacks in such a woeful state could not hope to compete with whites in the open marketplace and any attempt by them to do so would invite their almost certain extermination. According to Richard Edelen, the presence of free blacks in any occupation and their tendency to undercut wages robbed white laborers of their respectability and would force white retaliation. In support of his position, Edelen quoted from an 1859 speech by A. H. H. Steuart before the Agricultural Society of Virginia. "I can clearly see," Steuart had said,

> how the tendency to a "conflict" between the black and the white laborer would become "irrepressible." The white laborer whose avocation had heretofore been respectable, and who had been accustomed to earning wages adequate to the support of his family, would not tolerate the competition of those who would degrade the dignity of labor and underbid him in his business.[14]

Eli Henkle was equally convinced. "You elevate the negro," he said, "and in so doing you place the poor white laboring class upon an equality with him. . . . I think it will result in a war of the races, when the poor negro will go down in the struggle."[15] Thomas Swann argued in a similar fashion that "equality in [the] workshop" would lead to "the irrepressible conflict which is certain to ensue when the two races . . . shall stand in accepted antagonism towards each other."[16]

Convictions such as these led a few conservatives to call for an outright return to slavery. Montgomery Peters, for example, claimed "There is a manifest injustice . . . in releasing this poor being—the negro—from the control and protection of those who understand his nature." It was the duty of white Marylanders "not to place these human beings in this helpless condition. . . . [We] cannot declare [their] freedom."[17] Most other planters did not go so far. Accepting emancipation as a fait accompli, they argued instead that blacks' rights as free men and women should be legally restricted and that some form of paternalistic control over their ex-slaves should be maintained by the master class. According to this argument, blacks deserved every protection of their right to work, to make contracts, and to live in peace, but beyond that their affairs should be closely regulated.

Conservatives used such reasoning especially in their defense of the forced apprenticeship of black children. "I do think it is for the good of society," argued an 1864 constitutional convention delegate,

> that such a provision be incorporated into the constitution. This sudden turning loose of immense quantities of negroes, utterly unused to and unskilled and uneducated in a single means of taking care of themselves—they will be like uncaged birds; they will not know how to manage, they will not know what to do.[18]

"It is a reasonable supposition," added the *Chestertown Transcript* in December of the same year, "that the negro unaccustomed to provide for his own wants, thrown upon his own resources at such times as these will be unable to maintain his children. It is better for the child and the community that they should not become vagrants."[19] On the first of January 1865, in his annual message to the General Assembly, Augustus Bradford concurred and suggested the broader necessity of caring for blacks in a number of ways. "We shall . . . witness the wants of an ignorant and dependent class . . . unaccustomed to think or act for themselves, suddenly thrown upon the community whose duty it will be . . . to think and act for them."[20]

Nor did conservatives contemplate only a temporary tutelage for their black charges. In the eyes of most planters, freed slaves' incapacity and inferiority were such that permanent white control was essential. Anything less posed the threat of black "equality," which would guarantee the erosion of Maryland society. "There are no half-way measures possible," insisted the *Baltimore Gazette*. "The black must give way to the white."[21] As Benjamin Harris explained:

> The negro must be kept in subordination to the white man. . . . I say this with the kindest feelings and sympathy for the negro race. Full equality of rights will never exist between races so dissimilar that they cannot socially amalgamate, especially when they live together in large numbers.[22]

Maryland conservatives were especially vehement on this point when opposing radical demands for universal manhood suffrage. "It seems strange that sensible men," wrote a September 1865 correspondent to the *Baltimore American*, "should endeavor to blend two races together between whom such an antipathy exists. Yet the very fact of conferring upon the negro the right of suffrage is a step towards its consummation."[23] According to a *Baltimore Sun* editorial in November of that year:

> [Radicals] close their minds to the fact that the negro . . . is actuated by feelings and sympathies distinct from those of the white race amongst whom he lives. They take no heed of the fearful examples of anarchy and perpetual civil strife furnished for our warning by the Mexican and other neighboring nations, where the Indian and negro races have intermingled with the whites in a social and political equality which has degraded the latter without benefitting the former, and which has almost made their social structure a reproach among nations.[24]

Specifically, conservatives feared a number of consequences attendant upon the introduction of "equality." High on their list were education for blacks similar to that received by whites, the mixture of the races through marriage and sexual relations, and black exercise of political power. "I am unwilling to educate him [the Negro]," said William Purnell, "and prepare him for the higher walks of life—those which are occupied by his superiors, the white race."[25] On the topic of sexual "intermingling," the *Baltimore Gazette* was equally blunt. "It is an indisputable fact," it claimed in July 1865, "that a general intermarriage between the two [races] would result in the production of a feebler race which would rapidly degenerate and eventually die out."[26] And as for blacks' potential political influence, Thomas Swann warned that universal suffrage would precipitate Maryland "into the hands of the African race."[27] A convention of Maryland conservatives in February 1866 expressed similar alarm. "We do not object to his [the Negro's] freedom," it resolved,

> but to give him the right to make our laws . . . we do most energetically protest and object. . . . In view of the momentous interests involved we do by our manhood, our love of country, by our devotion to the best interests of the Union, solemnly, earnestly, and unitedly pledge ourselves and all we can influence, to arrest this baleful measure.[28]

Conservatives believed their ideology represented the best interests of everyone in the state, including blacks. "The liberated class are familiar with the duties required of them," said the *Baltimore Sun*, "and in the great majority of cases have not been intoxicated by their newly acquired freedom."[29] The *Sun* and others of a like opinion were sure that if left undisturbed, black behavior would remain docile and that planters and freedmen would come to terms without disrupting Maryland's traditionally white-dominated politics, economy, and society. According to the *Chestertown Transcript*, freed blacks, if "left to the management of those alone who have the right to control them . . . will enjoy all the privileges and protection of the laws of the State."[30]

Neither blacks nor white reformers could afford to treat the conservative ideology lightly. For one thing, it represented the opinions of most of the men and women for whom freed slaves had to work. For another, after radicals' defeat in the Maryland election of 1866, conservative politicians controlled the government of the state. For all practical purposes, then, the planter ideology constituted white Maryland's racial orthodoxy and as such, the reality that faced blacks and reformers and defined the dimensions of their maneuverability.

II

Countering the conservative philosophy was that of white radicalism. The property first of the emancipationist wing of the Maryland Union Party, this label increasingly defined those whites of Northern or Radical Republican sentiment who desired the elevation of blacks beyond simple emancipation. A minority in their own party, such extremists enjoyed political influence only to the extent they could persuade their more conservative or moderate colleagues that continued elevation of blacks was essential to secure their freedom, and only so long as conservatives in general were restrained by the presence of the United States Army, the Freedmen's Bureau, and a registration act that disfranchised Confederate sympathizers. Such a favorable combination of circumstances prevailed only until the defeat of the Union Party in 1866 but did not end before radicals had reached several important goals. Their principal accomplishment, of course, was the emancipation of Maryland's slaves, but they managed also to obtain the repeal of many statutes affecting the lives of free blacks, and to keep the issue of further black progress in the forefront of state politics even after their loss of political power.

At the forefront of the radical cause were a number of outspoken politicians whose consistent advocacy of black elevation won them considerable notoriety in a generally conservative state. Foremost nationally was Henry Winter Davis, United States Representative and Radical Republican whose early agitation of universal manhood suffrage predated that of even his closest Maryland colleagues.[31] Davis's death in 1865 robbed the radical cause in his state of its most powerful and articulate spokesman, a blow from which it never fully recovered. None of his followers possessed Davis's national constituency and without it lacked the means to bring real federal power to bear on Maryland conservatism. Of the survivors, the best known were John Creswell, United States Representative and Senator, 1863–66, and Hugh Lennox Bond, judge of the Baltimore Criminal Court between 1861 and 1867. Creswell did his best to sustain Davis's cause in Congress but lacked his influence and charisma. Bond did notably better. Although the loser by a wide margin to Democrat Oden Bowie in the Maryland gubernatorial campaign of 1867, he was clearly the state's most effective spokesman for radical views. Almost single-handedly, it seemed at times, he spearheaded the fight against apprenticeship, the drive to educate black children, and the effort to win black Marylanders the vote.[32]

Supporting Creswell and Bond were John L. Thomas, Jr., and Francis Thomas, both U.S. Representatives, and Archibald Stirling, Jr., Henry Stockbridge, Joseph M. Cushing, and James Valliant, all emancipationist delegates to the 1864 constitutional convention who went on to play prominent roles in state politics.[33] In addition, Maryland radicals enjoyed the steady backing of first the United States Army and then the Freedmen's Bureau, between 1861 and 1868. Almost to a man, federal officers supported radical attempts to win further rights and education for black Marylanders and sought to assist freedmen in every way they judged appropriate to establish themselves as free and self-reliant workers. Especially prominent were General Lew Wallace of the U.S. Army, who ordered county orphans' courts to cease binding black children in 1864, and Edgar Gregory, who commanded the Maryland district of the Freedmen's Bureau between 1866 and 1868. Finally, radicals received articulate assistance from a number of journals, the most influential being the *Baltimore American,* the *Easton Gazette,* and the *Frederick Examiner.*

Radicals pursued genuinely progressive goals and hoped to establish a society substantially different from that dominated by slavery. What set Maryland radicals apart from conservatives and at the same time defined the reform dimensions of their ideology was their conviction that emancipation marked a fundamental departure from the ways of slavery and that freedom offered their state the chance to build a more productive, informed, and civilized society. To such men as Bond, Creswell, and the Thomases, slavery had cast a pall over Maryland for too long, denying it the opportunity to advance economically, and socially, with its more ambitious northern neighbors. Theirs was a set of values predicated upon self-help, open competition, and industrial growth, all in the absence of what they described as planter inertia.

According to radicals, one of conservatives' biggest stumbling blocks was their obsession with "negro equality." Planters' fear of free blacks, they said, led them to resist change of any sort that threatened white hegemony and blinded them to prospects of future growth. Radicals, too, believed in a white-dominated society, but did not fear the consequences of black advancement in certain areas. Unlike conservatives who feared *any* form of black elevation, radicals felt that controlled uplift for freed men and women would benefit all Marylanders, and that ex-slaves animated by freedom possessed the capacity to raise themselves from degradation to become more productive citizens.

"They have the means of advancement within their own grasp," explained the *Baltimore American* as early as November 14, 1864. "Most of them, we have every reason to believe," added the Friends Association in Aid of Freedmen two weeks later, "are capable of doing this."[34] To the conservative claim that blacks were inherently incapable of independent initiative, radicals responded vigorously. "[A]way with the despicable trash," exclaimed Archibald Stirling in June 1864, "of maintaining the idea, in violation of all the instincts of human nature, that these people will not work when they can and cannot work when they will."[35] "A hundred thousand free blacks in Maryland can support themselves now," added Joseph Cushing in November of the same year. "They are abundantly able to support themselves."[36] Moreover, the incentive provided by their emancipation would ensure blacks' continued determination to improve their capacities. "As sure as it is the law of God for the white man that . . . freedom [is] better than slavery," argued Creswell, "so will experience vindicate the same great principle for the black man."[37] "The desire to rise, to ameliorate one's condition," added the *Baltimore American,* "is the mainstream of action, and activity is the source and cause of civilization."[38]

It was for this reason that radicals reserved their greatest praise for the benefits of black education. "Educated labor produces more than uneducated labor," claimed Hugh Lennox Bond in November 1864, "it is therefore in the interest of the State that all men should be instructed."[39] Most radicals agreed. "It is not only right that we should educate them," said the *Cambridge Intelligencer* in March 1865, "but it is also to our interest. By improving them we benefit ourselves. Ignorance is a curse to any people and no community can prosper which tolerates the presence of a large uneducated class."[40] Radicals believed that black workers thus elevated would assist greatly in overcoming the stagnation of plantation agriculture and in encouraging new patterns of economic development. As the *Baltimore American* explained, "We want their help on our farms; we need their services in our manufactures; we require their aid in our renewed efforts to place industrial interests of the State upon a permanent basis of prosperity."[41]

According to radicals, education would rid blacks of the debilitations that characterized their status as slaves. In a public address in Wilmington, Delaware, Bond told his listeners that

> . . . education enhances the value of labor. The workman who is so ignorant that he cannot kill his pig because the moon is not of the right age, will lose two days waiting for fear the meat will shrink, or he will not set his fence at another time of the moon for fear the bottom rail will sink into the ground, and so he waits for a week; or perhaps he fancies he is bewitched, wears salt in his boots, and spends much time visiting a conjuror. Such labor is not valuable, and yet it is what Delaware and Maryland have.[42]

In an editorial probably written by Bond, the *Easton Gazette* in January 1865 bemoaned the fact that the presence of workers so ignorant frightened prospective immigrants away. The latter, it warned, "must see about them educated labor. If they take notice that the colored people are left in hopeless ignorance . . . they will not remain among us."[43] Once educated, blacks would become valuable assets to Maryland's economy, "for when cultured and educated," explained Bond, "our people will not let them go away, so valuable will be their services to the country."[44]

But the radical commitment to blacks' progress consisted of more than their education, no matter how important that might be. As part of their search for a new and more enlightened society, radicals called upon white Marylanders to cast off the "yoke" of slavery and to recognize a new "tendency toward freedom" with *all* its implications, including full rights of citizenship for blacks. To Bond and other radicals this meant several things, starting with the assumption that blacks were human beings who deserved to be treated as such, moving on to blacks' enjoyment of the same civil rights as whites, and concluding with their exercise of the ultimate privilege, the franchise. Anything less, radicals argued, doomed Maryland to the same social and economic inertia that had characterized the years of slavery. "The absurd prejudices of the past are abandoned," claimed the *Baltimore American*. "What we contend is that the utmost freedom of individual action . . . is for the highest good of the community."[45]

Radicals' insistence that blacks be treated as fellow human beings with needs and desires like those of whites stopped short of racial equality but ascribed to blacks all the qualifications necessary to share in the building of a better Maryland. "The chief end of man, black or white," explained Joseph Pugh, an 1864 constitutional convention delegate, "is to secure his own happiness. . . . No man can show . . . that the negro race are so deficient by *nature* in those natural attributes."[46] To deny the accuracy of this statement was to James Valliant "absurd, monstrous, inhuman and unchristian." "The negro is a man, not a brute," claimed Valliant. "He is endowed with the same moral attributes as other men."[47] And that such endowment fitted blacks with the prerequisites conducive to social progress there could be no doubt. "Give them proper encouragement," advised the *Baltimore American*, "then trust to their natural instincts for the result. . . . Open to the negro the avenue of wealth . . . and you will thus excite his emulation to obtain a respectable footing."[48]

"If liberty means anything, it must mean this," said the *Baltimore American*. "[I]t must consist in the absence of restraint . . . ; it must be an equal chance for all to labor, and receive the reward of their labor."[49] To accomplish this aim, argued the *American*, "the black code must be abolished, negro testimony must be admitted in courts, contracts for labor must be observed by employers, [and] fair compensation must be allowed for work."[50] And federal laws must be obeyed. "Congress has granted to him [the Negro] such civil rights," explained the *American*, "as shall enable him to remain peaceably where he is . . . without which privileges he would be powerless either to hold that which he has acquired or to collect the claims which are jointly [*sic*] due him."[51]

Behind radicals' advocacy of such protection for blacks were principles as well as practical considerations. For one thing, blacks surely deserved these rights after fighting for the Union cause in the Civil War. But secondly, and more importantly, radicals believed that blacks possessed a basic claim to equal treatment under the law guaranteed by no less a document than Thomas Jefferson's Declaration of Independence. As American citizens, blacks were entitled to the same legal privileges as whites, and although most radicals agreed with conservatives that statutes could not affect social or racial distinctions, there was no gainsaying this commitment to an elevated place for blacks in Maryland society. It was a principle to which radicals constantly returned in their speeches, and none was more eloquent than Hugh Lennox Bond. "We have come back to the fundamental ideas of the founders of the Republic," he said in June 1867,

> and herald today the creed which was the belief common to them all. . . . In that declaration they declared that . . . all men were born free and equal, and that they were endowed with inalienable rights. . . . That is the Radical platform we advocate—a return to the principles which inspired our fathers, which were placed at the foundation of the Republic.[52]

Others concurred. "Certainly all residents must surrender a portion of their natural rights to the community for the good of the whole," commented a correspondent to the *Baltimore American.* "But no one man or class should be called upon to surrender any right which may be retained by others in the same community."[53] In a July 1866 editorial, the *American* added, "The Declaration of Independence declares that all men—not all white men—are endowed with the right to 'life, liberty, and the pursuit of happiness.' Those who disbelieve in this doctrine must ignore the fundamental principles on which our Government is founded."[54] Marylanders must, the *American* declared later, "place it among the irreversible laws of the land that liberty recognizes no distinction among men."[55] Only then would their state enjoy "a pure democracy, founded upon equal laws and giving to every man an opportunity to be all God made him capable of being."[56]

To radicals, the application of these principles would guarantee Maryland the progressive society they sought. "[I]n qualifying him [the Negro] for the duties of a citizen," wrote "Junius" in September 1865, "we will secure the prosperity and happiness of both races, one of which can never be prosperous by the injury of the other."[57] By recognizing this truth, added the *American* in July 1867, "the last remnant of aristocracy will be abolished," and the way opened to "establish justice upon immovable foundations, and develop industry and energies of the people."[58] Two weeks later, the *American* elaborated. In defense of universal manhood suffrage, it said,

> we think it can be demonstrated by the clearest rules of logic that . . . [it] would be beneficial to the community, that it would promote virtue, industry, and intelligence, enhance the value of every piece of property, add thousands and millions to the aggregate wealth of the State, increase population, and increase our commerce. . . . It would operate like the pebble cast into the middle of the ocean, and would execute a motion whose influence would be felt everywhere and never be lost.[59]

Of course it was one thing for radicals to promote equal civil and political rights for blacks; quite another to persuade conservatives to agree with them. Radicals were fully aware of the awesomeness of this task and responded as vigorously as they knew how. Although they, too, regarded blacks as inferior to whites in some ways, radicals constantly decried the type of prejudice that denied the blacks their humanity, civil rights, or educational opportunity. White Marylanders had a "duty to overcome prejudice," declared Bond. "We must fight prejudice and decide in favor of 'nigger.' "[60] He knew that "Every ignorant man will be constantly afraid that his next door neighbor is a negro."[61] He understood the bias that dictated "that every negro, if educated would become a Brigham Young, and marry all the women he could find."[62] Still, Bond had little sympathy for those who believed that any assistance for blacks raised the specter of social equality. White superiority could take care of itself and required no help from racial prejudice. "Because I think myself either by the gift of God or accidental circumstances superior to the Darks it is no reason that I should stop the avenues of their egress."[63] Furthermore, "If a man can beat another in a race, why insist on tying a weight to the legs of his competitor?"[64]

Bond had no fear of "negro equality" and neither did his colleagues. As John L. Thomas explained, "Because I am an American citizen, I choose to give them [Negroes] what God has given me and every man. . . . When a negro raises himself I do not think that he is degrading me or that I am elevating him, and anyone afraid of negro equality is not as good as a negro."[65] And as Henry Stockbridge added, "I have no sympathy, no respect even, for that feeling, or that fear . . . that is so eternally afraid of negro equality. If with generations that [head?] start . . . we cannot maintain the race with them, then in all conscience let us give them the track."[66] Indeed, according to James Valliant, whites had no choice in their treatment of the Negro, for:

> He has the same virtues [as whites] and is addicted to the same vices. Being a man and not a brute, and being born on our soil, he has the same claim to it by the law of nature and nature's God that we have. His right to our sunlight and our atmosphere is identical to ours. . . . I say that the negro is a man. . . . As such how can we, how dare we, to deprive him of the exercise of those rights with which God has endowed him.[67]

But most white Marylanders were not prepared to accept such an idea, and those who did suffered constant attack. In November 1866 a correspondent called Bond a "black-hearted nigger-loving son of a bitch," and closed his message with a fervent "God damn you."[68] Another sent a warning that read "Judge and Negroes, your time draws nigh," with a picture of a gallows underneath.[69] The *Baltimore Gazette* dismissed Bond as an "unscrupulous demagogue . . . of the most malignant partisanship," and scorned his "unctious discourses to our colored brethren."[70] His was, as Bond knew, a difficult struggle against great odds. "It will take a moral Ajax," he complained, "to wrest from these people the accumulated prejudice of two centuries and make them believe in the common brotherhood of man."[71] Bond and other radicals realized they had to revolutionize ways of life familiar to generations. But if Maryland were to change, its people must too.

> I know it is difficult to get out of a net, to change ideas after you are fifty or sixty years old. It would be the death of some men of that age if they did, but they have no right to force us younger people, who have new ideas and are to live under a new system, to hold their exploded views. They must not expect to put our new wine into their old bottles; they must not expect me to go the gait they paced fifty years ago; they must not expect to make the Eastern Shore like a province of China, where men do the same things, father and son for a thousand years.[72]

Politically, Bond lost his battle. He and his colleagues pushed too hard and suffered their second defeat in as many years in the state election of 1867.[73] Nevertheless, the effectiveness of the radical position was not confined to politics. In the emancipation of the slaves, the repeal of black code legislation, the establishment of schools, and the assistance given the U.S. Army and Freedmen's Bureau, radicals lent powerful support to black Marylanders' efforts to improve their lives. More importantly, radical racial attitudes themselves, while failing to become white Maryland's racial orthodoxy, served as a bridge between the white reform mentality and black aspirations. Together they defined the areas of progress possible in the search for a new society.

III

Nonetheless, despite the obvious thrust toward change in radical ideology, George Fredrickson and others are quite correct in pointing to serious reservations in radicals' commitment to black progress which, alongside conservative views helped define the restraining characteristics of white attitudes in general. Briefly stated, white radicals shared with their conservative counterparts several assumptions about blacks and their place in Maryland society that helped confine freedmen in their search for equality. Like conservative planters, radical politicians and federal agents were white men of their times accustomed to regarding blacks as distinct people with problems attributable to the peculiarities of their race and circumstance. And although radicals obviously transcended many more such mental obstacles than conservatives in their search for a post-emancipation society to their liking, they did not conquer them all. Blacks remained lesser beings than whites to the radical mind and deserving of special treatment, albeit of a more progressive sort than that envisioned by conservatives.

From the outset, radicals shared with conservatives the idea that freed slaves were degraded people. Although they attributed such a condition to the influences of slavery rather than to blacks' inherent characteristics, radicals remained singularly unimpressed with newly freed men and women as individuals with social conscience, moral values, or human dignity. Studies by Lawrence Levine, Eugene Genovese, Herbert Gutman, John Blassingame, Philip Morgan, and others, tell us of slaves throughout the south who possessed these virtues as part of a black community and consciousness that grew despite the restrictions of slavery.[74] Maryland radicals perceived little or nothing of this "world the slaves made," and were convinced that what they had before them was an inchoate mass of ignorant, demoralized people. "[T]he brand [is] upon them," explained Henry Stockbridge in August 1864, "the degradation of generations of servitude, [and] the stupidity and ignorance begotten of that servitude."[75] "Their mental condition is blank and vacant," said the *Baltimore American* in November 1864, and eighteen months later, the message was the same. "[The Negro's] moral character is very low," it asserted in April 1866.

> Lying, thieving, and licentiousness are the natural vices of slavery. Indo-
> lence and thriftlessness are inevitable where industry meets with no re-
> ward. Here, then, we see the great props of manhood broken down.
> Ignorance now comes in to cast a deeper shade over the picture and sink
> the man more nearly to the brute. . . . Self respect is destroyed; the link
> that binds man to honor and virtue is broken. . . . Hence there ensues a
> social and moral degradation, sad and pitiable to behold.[76]

Moreover, like conservatives, radicals feared the consequences of releasing such a degenerate people upon the state in their present condition. "For the most part they are ignorant," explained Hugh Lennox
Bond in the opening statement of the Baltimore Association for the
Moral and Educational Improvement of the Colored People. "Thrown
upon their own resources . . . they cannot be expected to know the
necessity of industry. . . . [I]gnorance is the mother of vice, and unless
these people are taught their duties . . . the necessity for almshouses,
jails, and penitentiaries will teach the folly of such economy."[77] "The
slave . . . is a more dangerous element as a free man now," added
J. F. W. Ware, a member of the Association's board of management.
"He is ignorant, he may become vagabond, and then vicious." According to Ware, education for blacks was essential, or else "the horde of
ignorant, unrestrained men, women, and children will be upon you—
your city [Baltimore] will be the charnel house of vagabondism, vice,
and crime."[78]

Of course, as these and earlier statements indicate, radicals believed
in blacks' capacity to improve—something few conservatives were prepared to admit. Nevertheless, there was something about these statements that undermined radicals' professed respect for blacks as human
beings. Such words as "degraded," "demoralized," "vicious," and "brut-
ish" appear too often in their language to be explained simply as radical
explanations of the results of slavery. Radicals' failure to see black culture, consciousness, or dignity in Maryland's freed population indicated

their shared opinion with conservatives that blacks were a distinct or peculiar people whose patterns of social and intellectual behavior were inferior to those of whites and desperately in need of improvement. For example, this point was made eminently clear in radicals' telling assumption that free slaves could or would not honor the sanctity of marriage and the family. As Creswell explained, "The slave could sustain none of those relations which give life all its charms. He could not say my home, my father, my mother, my wife, my child, my body."[79] Or as the *Baltimore American* put it:

> Self-respect is destroyed [in the slave]: the link that binds man to honor and virtue is broken. He has neither home, nor wife, nor children. He is deprived of all those tender and endearing relations that cultivate the affections and develop the nobler part of human nature.[80]

Admittedly, there may have been something self-serving about radicals' denigration of blacks. Some may have deliberately overemphasized the point to attract support for their educational and other rehabilitative programs. By publicly accepting a part of conservatives' assessment of blacks' capacity, radicals may have hoped to convince some of the former of the need for blacks' moral improvement. Interestingly, when it served their purpose, radicals could soften their image of black demoralization. Illustrating this point, and again on the question of the black family, radicals often attacked the apprenticeship of black minors because it undermined family integrity, the assumption being, for the purpose of this argument at least, that such integrity was there in the first place.

There was, however, too much in radicals' general approach that was critical toward blacks to suggest that their ideology was so subtly opportunistic. Despite their relatively high opinion of blacks' capacity to improve, radicals made it quite clear in a number of ways that they thought blacks inferior to whites. Intellectually, for example, few friends of blacks' progress thought them capable of reaching the level of whites. "I have no sympathy for that feeling," said Henry Stockbridge.

> Was such a thing ever known as any negro becoming intellectually the equal of the white man, save in those occasional, those rare, those sporadic cases which everyone looks upon as a phenomenon . . . where it seems to be rather an intuition, an instinct than the result of intellectual power.[81]

"It will be impossible for the negro to become the intellectual equal of the white man," added the *Baltimore American*, "if the white man by studious and prudent care holds himself the superior in intellect, in manners, and in all the virtues of the citizen."[82]

Belief in the intellectual inferiority of blacks suggested their inadequacy in other areas too, and in no instance were radicals more concerned with establishing this fact than on the question of social equality. At no point in their attack against conservative ideology did they argue that blacks were the social equals of whites or advocate racial "intermingling" of the type so feared by conservatives. Radicals opposed racial intermarriage, refrained from supporting integrated schools, and in most instances confirmed whites' right to exclude blacks from meetings and places where their presence was undesired. "If a natural antipathy to amalgamation acts as a barrier against . . . 'homogeneity,' " explained the *Baltimore American*, "[then] socially the whites and the blacks cannot intermingle."[83] "It is as impossible," added John Thomas, "to place the black man on the same social level with the white man as it is to make darkness light."[84] As for conservative fears that the Civil Rights Act or universal suffrage would equalize the races socially, radicals were quick to argue that custom, not statutes, dictated such relationships. "Every man associates with whom he pleases, when he pleases," said Francis Thomas.[85] "To make a man equal before the law," added Hugh Lennox Bond, "does not make it obligatory on me to eat, sleep, or drink with him."[86] It was "a question of ethics," concluded the *Frederick Examiner*. "This is a matter over which the law has no control."[87]

Indeed, some radicals made no effort to hide the distaste with which they viewed the prospect of social intercourse on an equal level with blacks. "Maryland is [as] unprepared now as she ever will be," asserted Lieutenant Governor Christopher C. Cox in January 1867, "for the adoption or sanction of any measure tending to so absurd and revolting a result as the social equality of the races."[88] Most radicals were neither so outspoken nor perturbed at the prospect of social contact with men and women of the other race, but even the respectably moderate joked about it in a revealingly patronizing manner. In jesting about conservative fears that the Civil Rights Act would "make the negro white," John Thomas allowed, "I was wonderfully surprised the day after the bill was passed in going up Pennsylvania Avenue to find the negro just the same and as black after the passage of the bill as before it."[89] "I was asked day after day," laughed Hugh Lennox Bond, "whether I wanted him [the Negro] to marry my sister or daughter. *I* took the precaution to get married before I joined this association and as much as you may be surprised at the fact, I have not had a single proposal since made to me."[90]

The acceptance by radicals of black separateness and inferiority helped undermine even their most ambitious program to improve the condition of Maryland's freed slaves. In providing schools and education for blacks, white reformers hoped to lift their charges out of the moral degradation so deplored by both conservatives and radicals, and to contribute to a more progressive society. Yet, without a more generous assessment of blacks' intellectual capacities and a greater willingness to countenance an end to social restrictions, radicals had difficulty seeing their schools as anything more than training or control centers for a people different from and subordinate to whites. Indeed, most radicals supported the provision of schools for blacks in large part to save Maryland from crime and economic stagnation by improving blacks' moral behavior and their capacity as agricultural or urban laborers. There was no apparent desire to educate blacks for the sake of their intellectual, occupational, or social mobility.

"The plainest dictates of duty urge upon us the work of their improvement," explained the *Baltimore American,*

> to raise them from their abject condition and by a judicious course of moral and intellectual culture, to train them for the duties of citizenship. If they are to live among us, let them form an intelligent and well disposed community and be fitted for the various positions of usefulness. . . . [It] is incumbent upon us to educate them beyond the temptations of vagabondism, vice and criminality to which they are liable."[91]

The choice confronting white Marylanders was, according to Bond, simple.

> There are but two courses to be pursued. The one is to leave these persons in the ignorance and moral destitution in which many of them now, unhappily are, and the other to endeavor by education to improve their habits, instruct them in their industry, make diligent the idle, reform the vicious and stimulate the good, that they may rise in the scale of being, and be better fitted for the varied duties they are called upon to perform.[92]

Among other radicals, Bond's attitudes were widely accepted. The purpose of education, said the *Frederick Examiner* in January 1865, was "[t]o make the large class of freed men in our midst moral and useful."[93] "They must be taught to be useful to themselves and to those around them," added James Valliant, and in words echoing those of Bond's, Joseph Cushing, secretary of the Baltimore Association invited the co-operation of all persons "who believe with us . . . that intelligent labor is more valuable to the State than ignorant drudgery . . . , that igno-rance breeds vice, and that prevention and punishment of crime is more costly than a common school system."[94] "You must either raise them up or they will drag you down," concluded Cushing. "The advantages of educating them are great and we can see no disadvantages."[95] And, as Bond himself pointed out, no one need fear that such education might result in racial equality. "If I could lift . . . [a] tree up ten feet," he asked, "would the top be any nearer to the bottom?"[96]

Finally, radicals' approach to black Marylanders was restricted by the nature of their personal contact. Too often white reformers spoke down to the people they sought to help, treating them like children in need of the most rudimentary social instruction. Thus, Edgar Gregory could advise an audience of black farm laborers to be "polite, humble, honest, and industrious," and the *Baltimore American* preach that "Every free-man ought to cultivate a spirit of dignity and self respect."[97] "Will you ever learn how to labor?" Bond at his unctuous best asked blacks. "You cannot lay down on the shovel and hoe and subsist upon the mere empty title of freedom. . . . Eschew intoxicating drinks, avoid thieving, get homes for yourselves."[98]

IV

It was through the mixture of conservative rigidity and radical promise and shortcomings that black Marylanders had to pick their way in de-veloping their own attitudes toward change. Basically, they did the only thing possible under the circumstances. They capitalized on available opportunities in radical positivism while rejecting or deflecting the pe-jorative assumptions of both white philosophies. It was a delicate task, one that called for considerable subtlety and tact on the part of Mary-land's black leaders. The blatantly racist opinions of conservative plant-ers were easy to dismiss but the views of radicals were more difficult to handle. Enthusiastic about the latter's support for civil rights, suffrage, and education, blacks remained troubled with radicals' low opinion of their intellectual capacity. As a result, their leaders walked a tightrope of sorts, promoting their own positive assessment of their race whenever possible, while trying not to jeopardize radicals' commitment to black progess in other areas.

Apart from Frederick Douglass and Henry Highland Garnet, Maryland's black leaders were relatively unknown outside their own community. Neither Douglass nor Garnet were, in the context of post-emancipation events, true Marylanders, but the famed abolitionist-orators made several important speeches in Baltimore in 1864 and 1865 that received widespread approval. Next to Douglass and Garnet in reputation were several black Baltimoreans, the most prominent being Isaac Myers, the ship caulker and labor leader; George Hackett, coal dealer; Reverend Benjamin T. Tanner of the African Methodist Episcopal Church; and Doctor H. J. Brown, William E. Matthews, and William F. Taylor. Myers was well known for his participation in the Chesapeake Marine Railway and Drydock Company. Hackett was captain of the black military club known as the Henry Winter Davis Guards, a high official in the United Order of Odd Fellows, and a director of the Douglass Institute.[99] Benjamin T. Tanner was pastor of the Bethel A.M.E. Church, the largest single black church in Baltimore and meeting place for many organizations and functions.[100] Doctor Henry J. Brown, a phrenologist, was a noted public lecturer who spoke throughout the state on the topics of black civil rights and education.[101] William E. Matthews served as a lobbyist in Washington for the interests of black Marylanders, and William F. Taylor, a caulker, toured rural Maryland in much the same fashion as Brown.[102]

In the areas of civil, political, and educational rights, blacks could proceed without restraint. White radical commitment was strong enough here to permit an equally positive response. The Colored State Convention of December 1865 demanded of the Maryland General Assembly that it "extend to them [the] manhood rights which are enjoyed by the white citizens of this State."[103] Such privileges were owing, claimed twenty black leaders in a petition to President Andrew Johnson, to the "loyal colored men of Maryland who during the national struggle for liberty sent eight regiments to the field."[104] And as John M. Langston said of the Declaration of Independence, "The black man . . . [can now state] that the assertions of that instrument are entirely true. . . . Liberty is now shielded, guarded and defended by American law; it knows no man by the curl of his hair, the color of his countenance, the chiseling of his lips, the carving of his nose, by his birth place or his lineage; our law asks but one question—is he a man . . . ?"[105]

Indeed, it was primarily on the basis of civil rights, suffrage, and education that black Marylanders and white radicals forged their most effective alliance. In their mutual desire to raise the economic and intellectual standards of Maryland's freed slaves and to create a new society based on the principle of equality under the law, they combined in pursuit of several important goals. It was an impressive biracial reform dynamic, one that made serious efforts to change the nature of Maryland society. Moreover, the ready availability of such white cooperation won the lasting gratitude of Maryland's black leaders. "The colored man is aware," said William Sanders, a delegate to the 1867 Republican state convention, "that the Radicals of Maryland were the first to place him in the position of a man and clothe him with the livery of a freeman."[106]

Still, this reform dynamic suffered from its narrowness. It was ideally conceived to accomplish some things but not others. It sought recognition of blacks' rights as citizens but hesitated to widen the definition of that citizenship to include social and racial equality. In large part the constraints of white racial attitudes were responsible for such a limitation but the caution characteristic of black attitudes was also important. In their disinclination to push white radicals further toward the breakdown of Maryland's racial and social barriers, black leaders acquiesced in the maintenance of distinctions akin to those of slavery.

Of paramount concern was blacks' assertion of racial equality with whites. "I hold that all men are equal naturally," claimed Douglass. "The black man is just as capable of being great as the whites." Admittedly, whites had a head start. "They can build ships," said Douglass, "while we can scarcely build a canoe." But it would not always be so. By "persistent, untiring effort," blacks could raise themselves to the level of whites.[107] Among blacks this was an opinion widely shared. "We affirm that there is no such thing," declared an 1867 A.M.E. Church conference in Baltimore, "as Caucasian blood . . . or African blood. God made of one blood all nations."[108] In a definitive comment on the question before the Republican state convention of May 1867 Henry J. Brown concluded:

> You will find the colored man who has had all the advantages of education, of science, of literature, of philosophy, and of schools of learning,

will compare favorably with the other races of mankind. . . . [T]he colored man has the same capabilities, the same intellectual and moral powers. . . . All men are alike in regard to their education, their capacity, their influence and their moral capability, providing they have surrounding them the same influences.[109]

But at the same time that Maryland's black leaders asserted the *principle* of racial equality, they refrained from demanding its immediate recognition. In an obvious effort to skirt radical hesitation on the subject most black spokesmen defined equality as something blacks had to earn through diligent application. Dovetailing their own ideas of self-reliance with radicals' insistence that blacks learn to cope by themselves, these leaders strove to convince white reformers of their inherent equality by its demonstration. "If we wish to enjoy the same privileges of the white man," explained Douglass, "we must labor to become his equal."[110] The purpose of the Douglass Institute, he said, was "to develop manhood, to build up manly character among the colored people of this city and State. It is to teach them the true idea of manly independence and self-respect."[111] The Colored State Convention of December 1865 advised blacks to become first "men of virtuous habits, disdaining to do anything beneath the dignity of men," before expecting full enjoyment of their rights.[112] "We must learn to labor and to wait," added John Langston before an overflow audience in Bethel Church, "and to imitate the lives of good white men."[113]

Douglass, Garnet, and others looked honestly to the impression black diligence would make upon its white audience and the effect it would have in widening blacks' social and economic opportunities. What they failed to treat with due respect was the tendency among whites—both conservative and radical—to applaud the concept of self-help as a way of *limiting* their obligation to black progress, and to believe that blacks would retain their second-class status in these areas more or less permanently. In the efforts of black leaders to avoid unnecessary "precipitation," they placed their faith in whites' future capacity to soften their racial or social theories in response to black self-improvement. Given the progressive character of much of radical ideology, black leaders understandably took this gamble, but on the basis of what white reformers were actually saying between 1864 and 1870, it was not justified. Significantly, some black Marylanders sensed the nature of this problem and objected to the policies of those "who are so much attached to the old servile system of hat-under-the-arm, that the least departure from it is sufficient to fill them with alarm," but their voices were in a distinct minority.[114]

Blacks were equally hesitant in pushing the question of social equality. Here, too, they took a higher road than radicals in insisting that race had nothing to do with social intercourse but softened the implication of such a principle by dismissing its immediate importance. "There is no such thing as social or moral equality," argued Henry J. Brown. "A man makes his equality in proportion as he studies, reads, and learns. . . . [A]s the colored man advances in education and intellect, and achieves wealth, just so in proportion will he become the social equal of the white man and not till then."[115]

Such caution characterized blacks' approach to the entire white reform mentality. Maryland radicals and federal officials were the only people to whom blacks could turn for assistance in the realization of their goals and thus had to be treated carefully. Most black leaders tried to make sure that the demands of their people did not run ahead of current radical thinking. According to William Taylor, "the steps of the colored people should be measured, and . . . they should avoid precipitation."[116] In an 1868 letter to the *Baltimore American*, "Many Colored Citizens" objected to too sudden a push for racial equality and said:

> under the present condition on the political horizon, [we] wish to be quiet lookers-on at the same time not unmindful of the great revolution working in politics, and soon to burst forth in all the splendor of the political equality of all men.[117]

Finally, the success of Maryland's reform impulse was mitigated by the inadequate communications between black leaders and freed slaves. Although several of the leaders toured southern Maryland and the Eastern Shore and spoke before large audiences of farm laborers, none of them were of that class. Understandably, their ideas drew more from their own experience as members of a long-standing urban, free black community than from that of recently freed slaves. Black Baltimoreans had long since learned to protect their position by agitating for those rights they knew reform-minded whites were prepared to support and by de-emphasizing those that threatened their tenuous status. Such an approach was tailor-made for the protection of the many privileges already gained by the free black community in Baltimore and for the gradual accumulation of others. It proved less effective in dealing with the problems of people with no rights or privileges to start with.

NOTES

1. A. W. Bradford to Major General O. O. Howard, October 4, 1865, State Papers [1865], Maryland State Archives, Annapolis, Md. Augustus W. Bradford was born in 1806 in Bel Air, Md. He graduated from St. Mary's College, Baltimore, in 1824, and was admitted to the Maryland bar in 1827. He became a prominent Whig and a strong supporter of the Union from the outset of the war. In 1861 he was elected governor of Maryland. He opposed slavery but also opposed federal interference in Maryland (*Dictionary of American Biography*, 2:553; *Who Was Who in America, Historical Volume, 1607–1896*, 69; *Who Was Who in American Politics*, 105).

2. "Message of Governor Swann to the General Assembly of Maryland" (Annapolis, 1866), 21–23; "Inaugural Address of Governor Oden Bowie to the General Assembly of Maryland, January, 1868" (Annapolis, 1868), 7, which appears as Document D in *Public Documents of the House of Delegates of Maryland January Session, 1868* (Annapolis, 1868). Born in Prince George's County, Md., in 1826, Oden Bowie attended St. Mary's College in Baltimore, graduating in 1845. After serving in the Mexican War, he was elected to the Maryland House of Delegates in 1849. In 1860, he became president of the Baltimore and Potomac Railroad. A leading Democrat throughout the Civil War, he was elected governor of Maryland in 1867 (*Dictionary of American Biography*, 2:510; *Who Was Who in America, Historical Volume, 1607–1896*, 67).

3. *Congressional Globe*, 39 Cong., 1 Sess., 373–74, 3172–75 (January 23 and June 14, 1866).

4. *Baltimore Gazette*, July 3, 1865.

5. *Baltimore Sun*, July 27, 1865.

6. *Baltimore American*, September 5, 1865.

7. *Baltimore Gazette*, April 18, 1866.

8. *Baltimore American*, August 7, 1867.

9. *Debates of the Constitutional Convention of the State of Maryland [1864]*, 3 vols. (Annapolis, 1864), 3:1580.

10. Ibid., 1:625.

11. Ibid., 1:735.

12. Ibid., 1:598.

13. *Maryland Farmer and Mechanic* 3 (January 1866): 8.

14. *Debates of the Constitutional Convention [1864]*, 1:577.

15. Ibid., 1:627.

16. "Message of Governor Swann to the General Assembly of Maryland" (Annapolis, 1866), 23.

17. *Baltimore American,* May 31, 1867.

18. *Debates of the Constitutional Convention [1864],* 3:1583.

19. *Chestertown Transcript,* December 17, 1864.

20. "Message of Governor Bradford to the General Assembly of Maryland at the January Session, 1865" (Annapolis, 1865), 4–5, which appears as Document A in Maryland, General Assembly House of Delegates, *Journal of Proceedings, January Session 1865* (Annapolis, 1865).

21. *Baltimore Gazette,* November 25, 1865.

22. *Congressional Globe,* 39 Cong., 1 Sess., 3172–75 (June 14, 1866).

23. *Baltimore American,* September 5, 1865.

24. *Baltimore Sun,* November 14, 1865.

25. *Debates of the Constitutional Convention [1864],* 3:1580.

26. *Baltimore Gazette,* July 3, 1865.

27. *Baltimore Sun,* June 22, 1866; *Baltimore American,* June 22, 1866.

28. *Baltimore Sun,* February 12, 1866.

29. Ibid., April 27, 1865.

30. *Chestertown Transcript,* December 16, 1865.

31. As early as May 27, 1865, Davis made his views on universal manhood suffrage clear. "Negroes are as integral a part of this state as whites," he said. "Both are citizens. Neither can speak in the name of the state for the other ... [and] it is the equal right of both to be heard and represented in constituting their common government" (*Baltimore American,* March 19, 1866. From a letter written in May 1865 but not released by Mrs. Davis until March 1866). For an excellent discussion of Davis's role in Maryland politics see numerous references in Charles L. Wagandt, *The Mighty Revolution: Negro Emancipation in Maryland, 1862–1864* (Baltimore, 1964).

32. For the best representation of Creswell's views see *Congressional Globe,* 38 Cong., 2 Sess., 120–24 (January 5, 1865). For a discussion of Hugh Lennox Bond see Richard Paul Fuke, "Hugh Lennox Bond and Radical Republican Ideology," *Journal of Southern History* 45 (November 1979): 570–86.

33. John L. Thomas was born in Baltimore in 1835. He studied law, was admitted to the Maryland bar in 1856, and moved to Baltimore in 1857. He was the city solicitor of Baltimore between 1860 and 1862, and state's attorney, 1863–65. He was a member of the 1864 state constitutional convention and in 1864 was elected to the United States House of Representatives (*Who Was Who in America: Historical Volume, 1607–1896,* 526). Born in 1799 in Pennsylvania, Francis Thomas was admitted to the Maryland bar in 1820. He became a member of the Maryland General Assembly in 1822, and served in the House of Representatives, 1831–41. He was governor of Maryland 1841–44. He was a strong Unionist during the Civil War and enlisted a volunteer

regiment of three thousand men. He served again in the House of Representatives, 1861–69 (*Dictionary of American Biography*, 18:429–30; *Who Was Who in America, Historical Volume, 1607–1896*, 526).

34. *Baltimore American*, November 14 and 26, 1864.

35. *Debates of the Constitutional Convention [1864]*, 1:739.

36. Ibid., 3:1596.

37. *Congressional Globe*, 38 Cong., 2 Sess., 120–24 (January 5, 1865).

38. *Baltimore American*, April 4, 1866.

39. Baltimore Association Broadside, Bond-McCulloch Family Papers (MS 1159), Maryland Historical Society.

40. From the *Cambridge Intelligencer* as printed in the *Easton Gazette*, March 11, 1865.

41. *Baltimore American*, August 7, 1867.

42. American Freedmen's Union Commission, New York Branch, *Annual Report . . . [1867]* (New York, [1867]), 14–16.

43. Clipping from the *Easton Gazette*, January 7, 1866, in Bond-McCulloch Family Papers (MS 1159), Maryland Historical Society.

44. *Baltimore American*, November 24, 1866.

45. Ibid., May 15, July 22, 1867.

46. *Debates of the Constitutional Convention [1864]*, 1:674, emphasis in original.

47. *Baltimore American*, August 31, 1865.

48. Ibid., July 2, 1866.

49. Ibid., July 22, 1867.

50. Ibid., August 18, 1865.

51. Ibid., July 2, 1866.

52. Ibid., July 1, 1867.

53. Ibid., June 26, 1865.

54. Ibid., July 2, 1866.

55. Ibid., July 9, 1867.

56. Ibid.

57. Ibid., September 14, 1865.

58. Ibid., July 9, 1867.

59. Ibid., July 22, 1867.

60. Ibid., November 24, 1866.

61. Ibid., April 21, 1866.

62. Ibid., November 24, 1866.

63. H. L. Bond to K. Bond, n.d., Bond-McCulloch Family Papers (MS 1159), Maryland Historical Society.

64. *Baltimore American*, May 13, 1867.

65. Ibid., May 15, August 14, 1866.

66. *Debates of the Constitutional Convention [1864]*, 3:1589.

67. *Baltimore American*, August 31, 1865.

68. Anonymous correspondent to Bond, November 1866, Bond-McCulloch Family Papers (MS 1159), Maryland Historical Society.

69. Anonymous correspondent to Bond, n.d., 1866, ibid.

70. *Baltimore Gazette*, January 9, 1867.

71. H. L. Bond to J. M. McKim, December 5, 1867, Antislavery Collection, Cornell University, Ithaca, New York.

72. *Baltimore American*, July 1, 1867.

73. See below.

74. Lawrence W. Levine, *Black Culture and Black Consciousness: Afro-American Folk Thought from Slavery to Freedom* (New York, 1977); Genovese, *Roll Jordan Roll*; Herbert Gutman, *The Black Family in Slavery and Freedom, 1750–1920* (New York, 1976); John W. Blassingame, *The Slave Community: Plantation Life in the Antebellum South* (Chicago, 1972); Philip D. Morgan, *Slave Counterpoint: Black Culture in the Eighteenth-Century Chesapeake and Low Country* (Chapel Hill, 1998).

75. *Debates of the Constitutional Convention [1864]*, 3:1589.

76. *Baltimore American*, November 14, 1864, April 4, 1866.

77. Baltimore Association Broadside, Bond-McCulloch Family Papers (MS 1159), Maryland Historical Society.

78. *Baltimore American*, March 15, 1865. John F. W. Ware was born in 1818 in Boston, Mass. He graduated from Harvard in 1838 and became a Unitarian minister in 1843. In 1864 he became the minister of the First Independent Society of Baltimore, and in 1867 of the new Church of the Saviour (*Dictionary of American Biography*, 19:450; *Who Was Who in America, Historical Volume, 1607–1896*, 562).

79. *Congressional Globe*, 38 Cong., 2 Sess., 120–24 (January 5, 1865).

80. *Baltimore American*, April 4, 1866.

81. *Debates of the Constitutional Convention [1864]*, 3:1589.

82. *Baltimore American*, August 17, 1867.

83. Ibid., August 17, 1865, May 7, 1867.

84. Ibid., May 24, 1866.

85. Ibid., May 15, 1866.

86. H. L. Bond to K. Bond, n.d., Bond-McCulloch Family Papers (MS 1159), Maryland Historical Society.

87. *Frederick Examiner*, May 22, 1867.

88. *Baltimore Sun*, January 3, 1867.

89. *Baltimore American*, May 15, 1866.

90. Ibid., November 24, 1866.

91. Ibid., March 15, 1865.

92. Baltimore Association Broadside, Bond-McCulloch Family Papers (MS 1159), Maryland Historical Society.

93. *Frederick Examiner,* January 4, 1865.

94. *Baltimore American,* August 31, 1865; *Second Annual Report of the Baltimore Association,* 6.

95. *Second Annual Report of the Baltimore Association,* 12.

96. *Baltimore American,* July 1, 1867.

97. *Baltimore American,* April 25, July 9, 1867.

98. *St. Mary's Beacon,* September 5, 1867. Quoted in Baker, *The Politics of Continuity,* 183.

99. *Journal of Proceedings of the First Branch City Council of Baltimore at the Sessions of 1864 and 1865,* 731; *Baltimore Gazette,* October 7, 1865; *Baltimore Sun,* October 7, 1865; *Baltimore American,* October 7, 1865, August 5, 1867.

100. Tanner, *An Apology for African Methodism.*

101. *Cecil Whig,* January 28, 1865; *Easton Gazette,* May 13, 1865.

102. Testimony of William F. Taylor, Testimony in Investigation of the Government of Maryland, 1867, Records of the House of Representatives, Committee on the Judiciary, Record Group 233.

103. *Baltimore American,* December 29, 1865.

104. W. E. Matthews et al. to Andrew Johnson, March 17, 1866, Andrew Johnson Papers, Manuscripts Division, Library of Congress, Washington, D.C; *Baltimore American,* March 19, 1866.

105. *Baltimore American,* August 27, 1867.

106. Ibid., May 15, 1867.

107. Ibid., December 5, 1864.

108. Ibid., April 18, 1867.

109. Ibid., May 15, 1867.

110. Ibid., December 5, 1864.

111. Ibid., September 30, 1865.

112. Ibid., December 29, 1865.

113. Ibid., August 27, 1867.

114. Ibid., June 1, 1866.

115. Ibid., May 15, 1867.

116. Ibid., May 15, 1868.

117. Ibid., May 21, 1868.

CONCLUSION

FOR BLACK MARYLANDERS, the ultimate confines of white racial attitudes lay in the inability of whites to meet the challenge of a society in transition. Neither conservatives nor radicals sought—as they saw it—to avoid the consequences of emancipation, but in the final analysis, both took refuge in a set of traditionally conservative or liberal ideas that effectively reimposed second-class citizenship upon black people. For conservatives, the process was deliberate; with radicals it was partly unintentional. The former applauded renewed signs of separation and subservience in blacks, the latter acquiesced in them as temporary or necessary. Radicals helped widen blacks' access to freedom, but their failure to confront squarely a full range of post-emancipation possibilities helped ensure that conservative attitudes prevailed.

The failure of whites to develop new solutions to what were, after all, new problems, grew basically from their inability to address the full implications of emancipation. Although they recognized that slavery had been abolished and that blacks were now free, few whites were prepared to contemplate anything much beyond that. To those who were, emancipation offered a gradual expansion of blacks' rights through a combination of beneficent legislation and self-help, which stopped well short of racial equality. Apart from blacks themselves, no one seemed to grasp that emancipation might be something quite different; that freedom might possess the potential to destroy racial prejudice and to place black Marylanders on an equal basis with whites.

At least blacks saw it this way. By their movement to Baltimore, Washington, and about the rural counties, their search for personal autonomy at home and at work, their participation in politics, and determination to educate or control the labor of their children, they pointed toward an agenda far more optimistic than that of whites. But given whites' apparent inability to transcend attitudinal restrictions that, after all, defined blacks solely as objects of white perceptions— inferior ones at that—it was hardly surprising that both conservatives and radicals should fail to get the point.

For blacks, such failure possessed profound implications, for it meant, essentially, that *their* aspirations for a newer and better Maryland stood little chance of impressing themselves upon those in power. Despite the unprecedented opportunity to develop social policy according to challenging new circumstances, both conservatives and radicals interposed assumptions about and definitions of black social behavior that concealed from them both the nature of black priorities and the need for innovative ideas to deal with them. For conservatives such blindness reinforced their already negative opinion of blacks' capacity. With radicals it undermined any chance of extending the liberal reform mentality into more socially democratic areas of change.

Black Marylanders strove valiantly to combat such obstacles by proving themselves responsible and able citizens. In finding new jobs, building schools, seeking the return of their apprenticed children, and struggling for civil and political rights, they sought to accomplish what they believed to be their full potential, and through it to open the door to racial equality. Indeed, between 1864 and 1870, blacks stood eager to participate with whites in building the rural and urban economy of their state. They confronted white society with a set of terms drastically changed since 1860 but totally predicated upon mutual success.

Through such effort, blacks made several real and legitimate advances. These—and others won with the help of white radicals—would benefit them for years to come. There was nothing temporary about gains in education, nor could blacks' enemies reverse the Civil Rights Act of 1866, Salmon P. Chase's apprenticeship decision, and the Fourteenth Amendment to the United States Constitution. Even blacks' flirtation with political power in the 1867 Republican Party stood them in good stead for the future. In 1870, the Fifteenth Amendment gave black men the franchise, and it was a prepared and informed electorate that assumed this new responsibility.[1]

But none of these accomplishments won any white support beyond the cautious applause of radical Unionists and Republicans. In fact, from the vast majority of white Marylanders black achievements encountered open hostility. In almost every instance, either the substance of what blacks sought or the manner in which they and their supporters went about getting it alienated most whites. Put simply, most rejected racial equality—and the measures they saw as being designed to bring it about—and it was this insistence that fed their determination to establish new social and economic controls. The result was a caste system similar in many ways to that of slavery, built upon black subservience and separation.

In the face of such rejection, black leaders emphatically denied their inferiority. In September 1865, in Baltimore, Frederick Douglass asserted that "the colored people not only have the higher qualities attributed to the white race, but . . . they are beginning to bring . . . [them] into vigorous exercise."[2] In Maryland's first interracial political convention in May 1867, Henry Brown insisted that "I do not stand before you as a black man, nor . . . as a white man, but . . . as a *man*:

All men are alike in regard to their education, their capacity . . . and their moral capability, provided they have surrounding them the same influences. . . . There is no such thing as social or moral equality. A man makes his equality in proportion as he studies, reads and learns.[3]

It was a sentiment that the *Baltimore American* professed to share, although with typical restraint:

The law which guarantees to the negro life, liberty and the pursuit of happiness . . . grants him an equal chance in the race of life. . . . Open to the negro the avenue of wealth; allow him where he has the ability to accumulate property, and to acquire an education, and you will thus excite his emulation to obtain a respectable footing in society.[4]

But the arguments of blacks and their supporters were largely in vain. Most whites did not listen to blacks and those who did possessed insufficient numbers or power to enjoy long-lasting impact. Radical politicians owed whatever influence they had to the United States Army, the Freedmen's Bureau, and a strict voter registration law. By 1868, they had lost the support of all three and the conservative Democratic Party emerged victorious with its basic, racist assumptions intact. Indeed, if anything, black and radical efforts had hardened whites' attitudes. In response to such efforts, conservatives closed ranks and began to define, articulate, and institutionalize a philosophy of racial supremacy for their post-emancipation society.

In doing so, they branded all black or radical talk of violence, discrimination, or prejudice as false. In April 1866, the *Baltimore Sun* informed its readers that "the two races are rapidly adjusting to altered circumstances. . . . An excellent regard on both sides for mutual interest is solving . . . [quickly] and happily the social problems of our time."[5] In January 1867, Thomas Swann told the General Assembly, "There is not a single free state where more earnest efforts are being made to improve and ameliorate their . . . condition."[6] And, according to the *Sun,* black Marylanders agreed. In words that revealed much it explained:

> The tractableness exhibited by the colored man in a state of slavery is characteristic of the race whether bond or free. The bent of his disposition if left to himself, inclines him to be guided by the white race, and to cooperate in his own sphere of labor with the general industry and progress.[7]

The only thing that stood in the way of complete racial harmony, claimed the *Chestertown Transcript* in June 1867, was "the meddling . . . [of] Radical fanatics . . . who are constantly false representing the relation between the races in our state."[8]

In the face of such willful opposition and in the absence of more effective support from their friends, black Marylanders found themselves most of the time left to their own devices. With what help they could get from the United States government and radical supporters, they built a community based on as much self-reliance and autonomy as they could extract from their employers. Much as slaves and free blacks before emancipation had fashioned a society amidst whites who were determined to restrict it, freed Marylanders sought to influence the conditions in which they worked and lived. By necessity, blacks pursued pragmatic goals shaped by a combination of their own priorities and those of the whites with whom they lived and worked. When all was said and done, they faced a broad, systemic white refusal to countenance an end to dependent black labor, a refusal that included almost every white in the state. Black Marylanders neither enjoyed total freedom nor suffered absolute coercion, but their struggle made two things clear: much of whatever they might accomplish, they would have to do by themselves; and such efforts would remain confined by white attitudes determined to regulate them.

Notes

1. Callcott, *The Negro in Maryland Politics.*
2. *Baltimore American*, September 30, 1865.
3. Ibid., May 15, 1867.
4. Ibid., July 2, 1866.

5. *Baltimore Sun*, April 9, 1866.

6. *Journal of Proceedings of the House of Delegates, January Session, 1867* (Annapolis, 1867), Document A, *Message of Governor Swann to the General Assembly of Maryland* (Annapolis, 1867), 18.

7. *Baltimore Sun*, January 9, 1867.

8. *Chestertown Transcript*, June 29, 1867.

BIBLIOGRAPHY

PRIMARY SOURCES

Government Documents, United States

1. Record Group 101, Records of the Bureau of the Comptroller of
   the Currency, Freedmen's Savings and Trust Company [Baltimore
   Branch], National Archives, Washington, D.C.
   a. Signature Book [Baltimore], 1866–
   b. Index, Deposit Ledger A, F. S. & T. Co., Baltimore
2. Record Group 105, Bureau of Refugees, Freedmen, and Abandoned Lands, District of Columbia, National Archives, Washington, D.C.
   a. Book Records
      Volume 1: Letters Received, Assistant Commissioner, Sep-
      tember 1865, to October 27, 1866.
      Volume 2: Letters Received, Assistant Commissioner, Octo-
      ber 27, 1866–
      Volumes 26, 27: Special Orders and Circulars, June 22,
      1865, to September 3, 1868.
      Volume 28: Monthly Reports to the Bureau of Abandoned
      or Confiscated Lands in Possession of the Assistant Com-
      missioner, August 1865 to March 1867.
      Volume 29: Land Reports, 1865 to 1867.
   b. Box Records
      i.   Letters Received, Assistant Commissioner.
      ii.   Letters Received, Superintendent of Education.
      iii. Land Reports.
      iv.   Miscellaneous Contracts.
3. Record Group 105, Bureau of Refugees, Freedmen, and Abandoned Lands, District of Maryland, National Archives, Washington, D.C.
   a. Book Records
      Volume 1: Letters Received, Assistant Commissioner, April
      1, 1866, to August 17, 1868.

Volume 3: Letters Sent, Assistant Commissioner, April 1, 1866, to August 17, 1868.

Volume 16: Special Order Book, May 7, 1866, to August 15, 1868.

Volume 47: Letters Received, Annapolis, July 20, 1866, to September 11, 1868.

Volume 48: Letters Sent, Annapolis, June 28, 1866, to March 13, 1868.

Volume 49: Letters Sent, Annapolis, March 14, 1868, to September 17, 1869.

Volume 50: Letters Sent, Bladensburg, June 4, 1866, to September 18, 1867.

Volume 52: Letters Received, Rockville, May 19, 1866, to September 30, 1867.

Volume 53: Letters Sent, Rockville, June 5, 1866, to October 2, 1867.

b. Box Records
    i.   Letters Received, Assistant Commissioner.
    ii.   Reports.
    iii. Special Orders and Circulars.
    iv.   School Reports.
    v.   Miscellaneous Construction of Schools.
    vi.   Letters Received, Annapolis.
    vii. Letters Received, Bladensburg.
    viii. Letters Received, Rockville.
    ix.   Bounty and Pensions.

4. Record Group 233, Records of the House of Representatives, Committee on the Judiciary, Testimony in Investigation of the Government of Maryland, National Archives, Washington, D.C.

5. Record Group 393, United States Continental Commands, Department of Washington, St. Mary's District, National Archives, Washington, D.C.

a. Book Records
    Volume 254: Letters Sent, July 1864 to December 1864.
    Volume 255: Letters Sent, February 1864 to May 1865.
    Volume 258: Letters Received and Endorsements, January 1864 to July 1865.

b. Box Records
    i.   Oaths of Allegiance and Letters Received, 1863–1865.

6. Record Group 393, United States Continental Commands, Middle Department, National Archives, Washington, D.C.
   a. Book Records
       Volume 13 (Old Book 14): Letters Received, August to November 1864, L to Z.
       Volume 14 (Old Book 15): Letters Received, November to December 1864, A to K.
       Volume 34 (Old Book 37), Letters Sent, Lew Wallace, September to November 1864.
       Volume 35 (Old Book 38), Letters Sent, Lew Wallace, November 5, 1864, to January 7, 1865.
       Volume 35 (Old Book 39), Letters Sent, Lew Wallace, January 8 to March 15, 1865.
       Volume 36 (Old Book 40), Letters Sent, Lew Wallace, March 15 to May 10, 1865.
       Volume 36 (Old Book 41), Letters Sent, June 20, 1865, to July 18, 1865.
       Volume 36 (Old Book 42), Letters Sent, Lew Wallace, May 11, 1865, to June 20, 1865.
       Volume 37 (Old Book 43), Letters Sent, W. S. Hancock, July 19, 1865, to September 27, 1865.
7. United States Bureau of the Census, Eighth Census of the United States, 1860, National Archives, Washington, D.C.
   a. Population Schedules.
   b. Agricultural Schedules.
8. United States Bureau of the Census, Ninth Census of the United States, 1870, National Archives, Washington, D.C.
   a. Population Schedules.
   b. Agricultural Schedules.
9. Abraham Lincoln Papers, Presidential Papers Microfilm, Library of Congress, Washington, D.C.
10. Andrew Johnson Papers, Presidential Papers Microfilm, Library of Congress, Washington, D.C.

Government Documents, Maryland

1. State Papers, Maryland State Archives, Annapolis, Md.
   a. Book Records
       i.   Executive Letter Book, 1864–1866.

    ii.   Letter Book, Executive Department, 1854–1866.

    iii. Proceedings of the Governor of the State of Maryland, 1861–1869.

    iv. Letters Received, A. W. Bradford, Governor, 1864–1865.

  b. Box Records, 1864–1868

Government Documents, Baltimore

1. City Records, 1864–1870, WPA Collection, Baltimore City Archives, Baltimore, Md.

Government Publications, United States

1. [United States Census Office, 8th Census, 1860], *Population of the United States in 1860, Compiled from the Original Returns of the Eighth Census* . . . Washington, 1864.
2. [United States Census Office, 8th Census, 1860], *Agriculture of the United States in 1860, Compiled from the Original Returns of the Eighth Census* . . . Washington, 1864.
3. [United States Census Office, 9th Census, 1870], *Population of the United States in 1870, Compiled from the Original Returns of the Ninth Census* . . . Washington, 1872.
4. [United States Census Office, 9th Census, 1870], *A Compendium of the Ninth Census*. Washington, 1872.
5. [United States Bureau of the Census], *Negro Population, 1790–1915*. Washington, 1918.
6. *The Congressional Globe, Containing the Debates and Proceedings of the Second Session of the Thirty-Eighth Congress [1864–1865].* Washington, 1865.
7. *The Congressional Globe, Containing the Debates and Proceedings of the First Session of the Thirty-Ninth Congress [1865–1866].* Washington, 1866.
8. *The Congressional Globe, Containing the Debates and Proceedings of the Second Session of the Thirty-Ninth Congress [1866–1867].* Washington: Congressional Globe Office, 1867.
9. *The Congressional Globe, Containing the Debates and Proceedings of the First Session of the Fortieth Congress [1867].* Washington, 1867.
10. *The Congressional Globe, Containing the Debates and Proceedings of*

the Second Session of the Fortieth Congress [1867–1868]. Washington, 1868.

11. [United States Congress, Documents and Reports], *Senate Executive Documents for the First Session of the Thirty-Ninth Congress of the United States of America, 1865–1866.* Vol. 2. Washington, 1866. Serial No. 1238.
Senate Executive Document No. 27, "Message from the President of the United States, Communicating in Compliance with a Resolution of the Senate of February last, A Communication from the Secretary of War, together with Reports of the Assistant Commissioners of the Freedmen's Bureau made since December 1, 1865."

12. [United States Congress, Documents and Reports], *Executive Documents Printed by Order of the House of Representatives, during the First Session of the Thirty-Ninth Congress, 1865–1866.* Vol. 7. Washington, 1866. Serial No. 1245.
Executive Document No. 11, "Freedmen's Bureau, Message from the President of the United States Transmitting the Report of the Commissioner of the Bureau of Refugees, Freedmen and Abandoned Lands."

13. [United States Congress, Documents and Reports], *Executive Documents of the Senate of the United States, Second Session, Thirty-Ninth Congress, 1866–1867,* Vol. 1. Washington, 1867. Serial No. 1276.
Executive Document No. 6, "Letter of the Secretary of War, Communicating in Compliance with a resolution of the Senate of December 17, 1866, reports of the assistant commissioners of freedmen, and a synopsis of laws respecting persons of color in the late slave states."

14. [United States Congress, Documents and Reports], *The Miscellaneous Documents of the House of Representatives for the First Session of the Fortieth Congress, 1867,* Vol. 1. Washington, 1868. Serial No. 1312.
Miscellaneous Document No. 27, "Affairs in Maryland: Memorial from the General Assembly of Maryland Asking the Immediate Consideration by Congress of the Condition of Public Affairs in that State, printed March 27, 1867."
Miscellaneous Document No. 28, "Affairs in Maryland: Resolu-

tions Adopted by the Grand Union League of Maryland, March 20, 1867."

Miscellaneous Document No. 32, "Affairs in Maryland: Resolutions of the Republican State Convention of Maryland, March 27, 1867."

Miscellaneous Document No. 34, "Affairs in Maryland: Memorial from the Mayor and Members of the City Council of Baltimore Asking Congress to Assist the People of Maryland to Form a State Government, Republican in Form, and in Unison with the Spirit of the Age, Order Printed, March 30, 1867."

15. [United States Congress, Documents and Reports], *The Miscellaneous Documents of the House of Representatives, Second Session of the Thirty-Ninth Congress, 1866–1867.* Washington, 1867. Serial No. 1302.

Miscellaneous Document No. 38, "Resolutions of the Common Council of Baltimore."

16. [United States Congress, Documents and Reports], *The Miscellaneous Documents of the Senate of the United States for the Second Session of the Fortieth Congress, 1867–1868.* Washington, 1868. Serial No. 1319.

Miscellaneous Document No. 24, "Letter of C. H. Howard, Assistant Commissioner of Refugees, Freedmen and Abandoned Lands, in Relation to the Opinion of Attorney-General Jones of the State of Maryland, Pronouncing Void the Decision of the Chief Justice of the Supreme Court of the United States Releasing Apprentices Bound under the Laws of Maryland, February 1, 1868."

17. [United States Congress, Documents and Reports], *Executive Documents and Reports, Printed by Order of the House of Representatives during the Second Session of the Fortieth Congress, 1867–1868,* Vol. 2. Washington, 1868. Serial No. 1324.

Executive Document No. 1, Part 1, "Report of the Secretary of War," which includes "Report of the Commissioner of the Bureau of Refugees, Freedmen and Abandoned Lands, November 1, 1867."

18. [United States Congress, Documents and Reports], *Executive Documents, Printed by Order of the House of Representatives during the Third Session of the Fortieth Congress, 1868–1869,* Vol. 3. Washington, 1869. Serial No. 1367.

Executive Document No. 1, "Report of the Secretary of War," which includes "Report of Major General O. O. Howard, Commissioner of the Bureau of Refugees, Freedmen, and Abandoned Lands, October 14, 1868."

19. *Federal Cases, Comprising Cases Argued and Determined in the Circuit and District Courts of the United States from the Earliest Times to the Beginning of the Federal Reporter Arranged Alphabetically by the Titles of the Cases and Numbered Consecutively,* Book 24. St. Paul, 1896.

20. *The War of the Rebellion: A Compilation of the Official Records of the Union and Confederate Armies.* Series 1, Vol. 43, Part 1. Washington, 1893. Serial No. 90.

21. *The War of the Rebellion: A Compilation of the Official Records of the Union and Confederate Armies.* Series 1, Vol. 43, Part 2. Washington, 1893. Serial No. 91.

22. *The War of the Rebellion: A Compilation of the Official Records of the Union and Confederate Armies.* Series 3, Vol. 4. Washington, 1900.

23. [Adjutant General's Department], *Notes Illustrating the Military Geography of the United States, 1813–1880.* Washington, 1881.

24. *First Semi-Annual Report on Schools and Finances for Freedmen, January 1, 1866,* by J. W. Alvord, Inspector of Schools and Finances. Washington, 1868.

25. *Second Semi-Annual Report on Schools and Finances for Freedmen, July 1, 1866,* by J. W. Alvord, Inspector of Schools and Finances. Washington, 1868.

26. *Third Semi-Annual Report on Schools for Freedmen, January 1, 1867,* by J. W. Alvord, General Supt. Schools, Bureau of Refugees, Freedmen and Abandoned Lands. Washington, 1868.

27. *Fourth Semi-Annual Report on Schools for Freedmen, July 1, 1867,* by J. W. Alvord, General Supt. Schools, Bureau of Refugees, Freedmen and Abandoned Lands. Washington, 1868.

28. *Fifth Semi-Annual Report on Schools for Freedmen, January 1, 1868,* by J. W. Alvord, General Supt. Schools, Bureau of Refugees, Freedmen and Abandoned Lands. Washington, 1868.

29. *Sixth Semi-Annual Report on Schools for Freedmen, July 1, 1868,* by J. W. Alvord, General Supt. Schools, Bureau of Refugees, Freedmen and Abandoned Lands. Washington, 1868.

30. Thorpe, Francis N., comp., *The Federal and State Constitutions,*

Colonial Charters, and Other Organic Laws of the States, Territories, and Colonies . . . Vol. 3. Washington, 1909.

Government Publications, Maryland

1. *Journal of the Proceedings of the House of Delegates, January Session, 1865.* Annapolis, 1865.
    a. Document A: "Message of Governor Bradford to the General Assembly of Maryland at the January Session, 1865."
    b. Document C: "Inaugural Address of Hon. Thomas Swann, Governor-Elect of Maryland."
    c. Document J: "Communication from Major General Lew Wallace in Relation to the Freedman's Bureau to the General Assembly of Maryland."
    d. Document P: "Report of the State Superintendent of Public Instruction to the General Assembly of Maryland."
2. *Journal of Proceedings of the Senate of Maryland, January Session, 1865.* Annapolis, 1865.
3. *Journal of Proceedings of the House of Delegates, January Session, 1866.* Annapolis, 1866.
4. *Journal of Proceedings of the House of Delegates, Extra Session, 1866.* Annapolis, 1866.
    a. Document A: "Message of Governor Swann to the General Assembly of Maryland."
    b. Document B: "Annual Report of the Comptroller of the Treasury Department for the Fiscal Year Ending 30th September, 1865."
    c. Document E: "First Report of the State Superintendent of Public Instruction to the Governor of Maryland."
    d. Document F: "Annual Report of the President and Directors of the Maryland Penitentiary, January, 1866."
5. *Journal of the Proceedings of the Senate of Maryland, January Session, 1866.* Annapolis, 1866.
6. *Journal of Proceedings of the Senate of Maryland, Extra Session, 1866.* Annapolis, 1866.
7. *Journal of the Proceedings of the House of Delegates, January Session, 1867.* Annapolis, 1867.
    a. Document A: "Message of Governor Swann to the General Assembly of Maryland."

   b. Document E: "Annual Report of the Comptroller of the Treasury Department for the Fiscal Year Ending September 30, 1866, to the General Assembly."

   c. Document K: "First Annual Report of the State Superintendent of Public Instruction with the Reports of the Presidents of the Boards of School Commissioners and Statistical Tables and other Documents Showing the Condition of the Public Schools of Maryland, for the Year Ending June 30, 1866."

   d. Document N: "Report of the Commissioner of Immigration of the State of Maryland to the General Assembly."

   e. Document X: "Memorial of the Grand Jury of Baltimore City Praying that a Place of Punishment May be Provided for Minor Colored Children."

   f. Document AA: "Report of the Select Committee on the Penitentiary."

   g. Document DD: "A Succinct Exposition of the Industrial Resources and Agricultural Advantages of the State of Maryland, by James Higgins, Professor of Natural Sciences and Agriculture at Maryland Agricultural College."

8. *Journal of the Proceedings of the Senate, January Session, 1867.* Annapolis, 1867.

   a. Document Y: "Report of the Committee on Labor and Immigration."

9. *Journal of the Proceedings of the House of Delegates of Maryland, January Session, 1868.* Annapolis, 1868.

   a. Document A: "Message of Governor Swann to the General Assembly of Maryland, at its Regular Session, January 1868."

   b. Document C: "Annual Report of the Comptroller of the Treasury Department for the Fiscal Year Ending September 30, 1867 to the General Assembly."

   c. Document D: "Inaugual Address of Governor Oden Bowie to the General Assembly of Maryland, January 8, 1868."

   d. Document I: "Annual Report of the President and Directors of the Maryland Penitentiary Made to His Excellency Thomas Swann, Governor of Maryland, January 1868."

   e. Document K: "First Report of the Superintendent of Labor and Agriculture to the General Assembly of Maryland, January Session, 1868."

f. [Document?]: "Report of the Adjutant General of the State of Maryland for the Year 1867."

g. Document R: "Report of the Commissioner of Immigration."

h. Document X: "Report of the Committee on Education for Providing a General System of Free Public Schools for the State of Maryland."

i. Document AA: "Report of the Joint Committee to Examine into the Condition of the Reformatory and Benevolent Institutions of the State."

j. [Document ?]: "Second Annual Report of the State Superintendent of Public Instruction and Reports of Presidents of the Boards of County School Commissioners, for the Year Ending June 30, 1867, with a Summary of the Statistics of the Public Schools of the City of Baltimore for the Year 1867."

10. *The Maryland Code of Public General Laws [1860]*. Baltimore, 1860.

11. *The Maryland Code of Public Local Laws [1860]*. Baltimore, 1860.

12. *Laws of the State of Maryland [1861–1862]*. Annapolis, 1862.

13. *Laws of the State of Maryland [1864]*. Annapolis, 1864.

14. *Laws of the State of Maryland [1865]*. Annapolis, 1865.

15. *Laws of the State of Maryland [1866]*. Annapolis, 1866.

16. *Laws of the State of Maryland [1867]*. Annapolis, 1867.

17. *Laws of the State of Maryland [1868]*. Annapolis, 1868.

18. *Maryland Reports, Containing Cases Argued and Determined in the Court of Appeals of Maryland*, Vol. 23, April and October Terms, 1865. Annapolis, 1868.

19. *The Constitution of the State of Maryland [1864]*. Annapolis, 1864.

20. *The Constitution of the State of Maryland [1867]*. Annapolis, 1867.

21. *The Debates of the Constitutional Convention of the State of Maryland [1864]*. 3 vols. Annapolis, 1864.

22. *Debates of the Maryland Constitutional Convention of 1867, as Reprinted from Articles Reported in the Baltimore Sun*, edited by Philip B. Perlman. Baltimore, 1923.

23. Jacobsen, Phebe R. *Quaker Records in Maryland*. Annapolis, 1967.

24. Radoff, Morris L., Gus Skordas, and Phebe Jacobsen. *The County Courthouses and Records of Maryland*. Part 2, Annapolis, 1963.

Government Publications, Baltimore

1. *Journal of Proceedings of the First Branch City Council of Baltimore at the Sessions of 1864 and 1865*. Baltimore, 1865.

2. *Journal of Proceedings of the First Branch City Council of Baltimore at the Session of 1866.* Baltimore, 1866.
3. *Journal of Proceedings of the First Branch City Council of Baltimore at the Sessions of 1866 and 1867.* Baltimore, 1867.
4. *The Ordinances of the Mayor and City Council of Baltimore, Passed at the Sessions of 1864 and 1865.* Baltimore, 1865.
5. *The Ordinances of the Mayor and City Council of Baltimore, Passed at the Session of 1866.* Baltimore, 1866.
6. *The Ordinances of the Mayor and City Council of Baltimore, Passed at the Sessions of 1866 and 1867.* Baltimore, 1867.
7. *Thirty-Ninth Annual Report of the Board of Commissioners of Public Schools to the Mayor and City Council of Baltimore [1868].* Baltimore, 1868.

Unpublished Manuscript Collections

1. Bond Civil War Scrapbook, MS 59, Maryland Historical Society, Baltimore, Md.
2. Bond-McCulloch Family Papers, MS 1159, Maryland Historical Society, Baltimore, Md.
3. Briscoe Collection, MS 1089, Maryland Historical Society, Baltimore, Md.
4. John A. J. Creswell Papers, Library of Congress, Washington, D.C.
5. Harrison Journal, MS 432.1, Maryland Historical Society, Baltimore, Md.
6. Lloyd Papers, MS 2001, Maryland Historical Society, Baltimore, Md.
7. Scrapbook of Newspaper Articles, 1839–1890, Collected by Nathaniel Holmes Morison, Enoch Pratt Free Library, Baltimore, Md.
8. Stockbridge Scrapbooks, MS 788, Maryland Historical Society, Baltimore, Md.
9. Warfield, Susanna Diaries, MS 760, Maryland Historical Society, Baltimore, Md.
10. Wilson Account Book, MS 1067, Maryland Historical Society, Baltimore, Md.
11. Baltimore Normal School Minutes, 1867–1908, MS 95, Maryland Historical Society, Baltimore, Md.

12. Baltimore Yearly Meeting, Religious Society of Friends, Orthodox, Records Deposited at Homewood Meeting House, Filmed November–December 1963 by Hall of Records, State of Maryland.
   a. "Minutes, Meeting for Sufferings, 1829–1877."
   b. "Minutes, Friends Association in Aid of Freedmen."
13. Papers of the Washington Conference, Methodist Episcopal Church (North), Methodist Historical Society, Lovely Lane Museum, Baltimore, Md.
   a. "Journal of Proceedings, Washington Annual Conference, Methodist Episcopal Church, Session, October 27–31, 1864."
   b. "Journal of Proceedings, Washington Annual Conference, Methodist Episcopal Church, Session of October 18, 1865."
   c. "Journal of Proceedings, 3rd Session, Washington, Annual Conference, Held in John Wesley Church, Baltimore, Maryland [1866]."
   d. "Proceedings of the Washington Annual Conference M. E. Church, Fourth Session, Held in Sharp St. Church, Baltimore, Md. [March 6–12, 1867]."

Published Manuscript Collections, Diaries, Memoirs, and Autobiographies

1. *Autobiography of Oliver Otis Howard*, 2 vols. New York, 1908.
2. Basler, Roy P., ed. *The Collected Works of Abraham Lincoln.* 8 vols. New Brunswick, 1953.
3. Beale, Howard K., ed. *Diary of Gideon Welles.* Vols. 2 and 3. New York, 1960.
4. Coffin, L. J. *Unwritten History.* Philadelphia, 1919.
5. Davis, Noah. *A Narrative of the Life of Rev. Noah Davis, A Colored Man.* Baltimore, 1866.
6. Handy, James A. *Scraps of African Methodist Episcopal Church History.* Philadelphia, n.d.
7. Payne, Daniel A. *History of the African Methodist Episcopal Church.* Nashville, 1891.
8. Tanner, Benjamin T. *An Apology for African Methodism.* Baltimore, 1867.
9. Wallace, Lew. *Lew Wallace: An Autobiography.* Vol. 2. New York, 1906.

10. Wayman, Alexander W. *My Recollections of African M. E. Ministers*. Philadelphia, 1881.

Published Minutes, Proceedings and Reports of Private Organizations and Societies

1. *First Annual Report of the Baltimore Association for the Moral and Educational Improvement of the Colored People*. Baltimore, 1866.
2. *Second Annual Report of the Baltimore Association for the Moral and Educational Improvement of the Colored People*. Baltimore, 1866.
3. *Third Annual Report of the Baltimore Association for the Moral and Educational Improvement of the Colored People*. Baltimore, 1868.
4. *Journal of the General Conference of the Methodist Episcopal Church [North], 1864*. New York, 1864.
5. *Minutes of the Annual Conferences of the Methodist Episcopal Church [North], 1864*. New York, 1864.
6. *Minutes of the Annual Conferences of the Methodist Episcopal Church [North], 1865*. New York, n.d.
7. *Minutes of the Annual Conferences of the Methodist Episcopal Church [North], 1866*. New York, n.d.
8. *Minutes of the Annual Conferences of the Methodist Episcopal Church [North], 1867*. New York, n.d.
9. *Journal of the General Conference of the Methodist Episcopal Church [North], 1868*. New York, 1868.
10. *Minutes of the Annual Conferences of the Methodist Episcopal Church [North], 1868*. New York, n.d.
11. *Journal of the Eighty-First Annual Convention of the Protestant Episcopal Church in Maryland*. Baltimore, 1864.
12. *Journal of the Eighty-second Annual Conference of the Protestant Episcopal Church in Maryland*. Baltimore, 1865.
13. *Journal of the Eighty-fourth Annual Convention of the Protestant Episcopal Church in Maryland*. Baltimore, 1867.
14. New York Branch [American] Freedmen's Union Commission. *Fifth Annual Report [1867]*. New York, 1867.
15. *The Twentieth Annual Report of the American Missionary Association [1866]*. New York, 1866.
16. *The Twenty-First Annual Report of the American Missionary Association [1867]*. New York, 1867.

17. *The Twenty-Second Annual Report of the American Missionary Association [1868].* New York, 1868.

Newspapers, Journals, and Magazines

1. *American Freedman*
2. *American Missionary*
3. *Annapolis Gazette*
4. *Baltimore American and Commercial Advertiser*
5. *Baltimore Gazette*
6. *Baltimore Sun*
7. *Bel Air National American*
8. *Cecil Whig*
9. *Chestertown Transcript*
10. *Chicago Tribune*
11. *The Christian Advocate*
12. *Easton Gazette*
13. *Easton Journal*
14. *Frederick Examiner*
15. *Frederick Republican*
16. *Freedmen's Record*
17. *The Liberator*
18. *Maryland Farmer and Mechanic*
19. *The Nation*
20. *National Anti-Slavery Standard*
21. *National Freedman*
22. *National Savings Bank*
23. *New York Times*
24. *New York Tribune*
25. *Towsontown Advocate*
26. *Westminster American Sentinel*

City Directories

1. *Business Directory of the Principal Southern Cities, 1866 and 1867.* New York, 1866.
2. *Houston's Baltimore City Directory [1867].* Baltimore, 1867.
3. *Woods' Baltimore City Directory, Ending Year 1864.* Baltimore, Md.
4. *Woods' Baltimore City Directory, 1865–1866.* Baltimore, Md.

5. *Woods' Baltimore City Directory, 1867–1868.* Baltimore, 1868.
6. *Woods' Baltimore City Directory, 1871.* Baltimore, 1871.

Biographical Encyclopedias

1. *The Biographical Cyclopedia of Representative Men of Maryland and the District of Columbia.* Baltimore, 1879.
2. *Biographical Directory of the American Congress, 1774–1961.* Washington, 1961.
3. Bragg, George F. *Men of Maryland.* Baltimore, 1925.
4. Bragg, George F. *Heroes of the Eastern Shore.* Baltimore, 1939.
5. Essary, J. Frederick. *Maryland in National Politics.* Baltimore, 1932.
6. Hall, Clayton Coleman, ed. *Baltimore, Its History and Its People.* New York, 1912.
7. Morris, Dan, and Inez Morris, eds. *Who Was Who in American Politics.* New York, 1974.
8. Simmons, William J. *Men of Mark.* Cleveland, 1887.
9. Simpson, Matthew, ed. *Cyclopedia of Methodism.* Philadelphia, 1882.
10. *Who Was Who in America: Historical Volume, 1607–1896.* Chicago, 1963.
11. Wright, Richard R. *Centennial Encyclopedia of the African Methodist Episcopal Church.* Philadelphia, 1916.

Atlases

1. *Atlas of Fifteen Miles Around Baltimore, Including Anne Arundel County, Maryland.* Compiled by G. M. Hopkins. Philadelphia, 1878.
2. *City Atlas of Baltimore, Maryland and Environs.* Compiled by G. M. Hopkins. Philadelphia, 1876.
3. *New Topographical Atlas of the State of Maryland and the District of Columbia.* Compiled by Simon J. Martinet. Baltimore, 1872.

SECONDARY SOURCES

Books and Articles

Abbott, Edith. "The Civil War and the Crime Wave of 1865–1870." *Social Services Review* 1 (1929): 212–34.

Abbott, Martin. "The Freedmen's Bureau and Negro Schooling in South Carolina." *South Carolina Historical Magazine* 57 (April 1956): 65–81.

———. *The Freedmen's Bureau in South Carolina*. Chapel Hill, 1967.

Ahern, William H. "Laissez-faire vs. Equal Rights: Liberal Republicans and Limits to Reconstruction." *Phylon* 40 (March 1979): 52–65.

Alderson, William T. "The Freedmen's Bureau and Negro Education in Virginia." *North Carolina Historical Review* 29 (January 1952): 64–90.

Alexander, Roberta Sue. "Hostility and Hope: Black Education in North Carolina during Reconstruction, 1865–1867." *North Carolina Historical Review* 53 (January 1976): 113–32.

———. *North Carolina Faces the Freedmen: Race Relations during Presidential Reconstruction, 1865–1867*. Durham, 1985.

Anderson, Eric, and Alfred A. Moss, Jr. *The Facts of Reconstruction: Essays in Honor of John Hope Franklin*. Baton Rouge, 1991.

Anderson, James D. *The Education of Blacks in the South, 1860–1935*. Chapel Hill, 1988.

Armstrong, Thomas F. "The Building of a Black Church: Community in Post-Civil War Liberty County, Georgia." *Georgia Historical Quarterly* 66 (fall 1982): 346–67.

———. "From Task Labor to Free Labor: The Transition along Georgia's Rice Coast, 1820–1880." *Georgia Historical Quarterly* 64 (winter 1980): 432–47.

Ayers, Edward L. *Vengeance and Justice: Crime and Punishment in the 19th Century American South*. New York, 1983.

Baker, Jean H. *The Politics of Continuity: Maryland Political Parties from 1858 to 1870*. Baltimore, 1973.

Baltimore: A Picture History. Commentary by Francis F. Bierne. New York, 1957.

Baltimore: Its History and Its People, by Various Contributors. New York, 1912.

Bellesiles, Michael A. "The Origins of Gun Culture in the United States, 1760–1865." *Journal of American History* 83, no. 2 (September 1996): 425–55.

Belz, Herman. *Emancipation and Equal Rights: Politics and Constitutionalism in the Civil War Era*. New York, 1978.

————. *A New Birth of Freedom: The Republican Party and Freedmen's Rights, 1861–1866.* Westport, Conn., 1976.

————. "The New Orthodoxy in Reconstruction Historiography." *Reviews in American History* 1 (March 1973): 106–13.

————. "Origins of Negro Suffrage during the Civil War." *Southern Studies* 17 (summer 1978): 115–30.

————. *Reconstructing the Union: Theory and Practice during the Civil War.* Ithaca, 1969.

Benedict, Michael Les. "Preserving the Constitution: The Conservative Basis of Radical Reconstruction." *Journal of American History* 61 (June 1974): 65–90.

Bennett, Lerone Jr. *Black Power U.S.A.: The Human Side of Reconstruction, 1867–1877.* Chicago, 1967.

Berlin, Ira. *Slaves without Masters: The Free Negro in the Antebellum South.* New York, 1974.

Berlin, Ira, Barbara J. Fields, Thavolia Glymph, Joseph P. Reidy, and Leslie S. Rowland. *Freedom: A Documentary History of Emancipation, 1861–1867.* Series 1, Volume 1. *The Destruction of Slavery.* Cambridge, Eng., 1985.

Berlin, Ira, Stephen F. Miller, Joseph P. Reidy, and Leslie S. Rowland. *Freedom: A Documentary History of Emancipation, 1861–1867.* Series 1, Volume 2. *The Wartime Genesis of Free Labor.* Cambridge, Eng., 1990.

Berlin, Ira, Stephen F. Miller, and Leslie S. Rowland. "Afro-American Families in the Transition from Slavery to Freedom." *Radical History Review* 42 (fall 1988): 89–121.

Berlin, Ira, Joseph P. Reidy, and Leslie Rowland. *Freedom: A Documentary History of Emancipation 1861–1867.* Series 2. *The Black Military Experience.* New York, 1982.

Bethel, Elizabeth R. *Promiseland: A Century of Life in a Negro Community.* Philadelphia, 1981.

Blassingame, John W. "Before the Ghetto: The Making of the Black Community in Savannah, Georgia, 1865–1880." *Journal of Southern History* 6 (summer 1973): 463–88.

————. *Black New Orleans, 1860–1880.* Chicago, 1973.

————. "The Recruitment of Negro Troops in Maryland." *Maryland Historical Magazine* 58 (1963): 20–29.

————. *The Slave Community: Plantation Life in the Antebellum South.* Chicago, 1972.

―――. "The Union Army as an Educational Institution for Negroes, 1862–1865." *Journal of Negro History* 34 (1965): 152–59.

Blauch, L. E. "Education and the Maryland Constitutional Convention, 1864." *Maryland Historical Magazine* 25 (1930): 225–51.

―――. "The First Uniform School System of Maryland, 1865–1868." *Maryland Historical Magazine* 26 (1931): 205–27.

Blight, David W. *Frederick Douglass' Civil War: Keeping Faith in Jubilee.* Baton Rouge, 1989.

Bogue, Allan G. "Historians and Radical Republicans: A Meaning for Today." *Journal of American History* 70 (June 1983): 7–34.

Boles, John B. *Black Southerners, 1619–1869.* Lexington, 1983.

Bond, Carroll T. *The Court of Appeals of Maryland: A History.* Baltimore, 1928.

Borchert, James. *Alley Life in Washington: Family, Community, Religion, and Folklife in the City, 1850–1970.* Urbana, 1980.

Boyett, Gene W. "The Black Experience in the First Decade of Reconstruction in Pope County, Arkansas." *Arkansas Historical Quarterly* 51 (summer 1992): 119–34.

Brackett, Jeffrey R. *The Negro in Maryland: A Study of the Institution of Slavery.* Baltimore, 1889.

―――. *Progress of the Colored People of Maryland since the War.* Baltimore, 1890.

Bradley, Gladyce H. "The Education of Negroes in Maryland." *Journal of Negro Education* 16 (1947): 370–74.

Bragg, George F. *History of the Afro-American Group of the Episcopal Church.* Baltimore, 1922.

―――. *Men of Maryland.* Baltimore, 1925.

Bremner, Robert H. *The Public Good: Philanthropy and Welfare in the Civil War Era.* New York, 1980.

Brink, Dan C. "What Did Freedom Mean? The Aftermath of Slavery as Told by Former Slaves and Former Masters in Three Societies." *OAH Magazine of History* 4 (winter, 1989): 35–46.

Brown, Richard Maxwell. *Strain of Violence: Historical Studies of American Violence and Vigilantism.* New York, 1975.

Browne, Gary Lawson. *Baltimore in the Nation, 1789–1861.* Chapel Hill, 1980.

Browne, Joseph L. "The Expenses Are Borne by Parents': Freedmen's Schools in Southern Maryland, 1865–1870." *Maryland Historical Magazine* 86 (winter 1991): 407–22.

Bruce, Dickson D. *Violence and Culture in the Antebellum South*. Austin, 1979.

Brugger, Robert J. *Maryland: A Middle Temperament, 1634–1980*. Baltimore, 1988.

Bucholz, Heinrich E. *Governors of Maryland from the Revolution to 1908*. Baltimore, 1908.

Bullock, Henry Allen. *A History of Negro Education in the South from 1619 to the Present*. Cambridge, Mass., 1967.

Burton, Orville B. *In My Father's House are Many Mansions: Family and Community in Edgefield, South Carolina*. Chapel Hill, 1985.

———. "Race and Reconstruction: Edgefield County, South Carolina." *Journal of Social History* 12 (fall 1978): 31–56.

Burton, Orville B., and Robert C. McMath, Jr., eds. *Toward a New South: Studies in Post-Civil War Southern Communities*. Westport, Conn., 1982.

Butchart, Ronald E. *Northern Schools, Southern Blacks, and Reconstruction: Freedmen's Education, 1862–1865*. Westport, Conn., 1980.

Callcott, Margaret Law. *The Negro in Maryland Politics, 1870–1912*. Baltimore, 1969.

Callum, Agnes Kane, comp. *Slave Statistics of St. Mary's County Maryland, 1864, Commissioner George B. Dent*. Baltimore, 1993.

Campbell, Randolph B. "The Burden of Local Black Leadership during Reconstruction: A Research Note." *Civil War History* 39 (June 1993): 148–53.

Cantrell, Gregg. "Racial Violence and Reconstruction Politics in Texas, 1867–1868." *Southwestern Historical Quarterly* 93 (January 1990): 333–56.

Cheek, William, and Aimee Lee Cheek. *John Mercer Langston and the Fight for Black Freedom, 1829–1865*. Urbana, 1989.

Christensen, Lawrence O. "Schools for Blacks: J. Milton Turner in Reconstruction Missouri." *Missouri Historical Review* 76 (January 1982): 121–35.

Cimbala, Paul A. "A Black Colony in Dougherty County: The Freedmen's Bureau and the Failure of Reconstruction in Southwest Georgia." *Journal of Southwest Georgia History* 4 (fall 1986): 72–89.

———. "The Freedmen's Bureau, the Freedmen, and Sherman's Grant in Reconstruction Georgia, 1865–1867." *Journal of Southern History* 55 (November 1989): 597–632.

———. "Making Good Yankees: The Freedmen's Bureau and Education in Reconstruction Georgia, 1865–1870." *Atlanta Historical Journal* 29 (fall 1985): 5–18.

———. "On the Front Line of Freedom: Freedmen's Bureau Officers and Agents in Reconstruction Georgia." *Georgia Historical Quarterly* 76 (fall 1992): 577–611.

Clark, Charles Branch. *Politics in Maryland during the Civil War.* Chestertown, 1952.

———. "Suppression and Control of Maryland, 1861–1865." *Maryland Historical Magazine* 54 (1959): 241–72.

Click, Patricia C. *The Spirit of the Times: Amusements in Nineteenth Century Baltimore, Norfolk, and Richmond.* Charlottesville, 1989.

Cohen, William. *At Freedom's Edge: Black Mobility and the Southern White Quest for Racial Control, 1861–1915.* Baton Rouge, 1991.

———. "Black Immobility and Free Labor: The Freedmen's Bureau and the Relocation of Black Labor, 1865–1868." *Civil War History* 30 (September 1984): 221–34.

———. "Negro Involuntary Servitude in the South, 1865–1940: A Preliminary Analysis." *Journal of Southern History* 42 (February 1976): 31–60.

Cohen-Lack, Nancy. "A Struggle for Sovereignty: National Consolidation, Emancipation, and Free Labor in Texas, 1865." *Journal of Southern History* 58 (February 1992): 57–98.

Colby, Ira C. "The Freedmen's Bureau: From Social Welfare to Segregation." *Phylon* 46 (September 1985): 219–30.

Cooper, Renee F. "Reconstruction and Education: Voices from the South, 1865–1871." *Prologue* 27 (summer 1995): 127–34.

Coryell, Janet L. *Neither Heroine nor Fool: Anna Ella Carroll of Maryland.* Kent, Ohio, 1990.

Cox, LaWanda. "The Promise of Land for the Freedmen." *Mississippi Valley Historical Review* 45 (December 1958): 413–40.

Crouch, Barry A. *The Freedmen's Bureau and Black Texans.* Austin, 1992.

———. "Guardian of the Freed People: The Texas Freedmen's Bureau Agents and the Black Community." *Southern Studies* 3 (fall 1992): 185–201.

———. "Hidden Sources of Black History: The Texas Freedmen's Bureau Records as a Case Study." *Southwestern Historical Quarterly* 83 (January 1980): 211–26.

———. "A Spirit of Lawlessness: White Violence; Texas Blacks, 1865–1868." *Journal of Social History* 18 (winter 1984): 217–32.

Crouch, Barry A., and Larry Madaras. "Reconstructing Black Families: Perspectives from the Texas Freedmen's Bureau Records." *Prologue* 18 (summer 1986): 109–22.

Cruden, Robert. *The Negro in Reconstruction.* Englewood Cliffs, N.J., 1969.

Culver, Dwight W. *Negro Segregation in the Methodist Church.* New Haven, 1953.

Currie, James T. "Benjamin Montgomery and the Davis Bend Colony." *Prologue* (25th Anniversary Issue, 1994): 73–86.

Curry, Ricard O., ed. *Radicalism, Racism, and Party Realignment: The Border States during Reconstuction.* Baltimore, 1969.

Daniel, Pete. "The Metamorphosis of Slavery, 1865–1900." *Journal of American History* 66 (June 1979): 88–99.

Davis, Ronald F. *Good and Faithful Labor: From Slavery to Sharecropping in the Natchez District, 1860–1890.* Westport, Conn., 1982.

DeCanio, Stephen. *Agriculture in the Postbellum South: The Economics of Production and Supply.* Cambridge, Mass., 1974.

Degler, Carl. "Rethinking Post-Civil War History." *Virginia Quarterly Review* 57 (spring 1981).

Della, Ray M., Jr. "The Problems of Negro Labor in the 1850's." *Maryland Historical Magazine* 66 (spring 1971): 14–32.

Donald, Henderson H. *The Negro Freedman.* New York, 1952.

Drago, Edmund L. "The Black Household in Dougherty County, Georgia, 1870–1900." *Journal of Southwest Georgia History* 1 (fall 1983): 38–40.

Dunlap, William C. *Quaker Education in Baltimore and Virginia Yearly Meetings.* Philadelphia, 1936.

Engerman, Stanley L. "Coerced and Free Labor: Property Rights and the Development of the Labor Force." *Explorations in Economic History* 29 (January 1992): 1–29.

———. "Slavery and Emancipation in Comparative Perspective: A Look at Some Recent Debates." *Journal of Economic History* 46 (June 1986): 317–39.

Engs, Robert Francis. *Freedom's First Generation: Black Hampton, Virginia, 1861–1890.* Philadelphia, 1979.

Evitts, William J. *A Matter of Allegiances: Maryland from 1850 to 1861.* Baltimore, 1974.

Fields, Barbara Jeanne. "Ideology and Race in American History." In J. Morgan Kousser and James M. McPherson, eds. *Region, Race and Reconstruction: Essays in Honor of C. Vann Woodward.* New York, 1982.

———. "The Nineteenth-Century American South: History and Theory." *Plantation Society in the Americas* 2 (April 1983): 7–28.

———. *Slavery and Freedom on the Middle Ground: Maryland during the Nineteenth Century.* New Haven, 1985.

Finley, Randy. *From Slavery to Uncertain Freedom: The Freedmen's Bureau in Arkansas, 1865–1869.* Fayetteville, 1996.

Fitzgerald, Michael W. "The Carpetbaggers Revisited: New Perspectives on Interregional Migration after the American Civil War." *Slavery & Abolition* 11 (September 1990): 227–35.

Fitzgerald, Michael W. *The Union League Movement in the Deep South: Political and Agricultural Change during Reconstruction.* Baton Rouge, 1989.

———. "Wager Swayne, the Freedmen's Bureau, and the Politics of Reconstruction in Alabama." *Alabama Review* 48 (July 1995): 188–218.

Fleming, Cynthia Griggs. "The Plight of Black Educators in Postwar Tennessee, 1865–1920." *Journal of Negro History* 64 (fall 1979): 355–64.

Foner, Eric. "The Continuing Evolution of Reconstruction History." *OAH Magazine of History* 4 (winter 1989): 11–13.

———. *Free Soil, Free Labor, Free Men: The Ideology of the Republican Party.* New York, 1970.

———. "The Meaning of Freedom." *Radical History Review* 39 (September 1987): 92–114.

———. *Nothing But Freedom: Emancipation and Its Legacy.* Baton Rouge, 1983, 74–110.

———. *Politics and Ideology in the Age of Civil War.* New York, 1980.

———. "Reconstruction and the Black Political Tradition," in *Political Parties and the Modern State*, Richard L. McCormick, ed. New Brunswick, 1983.

———. *Reconstruction: America's Unfinished Revolution.* New York, 1988.

———. "Reconstruction Revisited." *Reviews in American History* 10 (December 1982): 82–100.

Formwalt, Lee W. "The Camilla Massacre of 1868: Racial Violence as

Political Propaganda." *Georgia Historical Quarterly* 71 (fall 1987): 399–426.

———. "Petitioning Congress for Protection: A Black View of Reconstruction at the Local Level." *Georgia Historical Quarterly* 73 (summer 1989): 305–22.

Franklin, John Hope. "Mirror for Americans: A Century of Reconstruction History." *American Historical Review* 85 (February 1980): 1–14.

———. *Reconstruction after the Civil War.* Chicago, 1961.

Fredrickson, George M. *The Black Image in the White Mind: The Debate on Afro-American Character and Destiny, 1817–1914.* New York, 1971.

Fuke, Richard Paul. "The Baltimore Association for the Moral and Educational Improvement of the Colored People, 1864–1870." *Maryland Historical Magazine* 66 (winter 1971): 369–404.

———. "Blacks, Whites, and Guns: Interracial Violence in Post-Emancipation Maryland." *Maryland Historical Magazine* 92 (fall 1997): 326–48.

———. "Hugh Lennox Bond and Radical Republican Ideology." *Journal of Southern History* 45 (November 1979): 569–86.

———. "Peasant Priorities?: Tidewater Blacks and the Land in Post-Emancipation Maryland." *Locus* 3 (fall 1990): 21–46.

———. "Planters, Apprenticeship, and Forced Labor: The Black Family under Pressure in Post-Emancipation Maryland." *Agricultural History* 62 (fall 1988): 57–74.

———. "A Reform Mentality: Federal Attitudes toward Black Marylanders, 1864–1868." *Civil War History* (September 1976): 214–35.

———. "A School for Freed Labor: The Maryland 'Government Farms,' 1864–1866." *Maryland Historian* (spring/summer 1985): 11–34.

Gara, Larry. "Teaching Negro Freedmen in the Post-War South: A Document." *Journal of Negro History* 40 (July 1955): 274–76.

Garonzik, Joseph. "The Racial and Ethnic Make-up of Baltimore Neighborhoods, 1850–70." *Maryland Historical Magazine* 71 (fall 1976): 392–402.

Gates, Paul. "Federal Land Policy in the South, 1866–1888." *Journal of Southern History* 6 (1940): 303–30.

Genovese, Eugene D. *Roll, Jordan, Roll: The World the Slaves Made.* New York, 1974.

Gerteis, Louis. *From Contraband to Freedmen: Federal Policy Toward Southern Blacks, 1861–1865.* Westport, Conn., 1973.

Gillette, William. *Retreat from Reconstruction, 1869–1879.* Baton Rouge, 1979.

Glymph, Thavolia, and John J. Kushma, eds. *Essays on the Southern Postbellum Economy.* College Station, Texas, 1985.

Graham, Leroy. *Baltimore: The Nineteenth Century Black Capital.* Washington, D.C., 1982.

Graves, John William. *Town and Country: Race Relations in an Urban-Rural Context, Arkansas, 1865–1905.* Fayetteville, 1990.

Gutman, Herbert. *The Black Family in Slavery in Freedom, 1750–1920.* New York, 1976.

Hahn, Steven. *The Roots of Southern Populism: Yeoman Farmers and the Transformation of the Georgia Upcountry, 1850–1890.* New York, 1983.

Hall, Robert. "Slave Resistance in Baltimore City and County, 1747–1790." *Maryland Historical Magazine* 84 (winter 1989): 305–18.

Harlan, Louis R. "Desegregation in New Orleans Public Schools during Reconstruction." *American Historical Review* 67 (April 1962): 663–75.

Henig, Gerald S. *Henry Winter Davis: Antebellum and Civil War Congressman from Maryland.* New York, 1973.

Hennessey, Melinda Meek. "Racial Violence during Reconstruction: The 1876 Riots in Charleston and Cainhoy." *South Carolina Historical Magazine* 86 (April 1985): 100–12.

———. "Reconstruction Politics and the Military: The Eufaula Riot of 1874." *Alabama Historical Quarterly* 38 (summer 1976): 112–25.

Hermann, Janet S. *The Pursuit of a Dream.* New York, 1981.

Hickey, Damon D. "Pioneers of the New South: The Baltimore Association and North Carolina Friends in Reconstruction." *Quaker History* 74 (spring 1985): 1–17.

Higgs, Robert. *Competition and Coercion: Blacks in the American Economy, 1865–1914.* Cambridge, Eng., 1977.

Hirschfield, Charles. *Baltimore, 1870–1900: Studies in Social History.* Baltimore, 1941.

Hofstadter, Richard, and Michael Wallace, eds. *American Violence.* New York, 1971.

Holt, Sharon Anne. "Making Freedom Pay: Freed People Working for

Themselves, North Carolina, 1865–1900." *Journal of Southern History* 60 (May 1994): 229–62.

Hornsby, Alton, Jr. "The Freedmen's Bureau Schools in Texas, 1865–1870." *Southwestern Historical Quarterly* 76 (April 1973): 397–417.

Horowitz, Robert F. "Land to the Freedmen: A Vision of Reconstruction." *Ohio History* 86 (summer 1977): 187–99.

Howard, George W. *The Monumental City: Its Past History and Present Resources.* Baltimore, 1873.

Huffman, Frank J. "Town and Country in the South, 1850–1880: A Comparison of Urban and Rural Social Structures." *South Atlantic Quarterly* 76 (summer 1977): 366–81.

Humphrey, George D. "The Failure of the Mississippi Freedmen's Bureau in Black Labor Relations, 1865–1867." *Journal of Mississippi History* 45 (February 1983): 23–27.

Jaynes, Gerald David. *Branches Without Roots: Genesis of the Black Working Class in the American South, 1862–1882.* New York, 1986.

Johnson, Daniel M. *Black Migration in America: A Social Demographic History.* Durham, 1981.

Johnson, Whittington B. "A Black Teacher and Her School in Reconstruction Darien: The Correspondence of Hettie E. Sabattie and J. Murray Hoag." *Georgia Historical Quarterly* 75 (spring 1991): 90–105.

Jones, Jacqueline. *Labor of Love, Labor of Sorrow: Black Women, Work, and the Family from Slavery to the Present.* New York, 1985.

——. *Soldiers of Light and Love: Northern Teachers and Georgia Blacks.* Chapel Hill, 1980.

——. "Women Who Were More Than Men: Sex and Status in Freedmen's Teaching." *Historical of Education Quarterly* 19 (spring 1979): 47–59.

Kellogg, John. "The Evolution of Black Residential Areas in Lexington, Kentucky, 1865–1887." *Journal of Southern History* 48 (February 1982): 21–52.

Kent, Frank Richardson. *The Story of Maryland Politics [1864–1910].* Baltimore, 1911.

Kimball, Philip Clyde. "Freedom's Harvest: Freedmen's Schools in Kentucky after the Civil War." *Filson Club Historical Quarterly* 54 (July 1980): 272–88.

Klein, Mary O. " 'We shall be accountable to God': Some Inquiries into the Position of Blacks in Somerset Parish, Maryland, 1692–1865." *Maryland Historical Magazine* 87 (winter 1992): 399–406.

Koger, A. Briscoe. *Negro Baptists of Maryland.* Baltimore, 1946.

Kohl, Martha. "From Freedom to Franchise: The Debate over African American Enfranchisement, 1865–1870." *Gateway Heritage* 16 (spring 1966): 22–35.

Kolchin, Peter. *First Freedom: The Response of Alabama's Blacks to Emancipation and Reconstruction.* Westport, Conn., 1972.

Kousser, J. Morgan, and James M. McPherson, eds. *Region, Race, and Reconstruction: Essays in Honor of C. Vann Woodward.* New York, 1982.

Kremer, Gary R. "James Milton Turner and the Reconstruction Struggle for Black Education." *Gateway Heritage* 11 (spring 1991): 66–75.

Lane, Roger. *Roots of Violence in Black Philadelphia.* Cambridge, Mass., 1986.

Laurie, Murray D. "The Union Academy: A Freedmen's Bureau School in Gainesville, Florida." *Florida Historical Quarterly* 65 (October 1986): 163–74.

Lee, Jean Butenhoff. "The Problem of Slave Community in Eighteenth Century Chesapeake." *William and Mary Quarterly* 43 (July 1986): 333–61.

Levine, Lawrence W. *Black Culture and Black Consciousness: Afro-American Folk Thought from Slavery to Freedom.* New York, 1977.

Lewis, Ronald L. *Coal, Iron, and Slaves: Industrial Slavery in Maryland and Virginia, 1715–1865.* Westport, Conn., 1979.

Litwack, Leon F. *Been in the Storm So Long: The Aftermath of Slavery.* New York, 1979.

Lovett, Bobby L. "Memphis Riots: White Reaction to Blacks in Memphis, May 1865–July 1866." *Tennessee Historical Quarterly* 38 (spring 1979): 9–33.

———. "Some 1871 Accounts for the Little Rock, Arkansas, Freedmen's Savings and Trust Company." *Journal of Negro History* 66 (winter 1981–1982): 322–28.

Low, W. A. "The Freedmen's Bureau and Civil Rights in Maryland." *Journal of Negro History* 36 (1952): 221–47.

———. "The Freedmen's Bureau and Education in Maryland." *Maryland Historical Magazine* 47 (1952): 29–39.

Low, W. Augustus, and Virgil A. Clift, eds. *Encyclopedia of Black America.* New York, 1981.

Lowe, Richard. "The Freedmen's Bureau and Local Black Leadership [A Research Note]." *Journal of American History* 80, no. 3 (December 1993): 989–98.

———. "Local Black Leaders during Reconstruction in Virginia." *Virginia Magazine of History and Biography* 103 (April 1995): 181–206.

McDonald, Forrest, and Grady McWhiney. "The South from Self-Sufficiency to Peonage: An Interpretation." *American Historical Review* 85 (December 1980): 1095–1118.

McFeely, William S. *Frederick Douglass.* New York, 1991.

———. "Two Reconstructions, Two Nations." *Massachusetts Review* 32 (spring 1991): 39–53.

———. *Yankee Stepfather: General O. O. Howard and the Freedmen.* New Haven, 1968.

McGehee, C. Stuart. "E. O. Tade, Freedmen's Education, and the Failure of Reconstruction in Tennessee." *Tennessee Historical Quarterly* 43 (winter 1984): 376–89.

———. "Military Origins of the New South: The Army of the Cumberland and Chattanooga's Freedmen." *Civil War History* 34 (December 1988): 323–43.

McGlynn, Frank, and Seymour Drescher, eds. *The Meaning of Freedom: Economics, Politics, and Culture after Slavery.* Pittsburgh, 1992.

McKee, Irving. *"Ben-Hur" Wallace.* Berkeley and Los Angeles, 1947.

McKitrick, Eric. *Andrew Johnson and Reconstruction.* Chicago, 1960.

———. "Reconstructions Ultraconservative Revolution." In *The Comparative Approach to American History*, ed. C. Vann Woodward. New York, 1968, 146–59.

McPherson, James. "The New Puritanism: Values and Goals of Freedmen's Education in America." In *The University in Society*, ed. Lawrence Stone. Vol. 2. Princeton, 1974, 611–39.

———. "White Liberals and Black Power in Negro Education, 1865–1915." *American Historical Review* 75 (June 1970): 1357–79.

———. "Who Freed the Slaves." *Proceedings of the American Philosophical Society* 139 (March 1995): 1–10.

———. "Who Freed the Slaves." *Reconstruction* 2 (1994): 35–40.

McWhiney, Grady. "The Revolution in Nineteenth Century Alabama Agriculture." *Alabama Review* 31 (January 1978): 3–32.

Magdol, Edward. *A Right to the Land: Essays on the Freedmen's Community.* Westport, Conn., 1977.

Mahan, Harold E. " 'We Feel to Bee A People': Historiographical Perspectives on Blacks in Emancipation and Reconstruction." *Maryland Historian*, 16 (Spring/Summer 1985) 41–56.

Malone, Anne Patton. *Sweet Chariot: Slave Family and Household Structure in Nineteenth Century Louisiana*. Chapel Hill, 1992.

Manakee, Harold R. *Maryland in the Civil War*. Baltimore, 1961.

Mandle, Jay R. *Not Slave, Not Free: The African American Economic Experience since the Civil War*. Durham, 1992.

———. *The Roots of Black Poverty: The Southern Plantation Economy after the Civil War*. Durham, 1978.

Marks, Bayly E. "Skilled Blacks in Antebellum St. Mary's County." *Journal of Southern History* 53 (November 1987): 537–64.

Maryland: A Guide to the Old Line State Compiled by the Workers of the Writers' Program of the Works Projects Administration, in the State of Maryland. New York, 1940.

May, J. Thomas. "The Freedmen's Bureau at the Local Level: A Study of a Louisiana Agent." *Louisiana History* 9 (winter 1968): 5–20.

Medford, Edna Greene. "Land and Labor: The Quest for Black Economic Independence on Virginia's Lower Peninsula, 1865–1880." *Virginia Magazine of History and Biography* 100 (October 1992): 567–82.

Messner, William F. "Black Violence and White Response: Louisiana, 1862." *Journal of Southern History* 41 (February 1975): 19–38.

———. "Black Education in Louisiana, 1863–1865." *Civil War History* 22 (March 1976): 41–59.

———. *Freedmen and the Ideology of Free Labor: Louisiana, 1862–1865*. Lafayette, La., 1978.

Meyers, John B. "The Education of Alabama Freedmen during Presidential Reconstruction, 1865–1867." *Journal of Negro Education* 40 (spring 1971): 163–71.

Moneyhon, Carl. "From Slave to Free Labor: The Federal Plantation Experiment in Arkansas." *Arkansas Historical Quarterly* 53 (summer 1994): 137–60.

Morgan, Lynda J. *Emancipation in Virginia's Tobacco Belt, 1850–1870*. Athens, Ga., 1992.

Morgan, Philip D. *Slave Counterpoint: Black Culture in the Eighteenth Century Chesapeake and Low Country*. Chapel Hill, 1998.

Morris, Robert C. *Reading, 'Riting, and Reconstruction: The Education of Freedmen in the South, 1861–1870*. Chicago, 1976.

Myers, William Starr. *The Maryland Constitution of 1864*. Baltimore, 1901.

———. *The Self-Reconstruction of Maryland, 1864–1867*. Baltimore, 1927.

Nash, Horace D. "Blacks in Arkansas during Reconstruction: The Ex-Slave Narratives." *Arkansas Historical Quarterly* 48 (autumn 1989): 243–59.

Neverdon-Morton, Cynthia. "Black Housing Patterns in Baltimore City, 1885–1953." *Maryland Historian* 16 (spring/summer 1985): 25–39.

Nieman, Donald G. *To Set the Law in Motion: The Freedmen's Bureau and the Legal Rights of Blacks, 1865–1868*. Millwood, N.Y., 1979.

Novack, Daniel A. *The Wheel of Servitude: Black Forced Labor after Slavery*. Lexington, 1978.

Oakes, James. "A Failure of Vision: The Collapse of the Freedmen's Bureau Courts." *Civil War History* 25 (March 1979): 66–76.

Olson, Sherry. *Baltimore: The Building of an American City*. Baltimore, 1980.

Osthaus, Carl. *Freedmen, Philanthropy, and Fraud: A History of the Freedmen's Savings Bank*. Urbana, 1976.

Oubre, Claude F. *Forty Acres and a Mule: The Freedmen's Bureau and Black Landownership*. Baton Rouge, 1978.

Paisley, Clifton. *From Cotton to Quail: An Agricultural Chronicle of Leon County, Florida, 1860–1967*. Gainesville, 1968.

Parker, Marjorie H. "Some Educational Activities of the Freedmen's Bureau." *Journal of Negro Education* 23 (winter 1954): 9–21.

Pearce, Larry W. "The American Missionary Association and the Freedmen's Bureau in Arkansas, 1866–1868." *Arkansas Historical Quarterly* 30 (autumn 1971): 241–59.

———. "The American Missionary Association and the Freedmen's Bureau in Arkansas, 1868–1878." *Arkansas Historical Quarterly* 31 (autumn 1972): 246–61.

Peek, Ralph L. "Lawlessness in Florida, 1868–1871." *Florida Historical Quarterly* 40 (October 1961): 164–85.

Penningroth, Dylan. "Slavery, Freedom, and Social Claims to Property among African Americans in Liberty County, Georgia, 1850–1880." *Journal of American History* 84 (September 1997): 405–35.

Phillips, Paul David. "Education and Blacks in Tennessee during Reconstruction, 1865–1870." *Tennessee Historical Quarterly* 46 (summer 1987): 98–109.

Pope, Christie F. "Southern Homesteads for Negroes." *Agricultural History* 44 (April 1970): 201–12.

Powers, Bernard E., Jr. *Black Charlestonians: A Social History, 1822–1885.* Fayetteville, 1994.

———. "Community Evolution and Race Relations in Reconstruction Charleston, South Carolina." *South Carolina Historical Magazine* 95 (January 1994): 27–46.

Preston, Dickson J. *Young Frederick Douglass: The Maryland Years.* Baltimore, 1980.

Pritchett, Jonathan B. "The Burden of Negro Schooling: Tax Incidence and Racial Redistribution on Postbellum North Carolina." *Journal of Economic History* 59 (December 1989): 966–973.

Putney, Martha S. "The Baltimore Normal School for the Education of Colored Teachers: Its Founders and Founding." *Maryland Historical Magazine* 72 (summer 1977): 238–52.

Quarles, Benjamin. " 'Fettered Freedom': Blacks in the Constitutional Era in Maryland, 1776–1810: An Introduction." *Maryland Historical Magazine* 84 (winter 1989): 299–304.

Rabinowitz, Howard N. "The Conflict between Blacks and the Police in the Urban South, 1865–1900. *Historian* 39 (November 1976): 62–76.

———. *The First New South, 1865–1920.* Arlington Heights, 1992.

———. "From Exclusion to Segregation: Southern Race Relations, 1865–1890." *Journal of American History* 63 (September 1976): 325–50.

———. "Half a Loaf: The Shift from White to Black Teachers in the Negro Schools of the Urban South, 1865–1890." *Journal of Southern History* 40 (November 1974): 565–94.

———. *Race Relations in the Urban South, 1865–1900.* New York, 1978.

Rable, George C. *But There Was No Peace: The Role of Violence in the Politics of Reconstruction.* Athens, Ga., 1984.

Rachleff, Peter J. *Black Labor in the South: Richmond, Virginia, 1865–1890.* Philadelphia, 1984.

Radoff, Morris L., ed. *The Old Line State: A History of Maryland.* Baltimore, 1956.

Rankin, David C. "The Impact of the Civil War on the Free Colored

Community of New Orleans." *Perspectives in American History* 11 (1977–1978): 379–416.

Ransom, Roger L., and Richard Sutch. "The Impact of the Civil War and Emancipation." *Explorations in Economic History* 12 (fall 1975): 6–11.

―――. *One Kind of Freedom: The Economic Consequences of Emancipation*. Cambridge, Eng., 1977.

Rapport, Sarah. "The Freedmen's Bureau as a Legal Agent for Black Men and Women in Georgia, 1865–1868." *Georgia Historical Quarterly* 73 (spring 1989): 26–53.

Rawick, George P., ed. *The American Slave: A Composite Autobiography*. 19 vols. Westport, Conn., 1972.

Reid, Joseph D. "Sharecropping as an Understandable Market Response: The Postbellum South." *Journal of Economic History* 33 (March 1973): 106–30.

Reidy, Joseph P. *From Slavery to Agrarian Capitalism in the Cotton Plantation South: Central Georgia, 1800–1880*. Chapel Hill, 1992.

Reilly, Wayne E., ed. *Sarah Jane Foster: Teacher of the Freedmen: A Diary and Letters*. Charlottesville, 1990.

Richardson, Joe M. "The American Missionary Association and Black Education in Civil War Missouri." *Missouri Historical Review* 69 (July 1975): 433–48.

―――. *Christian Reconstruction: The American Missionary Association and Southern Blacks, 1861–1890*. Athens, Ga., 1986.

―――. "The Freedmen's Bureau and Negro Education in Florida." *Journal of Negro Education* 31 (fall 1962): 460–67.

Richter, William L. *The Army in Texas during Reconstruction, 1865–1870*. College Station: Texas A&M University Press, 1987.

―――. *Overreached on All Sides: The Freedmen's Bureau Administrators in Texas, 1865–1868*. College Station, Texas, 1991.

Riddle, Wesley Allen. "The Origins of Black Sharecropping." *Mississippi Quarterly* 49 (winter 1995–1996): 53–71.

Ripley, C. Peter. *Slaves and Freedmen in Civil War Louisiana*. Baton Rouge, 1978.

Ripley, C. Peter, Roy E. Finkenbine, Michael F. Hembree, and Donald Yacovone. *Witness for Freedom: African American Voices on Race, Slavery, and Emancipation*. Chapel Hill, 1993.

Roark, James. *Masters without Slaves: Southern Planters in the Civil War and Reconstruction*. New York, 1977.

Robinson, Armstead L. "Beyond the Realm of Social Consensus: New Meanings of Reconstruction for American History." *Journal of American History* 68 (September 1981): 276–97.

Roediger, David R. *The Wages of Whiteness: Race and the Making of the American Working Class.* London, 1991.

Rose, Willie Lee. *Rehearsal for Reconstruction: The Port Royal Experiment.* New York, 1964.

———. *Slavery and Freedom.* Edited by William W. Freehling. New York, 1982.

Rouse, Michael Francis (Brother Bede C.F.X.). *A Study of the Development of Negro Education under Catholic Auspices in Maryland and the District of Columbia.* Baltimore, 1935.

Royce, Edward. *The Origins of Southern Sharecropping.* Philadelphia, 1993.

Saville, Julie. "Grassroots Reconstruction: Agricultural Labor and Collective Action in South Carolina, 1860–1868." *Slavery and Abolition* 12 (December 1991): 173–82.

———. *The Work of Reconstruction: From Slave to Wage Laborer in South Carolina, 1860–1870.* New York, 1994.

Scharf, J. Thomas. *The Chronicles of Baltimore.* Baltimore, 1874.

———. *History of Baltimore City and County.* Philadelphia, 1881.

———. *History of Maryland, 1879.* 3 vols. Reprint, Hartboro, 1967.

Schor, Joel. "The Rivalry Between Frederick Douglass and Henry Highland Garnet." *Journal of Negro History* 64 (winter 1979): 30–38.

Schultz, Edward T. *History of Freemasonry in Maryland.* 4 vols. Baltimore, 1884–1888.

Schweninger, Loren. "The American Missionary Association and Northern Philanthropy in Reconstruction Alabama." *Alabama Historical Quarterly* 32 (fall-winter 1970): 129–56.

———. *Black Property Owners in the South, 1790–1915.* Urbana, 1990.

Scott, Rebecca. "The Battle over the Child: Child Apprenticeship and the Freedmen's Bureau in North Carolina." *Prologue* 10 (summer 1978): 101–13.

Sefton, James E. *The United States Army and Reconstruction, 1865–1877.* Baton Rouge, 1967.

Sharkey, Robert P. *Money, Class and Party: An Economic Study of Civil War and Reconstruction.* Baltimore, 1967.

Shaw, Bevery F. *The Negro in the History of Methodism.* Nashville, 1954.

Sherwood, Grace H. *The Oblates' Hundred and One Years*. New York, 1931.

Shifflett, Crandall A. *Patronage and Poverty in the Tobacco South: Louisa County, Virginia, 1860–1900*. Knoxville, 1982.

Shapiro, Herbert. "Afro-American Responses to Race Violence during Reconstruction." *Science and Society* (summer 1972): 158–70.

———. *White Violence and Black Response: From Reconstruction to Montgomery*. Amherst, Mass., 1988, 5–29.

Sheldon, Randall G. "From Slave to Caste Society: Penal Changes in Tennessee, 1830–1915." *Tennessee Historical Quarterly* 38 (winter 1979): 462–78.

Shlomowitz, Ralph. " 'Bound' or 'Free'? Black Labor in Cotton and Sugarcane Farming, 1865–1880." *Journal of Southern History* 50 (November 1984): 570–96.

———. "On Punishments and Rewards in Coercive Labor Systems." *Slavery and Abolition* 12 (September 1991): 97–102.

———. "The Origins of Southern Sharecropping." *Agricultural History* 53 (July 1979): 557–75.

Small, Sandra E. "The Yankee Schoolmarm in Freedmen's Schools: An Analysis of Attitudes." *Journal of Southern History* 45, no. 2 (August 1979): 381–402.

Smallwood, James. "Black Education in Reconstruction Texas: The Contributions of the Freedmen's Bureau and Benevolent Societies." *East Texas Historical Journal* 19 (spring 1981): 17–40.

———. "Black Freedwomen after Emancipation: The Texas Experience." *Prologue* 27 (winter 1995): 303–17.

———. "Charles E. Culver, a Reconstruction Agent in Texas: The Work of Local Freedmen's Bureau Agents and the Black Community." *Civil War History* 27 (December 1981): 350–61.

———. "Perpetuation of Caste: Black Agricultural Workers in Reconstruction Texas." *Mid-America* 61 (January 1979): 2–24.

———. *Time of Hope, Time of Despair: Black Texans during Reconstruction*. Port Washington, N.Y., 1981.

Smith, Albert C. " 'Southern Violence': Arson as Protest in Black-Belt Georgia, 1865–1910." *Journal of Southern History* 51 (November 1985): 527–64.

Smith, John David. "More than Slaves: Less than Freedmen: The 'Share Wages' System during Reconstruction." *Civil War History* 26 (September 1980): 256–66.

Somers, Dale A. "Black and White in New Orleans: A Study in Urban Race Relations, 1865–1900." *Journal of Southern History* 40 (February 1974): 19–42.

Sparks, Randy J. " 'The White People's Arms Are Longer Than Ours': Blacks, Education, and the American Missionary Association in Reconstruction Mississippi." *Journal of Mississippi History* 54 (February 1992): 1–27.

Spivey, Donald. *Schooling for the New Slavery: Black Industrial Education, 1868–1915*. Westport, Conn., 1978.

Sprague, Stuart Seely. "From Slavery to Freedom: The Economic History of Northeastern Kentucky, 1850–1875." *Essays in Economic and Business History* 12 (1994): 245–49.

Stagg, J.C.A. "The Problem of Klan Violence: The South Carolina Upcountry, 1868–1871." *Journal of American Studies* 8 (December 1974): 303–18.

Stampp, Kenneth. *The Era of Reconstruction, 1865–1867*. New York, 1965.

Steiner, Bernard C. *Citizenship and Suffrage in Maryland*. Baltimore, 1895.

———. *History of Education in Baltimore*. Washington, 1894.

———. *Life of Henry Winter Davis*. Baltimore, 1916.

———. *Life of Reverdy Johnson*. Baltimore, 1914.

Sutch, Richard, and Roger L. Ransom. "The Ex-Slave in the Post-Bellum South: A Study of the Economic Impact of Racism in a Market Environment." *Journal of Economic History* 33 (March 1973): 131–48.

Sutherland, Daniel E. "A Special Kind of Problem: The Response of Household Slaves and Their Masters to Freedom." *Southern Studies* 20 (summer 1981): 151–66.

Swint, Henry Lee. *The Northern Teacher in the South, 1862–1870*. Nashville, 1941.

———. "Reports from Educational Agents of the Freedmen's Bureau in Tennessee, 1865–1870." *Tennessee Historical Quarterly* 1 (1942): 51–80, 152–70.

Taylor, Arnold H. *Travail and Triumph: Black Life and Culture in the South since the Civil War*. Westport, Conn., 1976.

Thomas, Bettye C. "A Nineteenth Century Black Operated Shipyard, 1866–1884: Reflections Upon Its Inception and Ownership." *Journal of Negro History* 59 (January 1974): 1–12.

————. "Public Education and Black Protest in Baltimore, 1865–1900." *Maryland Historical Magazine* 71 (fall 1976): 381–91.

Toll, William. "Free Men, Freedmen, and Race: Black Social Theory in the Gilded Age." *Journal of Southern History* 44 (November 1978): 571–96.

————. *The Resurgence of Race: Black Social Theory from Reconstruction to the Pan-African Conferences.* Philadelphia, 1979.

Towers, Frank. " 'A Vociferous Army of Howling Wolves': Baltimore's Civil War Riot of April 19, 1861." *Maryland Historian* 23 (fall/winter 1992): 1–28.

Trefousse, Hans L. *The Radical Republicans: Lincoln's Vanguard for Racial Justice.* New York, 1969.

Trelease, Allen W. *White Terror: The Ku Klux Klan Conspiracy and Southern Reconstruction.* New York, 1971.

Tunnell, Ted. *Crucible of Reconstruction: War, Radicalism, and Race in Louisiana, 1862–1877.* Baton Rouge, 1984.

————. "Free Negroes and the Freedmen: Black Politics in New Orleans during the Civil War." *Southern Studies* 19 (spring 1980): 5–28.

Tyack, David, and Robert Lowe. "The Constitutional Moment: Reconstruction and Black Education in the South." *American Journal of Education* 94 (February 1986): 236–56.

Vance, Joseph C. "Freedmen's Schools in Albemarle County during Reconstruction." *Virginia Magazine of History and Biography* 61 (October 1953): 430–38.

Vandal, Giles. "Black Violence in Post-Civil War Louisiana." *Journal of Interdisciplinary History* 25 (summer 1994): 45–64.

————. *The New Orleans Riot of 1866: Anatomy of a Tragedy.* Lafayette, La. 1983.

Vaughan, William P. *Schools for All: The Blacks and Public Education in the South, 1865–1877.* Lexington, 1974.

Wagandt, Charles L. "The Civil War Journal of Dr. Samuel A. Harrison." *Civil War History* 12 (1967): 131–46.

————. *The Mighty Revolution: Negro Emancipation in Maryland, 1862–1864.* Baltimore, 1964.

Wagstaff, Thomas. " 'Call Your Old Master "Master" ': Southern Political Leaders and Negro Labor during Presidential Reconstruction." *Labor History* 10 (summer 1969): 323–45.

Waldrep, Christopher. "Substituting Law for the Lash: Emancipation and Legal Formalism in a Mississippi County Court." *Journal of American History* 82 (March 1996): 1452–477.

Walker, Clarence E. *A Rock in a Weary Land: The African Methodist Episcopal Church during the Civil War and Reconstruction.* Baton Rouge, 1982.

Waller, Altina L. "Community, Class, and Race in the Memphis Riot of 1866." *Journal of Social History* 18 (winter 1984): 233–46.

Walvin, James. "Recurring Themes: White Images of Black Life during and after Slavery." *Slavery and Abolition* 5 (September 1984): 442–55.

Washington, Delo E. "Education of Freedmen and the Role of Self-Help in a Sea Island Setting, 1862–1982." *Agricultural History* 58 (July 1984): 442–55.

Wayne, Michael. *The Reshaping of Plantation Society: The Natchez District, 1860–1880.* Baton Rouge, 1983.

West, Earle H. "The Harris Brothers: Black Northern Teachers in the Reconstruction South." *Journal of Negro Education* 48 (spring 1979): 126–38.

Wheeler, Edward L. *Uplifting the Race: The Black Minister in the New South, 1865–1902.* Lanham, Md., 1986.

White, Howard A. *The Freedmen's Bureau in Louisiana.* Baton Rouge, 1970.

White, Kenneth B. "The Alabama Freedmen's Bureau and Black Education: The Myth of Opportunity." *Alabama Review* 34 (April 1981): 107–24.

Wiener, Jonathan. *Social Origins of the New South: Alabama, 1860–1885.* Baton Rouge, 1978.

Wiggins, William H. Jr. *O Freedom! Afro-American Emancipation Celebrations.* Knoxville, 1987.

Williams, Frank B. "John Eaton, Jr., Editor, Politician, and School Administrator, 1865–1870." *Tennessee Historical Quarterly* 10 (December 1951): 291–319.

Williams, Harold A. *The Baltimore Sun, 1837–1987.* Baltimore, 1987.

Williams, Loretta J. *Black Freemasonry and Middle Class Realities.* Columbia, Mo., 1980.

Williamson, Joel. *After Slavery: The Negro in South Carolina After Reconstruction, 1861–1877.* 1965.

———. "Black Self-Assertion before and after Emancipation." In *Key*

Issues in the Afro-American Experience, Nathan I. Huggins, Martin Kilson, and Daniel M. Fox, eds. Vol. 1. New York, 1971.

Wilson, James Grant, and John Fiske, eds. *Appleton's Encyclopedia of American Biography*. New York, 1898.

Wilson, Keith. "Education as a Vehicle of Racial Control: Major General N. P. Banks in Louisiana, 1863–1864." *Journal of Negro Education* 50 (spring 1981): 156–70.

Wood, Forrest G. *Black Scare: The Racist Response to Emancipation and Reconstruction*. Berkeley and Los Angeles, 1968.

Woodman, Harold D. *New South–New Law: The Legal Foundations of Credit and Labor Relations in the Postbellum Agricultural South*. Baton Rouge, 1995.

———. "Postbellum Social Change and Its Effect on Marketing the South's Cotton Crop." *Agricultural History* 56 (January 1982): 215–30.

———. "Post-Civil War Southern Agriculture and the Law." *Agricultural History* 53 (January 1979): 319–37.

———. "Sequel to Slavery: The New History Views the Postbellum South." *Journal of Southern History* 44 (November 1977): 523–54.

Woodward, C. Vann. "Seeds of Failure in Radical Race Policy." In *New Frontiers in American Reconstruction*, ed. Harold M. Hyman. Chicago, 1966, 125–47.

Wright, Gavin. *Old South, New South: Revolutions in the Southern Economy since the Civil War*. New York, 1986.

———. "The Strange Career of the New Southern Economic History." *Reviews in American History* 10 (December 1982): 164–80.

Wright, George C. *Life behind a Veil: Blacks in Louisville, Kentucky, 1865–1900*. Baton Rouge, 1985.

Wright, James M. *The Free Negro in Maryland, 1634–1860*. New York, 1921.

Wyatt-Brown, Bertram. "Black Schooling during Reconstruction." In *The Web of Southern Social Relations: Women, Family and Education*, Walter J. Fraser Jr., R. Frank Saunders Jr., and Jon L. Wakelyn. eds. Athens, Ga., 1985, 146–65.

Wynne, Lewis Nicholas. *The Continuity of Cotton: Planter Politics in Georgia, 1865–1892*. Macon, Ga., 1986.

Yacovone, Donald. "The Fruits of Africa: Slavery, Emancipation, and Afro-American Culture." *American Quarterly* 40 (December 1988): 569–76.

Unpublished Theses and Dissertations

Aidt-Guy, Anita Louise. "Persistent Maryland: Antislavery Activity between 1850 and 1864." Ph.D. diss., Georgetown University, 1994, DA9511255.

Battle, Thomas C. "Published Resources for the Study of Blacks in the District of Columbia: An Annotated Guide." Ph.D. diss., Georgetown University, 1982.

Caldwell, Joel L. "A Social, Economic, and Political Study of Blacks in the Louisiana Delta, 1865–1880." Ph.D. diss., Tulane University, 1989, DA9008725.

Cimbala, Paul A. "The Terms of Freedom: The Freedmen's Bureau and Reconstruction Georgia, 1865–1870." Ph.D. diss., Emory University, 1983.

Cole, Stephanie. "Servants and Slaves: Domestic Service in the Border Cities, 1800–1850." Ph.D. diss., University of Florida, 1994, DA9607048.

Corrigan, Mary Elizabeth. "A Social Union of Heart and Effort: The African-American Family in the District of Columbia on the Eve of Emancipation." Ph.D. diss., University of Maryland, 1996, DA9637633.

Cox, Thomas C. "Blacks in Topeka, Kansas, 1865–1915: A Social History." Ph.D. diss., Princeton University, 1980.

Davis, Dernoral. "Against the Odds: Postbellum Growth and Development in a Southern Black Urban Community, 1865–1900." Ph.D. diss., State University of New York, Binghamton, 1987, DA8720656.

Devlin, George A. "South Carolina and Black Migration, 1865–1940: In Search of the Promised Land." Ph.D. diss., University of South Carolina, 1984.

Edwards, Ellen Wheeler. "Maryland during the Reconstruction Period." M.A. Thesis, University of Minnesota, 1928.

Frankel, Noralee. "Workers, Wives, and Mothers: Black Women in Mississippi, 1860–1870." Ph.D. diss., George Washington University, 1983.

Fuller, C. Marchal. "Governmental Action to Aid Freedmen in Maryland, 1864–1869, with Special Emphasis on the Freedmen's Bureau." M.A. Thesis, Howard University, 1965.

Fuke, Richard Paul. "The Break-Up of the Maryland Union Party, 1866." M.A. Thesis, University of Maryland, 1965.

———. "Black Marylanders, 1864–1868." Ph.D. diss., University of Chicago, 1973.

Garonzik, Joseph. "Urbanization and the Black Population of Baltimore, 1850–1870." Ph.D. diss., State University of New York at Stony Brook, 1974.

Glymph, Thavolia. "The Second Middle Passage: The Transition from Slavery to Freedom at Davis Bend, Mississippi." Ph.D. diss., Purdue University, 1994, DA9523351.

Goodwin, Floetta. "Lew Wallace during the Civil War and Reconstruction." M.A. Thesis, University of Chicago, 1927.

Graham, Glennon. "From Slavery to Serfdom: Rural Black Agriculturalists in South Carolina, 1865–1900." Ph.D. diss., Northwestern University, 1982.

Griffin, Paul R. "Black Founders of Reconstruction Era Methodist Colleges: Daniel A. Payne, Joseph C. Price, and Isaac Lane, 1863–1890." Ph.D. diss., Emory University, 1983.

Hennessey, Melinda M. "To Live and Die in Dixie: Reconstruction Race Riots in the South." Ph.D. diss., Kent State University, 1978.

Hicks, Helena S. "The Black Apprentice in Maryland Court Records from 1661 to 1865." Ph.D. diss., University of Maryland, 1988, DA8818404.

Hildebrand, Reginal Francis. "Methodism and the Meaning of Freedom: Missions to Southern Blacks during the Era of Emancipation and Reconstruction." Ph.D. diss., Princeton University, 1992, DA9135834.

Hine, William C. "Frustration, Factionalism, and Failure: Black Political Leadership and the Republican Party in Reconstruction Charleston, 1865–1877." Ph.D. diss., Kent State University, 1979.

Holt, Sharon Ann. "A Time to Plant: The Economic Lives of Freedpeople in Granville County, North Carolina, 1865–1900." Ph.D. diss., University of Pennsylvania, 1991, DA9200345.

Hucles, Michael Edward. "Postbellum Urban Black Economic Development: The Case of Norfolk, Virginia, 1860–1890." Ph.D. diss., Purdue University, 1990, DA9031341.

Jacobs, Grace Hill. "The Negro in Baltimore, 1860–1900." M.A. Thesis, Howard University, 1945.

Jenkins, Wilbert Lee. "Chaos, Conflict, and Control: The Responses of Newly-Freed Slaves in Charleston, South Carolina, to Emancipation and Reconstruction, 1865–1877." Ph.D. diss., Michigan State University, 1991, DA9216316.

John, Beverly M. "Culture and Social Change: The Values and Behavior of African American People in the South Carolina Low-Country and Georgia Coastal Region in the Antebellum and Postbellum Periods." Ph.D. diss., University of California, Berkeley, 1991, DA9203601.

Johnson, Elliott McC. "The Influence of Blacks on the Development and Implementation of the Public Education System in South Carolina, 1863–1876." Ph.D. diss., American University, 1978.

Johnson, Josie R. "An Historical Review of the Role Black Parents and the Black Community Played in Providing Schooling for Black Children in the South, 1865–1954." Ph.D. diss., University of Massachusetts, 1986.

Johnson, Richard H. "A Critical Study of Religious Work among the Negroes of St. Mary's County, Maryland, since 1865, with Special Reference to the Catholic, Episcopal, and Methodist Churches." M.A. Thesis, Howard University, 1948.

Johnston, Allan J. "Surviving Freedom: The Black Community of Washington, D.C., 1860–1880." Ph.D. diss., Duke University, 1980.

Jones, Maxine D. "A 'Glorious Work': The American Missionary Association and Black North Carolinians, 1863–1880." Ph.D. diss., Florida State University, 1982.

McBride, William G. "Blacks and the Race Issue in Tennessee Politics, 1865–1876." Ph.D. diss., Vanderbilt University, 1989, DA8919704.

McDaniel, George W. "Preserving the People's History: Traditional Black Material Culture in Nineteenth and Twentieth Century Southern Maryland." Ph.D. diss., Duke University, 1979.

McKelvey, Kay Najiyyah. "Early Black Dorchester, 1776–1870: A History of the Struggle of African-Americans in Dorchester County, Maryland, To Be Free To Make Their Own Choices." Ph.D. diss., University of Maryland, 1991, DA9133192.

Mansfield, Betty. "That Fateful Class: Black Teachers of Virginia's Freedmen, 1861–1882." Ph.D. diss., Catholic University, 1980.

Newby, Cassandra Lynn. " 'The World Was All Before Them': A Study of the Black Community in Norfolk, Virginia, 1861–1884." Ph.D. diss., College of William and Mary, 1992, DA9304506.

Paul, William George. "The Shadow of Equality: The Negro in Baltimore, 1864–1911." Ph.D. diss., University of Wisconsin, 1972.

Phillips, Christopher William. " 'Negroes and Other Slaves': The African-American Community of Baltimore, 1790–1860." Ph.D. diss., University of Georgia, 1992, DA9235467.

Phillips, Paul D. "A History of the Freedmen's Bureau in Tennessee." Ph.D. diss., Vanderbilt University, 1964.

Richardson, Barbara A. "A History of Blacks in Jacksonville, Florida, 1860–1895: A Socio-Economic and Political Study." Ph.D. diss., Carnegie-Mellon University, 1975.

Roberts-Jackson, LaVonne. " 'Freedom and Family': The Freedmen's Bureau and African-American Women in Texas in the Reconstruction Era, 1865–1872." Ph.D. diss., Howard University, 1996, DA9700818.

Rowland, Leslie Suzanne. "Emancipation and the Black Military Experience during the American Civil War: A Documentary History." Ph.D. diss., University of Rochester, 1991, DA9128781.

Schwalm, Leslie Anne. "The Meaning of Freedom: African-American Women and Their Transition from Slavery to Freedom in Lowcountry South Carolina." Ph.D. diss., University of Wisconsin, Madison, 1991, DA9133415.

Thomas-Holder, Susan Alexis. "Henry Highland Garnet: His Life, Times, and an Afro-centric Analysis of His Writings." Ph.D. diss., Temple University, 1994, DA9512879.

Verney, Kevern J. "Contrast and Continuity: 'Black' Reconstruction in South Carolina and Mississippi, 1861–1877." Ph.D. diss., University of Keele, United Kingdom, 1987, BRDX87345.

Welch, Eloise T. "The Background and Development of the American Missionary Association's Decision to Educate Freedmen in the South, with Subsequent Repercussions for Higher Education." Ph.D. diss., Bryn Mawr, 1976.

Whitman, Torrey Stephen. "Slavery, Manumission, and Free Black Workers in Early National Baltimore." Ph.D. diss., Johns Hopkins University, 1993, DA9327686.

Williams, Lou Falkner. "The Great South Carolina Ku Klux Klan Trials, 1871–1872." Ph.D. diss., University of Florida, 1991, DA9209092.

Wilson, Emily W. "The Public Education of Negroes on the Eastern Shore of Maryland." M.A. Thesis, Howard University, 1948.

Windham, Joseph Edward. "Bondage, Bias, and the Bench: A Historical Analysis of Maryland Court of Appeals Cases Involving Blacks,
1830–1860." Ph.D. diss., Howard University, 1990, DA9134079.
Wright, C. T. "The Development of Education for Blacks in Georgia,
1865–1900." Ph.D. diss., Boston University, 1977.

INDEX